home front
directory

home front directory

Alison Reynolds

Sarah Childs-Carlile

This book is published to accompany the *Home Front* television series.
Series Editor: Franny Moyle

First published by BBC Worldwide Ltd in 1999
80 Wood Lane, London W12 0TT
Text © BBC Worldwide Ltd 1999
The moral right of the authors has been asserted

ISBN 0 563 38488 3

Commissioning Editor: Nicola Copeland
Project Editor: Charlotte Lochhead
Copy Editor: Susan Martineau
Art Editors: Ellen Wheeler and Lisa Pettibone
Design: Ben Cracknell Studios

Set in AES, Folio and Officina
Typeset by BBC Worldwide Ltd
Printed and bound in Great Britain by Butler and Tanner Ltd, Frome and London
Cover printed by Belmont Press Ltd, Northampton

A note from the authors:
The information given in this book has been researched as carefully as possible and, to the best of our knowledge, is correct at the time of printing. We apologise for any errors or misrepresentations that may have occurred and will be happy to make amendments in later editions. Let us know if your address has changed by writing to:

The *Home Front* Directory, c/o *Home Front*, Room E304, BBC Television Centre, Wood Lane, London W12 7RJ

Always follow manufacturers guidelines on cleaning or caring for products.
The authors/publisher take no responsibility for advice given herein.

notes on using this book

Use the contents guide on pp.6–7 to find the chapter you need. All the chapters and their sub-sections have introductions to help you find what you're looking for, so it's worth taking a few moments to read them. Where it seemed more helpful to do so, some chapters or sub-sections have been divided into geographical regions to make it easier for you to locate a supplier near you. (It's a good idea to scan the other regions, too, as you may find just what you are looking for elsewhere!) If your region is not listed then there is no supplier we know of there. If the majority of companies in a section are manufacturers who stock other outlets throughout the UK, then we may have opted for a non-regional listing because the company's location is not so relevant and you can call them to find out where your nearest stockist is. The regions are:

south west: Bristol, Cornwall, Devon, Dorset, Somerset, South Gloucestershire and Wiltshire

south east: Bedfordshire, Berkshire, Buckinghamshire, Hampshire, Hertfordshire, Isle of Wight, Kent, London, Surrey and Sussex

east: Cambridgeshire, Essex, Lincolnshire, Norfolk and Suffolk

central: Derbyshire, Gloucestershire, Herefordshire, Leicestershire, Northamptonshire, Nottinghamshire, Oxfordshire, Shropshire, Staffordshire, Warwickshire, West Midlands and Worcestershire

north west: Cheshire, Cumbria, Lancashire, Liverpool, Manchester and Wirral

north east: Durham, Middlesborough and Teesside, Northumberland and Tyneside, and Yorkshire

wales & isle of man

scotland

northern ireland

We have chosen to list suppliers names alphabetically using their first given name so, for example, John Oliver is listed under 'J' for John, or C Brewer & Sons is under 'C'. Suppliers with names beginning with 'The' will be found under their first given name, too, so, for example, The Dwelling is listed under 'D' for 'Dwelling'. Some companies have chosen not to give an address but with a quick phone call they will provide you with your nearest branch or stockist.

The following symbols have been used throughout the book to highlight certain features:

hf shows a company's product has been featured on *Home Front*

hfg shows a company's product has been featured on *Home Front in the Garden*

✉ shows a company offers a mail order service. We have tried to alert you in the text if they *only* do mail order, i.e. are not a shop premises you can actually visit.

contents

introduction

Home Front is BBC2's leading programme about interior design and decoration. We've been on air since 1994 providing know-how, top tips and expert advice in all areas of home decorating, and have inspired a whole generation of enthusiasts to create stylish effects in their own homes. No longer content with off-the-peg solutions, people are increasingly using their homes to express themselves. And no wonder – whether it's a simple stencil used to enhance a room, a bold change to brighter colours or even designing a whole kitchen, there is nothing as satisfying or rewarding as completing a home project and sitting back to enjoy the admiration from your buddies.

Ever since *Home Front* started we've been inundated with letters, calls and enquiries from our viewers, keen to try out our ideas for themselves and track down suppliers of the innovative materials and products we use in our room makeovers – a mosaic panel, a rubber floor, slate splashbacks or an MDF table with birch veneer finish. In answering all your queries we built up an enormous database of addresses and information and it seemed a good idea to compile it in some way, and so the *Home Front Directory* came about.

This book is designed to inform you of the many products and services available to you all over the UK. We hope this directory will enable you to source the kind of stuff you need to get on and create those interior designs and decorative finishes you really want. Some of the retailers and manufacturers listed in the book are featured in our series factsheets, as their products or services have been used by the *Home Front* team for our tv projects. Others have been included after extensive research, in order to provide a nationwide listing and a comprehensive guide reflecting the diversity of projects we undertake on the programmes. You'll find everything from salvage yards and stockists of traditional paints, to suppliers of the most contemporary designer lighting and those providing the more unusual industrial materials that designers are increasingly using to reshape domestic interiors. Undoubtedly there were hundreds more we could have included ... maybe next time! Although we can't vouch for the products or services of those published here, we have tried to pick the ones we think you will find most useful.

I hope that using this directory you'll now be able to source the materials you need to get started on something amazing. I hope, too, that this book will become as useful a tool in your design and decorating projects as your faithful tape measure or favourite paint brush.

Happy decorating!

Franny Moyle
Home Front Series Editor

1 what

This perplexing question is usually the first thing you address when you move into a new house and its solution is often the defining decision that influences all the rest. What to put on the walls is frequently dictated by fashion – paint seems to be perennially popular, whereas wallpaper teeters on the brink and every so often makes a major comeback. Paint in itself is a maze of choices – you can colourwash, rag roll, stipple and distress – the list is endless. And although some sneer at stencilling, it can still look very effective. There are hundreds of designs available, traditional and modern, plus the scope for making your own.

But the fun of decorating today is that there are so many other alternatives out there – things that are not usually even considered for interiors that could be, if people knew where to get hold of them easily. Metal sheeting, plastic, wood, blackboard paint, spray-on glitter, even brown paper can all be used. And, because some of these are relatively inexpensive, if you get bored with the look you can get rid of it and start again. Fabrics shouldn't be overlooked either – hessian, suede and silk can be used to stunning effect – but be careful with the seams. Real leather is perhaps one of the most luxurious choices, but there are imitation leathers available which look equally good. Don't be put off by the choices on offer. Instead, be liberated by them and you can let your walls do the talking.

This chapter includes just about everything you can put on your walls and is divided into self-contained sections beginning with paint, as this is the most popular wall covering. External walls shouldn't be overlooked either. A coat or two of masonry paint (found in the specialist paint section) will not only preserve the longevity of your house but make it more saleable if you're thinking of putting it on the market. To use this chapter, turn to the particular wall covering you are interested in and there will be notes to explain particulars like what the difference between our categories of standard and specialist paints are, or what constitutes modern and groovy wallpaper.

about walls?

key:  shows the product has appeared on *Home Front*

✉ shows the company offers a mail order service

paint

Paint is still the cheapest and most dramatic way of creating a colour scheme and the majority of people opt for it. The enormous range of paints available on the market today can sometimes be bewildering. Faced with scores of different shades of white, it is easy to be put off and go for the safest option. Sales of magnolia do still dominate, but other colours are now creeping up, reflecting our growing sense of adventure.

When considering colour, the basic rules are to work out which way your room faces. Think about whether it gets the morning or evening sun; rooms that don't get much sun can be made to appear brighter by clever use of warm tones. Remember that colour can play all sorts of visual tricks – high ceilings can appear lower if they are painted in a darker shade, and the reverse is also true. Horizontal stripes can make a room appear wider and, if your room is badly proportioned, using the same colour on ceilings, walls, and woodwork can reduce this effect. Matchpots, which most companies now do, help avoid costly mistakes. It's crucial that you first paint a largish area using the entire pot and live with until you are sure – a colour can vary wildly according to what time of day it is and what sort of light is on it. A good trick is to paint the inside of a cardboard box the colour you propose and see how the changing light affects the colour.

Besides settling on a colour, there is also a whole barrage of other questions to face – what type of paint should you use where, should you use a primer or not, can you use distemper and limewash in modern properties, and what do the terms 'historic' and 'authentic' actually mean? The most important things to take into consideration when choosing paint for your home is where you intend to use the paint, what type of finish you need, and what sort of walls you have. Limewash, for example, is part of the distemper family along with whitewash and oil-bound distemper. It will not stick to surfaces with which it is chemically incompatible and if you try to use limewash on a wall in a modern house, it will not only look odd, but may be incompatible with your surfaces. It's best used on walls with old, untreated plaster – preferably those that were built before the nineteenth century but, if in doubt, consult an expert. Similarly, if you use a petro-chemical oil paint straight on to old walls that are prone to damp it may make the situation worse as the walls won't be able to breathe.

The advent of so-called 'heritage' and 'historic' colours have been one of the success stories of the last decade. Sales have gone through the roof and nearly all the major paint companies now have their own range. However, there is still a lot of snobbery and confusion about them, about what's 'authentic' or not. Basically, it's all a matter of taste. The range of colours actually available in the eighteenth century was limited by the availability of natural pigments and you couldn't buy ready-made paints as we know them today. The whole process of making paints and what conditions they have to stand up to has totally changed since then. Today's vinyl silks, with their ability to be wiped clean of everything from greasy fingermarks to water splashes must surely be a good invention, so why regress? As long as you remember that some licence is taken with the word 'authentic' and that unless you are involved in the detailed and complex matter of restoration or conservation where analyzing how that precise colour was achieved is of significance, then you won't get bogged down in whether the colour of paint you adore is historically suitable for your type of house or not.

Lastly, there is a whole range of specialist paints on the market with which you can create endless variations. Metallic spray paints are probably best used sparingly but they can give an unusual finish, as can small highlights of gold or silver leaf. If you're environmentally conscious, there are now organic paints and 'green' paints with a low VOC (volatile organic content – the chemicals given off during the manufacturing process), although you need to be prepared to apply a few extra coats of these.

Above all, do what's right for you and your style of living. Let the list below help to guide you through the myriad choices. The paints have been categorized as either standard or specialist and the section introductions will explain what each of these categories contains.

standard

For the purposes of this directory we have divided paint, which is an enormous topic, into two sections – namely standard and specialist. It is not always easy to decide which category a paint should be placed in. What one person may call specialist, another may call standard. In this section, however, you will find ready-to-use, off-the-shelf paints in the standard finishes of emulsion and eggshell. Historic colours that you buy ready mixed have now become so popular that they warrant being included in the standard section, too.

Cole & Son

144 Offord Road, London N1 1NS
tel: 0171 607 4288 • fax: 0171 607 3341

A subtle range of colours, from a company that has been manufacturing paint since 1875, is available from their showroom. There are about twenty-five colours in all – half of which are available in vinyl matt emulsion and the other half in oil-based eggshell, as well as emulsion.

Crown Decorative Products Ltd

PO Box 37, Crown House, Hollins Rd, Darwen, Lancs BB3 0BG
tel: 01254 704951 for stockists • fax: 01254 774414

Crown is still one of the leading brand names and have a whole host of paints on offer. Available from most large DIY outlets, new ranges are being launched all the time to keep up with modern needs. One of their latest additions is a range of textured paints in Smooth Velvet or Sand, which feels rough and grainy to the touch and is great for adding a bit of interest.

Designer's Guild

267–271 & 275–277 Kings Rd, London SW3 5EN
tel: 0171 243 7300 for the store • fax: 0171 243 7710
tel: 0171 351 5775 for general enquiries
Launched in spring 1998, Designer's Guild colours have been specifically designed to work alongside the Guild's distinctively colourful fabrics and wallpapers. The paints are manufactured by Farrow & Ball. As well as vibrant shades of cornflower and lime, there are some more muted colours, such as Tuscan Olive and Zinc Blue, all of which are available in matt emulsion or eggshell.

Farrow & Ball

33 Uddens Trading Estate, Wimbourne,
Dorset BH21 7NL
tel: 01202 876141 for stockists • fax: 01202 873793
e-mail: farrow-ball@farrow-ball.co.uk
tel: 0171 351 0273 for London showroom

One of the success stories of the nineties although
they had, in fact, been manufacturing paint for years.
The palette of colours was created for the National
Trust and, although they are not strictly historically
accurate, they look like the colours of the past would
have done when they aged and mellowed. They were
chosen for all the room sets in the BBC's adaptation of
Pride and Prejudice. Their strange names have become
almost legendary including Dead Salmon and
Mouse's Back.

Fired Earth

Twyford Mill, Oxford Rd, Adderbury,
Oxon OX17 3HP
tel: 01295 812088 for stockists • fax: 01295 810832
e-mail: enquiries@firedearth.com

The Victoria & Albert Museum worked in conjunction
with Fired Earth to produce their palette of Historic
Colours based on eighteenth- and nineteenth-century
colours. *Home Front* designer Lloyd Farmar chose their
Dragon's Blood Red to create a medieval look. In the
summer of 1998 Fired Earth added to this very popular
range with a palette of Contemporary Colours –
vibrant, modern shades that look set to be every bit as
popular as their historic ones.

Habitat

196 Tottenham Court Rd, London W1P 9LD
tel: 0171 255 2545
tel: 0645 334433 for branches

Habitat have only started selling their own brand paint
in the last few years but it seems to have done very
well. There is a limited palette of colours produced
usually dependent on what colour is 'in' that season.
It's relatively expensive per litre compared to the
larger DIY stores so you could be paying for the name.

ICI Dulux Paints

Wexham Rd, Slough, Berks SL2 5DS
tel: 01753 550555 for advice and product information

Dulux is one of the largest brand names around and
has literally hundreds and hundreds of colours. They
can mix virtually any colour to order using a base coat

and various tints and it is well worth investing in one
of their colour charts – a chunky A5 book showing all
the colours available – which many interior designers
carry around with them. Their Heritage range has a
good selection of colours.

Jane Churchill Paints

118 Garratt Lane, London SW18 4DJ
tel: 0181 877 6400 for stockists

If you like Jane Churchill's subtle and traditional,
yet still contemporary, fabrics, choosing a paint to
go with them couldn't be easier. These paints have
been specially formulated to complement their fabric
and wallpaper ranges. They are manufactured by
nineties success story Farrow & Ball and are available
through many outlets, including Farrow & Ball
themselves.

John Oliver

33 Pembridge Rd, London W11 3HG
tel: 0171 221 6466 • fax: 0171 727 5555

John Oliver Paints have been in business for nearly
forty years and they have always been up to date with
the latest colours. There are around forty-six colours.
The paint chart, for which there is a nominal charge,
shows them in matt emulsion but other finishes can
be produced to order. They have great names – Betty
II Blue, Imperial Chinese Yellow, and Kinky Pink
(a fantastic fuchsia). You can visit their showroom at
the above address.

Johnstone's Paints

Huddersfield Rd, Birstall, Batley, W.Yorks WF17 9XA
tel: 01924 354000 for stockists • fax: 01924 354001

There are over a thousand shades to choose from here
and, if you still can't find the one you want,
Johnstone's operate a free matching service. Send in
a sample of fabric or wallpaper and they will find an
exact colour match. Anne McKevitt chose their muted
shades of aubergine and kelp green for a kitchen/diner.

Macpherson Paints

Unit 2–3, Brough Parkway, Newcastle,
Newcastle-upon-Tyne NE6 2YF
tel: 0191 265 7321

Macpherson have a good range of colours, from subtle
shades to vibrant ones, suitable for all types of home.
Home Front designer Kevin Allan chose two tones of a
heathery pinky-beige, the Bugle and Consul shades

from their range (one paler than the other) to show that you needn't always choose white if you want to create a relaxing, modern and minimalist bedroom.

Sanderson

100 Acres, Sanderson Rd, Uxbridge, Middx UB8 1DY
tel: 0171 584 3344 for stockists • fax: 0171 584 8404
and
112–120 Brompton Rd, London SW3 1JJ (showroom)

Sanderson have been manufacturing paint for years and is a company with an air of reliability and tradition. There are hundreds of colours in their Spectrum range which are available in all standard finishes.

specialist

Metallic, masonry and environmentally friendly paints, fluorescent, heavy-duty floor paints, and materials used for gilding and paint effects are all included in this section. Anything that needs to be mixed or weighed, such as limewash and distemper, can also be found here.

Ardenbrite

c/o Tor Coatings Ltd, Portobello Industrial Estate
Birtley, Chester-le-Street, Co Durham DH3 2RE
tel: 0191 410 6611 for stockists • fax: 0191 492 0125
e-mail: enqs@tor-coatings.com

Specialist paints including a good range of masonry paints, anti-graffiti paints, and black enamel for railings and fireplaces. They make twelve metallics in traditional colours: choose from five different golds, light and dark copper, two different bronzes, two silvers and a pewter. The gold ones are a good replica for gold leaf – and less expensive.

Artex-Blue Hawk Ltd

Pasture Lane, Ruddington, Nottingham NG11 6AG
tel: 0115 984 5679 for stockists

Artex has unfortunately earned itself a reputation for tackiness, and most people want to know how to get rid of the dreaded stuff instead of where to get it from. However, used in unusual ways – perhaps just in patches – as *Home Front* has shown, it can look effective and perhaps it will even come back into fashion. You can buy Artex in bags, and get all the rollers you need to make different patterns (from stucco to stipples). There is also a version of artex

called Mediterranean Touch which produces a rustic-look rough plaster effect. It comes ready mixed and you use it straight from the tub.

Auro Organic Paint Supplies

Unit 1, Goldstone Farm, Ashdon, Saffron Walden, Essex CB10 2LZ
tel: 01799 584888 • fax: 01799 584042

All the paints are made from natural products – linseed oil, pine resin, chalk ... and so on – and imported from Germany. There is a good range of colours and the company has a total commitment to sustainable ecology. Because the paints are made without the use of bio-cides or petro-chemicals, they do not contribute to the 'greenhouse' effect. All the contents are declared on the labels.

B&Q Horizons Range

tel: 0181 466 4166 for branches

One of B&Q's own brands, the Horizons range has been specifically developed to be environmentally friendly and this was the paint Anne McKevitt chose to paint the striped walls on the *Home Front* Ecohome. The paint has a low VOC (volatile organic compounds) content and is marked with the VOC symbol.

Benetton Paints

c/o B&Q
tel: 0181 466 4166 for branches

Not content with just selling clothes, Benetton launched their own paint range in 1998 which is sold within the larger B&Q stores. There are currently eighteen colours in all, with names like Jeans, plus several metallic shades. There are also three fun finishes for creating easy paint effects, such as Rag & Roll which you simply apply directly on to the base coat.

Brats

281 King's Rd, London SW3 5EW
tel: 0171 351 7674 • fax: 0171 349 8644
and
624c Fulham Rd, London SW6 5RS
tel: 0171 731 6915

A range which is exclusive to Brats but available by mail order. Their Mediterranean Palette consists of water-based emulsion in vibrant colours which dry to a chalky finish. Based on traditional Turkish paints, the colours conjure up memories of exotic places – Corsica,

Constantinople, Seville. They're not suitable for external walls in the British climate and be prepared for the finish to appear more irregular than manufactured emulsions. The paint also retains brushstrokes when dry, so paint carefully.

C Brewer & Sons

327 Putney Bridge Rd, London SW15 2PG
tel: 0181 788 9335 • fax: 0181 788 8285

This is a good supplier of scumbles and glazes, and unusual metallic paints, as well as standard paints such as Dulux, and well worth a visit.

Casa Paint Company

PO Box 77, Thame, Oxon OX9 3FZ
tel: 01296 770139 for stockists (and also available in Homebase stores)

There are eighteen striking shades based on Mediterranean colours that make up the World Colours range – all handmade to a traditional recipe. You can use them neat as stencil paints or diluted with water for an easy colourwash and other paint effects. They were the first chalky textured paint to be widely available and the first paint company within Homebase to have a hand-painted colour chart. The packaging is also recyclable.

Colourman Paints

Pine Brush Products, Coton Clanford, Stafford, Staffs ST18 9PB
tel: 01785 5541131 for stockists • fax: 01785 282292

These are water-based paints which have been developed to mimic the look of paints used in the eighteenth and nineteenth centuries. They have a flat, chalky finish when dry and can be used on walls and woodwork, although they should be protected with varnish if you're using them on furniture or anywhere where they are likely to be splashed with water.

Coo-Var

Ellenshaw Works, Lockwood St, Hull, E.Yorks HU2 0HN
tel: 01482 328053 for stockists • fax: 01482 219266

An excellent range of specialized coatings, primers and paints including the superbly named Anti-Climb Paint that, when applied to walls and sills, looks perfectly normal but is in fact very slippery, making the surface almost impossible to scale. It also leaves tell-tale marks on the suspect's clothes! They also do luminous paint, anti-graffiti paint, and a wide range of yacht varnishes and wood preservatives.

Craig & Rose

172 Leith Walk, Edinburgh EH6 5EB
tel: 0131 554 1131 for stockists • fax: 0131 553 3250

Craig & Rose are probably best known for their quality range of varnishes which are perfect for achieving that 'flat look' typical of Victorian walls. They have an excellent range of glazes and scumbles, plus more unusual things like chlorinated paint, which is useful if you've got a swimming-pool. They have thier own showroom and are also stocked in most branches of Paint Magic. Craig & Rose have been in business for over 150 years and their products can always be relied on to acheive the effect you want.

Cy-Près

14 Bells Close, Brigstock, Kettering, Northants NN14 3JG
tel: 01536 373431 • fax: 01536 373431

This mail order only supplier will make up quantities of limewash and soft distemper to specific quantities. Kevin McCloud used their products literally to cook with paint when *Home Front* was helping restore a three-hundred-year-old cottage in Northamptonshire and the owners wanted to achieve a traditional look that would allow their old walls to breathe.

Dial-a-Colour

538 Stirling Rd, Riggend, Airdrie Ml6 7SS
tel: 0800 731 6063 • fax: 0800 731 6063

All your decorating needs are met by this small company from stencils to scaffolding. At the moment, the service is only available if you live in the Glasgow or Lanarkshire areas but they have plans to expand further. Phone for a colour chart.

E Ploton (Sundries) Ltd

271A Archway Rd, London N6 5AA
tel: 0181 348 2838

A good place to go if you're looking for gilding materials and artists' acrylics. They have a huge selection of brushes and other artists' equipment and helpful staff.

Flexicote Ltd

Specialty Coatings Division, Gerrard House, Worthing Rd, East Preston, W. Sussex BN16 1AW
tel: 01372 720780 for stockists • fax: 01372 720780

If you have a bathroom, cellar, kitchen or even swimming-pool that is prone to damp, this manufacturer has a range of speciality coatings and paints for both domestic and industrial purposes.

Francesca's Limewash

Unit 24A Battersea Business Centre, 99/109 Lavender Hill, London SW11 5QL
tel: 0171 228 7694 • fax: 0171 228 8067

If you don't want to go to the trouble of mixing up your own limewash, this range comes ready prepared and poured. Reminiscent of the colours of the Italian countryside, the paint dries to give a warm, velvety feel. The colour chart is hand-painted (there is a small charge for it) and there is also a matching service if you have a particular colour in mind. Buy all that you need at the same time as the colour pigments tend to vary from batch to batch. The studio is open by appointment only.

Grand Illusions

2–4 Crown Rd, St Margaret's, Twickenham, Middx TW1 3EE
tel: 0181 892 2151 for mail order
tel: 0181 607 9446 for specific enquiries and for details of two other branches • fax: 0181 744 2017

These water-based paints have been sourced from historic paint charts from all round the world and are made from earth pigments and china clay to emulate the milk paints of the nineteenth century. They are designed primarily for using on wood. You can use them on walls and floors, although they do warn that as the paints have a high chalk content, they tend to mark easily and should be given a layer of protective varnish.There are around forty colours to choose from but new ones are being developed all the time – the latest range is called the Long Island Collection which they say 'perfectly replicates the charm of seaside houses'.

Hammerite Products

Prudhoe, Northumberland NE42 6LP
tel: 0161 830000 for stockists

Suitable for surfaces like metal railings and gates, or if you have an old iron bed that could do with a lick of paint, Hammerite do a range of enamel paints in lots of different colours that will give it a new lease of life. You can also use it on radiators and garden furniture.

Heritage Village Colors

The Old Village Paint Store, Shop 3
Heart of the Country, Home Farm, Swinfen, nr Lichfield, Staffs WS14 9QR
tel: 01543 480669 for stockists • fax: 01543 481684

In this delightful little 'village', a cluster of converted farm buildings selling everything from hand-made jewellery to crêpes, you will find the Old Village Paint Store selling a range of heritage paints based on the paint used by American craftsmen in the early 1800s. There is simulated milk paint which is designed for stencilling, painting wooden furniture and internal walls, and they say it covers in one coat. There are also the Heritage Village Colors, again based on original formulas. The paint is charmingly sold by the pint and the quart but the staff should be able to convert that to litres if you're not sure. They are closed on Mondays.

Holman Specialist Paints

15–16 Central Trading Estate, Signal Way, Swindon, Wilts SN3 1PD
tel: 01793 511537 for stockists • fax: 01793 431142

If you want to give an exterior wall a vibrant makeover, this company supply the Vallti range from Finland, which includes opaque paints in shades of fuschia pink and cobalt blue amongst others.

Humbrol DIY Ltd

Marfleet, Hull, E.Yorks HU9 5NE
tel: 01482 701191/0800 132379 for stockists
fax: 01482 712908

A whole host of products including a spray that simulates the look of sandblasted glass called Glass Etch. It has been used on *Home Front* on numerous occasions. Anne McKevitt used it on a kitchen window that was overlooked, and Lloyd Farmar created a stylish front door panel with it. Its only drawback is that, unlike proper sandblasting, it doesn't last forever and can get weather-beaten in an external setting, but it's good for an instant effect.

International Paint

tel: 01703 226722 for stockists

Available in most major DIY outlets, International do a great range of floor paints in mouth-watering colours such as caramel and terracotta. They also do a Melamine Primer that can be used on tired kitchen units before you give them a coat of emulsion for an instant face-lift, and Tile Primer that should be applied to ceramic tiles before you paint over them.

JW Bollom & Co Ltd

PO Box 78, Croydon Rd, Beckenham, Kent BR3 4BL
tel: 0181 658 2299 for stockists
fax: 0181 658 8672
e-mail: sales@bollom.com

Manufacturer of all types of paint including a useful range of Childsafe paint which is good for nursery furniture, toys and playground equipment. They also do enamels, floor paint, and a very useful product that can remove graffiti from brick, or remove lipstick, crayon and marker pen inks. There are depots all over England and one in Northern Ireland. Phone the head office number and they will put you in touch with your nearest depot or stockist.

L Cornelissen & Son

105 Great Russell St, London WC1B 3RY
tel: 0171 636 1045 • fax: 0171 636 3655

If you want to try your hand at gilding, this shop sells books of aluminium, silver and gold leaf plus everything else you need. *Home Front* designer Fiona Samler used their aluminium leaf on a mantelpiece to create a seductive bedroom. They also supply artists' acrylics, powder pigments, and an extensive range of artists' brushes.

Lawrence T Bridgeman

1 Church Rd, Roberttown, Liversedge, W.Yorks WF15 7LS
tel: 01924 413813 for stockists • fax: 01924 413801

For a traditional Shaker or American Colonial look, this company has a range of Buttermilk, Old Village and Vintage Paints based on traditional recipes in use in America since 1816. Imported from America, the Buttermilk paints are the only milk paints authenticated by the Colonial Williamsburg Foundation.

Leyland Paint Company

Kalon Decorative Products, Huddersfield Rd, Birstall, Batley, W.Yorks WF17 9XA
tel: 01924 477201 for colour advisory service and stockists • fax: 01924 422210

There are over 3000 shades available with some fantastic names – Moon Carrot and Moose Bark – and some specialist products such as Heavy Duty Floor Paint, which come in unusual colours, plus a good range of masonry paints.

Nutshell Natural Paints

Hamlyn House, Mardle Way, Buckfastleigh, Devon TQ11 0NR
tel: 01364 642892 helpline and orders
fax: 01364 643888

Made principally from casein – the curd that separates off when milk is left to go sour – these traditional paints are completely environmentally friendly. Treated properly, they can be surprisingly hard-wearing although you may find you need a few more coats than you would with conventional chemically processed paints. You can visit Hamlyn House in person, but it's best to ring first.

Paint Creative

17 Holywell Hill, St Albans, Herts AL1 1EZ
tel: 01727 836338 for mail order • fax: 01727 875872

With over forty-eight colours, available by mail order only, choose from subtle eighteenth century to dramatic 1960s. This company prides itself on being able to provide any colour for your home whatever the period and whatever your taste. They do a range of acrylic metallics (in silver, copper, pewter etc.) which you can add to a colourwash or scumble glaze if you want a shimmery finish, and The Old Masters Collection uses colours reminiscent of those used in great masterpieces. (See also Furniture You Paint Yourself p.161.)

Paint Library

5 Elystan St, London SW3 3NT
tel: 0171 823 7755 • fax: 0171 823 7766

A range of paints in mostly muted, subtle shades – the mail order colour chart, for which there is a charge, is all painstakingly hand-painted and bound containing individual cards, with mounted samples arranged according to the colour spectrum. In direct contrast, they also do a funky range of glitter and metallic paints with names like Skywalker, Goldfinger and Modesty Blaze which are great fun, and an unusual range of pearlescent glazes that look like liquid mother-of-pearl. They do a matching range of glitter fabrics for which samples are available upon request.

Paint Magic

48 Golborne Rd, Notting Hill, London W10 5PR
tel: 0181 960 9960 • fax: 0181 960 9655

Jocasta Innes, a regular presenter on *Home Front*, wrote her best-selling book *Paint Magic* and inspired a decade of paint effects. Still going strong, there are now many branches of Paint Magic both in Britain and overseas selling everything from woodwash, stencil paint, historic colours, liming paste and crackle glaze, plus all the tools you could need. (See also Courses p.265.)

Papers & Paints
4 Park Walk, London SW10 0AD
tel: 0171 352 8626 • fax: 0171 352 1017

True colour experts for over forty years who have the largest collection of colour stored on computer in their shop. This means that they can run through colours and match any for you from their database. If the colour you had in mind is still not there, which is unlikely, bring a sample which is smooth, flat, and bigger than a thumbnail and, for a charge, the computer will match it.

Potmolen Paint

27 Woodcock Industrial Estate, Warminster, Wilts BA12 9DX
tel: 01985 213960 • fax: 01985 213931

If you live in an old house this company sells a range of products that are probably suitable for the walls including distemper, limewash, size, lime putty, and whiting. You need to know what you are doing if you're planning on making it up yourself, otherwise it could end up being a very costly process but, if you do, it's hugely satisfying. Paints are available by mail order only.

Ray Munn
861–863 Fulham Rd, London SW6 5HP
tel: 0171 736 9876

This is a great shop crammed with useful products and they also offer a colour-matching service. This is a good outlet for ESP (Easy Surface Prep), which is ideal for priming tiles, laminates, glass and plastics before you paint them.

The Real Paint Shop
122 Sheen Rd, Richmond, Surrey TW9 1UR
tel: 0181 940 7539 • fax: 0181 288 1501

This is currently the only outlet for non-toxic paint from manufacturer Worldcare. The paints don't produce any fumes so you should literally get a headache-free job. You do have to let them dry for far longer than you would if using chemically manufactured paints, as

there is nothing in them to help speed up the drying process, but as long as you're not in a hurry, you still get a good effect. The Real Paint Shop also sells overglazes, colourwash and non-toxic paint, suitable for use on interior and exterior wood, made from linseed oil.

Relics of Witney

35 Bridge St, Witney, Oxfordshire, Oxon OX8 6DA
tel: 01993 704611

This shop sells Annie Sloan's range of decorative paints which come in two distinct collections: the Traditional Range – colours inspired by eighteenth- and nineteenth-century European Decorative Painting; and the Impressionist Range – inspired by Decorative Painting of the twentieth century. Both are perfect for a number of techniques including colourwashing, stencilling, stamping, gilding and ageing. You can mix the two to create a whole new palette and suggestions for this are given on the back of the paint cards, as well as a useful guide to colours that work well together. Relics also sell just about everything you could ever need for specialist paint effects and their mail order catalogue is a must.

Roscolab Ltd
Blanchard Works, Kangley Bridge Rd, Sydenham, London SE26 5AQ
tel: 0181 659 2300 for stockists • fax: 0181 659 3153
e-mail: 100750.1474@compuserve.com

Although largely suppliers to the theatrical and film industry, this company nevertheless makes a fascinating range of paints that can be imaginatively adapted for domestic use. There are fluorescent paints, one of which is 'invisible' under normal lighting conditions but magically appears under UV light, and a range of lovely bright scenic paints called Off Broadway which *Home Front* designer Stewart Walton used when he created a mini-theatre for a toddler's room.

Rose of Jericho
St Blaise, Westhill Barn, Evershot, Dorchester, Dorset DT2 0LD
tel: 01935 83676 for stockists • fax: 01935 8301

The delightfully named Rose of Jericho has a small but quality range of traditional paints based on original recipes and in attractive muted colours. They also manufacture limewash, both soft and oil-bound distemper, plus suitable undercoats and mortars.

Shaker

322 King's Rd, London SW3 5UH
tel: 0171 352 3918 • fax: 0171 376 3494
and
25 Harcourt St, London W1H 1DT
tel: 0171 724 7672 • fax: 0171 724 6640

The Shaker Old Village Paint range comes in eight
colours with names like Wild Bayberry, South Family
Green and is suitable for woodwork, furniture and
metal. Imported from America and sold in pints and
quarts, Shaker recommends that you stir the paint for
at least seven minutes before applying, that you use
an oil-based undercoat and allow at least thirty-six
hours for it to dry (more in cold weather). You can buy
the paint at either store or by mail order through the
Harcourt St branch, but the delivery cost does tend to
bump the price up considerably.

Zoffany Paints

Talbot House, 17 Church St, Rickmansworth,
Herts WD3 1DE
tel: 01923 710680 • fax: 01923 710694
and
63 South Audley St, London W1Y 5BF (showroom)
tel: 0171 495 2505 • fax: 0171 493 7257

Zoffany has a limited but carefully chosen palette of
colours designed to complement their stylish range of
fabrics and wallpapers.

stamps & stencils

Stencilling had its real heyday in the eighties when it seemed that everything in sight was
given a bunch of grapes or a wreath of ivy. Although it has lost some of its popularity,
stencilling on walls can still give a room real individuality. If it is kept to a minimum or just
used to highlight certain features, it can look both stylish and timeless. *Home Front* has
shown, for example, how the clever use of a single Scandinavian-inspired motif, interspersed
at intervals to resemble wallpaper, can look stunning. At the opposite end of the scale,
stencilling can also be really wacky and original – adorning your walls with a Marilyn Monroe
stencil can really make more of a statement than simply having a poster that thousands of
other people also have. Stencilling can also be great for children's rooms and one way of
letting them have a hand in their own decor. Stamps with patterns cut out of wood or metal,
which are really just an advanced form of the potato print, are also great fun and the designs
they now come in are endless. Use them to create your own unique wallpaper patterns
and borders.

Annie Sloan

Knutsford House, Park St, Oxford OX20 1RW
tel: 0870 601 0082 for shops and stockists
fax: 01993 813710 for orders

As well as selling Annie Sloan's range of stencils, you
can also buy gilding materials, products to age and

distress, waxes and polishes ... in fact anything that is
used in her phenomenally successful rage of craft
books can be purchased by mail order or at one of the
shops. Phone the main number for details of your
nearest outlet.

Design-Warehouse Ltd
Kingfisher House, Copse Lane, Hayling Island,
Hampshire PO11 0QB
tel: 01705 466060 • fax: 01705 466262
e-mail: sales@design-warehouse.com

A whole host of products for stencilling and stamping
here, from stencil cutters, rubber stamps, paint sticks,
ink pads and all the accompanying paraphernalia. Mail
order only.

The Dwelling
76 Park St, Camberley, Surrey GU15 3PT
tel: 01252 336777 or 0800 854 882
fax: 01252 316767

Lots of different stencil designs are on offer or you can
have your own design made up – they make them for
you using a laser cutter. They also sell gilding
materials, liming wax, oil sticks, etc, all of which are
also available through mail order.

The English Stamp Company
Worth Matravers, Dorset BH19 3JP
tel: 01929 439117 for stockists • fax: 01929 439150

Choose from hundreds of different designs of stamp
pads from Tudor Roses to giraffes. They will also
custom make stamps if you want something particular.
They sell all the coloured ink pads plus plaster and
stonewall kits.

Mad Hatters
26 High St, Otford, Kent TN14 5PQ
tel: 019959 525578

A retail outlet for stencilling equipment including a
range of stencils themselves, plus acetates and heat
pens for creating your own.

Painted Finish
Unit 6, Hatton Country World, Hatton,
Warks CV35 8XA
tel: 01926 842376 • fax: 01926 842660

You can order from the comfort of your own home
anything you might need for stencilling through this
mail order only company. They have things like crackle
glaze and gold leaf too.

Pavilion Originals
6a Howe St, Edinburgh EH3 6TD
tel: 0131 225 3590 • fax: 0131 225 9913

Here you will find everything you could possibly need
for stencilling, including the varnishes, glazes and
the tools.

Personal Impressions
Curzon Rd, Chilton Industrial Estate, Sudbury,
Suffolk CO10 6XW
tel: 01787 375241 for stockists

This company has been making stamps since 1878 and
also distributes brass stencils from the company
Dreamweaver through craft shops. The brass stencils
are small in size (approx 5 x 7.5 cms/2 x 3 inches) and
feature everything from bears to boats. Dreamweaver
also do the entire alphabet on one stencil, which is
useful.

The Stamping Ground
PO Box 1364, London W5 5ZH
tel: 0181 840 0040 • fax: 0181 840 4060

This mail order company has lots of stamp pads in
many different designs plus all the coloured inks you
could possibly need.

Stencil Library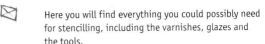
Stockfield Hall, Stocksfield,
Northumberland NE43 7TN
tel: 01661 844844 for stockists • fax: 01661 843984

Stencilling needn't always be about grape vines,
flowers and fruit and the Stencil Library proves it. If
you want to create a Warhol-inspired picture, they sell
a brilliant Marilyn Monroe stencil which Anne McKevitt
used on *Home Front* on the walls of a teenage
boudoir. The catalogue costs £5 but it's refundable
with your first order. They also do themed packs for
decoupage.

The Stencil Store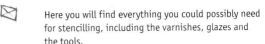
29/31 Heronsgate Rd, Chorleywood,
Herts WD3 5BN
tel: 01923 285577 • fax: 01923 285136
e-mail: mail@stencilstore.com

The owner of the company returned from America ten
years ago with a stencil and decided to set up his own
business. There are now more than twenty Stencil
Stores nationwide, including branches in Paris and
Amsterdam. The stencils themselves are fairly
traditional – like grapes, vines and Greek key – and
include some charming nursery motifs. (See also
Courses, p.265.)

wallpaper

It's incredible to think that wallpaper was first used as far back as the fifteenth century when small pieces were used to adorn walls or to bring interest to furniture. It was not until the dawn of the seventeenth century that printers struck upon the novel idea of pasting the paper together. Printed entirely by hand and gradually introducing colour, by the eighteenth century the technique had been perfected and highly patterned florals and Chinese-influenced papers came into vogue. With the advent of mechanization in the nineteenth century, wallpaper really took off.

Since then, the humble wallpaper has undergone numerous transformations and has gone in and out of favour countless times. Almost entirely banished in the 1980s, when the craze for paint effects really came into its own, wallpaper seemed outmoded and old-fashioned, something to be found only in stately homes. But recently, it has come back into fashion in a big way and today there are more ranges on offer than ever before. There are companies handmaking wallpaper from traditional hand block designs by designers such as Pugin and William Morris originating from the 1870s, who are reporting a great deal of renewed interest. But you can also get more modern and groovy rolls of funky metallic colours, ones made from bamboo or made to look like bamboo, and even wallpapers created to resemble concrete or wood. And it has come full circle: if you don't fancy attempting one of the many paint finishes – such as rag rolling, stippling or colourwashing – you can now buy papers that mimic these effects.

Another good thing about wallpaper is that it covers a multitude of sins if your walls are less than perfect, although it always pays to prepare the walls properly to ensure a smooth finish. It can make a room look instantly cosy, which is not always the case with paint, and can make a really striking impression – so much so that you won't need to put pictures up but let the wallpaper speak for itself!

traditional

Traditional wallpapers encompass those that are still being made to designs originating from hundreds of years ago – sometimes even using the same blocks and printing presses! This section also covers designs that aren't instantly recognisable but sum up 'period style' and would not look out of place in any traditionally styled home.

Alexander Beauchamp
Unit 2/12, Chelsea Harbour Design Centre, Chelsea Harbour, London SW10 0XE
tel: 0171 376 4556 • fax: 0171 376 3435

Experts in reproducing hand-printed wallpapers that are all screen-printed by hand. Many of the original screens used to make up the designs still exist but they can make up new ones, although this is, of course, a highly specialized service so expect to pay for their expertise. They also stock rolls of wallpaper, including a charming Chinoiserie collection.

Anna French

343 King's Rd, London SW3 5ES
tel: 0171 351 1126 for stockists • fax: 0171 351 0421

Anna French wallpapers are striking and beautifully designed to complement her range of fabrics. They have a curious timeless feel and, although some are inspired by traditional designs, they still retain a contemporary feel. They are available in hundreds of stores nationwide and the London showroom will be able to tell you your nearest stockist.

Baer & Ingram

273 Wandsworth Bridge Rd, London SW6 2TX
tel: 0171 736 6111 for showroom
tel: 01373 812552 for stockists • fax: 0171 736 8581

Browse through wallpaper books from most of the recognized names here. They offer a useful research service if you're trying to match an elusive wallpaper. They also have their own range of matching fabrics and papers including a *Wallace & Gromit* one.

Brunschwig & Fils

10 The Chambers, Chelsea Harbour Design Centre, London SW10 0XF
tel: 0171 744 1440 for stockists • fax: 0171 351 2280

Brunschwig & Fils are perhaps best known for their fake book paper, which has graced the walls of hundreds of rooms, but they also do many other designs, both traditional and contemporary.

Cole & Son

144 Offord Road, London N1 1NS
tel: 0171 607 4288 • fax: 0171 607 3341

Wallpapers are still hand printed in the traditional way using historic designs and they have been doing so in the John Perry factory since 1875. Their papers grace the walls of Buckingham Palace and Balmoral but don't be intimidated – they do stock cheaper rolls of prints, including a pretty butterfly one, in their showroom.

Colefax & Fowler

39 Brook St, London W1Y 2JE
tel: 0171 493 2231 for stockists • fax: 0171 355 4037

Colefax & Flower are one of the most recognized and long-established names in the business. Country cottages come to mind with their range of chintzes and florals and they seem to sum up all that is quintessentially English. Mixed with other things, they can still look bright and fresh and not at all grannyish.

Farrow & Ball

33 Uddens Trading Estate, Wimbourne, Dorset BH21 7NL
tel: 01202 876141 for stockists • fax: 01202 873793

A huge range of wallpapers which would look good in both period and modern homes and using colours from their paint collection. Their Paper 3 Collection is made using traditional nineteenth-century methods of dragging the paper through troughs filled with paint to produce the stripe with blurry edges.

Hodsoll McKenzie

52 Pimlico Rd, London SW1W 8LP
tel: 0171 730 2877 for stockists • fax: 0171 823 4939

Papers that are perfect for the period home can be found here, including Regency stripes in traditional colours, as well as a range of archive wallpapers.

Laura Ashley

PO Box 19, Newtown, Powys SY16 1DZ
tel: 0990 622116 for mail order and branches
tel: 0800 868100 for their Home Furnishing Catalogue

Laura Ashley Ltd suffered somewhat under the craze for getting rid of chintz and the trend for minimalism. But whilst still doing what it does best, in recent years it has lost its 'pretty pretty' image and become more contemporary and you may be surprised at the range on offer from striking ginghams to bold stripes.

Osborne & Little

304 King's Rd, London SW3 5UZ
tel: 0171 352 1456/0181 675 2255
fax: 0181 673 8254

Their showroom on the King's Rd is quite ostentatious and it can feel like you are being weighed down by tradition. However, don't be put off. If you're after real quality, they are definitely one of the names to trust. One of their bestsellers is a paper called Secret Garden, which is covered in topiary. *Home Front* designer Peter Plaskitt used their gold Oratorio and their silver Nocturne paper – part of their Coloratura collection – on a ceiling to stunning effect.

Sanderson

112–120 Brompton Rd, London SW3 1JJ
tel: 0171 584 3344 for stockists • fax: 0171 584 3344

The Brompton Rd showroom houses Sanderson's own collection as well as at least sixty other names. It's a good place to go and browse in to see what's on offer.

Sanderson's supply stock to a number of outlets so ring to find out your local stockist.

Timney & Fowler
388 King's Rd, London SW3 5UZ
tel: 0171 352 1456 for stockists • fax: 0171 352 0351

A Timney & Fowler wallpaper is almost always instantly recognizable for its striking black and white designs with classical motifs such as urns, calligraphy, and heraldic signs. Decorating a whole room with one of their designs would really make a bold statement. They have a showroom as well as supplying elsewhere.

Zoffany
Unit 12, Chelsea Harbour Design Centre, Chelsea Harbour, London SW10 0XE
tel: 0171 349 0043 for stockists • fax: 0171 351 9677

Zoffany specialize in hand-printed wallpapers spanning over three centuries, which are kept in their archive. They can reproduce them to order although they do have stock rolls available as well.

modern & groovy

Wallpaper doesn't have to be reserved for period style homes; if you want something eye-catching and unusual, try covering your walls in one of the faux effects that are around now – from fake bamboo to fake wood. Tradition is out, retro is in!

Altfield
Unit G4 & 2/22, Chelsea Harbour Design Centre, Chelsea Harbour, London SW10 0XE
tel: 0171 351 5893 for stockists • fax: 0171 376 5667

Altfield has lots of unusual finishes including bronze, metallic, lacquered silver, stone and wood veneers, and one called Island Weaves, which is made from natural fibres.

Bruno Triplet
Unit 1/1, Chelsea Harbour Design Centre, Chelsea Harbour, London SW10 0XE
tel: 0171 795 0395 for stockists • fax: 0171 376 3070

If you want to try out a fabric look on your walls, this company manufactures a great wallpaper made from

linen that looks contemporary and can act as a natural canvas for pictures.

Cath Kidston
8 Clarendon Cross, London W11 4AP
tel: 0171 221 4000 • fax: 0171 229 1992

Cath Kidston's designs are inspired by the fifties and here in this little shop you will find lots of pink roses set against a background of candy stripes. They always manage, however, to look fresh and modern. She also does a range of fake wood wallpaper.

Designer's Guild
267–271 & 275–277 Kings Rd, London SW3 5EN
tel: 0171 243 7300 • fax: 0171 243 7710
tel: 0171 351 5775 for enquiries and stockists

The wallpaper and fabric showroom (at No. 275–277) is packed with vertical racks and racks of wallpapers all in designer Tricia Guild's distinctive palette of vibrant colours. She takes a lot of inspiration from flowers, which are highly stylized, as well as stripes, spots and swirls. They're good to mix and match with the fabrics and you can see them in room sets at the home store a couple of doors down, at No. 267–271.

Donghia
Unit 23, Chelsea Harbour Design Centre, Chelsea Harbour, London SW20 0XE
tel: 0171 823 3456 for stockists • fax: 0171 376 5758

Making wallpaper out of raffia, grass cloth and hemp sounds like something out of the hippy seventies, but they're actually incredibly effective and with today's desire for 'sensual living', are bang up to date.

John Oliver
33 Pembridge Rd, London W11 3HG
tel: 0171 221 6466 for stockists • fax: 0171 727 5555

Leafing through their Metallics range book is like a trip down memory lane from the seventies. There are wallpapers covered in pampas grass and bamboo, lurid flowers, swirls and geometric patterns. *Home Front* designer Kevin Allan chose their Honeycombe Jo – a silver and blue metallic paper when he made over a lounge in seventies style. They don't, however, always have the old patterns in stock but they will try their best to help. The papers are definitely not cheap. Kevin's tip was to perhaps paper only one wall so as not to overdo it.

Muraspec
Zoffany House, 74–78 Wood Lane End, Hemel
Hempstead, Herts HP2 4RF
tel: 0990 117118 for stockists • fax: 0990 329020

If you fancy the smooth velvety feel of suede on your
walls, this company sell it in a range of colours with a
paper backing for application. They also do hessian
and silk fabrics suitable for walls.

Nobilis-Fontan Ltd
Unit G3, Chelsea Harbour Design Centre,
Chelsea Harbour, London SW10 0XE
tel: 0171 351 7878 for stockists • fax: 0171 376 3507

The trend for creating wallpapers to mimic other
effects is rife here. If you want your walls to look as if
they are covered in concrete, try their Concrete MAT23
wallpaper. They also do ones that look like wood.

Ornamenta Ltd
Unit 3/12 Chelsea Harbour Design Centre,
Chelsea Harbour, London SW10 0XE
tel: 0171 352 1824 for stockists • fax: 0171 376 3398

This company specializes in making wallpapers that
imitate other things, for example Woodgrain, which is
not to be confused with woodchip!

Tracy Kendall
116 Greylord Lane, London SW16 5RN
tel: 0181 769 0618

Very striking hand-printed wallpaper featuring one
strong image – a massive single feather or dandelion
head. They look stunning used as a single drop. You
get three images per roll and she will make them in
any colour on any kind of wallpaper.

specialist services

These people can help if you are trying to match up an
old wallpaper and replace it, or acquire specialist
accessories.

Hamilton-Weston Wallpapers
18 St Mary's Grove, Richmond, Surrey TW9 1VY
tel: 0181 940 4850 • fax: 0181 332 0296

If you find a little piece of wallpaper behind an old
wardrobe when you move in and would like to know
what it was and perhaps even match it, this company
offers a good sourcing service.

Troy North
High Ardley, Hexham,
Northumberland NE46 2LG
tel: 01434 607366 for stockists

Gimp is the co-ordinating braid that you can use to
finish off the edges of wallpaper where it meets the
dado rail and make it look really classy and
professional. Troy North sells it in every conceivable
colour and, although it's technically a traditional
thing, it's coming back into fashion.

wood panelling

In the seventeenth century, the skirting, dado and cornicing would all have been integral to
a fully panelled wall covered entirely in wood. It was not until plaster began to become more
popular that the use of wood began to decline and gradually disappear, leaving the skirtings
and cornicing behind as a legacy. Wooden panelling was then thought outmoded and old-
fashioned and, although its use continued to varying degrees in the Victorian period and
during the Arts & Crafts movement, it has remained so. Apart from a period in the seventies
and eighties when wooden cladding seemed to be going up everywhere, especially in
bathrooms, panelling was ripped out in favour of smooth plaster and paint.

Today, however, many people are now deliberately putting it up or at least trying to preserve what they may already have in their home. If you have any original wooden panelling it may need restoring and some of the companies listed below will be able to advise you. It is more likely you will have, or be considering, tongue and groove panelling. Painted white or stained, it can make your house look like a seaside beach hut or left in its natural state it can evoke a period feel. It looks great in a bathroom or below the dado rail in a hallway, and is also a good way of masking walls that are uneven and unsightly. If you're putting it up yourself using new wood from a timber merchant, be warned – if you want to avoid ugly gaps between the planks, you should allow the wood to acclimatize in your home for a few days. Below you will find everything from suppliers of the cheapest tongue and groove to experts in restoring Jacobean panelling. In all cases, phone first to discuss your requirements as these are not really shops you can visit.

Architectural Heritage

Taddington Manor, Taddington, nr Cutsdean,
Cheltenham, Glos GL54 5RY
tel: 01386 584414 • fax: 01386 584236
e-mail: puddy@architectural-heritage.co.uk

Set in the grounds of seventeenth-century Taddington Manor House with barns full of stock, there are at least four rooms full of reclaimed antique panelling.

Bernard Dru Oak

Bickham Manor, Timberscombe, Minehead,
Somerset TA24 7A
tel: 01643 841312 • fax: 01643 841048

The National Trust come to this company for restoration work on properties. Specialists in their field, they will also supply oak panelling for specific architectural projects.

CF Henderson

36 Graham St, London N1 8JX
tel: 0171 226 1212 • fax: 0171 490 4913

CF Henderson can supply you with wall panels in beech, oak or cherrywood for top of the range projects.

Charles Hurst

Unit 21, Bow Triangle Business Centre,
Eleanor St, London E3 4NP
tel: 0181 981 8562

A good provider of reasonably priced pine tongue and groove panelling that is dried in a kiln so that is takes on a weathered look. It comes in four different designs.

Crowther of Syon Lodge

Busch Corner, London Rd, Isleworth, Middx TW7 5BH
tel: 0181 560 7978 • fax: 0181 568 7572

If you live in a real Jacobean, Queen Anne or Tudor property and would like to restore it to its original state, this well-established company has a team of experts who can advise you and make period panelling to suit.

Deacon & Sandys

Hillcrest Farm Oast, Hawkhurst Rd, Cranbrook,
Kent N17 3QD
tel: 01580 713775 • fax: 01580 714056

This company has a team specializing in the seventeenth and eighteenth centuries, who have a stock of period panelling for walls and floors.

Do-It-All

tel: 0800 436436 for branches

If you want something cheap and cheerful that will still look good, Do-It-All have a good range of inexpensive tongue and groove panelling that is sold in packs. The job won't cost the earth – depending on how much you need!

Hallidays
The Old College, Dorchester-on-Thames, Wallingford,
Oxon OX10 7HL
tel: 01865 340028 • fax: 01865 341139

If you like the look of limed oak or 'antique' pine, this
company could be the answer as it has a good range of
both that are suitable for panelling.

Roy Blackman Associates
150 High Rd, Chadwell Heath, Romford, Essex RM6 6NT
tel: 0181 599 5247 for stockists • fax: 0181 598 8725

If you'd like the look of authentic wood panelling
but can't afford the real thing or can't find what you
want in a salvage yard, try this company's panelling
which looks like wood but is actually made from
polyurethane. Sit back and see if people can tell
the difference.

Thornhill Galleries
78 Deodar Rd, London SW15 2NJ
tel: 0181 874 2101 • fax: 0181 877 0313

This company has been established for more than a
hundred years and specializes in original period

panelling, particularly French and English. Phone first
to discuss your requirements.

Victorian Wood Works
Gilksten Trading Estate, 118 Carpenter Rd,
London E15 2DY
tel: 0181 985 8280 • fax: 0181 986 3770

Masses and masses of reclaimed timber is kept in
stock here and you'll probably be spoilt for choice. The
wood is mostly oak and pine although they also have
some more unusual things such as jarrah – a wood
from Australia.

Wickes
Head Office, 120–138 Station Rd,
Harrow, Middx HA1 2QB
tel: 0870 608 9001 for customer services
tel: 0500 300328 for branches

Wickes sell a very reasonably priced tongue and groove
cladding that you could put in a hall or in a bathroom.
They also sell useful pre-cut battens to put the
cladding up with.

cornicing & moulding

If you live in a period house and like period features, you may be lucky enough to have some
of the original cornicing and moulding. It is a fascinating way of dating your house and also
may tell you something about the house's previous owners – corbels (the decorative stone or
wooden supports which project from a wall) for example, were often made to depict the trade
of the family so you may discover they were a seafaring family or farmers. If you've got lots
of decorative-style plaster mouldings in the form of mythical beasts, your house is probably
Victorian whereas by the Edwardian era they had become much more simple with stylized
flowers and animals predominating.

Cornicing is there to disguise the join between the wall and the ceiling and can be made
either from wood or plaster, but, if it's been painted many times over the years, it may have
lost its definition. If your cornicing is damaged, it can usually be repaired on site by an expert.
Alternatively, you could go out and buy a ready-made section from a large DIY outlet. If your
style was one that was commonly used, the chances are you will still be able to find the
pattern. Ceiling roses were introduced in the nineteenth century principally as a way of covering

up unsightly gas piping in the ceiling and, if you suspect there was once a ceiling rose up on your ceiling, you can have reproduction ones specially made.

If your decorative mouldings have been ripped out and you'd like to replace them, you can buy certain pieces off the shelf – most DIY stores now do a selection. But if you think they look a bit plasticky, or you have a bit more money to spend, you can also enlist specialist companies to make new ones. If your decorative mouldings are intact but have been damaged over the years – maybe the nose has come off your cherub, or your lion's mane has become clogged with layers of paint – the specialist companies can also restore them.

There are some things you can do yourself to protect your period features – take extreme care when dusting or vacuuming. Either dust with a small paintbrush or, if you must use a vacuum, protect the mouldings by covering the cleaning head with a piece of foam. Don't use water on them as the plaster may dissolve.

Most companies listed below will send you a brochure on request so that you can see the type of thing they do. You can then specify to the company what items you want, and they will either fit them for you or you can order them to be delivered by post and you can fit them yourself.

Articole Studios
9 Alexander Rd, Stotfold, Hitchin, Herts SG5 4NA
tel/fax: 01462 835640
e-mail: articole@globalnet.co.uk

A specialist company who do lots of work for the theatre and film industries, making props out of plaster and resin castings. They undertake repairwork on stonework such as carved figures and make specialist moulds for companies like Artex. Phone to discuss your requirements.

Artistocast
14a Orgreave Close, Dorehouse Industrial Estate, Handsworth, Sheffield, S.Yorks S13 9NP
tel: 0114 269 0900 for a catalogue
fax: 0114 269 0955

If your decorative mouldings are chipped, broken or missing altogether, this company can design and manufacture you new ones in keeping with the style of your house as well as restore existing ones. Phone to discuss your requirements.

Belfast Mould Company
6 Florenceville Drive, Ormeau Rd,
Belfast BT7 3GY
tel: 01232 646699

Belfast Mould Company can come to the rescue if your mouldings have seen better days and need some TLC. Specialists in reproduction, they also offer a fitting service. Phone for an appointment.

British Gypsum Ltd
East Leake, Loughborough, Leics LE12 6HX
tel: 0990 456123 for stockists • fax: 0990 456356

Their Gyproc cove and cornice range is good for hiding ugly surface cracks or cables and come with full fixing instructions. If you have a corbel that is badly damaged and can't afford to have it repaired their cornice batten bridges the old one without having to remove it. Phone to discuss your requirements.

Cliveden Conservation Workshop
The Tennis Courts, Cliveden Estate, Taplow, Maidenhead, Berks SL6 0JA
tel: 01628 604721 • fax: 01628 660379

Specialists in the conservation of stonework and statuary, this company also undertakes large-scale commissions for plasterwork such as Elizabethan ceilings. They are mostly concerned with stately homes, but worth contacting if you have a property of particular interest and a budget of between £5000–10 000. They also do restorative work on floors – for example, the medieval tiles of Westminster Abbey and Winchester Cathedral.

Copley Decor Mouldings
Copley Decor Ltd, Leyburn, N.Yorks DL8 5QA
tel: 01969 623410 for stockists • fax: 01969 624398

All types of cornices, ceiling roses, dado rails, corbels, 'mouldings. They are made from hard cellular resin rather than fibrous plaster which is lighter and more flexible and therefore easier to fix to uneven walls and ceilings. They can be painted with any decorative paint.

The Decorative Plasterwork Company
Brunswick Industrial Estate, Brunswick Village, Newcastle-upon-Tyne NE13 7BA
tel: 0191 236 4226 for brochure • fax: 0191 236 2242

A good range of niches, corbels, panel moulds and sixteen different types of centrepiece for the ceiling. The experienced staff will give advice as to which would best suit your type and period of house.

Designed Plastercraft Associates
35 Shore Rd, London E9 7TA
tel: 0181 985 8866 • fax: 0181 986 3168

Specialists in fibrous plasterwork who usually undertake large restoration projects, often commissioned by English Heritage. They will consider smaller projects on occasion depending on the nature of the job.

Fine Art Mouldings
Unit 6, Roebuck Rd Trading Estate,
15–17 Roebuck Rd, Hainault, Ilford, Essex IG6 3TU
tel: 0181 502 7602 • fax: 0181 502 7603

All the products are made in the company's own workshops and you can either fix them up yourself as they come complete with full instructions, or pay for one of the firm's City & Guilds Craftsmen to do it for you. As well as the usual niches, corbels and cornicing, there is an attractive range of decorated ceiling roses (which are delicately shaded), overdoors, ceiling domes and columns in classical designs. You can visit the site during normal office hours.

G Jackson & Sons
Clark & Fenn, Unit 19, Mitcham Industrial Estate, Streatham Rd, London CR4 2AJ
tel: 0181 648 4343 • fax: 0181 640 1986

One of the oldest plasterwork specialists in operation originally founded by Robert Adam. They are often called in to historic sites that have suffered extensive damage through fire or flood. They will occasionally take on domestic commissions. Phone to discuss your requirements.

Grandisson
The Mill, Alansway, Ottery St Mary, Devon EX11 1NR
tel: 01404 812876

This company can reproduce all types of decorative mouldings including corbels, ceiling roses, columns and niches. Phone for advice on your particular needs.

H&F Badcock
Unit 9, 57 Sandgate St, Old Kent Rd, London SE15 1LE
tel: 0171 639 0304 for brochure • fax: 0171 358 1239

Established more than a hundred years ago, H&F Badcock produce high-quality fibrous plasterwork. They are able to create columns and half columns, corbels, friezes and bedmoulds – all in traditional designs featuring urns and swags, bunches of grapes – and all types of cornicing. They can reproduce damaged plasterwork or work to your own design. Phone to discuss your requirements.

Hayles & Howe
25 Picton St, Montpelier, Bristol, Avon BS6 5PZ
tel: 01179 246673 • fax: 01179 243928

Specialists in ornamental plasterwork who can restore and reproduce a period feature whether it is a large ceiling or a small statue.

Hodkin & Jones
Callywhite Lane, Dronfield, Sheffield, S.Yorks S18 6XP
tel: 01246 290890 • fax: 01246 290292

If your cornicing has come down or is damaged beyond repair, this company can make a copy in fibrous plaster and re-install it for you.

Lindman
Tower Lane, Warmley, Bristol, Avon BS15 2XX
tel: 0117 947 7878 for brochure • fax: 0117 961 0901

If your room is lacking in traditional features, this company makes wood cornicing in two different period styles – baroque and classical – which is easy to put up yourself. It comes with hidden tracks and you simply snap the cornicing into place. They also do panelling which can be painted or stained and is more affordable than hardwood panelling.

Locker & Riley
23 Faraday Rd, Leigh-on-Sea, Essex SS9 5JU
tel: 01702 528803 • fax: 01702 526125

Everything for the period home here from dado rails to columns and cornices that the company will also install for you.

Richard Burbridge Ltd
Whittington St, Oswestry, Shropshire SY11 1HZ
tel: 01691 678201 for stockists • fax: 01691 659091

Wooden decorative mouldings and ornaments in the shape of fleur de lys, scrolls etc. Phone for your nearest stockists – available in most large DIY stores such as B&Q and Homebase.

Stevensons of Norwich
Roundtree Way, Norwich, Norfolk NR7 8SQ
tel: 01603 400824 • fax: 01603 405113

If your existing plasterwork is damaged and cannot be easily restored or has come off altogether, this company provides a useful matching service.

Troika Architectural Mouldings
Troika House, 41 Clun St, Sheffield, S.Yorks S4 7JS
tel: 0114 275 3222 • fax: 0114 275 3781

If your ceiling is plain and featureless, this company will consider turning it into a decorative feast. They take larger projects, and did the oriental ceilings in London's Dorchester Hotel, which gives you some idea of their craftsmanship and the scale of work they undertake.

metal

Putting metal on walls used to be the exclusive preserve of trendy cafés and bars, but now the look is spilling over into home use. However, using metal can be costly and you can overdo it. On limited areas, such as kitchen worktops and splashbacks, it can look amazing. It does take some looking after as marks show up quite easily and you may have to spend some time regularly buffing up the surface area. Metal, which includes aluminium, zinc, tin and the most costly of all, stainless steel, normally comes in sheets or tiles and can be solid or perforated. Most companies will cut to size. It can be fixed directly to plaster but it is probably safer to fix it to wood first and, if you're not sure, get a specialist recommended from the company you purchase it from. You don't want the bare plaster coming away in your hands.

Aluminium sheeting is considerably cheaper than stainless steel but can look just as good in a kitchen or even a lounge. Remember that the edges may be sharp and will have to be sunk into something. It is still quite expensive so use it sparingly. One of the biggest responses *Home Front* had to an item was when Amateur Decorator of the Year winner, Danielle Dax, put silver plastic sheeting on the walls of a Barratt house sitting-room. She was actually using Mylar – a substance used for plant propagation – which is available from good plant nurseries.

The companies listed below are not really shops that you can just walk into, they are workshops. Phone first and they will be happy to discuss your needs and will usually be able to cut products to size for you.

AJ Fabrications
9 Manfield Park, Cranleigh, Surrey GU6 8PT
tel: 01843 276016

If you've considered using aluminium treadplate (the cross-hatched metal you see everywhere – especially on the backs of doors and in lifts) for your walls or floor, this company can supply it. Taken up the walls it can look really unusual, although it's best not to go too overboard. You don't want to feel as if you're living in a tin hut. It could also be used for kitchen splashbacks.

Bragman Flett
30 Gwynne Rd, London SW11 3UW
tel: 0171 228 8855 • fax: 0171 228 2312

This company sells all types of metal including copper, brass, aluminium, and the pricey stainless steel. The metals can be perforated or supplied in galvanized sheets.

Builders, Iron & Zincworth
Millmarsh Lane, Brimsdown, Enfield, Middx EN3 7QA
tel: 0181 443 3300 • fax: 0181 804 6672

As their name suggests, this company is a good outlet for zinc, which can be used for worktops in the kitchen. Sold in sheets, you'll need a specialist to cut and fit it for you.

County and Capital Metals
Lockfield Ave, Brimsdown, Enfield, Middx EN3 7PY
tel: 0181 805 7277 • fax: 0181 805 7308

A good supplier of stainless steel that comes in sheets. Fitting stainless steel on kitchen worktops is a specialist job but it can look amazing. They also do other metals.

DZ Designs
The Old Mill House, Stanwell Moor, Staines, Middx TW19 6BJ
tel: 01753 682266 • fax: 01753 685440

If you like the look of chicken wire – perhaps in the cupboard doors of a country-style cabinet or even a bathroom one – this company supplies it in various different finishes, dull or shiny, and with various gauge holes.

The Expanded Metal Company
PO Box 14, Longhill Industrial Estate, Hartlepool, N.Yorks TS25 1PR
tel: 01429 867388 for stockists
fax: 01429 866795

Steel mesh is an innovative way to dress your walls but, used in the right setting, it can be extremely effective. The Expanded Metal Company can supply it in many different finishes.

Gooding Aluminium
1 British Wharf, Landmann Way, London SE14 5RS
tel: 0181 692 2255 • fax: 0181 469 0031

A good supplier of aluminium sheeting who will cut to size and finish off the edges for you if they are not being 'sunk' into something else.

JD Beardmore & Co
17 Pall Mall, London SW1Y 5LU
tel: 0171 637 7041 • fax: 0171 436 9222

If you want to conceal ugly radiators or even unsightly central heating pipes, this long-established company supplies lots of attractive perforated grilles and meshes in brass and steel that you can view in their showroom.

Metra Non-Ferrous Metals
Pindar Rd, Hoddesdon, Herts EN11 0DE
tel: 01992 460455 • fax: 01992 451207

A good supplier of zinc sheeting that can be cut to size.

Smiths Metal Centre
42–56 Tottenham Rd, London N1 4BZ
tel: 0171 241 2430 • fax: 0171 254 9608

This outlet sells all types of metal but particularly aluminium and tinplate. *Home Front* designer Stewart Walton used a sheet of tinplate with its magnetic qualities, and a polished finish smooth to the touch, to make a magnetic pinboard for a teenage boy's bedroom. The helpful staff will be able to advise you – phone to discuss requirements first.

glass

Glass brick walls and features have been around for a long time, but it seems that it is only recently that they have come into the limelight. If you are keeping your eye out for them you will suddenly see them everywhere – in shops, banks, department stores, stations, and in the pavement you are walking on.

The beauty of glass brick walls is that you can partition off areas without blocking out the light. You can create dappled light effects or, if you use coloured glass, mini rainbows from the refracted light. But be careful about where they go – not all the bricks or blocks available conform to standard fire regulations and if you're constructing a free-standing wall make sure it will be safe with whatever method of construction you employ. Steel-rod assembly is where the glass bricks are slotted together using tiny steel rods that are invisible once the wall is built, others are plastered together and held in place by plastic pegs. The individual suppliers should be able to advise you.

Colourwash
63–65 Fulham High St, London SW6 3JJ
tel: 0171 371 0911 • fax: 0181 459 4280

This bathroom stockist also sells glass blocks of the steel-rod assembly type and they come in clear, a frosted finish, or blue, green and brown.

Focus Ceramics Ltd
Unit 4, Hamm Moor Lane, Weybridge Trading Estate, Weybridge, Surrey KT15 2SD
tel: 01932 854881 for stockists • fax: 01932 851494
e-mail: focus@dial.pipex.com

Focus distribute a huge range of glass blocks in all the colours of the rainbow as well as clear. *Home Front* used them to create a stunning wall in a riverside apartment that reflected the light glinting off the water and made a really special internal feature.

Luxcrete
Premier House, Disraeli Rd, London NW10 7BT
tel: 0181 965 7292

Luxcrete are experts in all types of glass and have a wide range of glass blocks which are the steel-rod assembly kind. Choose from twenty-nine different patterns and textures to create unique walls.

Shackerley (Holdings) Group Ltd
PO Box 20, Wigan Rd, Euxton, Lancs PR7 6JJ
tel: 01257 273114 for stockists
fax: 01257 262386

The Solaris range of glass blocks, which Shackerley distribute, come in blue, grey, light green, pink and turquoise. The clear ones come in a huge range of different finishes – from ribbed, cross-ribbed and cross-hatched to ones that look as if bubbles have been trapped inside. If you want to create glass panels in the floor, they also do glass paving blocks which look incredible.

Wickes
Head Office, 120–138 Station Rd, Harrow, Middx HA1 2QB
tel: 0870 608 9001 for customer services
tel: 0500 300328 for branches

Wickes' glass blocks are extremely good value and they use the white plaster method rather than steel rods. Anne McKevitt chose them to create a circular wall around the shower room in the loft conversion which appeared on *Home Front*.

unusual wall coverings

Here are a couple of companies who offer really fun wall coverings – if you're really adventurous or want something out of the ordinary to be really different.

AJL Displays
Enterprise House, Inkerman St, Llanelli,
Carmarthenshire SA15 1SA
tel: 01554 758913 for stockists • fax: 01554 777760

If you get bored easily, this company does spray on wall coverings that can be washed off. Their 'disco glitter' is available in hundreds of colours.

JW Bollom
PO Box 78, Croydon Rd, Beckenham, Kent BR3 4BL
tel: 0181 658 2299 for stockists • fax: 0181 658 8672

Bollom are full of ideas for unusual things to go on walls such as felt, hessian, glass fibre, suede, metallics and vinyls.

under

What you choose for the floor has an enormous impact on the rest of the house; not only does it pull the room together as a whole but it also sets the tone and will, hopefully, last for years. Choosing the right type of flooring depends largely on what you are using the room for. For example, something hard-wearing is an obvious choice if it is going to be taking a battering from people constantly charging up and down the stairs or coming in with muddy shoes from the garden.

Carpets available today come in all sorts of colours and textures, cut into tiles and with a range of piles. But carpet is not the only solution to covering your floors. Natural floor coverings made from products such as seagrass, jute or coconut husks have become hugely popular in the nineties. Wood is an option, even if your floorboards are in bad condition, with the range of new laminated and parquet floorings that can now be fitted over your existing floor. Linoleum has had a revival and there are hundreds of patterns and colours to choose from, and there is rubber, vinyl, stone of all varieties and even leather flooring for use underfoot.

This chapter guides you through the choices and also some options you may not have considered. Although you always need to bear in mind the purpose of the floor, don't be afraid to try out more unusual floor coverings. And remember – whatever you spend, you will reap in quality.

foot

key: 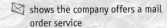 shows the product has appeared on
Home Front

✉ shows the company offers a mail
order service

carpet

Gone are the days when carpet was a measure of wealth – remember shag pile? For a while carpet seemed to plummet out of fashion and was ripped up, to be replaced with bare floorboards. But sometimes all you really want is a little bit of warmth and comfort underfoot.

Today there are more types, colours and textures than ever before. Deciding on carpet is really dependent on where you intend to use it. Fitted carpets are not really practical for bathrooms or kitchens, although carpet tiles are. If you scorch a patch with an iron, or your pet has a little accident, you can simply replace the affected area. It can be frightening to decide on a block of colour, knowing it will take up the majority of the space and therefore the eye. Remember these simple guidelines: if your room is large and you want to make it appear smaller or cosier, then go for a darker shade but, be warned, darker shades show up as much dirt as lighter ones do; conversely, if you have a small room and wish to make it appear larger, then choose a lighter colour; if your room is small don't choose a design with a large, jazzy pattern that will only serve to dominate the room; above all, consider what the room is going to be used for or whether you need a particularly stain-resistant or hard-wearing carpet, such as short needlecord.

With carpet you really do get what you pay for – if you skimp on the underlay it will show. Rubber underlay is the best as it will give you a lovely spring in your step whilst absorbing pressure. Pure wool is the most hard-wearing material, which is reflected in the price, although a small ratio of nylon mixed in (say 80 per cent wool, 20 per cent nylon) will also give your carpet lasting durability. Check whether the tufts are woven in or are just stuck on to a backing. The former will obviously withstand more wear but, again, will cost more because of the work that has gone into its manufacture.

The term 'carpet pile' refers to the way individual strands of wool or nylon are knotted one by one into the warp (the threads running lengthways on a loom) to form tufts. The number of knots per square inch determines the final softness of the carpet. Carpets that are flatwoven have no pile as such. In these the crosswise, or weft, threads are just threaded over and under the warp and pulled taut. There are hand- and machine-made carpets but you only really need to know all this to help you understand why carpets can vary wildly in price.

It is possible to lay carpet yourself and you could save yourself some money, but in the long run it's usually best to call in the experts. They know how to cut the carpet with the minimum wastage, and will be able to supply the gripper rods, underlay and other bits and bobs needed for the job (always check what is included in your quote) and save you a lot of time.

Because there are showrooms all over the country displaying carpets from many different manufacturers, we have listed the manufacturers and/or companies we think are particularly good. They will be able to tell you where your nearest showroom or stockist is.

Afia Carpets
Unit 11/12, Chelsea Harbour Design Centre,
Chelsea Harbour, London SW10 0XE
tel: 0171 351 5858 for stockists • fax: 0171 351 9677

All their carpets are made from pure wool and flat woven. If you want a groovy leopard-skin design, this is where to look.

Allied Carpets Group
Head Office, Allied House, 76 High St, Orpington,
Kent BR6 0JQ
tel: 0800 192192 for branches

Allied Carpets is still one of the biggest names in the carpet industry and has literally hundreds of designs, colours, patterns, textures and weaves on offer. Available from most major outlets as well as their own superstores, you should be able to find something you like here.

The Alternative Flooring Co Ltd
14 Anton Trading Estate, Andover, Hants SP10 2NJ
tel: 01264 335111 • fax: 01264 336445

There are some lovely carpets to choose from here in fine knit weaves and ribs. *Home Front* designer Kevin Allan chose their Silver Birch Wool to create a really classy look for a lounge. The staff are extremely helpful and knowledgeable.

Anta Scotland
Fearn, Tain, Ross-shire IV20 1XW
tel: 01862 832477 for stockists • fax: 01862 832616
e-mail: antascot@acl.com
and
32 High St, Royal Mile, Edinburgh EH1 1TB
tel: 0131 557 8300

Anta have been making carpets using traditional methods for years and they are all top quality using wool from the Shetlands. Whether you're a true Scot or not, their tartan designs are bold and fun.

Blenheim Carpets
Unit 2A, Salter St, London NW10 6UL
tel: 0181 964 2700 • fax: 0181 960 8051
and

555 Kings Rd, London SW6 2EB
tel: 0171 384 2773 • fax: 0171 731 6568

If you are looking for a quality carpet, visit either one of these showrooms to see a good selection mostly in wool, with tweeds and herringbones. It is also a good place to go for high-quality entrance matting.

Brintons Ltd
PO Box 16, Exchange St, Kidderminster,
Worcs DY10 1AG
tel: 01562 820000 • fax: 01562 515597

The largest carpet manufacturer in the UK for Axminster and Wilton, both of which are woven carpets and therefore high quality. There are over 500 different styles available and they all come in the recommended 80:20 wool to nylon ratio.

The Carpet Library
148 Wandsworth Bridge Rd, London SW6 2UH
tel: 0171 736 3664 • fax: 0171 736 7554

The Carpet Library is a good name for this company as you can browse through endless books full of examples. They will send out smaller pocket-sized books of photos on request although you really should see the carpets in the flesh, as it were. There are all sorts of things here, from traditional to modern, including some reproductions of William Morris designs.

Chatsworth
227 Brompton Rd, London SW3 1PY
tel: 0171 584 1386 • fax: 0171 581 3053

A good showroom for printed and plain carpets, which are nearly all woven rather than stuck onto a backing.

Custom Carpet Company
PO Box 167, Tadworth, Surrey KT20 6WH
tel: 01737 830301 for details • fax: 01737 833785

From the smallest rug to a large fitted floor covering, this company can make a carpet to suit your needs. Design is the major element of their approach, whether hand-tufted, passmachine or woven, and their designers will prepare art samples for you and sample tufts before beginning your individual project.

Heuga

hf

Ashlyns Hall, Chesham Rd, Berkhamstead,
Herts HP4 2ST
tel: 0990 304030 for stockists

Heuga have an excellent range of carpet tiles in all
sorts of types. Don't be put off by the fact that they
are 100 per cent nylon – they are actually extremely
hard-wearing. The Tundra range comes in ten different
colourways: five in natural hues and five vibrant ones.
There are also tiles with deep piles and short-tufted
ones which would be suitable for a kitchen.

Ryalux Carpets Ltd

Ensor Mill, Queensway, Castleton, Rochdale,
Lancs OL11 2NU
tel: 01706 716000 for stockists • fax: 01706 860618
tel: 0800 163632 for more information

Made with top-quality New Zealand wool, these carpets
come in hundreds of plain colours and a lesser number
of subtly patterned ones. Tufted on modern looms, you
can order the carpets in any width, which means you
will not pay for any wastage. The company also offers
an invaluable Special Dye Service where they can
match any colour you would like for your colour
scheme.

Tomkinson's Carpets Ltd

PO Box 11, Duke Place, Kidderminster, Worcs DY10 2JR
tel: 0800 374429 for stockists

Masses of colours and patterns that you can mix and
match. They do a fun zebra-striped border called Safari
that you could use to edge another strong colour, as
well as more than thirty others. They are also one of
the main distributors for Axminster – they produced
the first piece of Royal Axminster way back in 1878.

Tretford

Joseph Hamilton & Seaton Ltd, JHS House, Gerard,
Lichfield Rd Ind Estate, Tamworth, Staffs B79 7UW
tel: 01827 312414 for stockists • fax: 01827 52092

Heavy contract carpet and tiles in plain blocks of
colour – Pomegranate, Curry Powder, Lobster – which
can be cut and combined without the pieces fraying.
They all have a five-year guarantee and are
manufactured using environmentally friendly
systems and processes.

Wools of New Zealand

Design and Development Centre, Little Lane, Ilkley,
W.Yorks LS29 8VG
tel: 01943 603 888 for stockists

Decorwool is their trademark and it comes in every
conceivable colour from orange and lime to rich blues
and purples. They also have a sisal-look weave which
combines the look of bleached wood with the comfort
of carpet.

natural coverings

Natural floor covering such as coir, jute, seagrass, and sisal enjoyed a massive splurge in
popularity in the nineties and their popularity looks set to endure. The reason perhaps for this
is that they are cheaper than carpet but answer the need for something soft underfoot, and
they look good in every type of house from country cottages to industrial-style lofts.

Coir is made from coconut husks, and can therefore be quite rough although it very hard-
wearing. Naturally brown in colour, it can be dyed and woven into lots of different designs.
Jute is the softest of the four, made from the fibrous stalks of the jute plant, and is perfect
for bedrooms or children's rooms. If your room is particularly sunny, be careful as it is prone
to fade under direct exposure to sunlight, and water spilled on to it will leave marks. Seagrass,
grown in paddy fields, has a natural in-built stain resistance but cannot be dyed and retains
a wonderful smell for some time after it has been laid. Finally, sisal, taken from a plant

resembling a yucca, is quite coarse in texture and individual strands can be dyed before it is spun, giving a textured look.

The only drawback with natural floor coverings is that they can sometimes be difficult to clean. Try and choose one that comes with an in-built stain protection and protective backing that will prolong its life. Some of the rougher ones are quite prickly if you're in bare feet or have young children crawling about, but there are plenty of softer ones on offer. If you are using any of them as stair coverings or as a runner, a useful tip is to make sure whoever fits them lays them with the warp threads of the weave running parallel to the stair treads and the weft threads running in the direction of the stair traffic. This will help make them last.

The Alternative Flooring Co Ltd
14 Anton Trading Estate, Andover,
Hants SP10 2NJ
tel: 01264 335111 for stockists • fax: 01264 336445

As well as a good selection of colours in seagrass, coir, sisal and jute, you will also find a range of coir rugs in a choice of plain or tapestry borders. These will give you the look without having to worry about the fitting. Phone for details of local stockists.

Bery Designs
157 St John's Hill, Battersea, London SW11 1TQ
tel: 0171 924 2197 • fax: 0171 924 1879

You can really buy an unusual natural runner or rug from this shop. The runners and rugs are made from sisal and jute and then hand-painted with fast-drying industrial paint for a hard-wearing surface. Colours can be mixed and matched to your choice and original commissions are welcome.

Bruno Triplet
Unit 1/1, Chelsea Harbour Design Centre,
Chelsea Harbour, London SW10 0XE
tel: 0171 795 0395 for stockists • fax: 0171 376 3070

These are seriously trendy natural floor covering designs in a host of subtle colours and weaves. One of the materials used is linen which comes in five different patterns. In other ranges subtle colours are mixed in interesting weaves to give a very contemporary look.

Crucial Trading
PO Box II, Duke Place, Kidderminster DY10 2JR
tel: 01562 825200 for stockists • fax: 01562 825177

One of the original companies to sell natural floor coverings, they now have a huge range of different colours, weaves and fibres. They even have a floor covering made from 100 per cent paper yarn. Or you can have rugs or mats with a selection of more than thirty different tapestry borders. Phone for details of more than local stockist.

Fired Earth
Twyford Mill, Oxford Rd, Adderbury,
Oxon OX17 3HP
tel: 01295 812088 for stockists
fax: 01295 810832

A distinctive range of natural floor coverings in different weaves and materials. If you are looking for something smart and eye-catching take a look at the herringbone weaves. They also make natural fibre rugs with either whipped edges or braided edges.

IKEA
Brent Park, 2 Drury Way, North Circular Rd,
London NW10 0TH
tel: 0181 208 5600 for enquiries and branches

There are some incredibly low prices here for cotton dhurries. The coir, sisal and jute mats are more expensive, but they are larger and still extremely good value. There isn't an enormous selection, but there are some trendy, unusual designs.

Kersaint Cobb & Co Ltd
Unit A02, Tower Bridge Business Complex,
Clements Rd, London SE16 4DG
tel: 0171 237 4270 for stockists
fax: 0171 252 0073
tel: 0800 163716 for information

A relatively small but varied collection of natural floorcoverings are manufactured by this company. One collection, called the Savannah Wool Collection, weaves jute, sisal and wool together, backed with hessian, to make a carpet-like texture. The company doesn't go in for dyeing with bright colours and leaves the majority of their floorcoverings in their natural earthy tones.

Lloyd Loom of Spalding
Wardentree Lane, Pinchbeck, Spalding, Lincs PE11 3SY
tel: 01775 712111 for stockists • fax: 01775 710571

Famous worldwide for their paper yarn furniture, Lloyd Loom now also make paper yarn natural floor coverings. The range comprises four designs in a choice of eight colours and looks quite different from many other natural floor coverings.

Marston & Langinger
192 Ebury St, London SW1W 8UP
tel: 0171 824 8818 for stockists
fax: 0171 824 8757

Better known for their conservatories, Marston & Langinger have a small selection of Moroccan rugs and hand-painted sisal rugs. The hand-painted rugs are in delicate colours and the Moroccan rugs have patterns sewn on in wool.

Natural Flooring Direct
PO Box 8104, London SE16 4ZA
tel: 0800 454721 • fax: 0171 732 5815

If you are looking for natural floor coverings at a reasonable price, it is definitely worth checking these people out. Although their price list may seem to mirror everybody else's, they are actually much cheaper because they include fitting, underlay and door bars in their prices. They operate a mail order service which helps to keep costs down.

Roger Oates Design
The Long Barn, Eastnor, Ledbury,
Herefordshire HR8 1EL
tel: 01531 631611 for stockists
fax: 01531 631361

Smart rugs and runners, mostly in stripes in a palette of earthy reds, mossy greens and soft antique blues. They also do plain rugs in haircord and sisal and these can be finished with a choice of contrast binding.

Rooksmoor Mills
Bath Rd, Stroud, Glos GL5 5ND
tel: 01453 872577 for stockists • fax: 01453 872420

This company specializes in a full range of natural floor coverings such as a variety of sisals, coirs, seagrasses and jutes, but also has quite a vast collection of wool carpets which look like natural floor coverings and also wool/sisal mixtures.

Sinclair Till Flooring Company
791–793 Wandsworth Rd, London SW8 3JQ
tel: 0171 720 0031 • fax: 0171 498 3814

This is a real centre for natural floor coverings. As well as having a vast collection of the sisals, jutes, coirs and seagrasses it also has cork flooring, rubber and painted sisal rugs and runners.

Three Shires
2 Eastboro Court, Alliance Business Park,
Attleborough Fields, Nuneaton, Warks CV11 6SD
tel: 01203 370365 • fax: 01203 370896

This company offers a large range of natural floor coverings in different colours, weaves and fibres including sisal, jute, seagrass and coir. You can't actually go to a showroom, but they will send samples, prices and literature to your home and offer a full measuring, estimating and fitting service..

The Waveney Rush Industry
Common Rd, Aldeby, Beccles, Suffolk NR34 0BL
tel: 01502 677345 • fax: 01502 678134
e-mail: Wag@paston.co.uk

If you want the real, real, real McCoy in natural floor coverings you have to come here. In 1947 this company revived the craft of rush-weaving, which dates back to early Anglo-Saxon days. All the products are entirely handmade and plaited in strips to almost any shape or size you require.

Zoffany
Talbot House, 17 Church St, Rickmansworth,
Herts WD3 1DE
tel: 01923 710680 for stockists • fax: 01923 710694

If you are looking for something unusual, look here. The Rückstuhl collection of natural floor coverings includes linen, jute, flax, paper, horse hair and goat's hair as well as the more normal fibres. Many of these are woven into distinctive and chic designs.

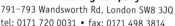

wood

It was not until after the middle of the eighteenth century that people began covering up their wooden floorboards. Until then they were deemed a feature and covered with beautiful rugs. Nowadays, with the huge impact Scandinavian style has had on British style, the first thing many people do when they move into a new property is to look under their carpets and see what state the floorboards are in. If they look sound, stripping and sanding is *de rigueur*.

Sanding is perhaps one of the worst DIY jobs going. It's noisy, physically exhausting, and time-consuming, but when you begin to reveal the beauty of the wood, it is definitely very satisfying. To seal floorboards you must apply at least three coats of varnish. It is tedious waiting for the layers to dry, but well worth it, and it will protect your floor for years to come. Make sure you hoover up all the remaining dust from the sanding process first, otherwise small specks will be fossilized forever in the varnish. Some people recommend wiping the floorboards first with white spirit applied with a soft cloth before varnishing – this does help to bring up the grain and get rid of any last remaining traces of dust.

But what do you do if your floorboards are not good enough to sand or you've got, as many people have in newer properties, boring old concrete? Don't despair because there are hundreds of alternatives if you still want the warm look of wood. Buying reclaimed wood from salvage yards is another good option and whether you choose pale birch or dark mahogany the results can look stunning. You also have the added satisfaction of knowing you're contributing to protecting the environment.

Alternatively, there is a huge choice of new wooden flooring from parquet to laminated wood. Laminate simply means that a coat of plastic has been bonded on to the base board or it has been constituted of layers of paper or cheap plywood impregnated with resin. Laminated wooden floors are great for thoroughfares such as hallways and can be laid on top of existing floors without having to nail them down – so-called 'floating floors' – fitting together rather like a jigsaw. The drawbacks are that they have a limited lifespan and you can't reseal them if they become damaged. Similarly, veneer floors are made by bonding a thin hardwood surface on to layers of softwood and you can't sand them either.

In this section you will find companies that manufacture and sell new wooden floors, although some use reclaimed wood. For more sources of old wood, see the Salvage chapter (p.190).

Activity Flooring Systems Ltd

Mill Lane, Westbury, Brackley,
Northants NN13 5JS
tel: 01280 705229 for stockists • fax: 01280 705992

This distributor has a wide range of hardwood timber
floorings and will also install them if required.

Agora London

123 Hurlingham Rd, London SW6 3NJ
tel: 0171 731 6327 • fax: 0171 736 3573

Agora use reclaimed oak from France to make beautiful
floors in a range of different classic designs. They will
also install them for you.

Bamboard

Church Nursery, East Carleton, Norwich NR14 8HT
tel/fax: 01508 570777 for details

Bamboard is a great new product which is both
beautiful to look at and touch. If you're wondering
how bamboo, which is technically a grass, can
withstand heavy traffic it is actually surprisingly tough
and resistant – as tough as hardwoods like maple and
oak. It is also environmentally sound. The wood comes
in a honey mellow colour but can be stained.

Bernard Dru Oak

Bickham Manor, Timberscombe, Minehead,
Somerset TA24 7UA
tel: 01643 841312 for stockists • fax: 01643 841048

If you're searching for a really rustic look, this
company manufactures a range which is called just
that, where the knots and the grain of the oak really
show through. There are three other 'grades' with
varying degrees of 'knottiness'. The one called Clean
has no knots at all. They will deliver nationwide.

Bruce Hardwood Floors (UK) Ltd

Unit 9, Moorbrook, Southmead Industrial Estate,
Didcot, Oxon OX11 7PJ
tel: 01235 515100 for stockists • fax: 01235 862255

This company, known simply as 'Bruce', is one of the
world's largest manufacturers of hardwood floors. The
wood can either be left unfinished so that you can stain
and seal it yourself, or finished in a variety of styles.

Campbell & Young

16 Lettice St, London SW6 4EH
tel: 0171 736 7191 • fax: 0171 731 2431
tel: 0171 795 0095 for stockists

Suppliers of parquet flooring in a choice of hard maple,
oak, beech, ash or birch. The tongue and groove can go
from left to right or vice versa allowing for an unusual
'fishbone' effect or can be laid in squares or you can
have the more standard 'shipdeck' pattern.

Campbell Marson & Company Ltd

34 Wimbledon Business Centre, Riverside Rd,
London SW17 0BA
tel: 0181 879 1909 for stockists • fax: 0181 946 9395
and
573 Kings Rd, London SW6 2EB (showroom)
tel: 0171 371 5001

As well as supplying new parquet flooring and a choice
of hardwood flooring, this company offers the useful
service of restoring existing parquet floors that have
suffered too much wear and tear over the years.

Chauncey's

15–16 Feeder Rd, Bristol, Avon BS2 0SB
tel/fax: 0117 971 3131

Chauncey's have a huge range of hardwood floors,
although they specialize in pitch pine and oak. They
also have reclaimed oak which you can buy in planks or
cut in tongue and groove boards.

David Gunton Hardwood Floors

Grange Lane, Whitegate, nr Winsford,
Cheshire CW7 2PS
tel: 01606 861442 • fax: 01606 861445

David Gunton is an international company that has a
huge range of timbers, as well as being experts at
installing floors in particularly awkward conditions,
perhaps where there are underfloor heating pipes to
negotiate. If you want a painstakingly crafted
marquetry floor, phone to discuss your requirements.

Designworkshop mfg

7–8 Denby Dale Industrial Park, Wakefield Rd,
Denby Dale, Huddersfield, W.Yorks HD8 8QH
tel: 01484 864455 for information
fax: 01484 861096

If you'd like wide planks in your laminated floor rather
than the standard shipdeck width, this company may
be able to help. They produce all their laminate and
hardwood flooring in-house.

Durabella Ltd

Eastways Industrial Estate, Witham, Essex CM8 3YQ
tel: 01376 535000 for stockists • fax: 01367 517217

One of the main manufacturers of strip flooring which can be purchased unfinished or finished. They are also trusted installers.

English Timbers
1A Main St, Kirkburn, Driffield, E.Yorks YO25 9DU
tel: 01377 229301 for stockists • fax: 01377 229303

This manufacturer uses traditional native timbers such as English oak, ash and elm and also American and dark woods such as danta and jatoba from West Africa and South America respectively. They take a great deal of care to use correctly seasoned timber and have a good technical back-up team.

Finewood Floors
5 Gibson Business Centre, High Rd,
London N17 0DH
tel: 0181 365 0222 • fax: 0181 885 3860

Choose from a massive selection of woods such as maple, walnut, oak and ash, as well as American red elm – they are one of the largest manufacturers in London. They will make you a parquet floor to order, and will also do more unusual floor finishes such as liming, oiling and antiquing the wood on request.

The Hardwood Flooring Company
146–152 West End Lane, London NW6 1SD
tel: 0171 328 8481 • fax: 0171 625 5951

This shop stocks many of the main suppliers including Junckers and Kährs.

Homebase
Head Office, Beddington House, Wallington,
Surrey SM6 0HB
tel: 0645 801800 for enquiries and branches

If you want the look of expensive parquet floors for a fraction of the cost, try their own-brand unfinished parquet block flooring, which can be stained or varnished using a colour of your choice.

IKEA
Brent Park, 2 Drury Way, North Circular Rd,
London NW10 0TH
tel: 0181 208 5600 for enquiries and branches

IKEA do very good, reasonably priced laminated flooring. Choose from Tundra, either in a beech stave or an alder pattern, Regel, which is more expensive and comes in birch, beech or oak veneer, or Stäpp, the cheapest of the three. None of the floors is recommended for use in bathrooms, conservatories or outdoors. All three versions have instructions on how to lay it yourself, and their sales gimmick is to offer you a money-back guarantee if you don't manage to do it!

Junckers Ltd
Wheaton Court Commercial Centre, Wheaton Rd,
Witham, Essex CM8 3UJ
tel: 01376 517512 for stockists • fax: 01376 514401

Junckers are one of the leading names in Europe for solid hardwood floors in oak, beech and ash. They do a Quick-Clip system that even a novice can lay easily.

Kährs
Kährs UK Ltd, Unit 1 Timberlaine Estate, Gravel Lane,
Quarry Lane, Chichester, W.Sussex PO19 2FJ
tel: 01243 778747 for stockists • fax: 01243 531237
e-mail: kahrs@mistral.co.uk

Kährs have lots of different new wooden floors which they have carefully selected to fit perfectly into many different settings. For example, their range includes Ash Stockholm, which is great for kitchens if you want that blond-wood effect to go with pale units; and they have darker floors, made from Australian jarrah wood; or two-strip beech and one-strip parquet, as well as many others. The majority of the wood they use comes from sustainable Swedish forests.

LBC Hardwood Flooring
100 Weston Grove, Upton, Chester, Cheshire CH2 1QN
tel: 01244 377811

This company uses both new and reclaimed wood for its floors and deals mostly in oak, pitch pine, and some elm and maple. You can buy the wood either in plank form, or cut into strips and blocks. They also do a range of laminated flooring.

Norske Skog Flooring
4b The Courtyard, Meadowbank, Bourne End,
Bucks SL8 5AU
tel: 01628 527298 for information • fax: 01628 529837

If you're loath to spend a lot on a new floor which you'll have to leave behind if you move, this is one revolutionary product you can take with you! Each section clips together in a mechanical locking system and so can easily be laid without a great deal of expertise and simply taken up again. Available in twenty colours, it is also ideal for allergy sufferers as it needs no fixing with glue or sealing with chemicals.

Penrose Hardwood Flooring
The Woodland Centre, Whitesmith, nr Lewes,
E.Sussex BN8 6JB
tel: 01825 872025 for stockists • fax: 01825 872971

This manufacturing company has around twenty-five
different woods including maple cherry, yellow birch
and black walnut. They also supply the more unusual
American white oak and bamboo.

Pergo Perstop Flooring UK Ltd
18–19 Cromwell Park, Chipping Norton,
Oxon OX7 5SR
tel: 01608 646200 for stockists • fax: 01608 644877
tel: 0800 374771 for catalogue

Pergo specialize in laminate flooring in beech, which
comes in narrow-blocked, pine-washed, oak-planked
and oak narrow-planked. The terms specify the
width of plank you should expect. They also do a
gorgeous laminated flooring in white pine for that
bleached-out look.

Richard Burbridge Ltd
Whittington Rd, Oswestry, Shropshire SY11 1HZ
tel: 01691 678214 for stockists • fax: 01691 659091

Laminated flooring is this company's speciality and
you have five different colour options. The floors of
many large shops are from here, which proves that
they can withstand enormous amounts of feet
trampling over them.

Solid Floor
128 St John St, London EC1V 4JS
tel: 0171 251 2917 • fax: 0171 251 2917

This shop stocks a wide range of hardwoods but
particularly specializes in importing more unusual and
exotic woods from abroad. If you're eco-friendly, they
stock sub-tropical hardwoods from Argentina and
Paraguay that are grown in environmentally sustainable

conditions, following strict conservation guidelines.
They also do great bamboo flooring where you can see
the pattern made from the nodes of the original cane.

Victorian Wood Works
Gliksten Trading Estate, 118 Carpenters Rd,
London E15 2ES
tel: 0181 534 1000

This is a well-known place to buy reclaimed wood floors
including wood block flooring and parquet. You can
even get such things as inlaid parquetry here. They also
have a good selection of old beams in a variety of woods.

Weldon Flooring Ltd
Hill Holt Farm, Norton Disney, Lincs LN6 9UP
tel: 01636 892772 • fax: 01636 892973

This company will design, supply and fit all types of
hardwood flooring. They'll even prepare the sub-floor
for you so that it goes down perfectly.

Wicanders
Amorim House, Star Rd, Partridge Green,
Horsham, W.Sussex RH13 8RA
tel: 01403 710001 for stockists • fax: 01403 710003

Their 'floating floors' can be laid quite easily in a day,
depending on the size of your room, and will instantly
give your room a warm look. They can be laid over
practically any existing surface – even carpet.

Wickes
Head Office, 120–138 Station Rd, Harrow,
Middx HA1 2QB
tel: 0870 608 9001 for customer services
tel: 0500 300328 for branches

Wickes have very reasonable prices for laminate
flooring as well as pine tongue and groove, and they
will deliver free if you place a decent-sized order. There
are over 122 branches nationwide.

lino, rubber & vinyl

Say the word 'lino' and many people think of school floors from the seventies – all a bit nasty
and coming up round the edges. But linoleum has undergone something of a revolution and
is now available in hundreds of tempting shades. The beauty of lino is that it is a completely

natural product, being made from linseed oil, wood that is ground down until it is as fine as flour, natural pigments and pine resin. It is also surprisingly warm underfoot, practical and easy to clean. Remember that if you choose a plain solid colour it will tend to show up marks quite easily – it is perhaps better to go for one with a slightly speckled tone.

Rubber is great for rooms in which you need a tough surface which will take a lot of traffic. It is just starting to catch on and is fantastically practical. It won't shrink or tear, and the patterns can lend it a design quality all of its own. Your floor must be absolutely level otherwise it will show all the lumps and bumps and the covering might start to lift. Get a professional in to lay a latex screed which will give you a lovely smooth surface.

Vinyl is actually short for polyvinyl chloride or PVC and, although it performs like lino, is made from chemicals. It is also water-resistant, but be careful of putting anything hot on it – unlike rubber and lino, it will scorch quite easily.

Lino, vinyl and rubber are all easy to clean and maintain and are a good choice if you suffer from allergies as they don't harbour dust in the way that carpets and natural floor coverings, such as jute and sisal, can.

Altro Floors
Works Rd, Letchworth, Herts SG6 1NW
tel: 01462 480480 for stockists • fax: 01462 480010
e-mail: info@altro.co.uk

Altro have a great range of vinyl flooring in funky colours. Their Prismastic vinyl looks like water with dappled light on it, and they also do a great range of swimming-pool tiles. They are very durable and come in a huge selection of colours, not just the primary ones you'd expect, with or without glittery-gravel set into them or with a marbled flecked appearance.

The Amtico Company Ltd
Kingfield Rd, Coventry, W.Midlands CV6 5PL
tel: 0800 667766 for stockists

Amtico have a fantastic range of truly novel products and are always at the cutting edge. They have a good range of coloured vinyls, one of which looks like fake wood with a metallic sheen. They recently launched a product which looks like glass but is actually plastic. *Home Front*'s Anne McKevitt chose their Monopoly board flooring when she was making the children's ward of a hospital a more fun place for the children to be, and she gave instant glamour to a small bathroom with some brightly coloured tiles sprinkled with silver glitter. New products are being launched all the time.

Armstrong World Industries Ltd
Fleck Way, Teeside Industrial Estate, Thornaby, Stockton-on-Tees, Cleveland TS17 9JJ
tel: 01642 763224 • fax: 01642 750213

You can choose from over 200 colours in this company's portfolio of PVC floor coverings. They are normally a supplier to the commercial sector, but they will do domestic work depending on the size of the order.

Dalsouple
PO Box 140, Bridgwater, Somerset TA5 1HT
tel: 01984 667233 for stockists • fax: 01984 667366

Rubber flooring need never be dull again as there are some really exquisite colours here such as the subtle Geranium, Lavender and Pistachio as well as in-your-face fuchsias and violets. The rubber comes in solid blocks of colour or you can have a marbled or terrazzo finish. Either have a smooth finish, or choose one of twenty-seven textures – such as raised bumps, leafs, or tiny grids. The rubber has to be imported from France and may take some weeks to arrive, but the very helpful telephone staff will advise you if anywhere else in the country has some in stock.

DLW Floorings Ltd
Centurion Court, Milton Park, Abingdon, Oxon OX14 4RY
tel: 01235 831296 for stockists • fax: 01235 861016

This manufacturer has a huge range of parquet flooring in hundreds of different colourways and marbled effects. There is also a range of inlays – for example, alphabet letters or charming animal motifs, such as hippos and snails, can be incorporated into the design to add fun in a child's room.

First Floor

174 Wandsworth Bridge Rd, London SW6 2UQ
tel: 0171 736 1123 • fax: 0171 371 9812

This is a good place to come to see samples of vinyl and rubber flooring from some of the main companies including Dalsouple (see p.45) and Forbo-Nairn (see below). They also have a good fitting service.

Flotex

Bonar Floor Ltd, High Holborn Rd, Ripley, Derbyshire DE5 3NT
tel: 01773 744121 • fax: 01773 744142

An odd one this, as Flotex, which is the trademark name, is neither vinyl nor carpet but has the best of both worlds. Their slogan is 'warm like carpet – tough like vinyl' and the product is made by fixing 66 million nylon fibres per square metre onto a reinforced glass fibre backing – a mind-boggling feat! The result is a floorcovering that can be as patterned as carpet, but that won't shrink or tear, and any spills can be mopped up instantly. It comes in loads of different patterns.

Forbo-Nairn Ltd

PO Box 1, Kirkcaldy, Fife, Scotland KY1 2SB
tel: 01592 643111/01592 643777 for stockists
fax: 01592 643999
e-mail: headoffice@forbo-nairn.co.uk

Forbo-Nairn have been manufacturing high-quality linoleum for years and their patience has paid off now it is undergoing a revival. They have two patented/trademarked products – Marmoleum and Artoleum. Both are hard-wearing but soft and easy to clean. When *Home Front* was following the Perry family restoring their thirties semi in Bristol, designer Peter Plaskitt chose Marmoleum for their family room precisely because of these qualities. He used it again for the floor of a school staffroom, which would need to withstand heavy traffic, but mixed different colours to create different areas.

Gerflor Ltd

Rothwell Rd, Warwick, Warks, CV34 5PY
tel: 01926 401500 for brochure • fax: 01926 401647

Lots of different coloured and patterned vinyl and rubber floorings here that are soft to walk on but can take quite a hammering. Their products are often in hospitals (they are noise-friendly), but don't be put off by the clinical image – they're warm and modern.

Homebase

Head Office, Beddington House, Wallington, Surrey SM6 0HB
tel:0645 801800 for enquiries and branches

Homebase stocks a very good, inexpensive range of floor tiles. Many are self-adhesive and so you can lay them yourself. Their Harmony blue was chosen by *Home Front* designer Kevin Allan for a seventies-style room.

Jaymart Rubber & Plastic

Woodlands Trading Estate, Eden Vale Rd, Westbury, Wilts BA13 3QS
tel: 01373 864926 for stockists • fax: 01373 858454

Specialists in contract flooring, Jaymart have a vast range of carpets, mats and matting which, with a little imagination, can be used for all sorts of domestic purposes. *Home Front* designer Stewart Walton chose their Grasshopper grass (softer than Astroturf) to cover bedroom walls for a football-mad blind boy, who wanted some fun and texture in his room. They do a good range of non-slip rubbers, usually seen on the side of swimming-pools, but that can be used in bathrooms, lounges or virtually anywhere that takes your fancy.

Karndean International

Ferry Lane, Offenham, Evesham, Worcs WR11 5RT
tel: 01386 49902 for stockists • fax: 01386 761249

If you'd like a vinyl floor installed in your kitchen or anywhere where it's going to take a battering from people constantly walking over it and from frequent cleaning, this company imports very heavy duty vinyl to do the job. It comes in either plank or tile form and, although the majority of their business is commercial, they are happy to supply for domestic purposes.

Pentonville Rubber Company

104 Pentonville Rd, London N1 9JB
tel: 0171 837 4582

A great source for rubber in bright primary colours, with or without patterns. Use it in a bathroom, a bedroom or a kitchen and it will look great. They usually supply to trade but will also deal with domestic orders.

stone

Limestone, marble, slate, quarry tiles, ceramic, sandstone and granite fall into this category and can all be used to spectacular effect within the home. Ceramic and encaustic tiles (where the pattern is inlaid into the tile) are probably the most frequently used because of their relative easiness to lay and their lower cost. Thus they have a whole chapter to themselves (see Ceramics on p.52). But this section on stone, divided into regional areas for ease of use, will help you consider the other options – they might not be as expensive as you'd think. (See p.5 if you are unsure what region to look under.)

Slate can look stunning. No two pieces are identical, and the hues range from a bluish grey to pinky tones. It has a wonderful silvery quality and is surprisingly easy to lay because the sheets are relatively thin, although it is still a job for a professional as it is prone to scratch easily. If limestone and marble are used sparingly they can look fantastic. Limestone mellows with age and will last a lifetime. Marble in particular can look fantastic in a bathroom, and is silky smooth to the touch although it can get stained if not looked after carefully. Sandstone has a warm honey-coloured tinge. It is found in the West Country and can be bought in tiles or flags. Granite, perhaps the most expensive hard floor covering and therefore out of many people's price range, can look spectacular.

The term 'quarry tiles' is used to refer to mass-produced terracotta rather than handmade. They are cheaper than the real thing because of this. Although they do lack some of the quality of real terracotta, they are very hard-wearing.

When caring for whatever type of stone floor you have, don't use wax. Although a silicone-based sealant could be used to seal it, ask the supplier what is suitable for maintenance of the surface. The best way to care for it is to sweep it regularly with a soft broom, and give it a clean every so often with hot water, a mop and a caustic-free detergent.

south west

Artisans of Devizes
36 The Nursery, Bath Rd, Devizes, Wilts SN10 2AG
tel: 01380 720007 • fax: 01380 728368

If you are environmentally conscious and patriotic, this could be the company for you as they look for quarries that use traditional methods in Britain if possible. Terracottas, limestones, slate tiles and flags, however, are brought in from abroad. If you are looking for the time-worn appearance of old stone floors, they have developed a special method to give new stone this look.

Classical Flagstones
Lyncombe Vale Farm, Lyncombe Vale, Bath, Avon BA2 4LT
tel: 01225 316759 • fax: 01225 482076

Replica flagstones you would be hard pressed to tell apart from the originals. Each is made by hand and there is a range of sizes. Finishes include Yorkstone, refined white limestone and distressed white limestone.

Delabole Slate
Pengelly Rd, Delabole, Cornwall PL33 9AZ
tel: 01840 212242 • fax: 01840 212948

Experienced craftsmen still split these handcrafted, natural slate floor tiles in the traditional way to expose their natural texture. The tiles come in a range of standard sizes and can be highly polished or left natural for a more traditional look.

Wellington Tile Co
Tone Industrial Estate, Milverton Rd, Wellington, Somerset TA21 0AZ
tel: 01823 667242 for stockists • fax: 01823 665685

A host of slates, flags and terracotta tiles with the added perk of local honey-coloured Ham stone flagstones available here. All the different stones come in a variety of colours and finishes.

south east

Albion Stone Quarries
Wray Coppice, Oaks Rd, Reigate, Surrey RH2 0LE
tel: 01737 224322 • fax: 01737 244584

It is quite refreshing to find a company that quarries British limestone – a stone that has its own unique qualities. It is fashioned into lovely floor tiles which will last a lifetime and only look better with age.

Attica
543 Battersea Park Rd, London SW11 3BL
tel: 0171 738 1234 • fax: 0171 924 7875
e-mail: tile@attica.co.uk

This showroom has an exciting mixture of antique stones such as antique Jerusalem stone and newly quarried stones which are treated to give them an old appearance. They also offer all kinds of decorative effects such as borders reminiscent of historic Italian marble and mosaics or *pavimenti* ceramic insets.

Capital Marble
Pall Mall Deposit, Unit 1, 124–128 Barlby Rd, London W10 6BL
tel: 0181 968 5340 for stockists • fax: 0181 968 8827

Capital Marble don't just distribute marble but also a wide range of other hard flooring, including limestone and the more expensive granite, as well as vitrified porcelain and mosaics suitable for underfoot.

Elon
66 Fulham Rd, South Kensington, London SW3 6HH
tel: 0171 460 4600 for stockists • fax: 0171 460 4601

Choose from a whole selection of handmade floor tiles in different colours, finishes and sizes at this showroom. There are terracotta, slate and Tuscan tiles and some lovely patterned ceramic inserts which measure 2 inches/5cm square.

European Heritage
48–52 Dawes Rd, London SW6 7EN
tel: 0171 381 6063 • fax: 0171 381 9534

As the name suggests, European Heritage specializes in European stone floors and sources products from all over the Continent. Some of the stone is quarried and some of it is reclaimed from old buildings. Their speciality is marble and granite, particularly unpolished, natural-looking finishes.

The Extra Special Tile Co
38 Albert Rd North, Reigate, Surrey RH2 9EG
tel: 01737 223030

If you are looking for a variety of natural stone floors, this is a good place to go and see. They supply ceramic tiles, plus a vast range of twenty different types of slate, ten different terracottas and ten different limestones.

Granite, Marble & Stone Ltd
Unit 7, Crown Yard, Bedgebury Rd, Goudhurst, Kent TN17 2QZ
tel: 01580 212222 • fax: 01580 211841

This company started importing Chinese slate more than ten years ago and now also brings in marble and limestone from all over the world. They sell direct to customers to keep costs down and have quite a large selection of different types of stone flooring.

H&L Marble
15a Wadsworth Rd, Perivale, Middx UB6 7JN
tel: 0181 810 9223 • fax: 0181 810 9718

This company supplies marble, granite and limestone flooring in many different shapes, sizes and finishes. They also offer kitchen worktops, vanity tops for the bathroom and a selection of marble tiles.

Hard Rock Flooring

Fleet Marston Farm, Fleet Marston, Aylesbury,
Bucks HP18 0PZ
tel: 01296 658755 • fax: 01296 655735

Hard Rock Flooring has a wealth of experience in
supplying natural stone and can help you to select the
right product and arrange for its fixing. They source
their natural stone and terracotta floorings from
Britain and other countries throughout the world and
have an impressive range of terracottas, sandstones,
slate, limestones and Venetian marble.

Limestone Gallery

2 Plimsoll Rd, London N4 2EW
tel: 0171 359 4432 • fax: 0171 359 5481

If you are looking for limestone, this showroom has
more than 150 types gathered together. They also do
unusual materials suitable for flooring, including real
terracotta tiles imported from France, and volcanic
lava slabs.

Magnificent Marble

276 High St, Sutton, Surrey SM1 1PG
tel: 0181 643 1723 • fax: 0181 770 7801

Magnificent Marble don't just stock marble, granite
and other stone products are available from this
company. They can provide floor or work surfaces for
the kitchen or bathroom in a variety of patterns and
colours, both in granite and marble.

Marble Arch Ltd

431 & 432 Gordon Business Centre, Gordon Grove,
London SE5 9DU
tel: 0171 738 7212 • fax: 0171 738 7613

This company are experts in marble for all
household applications and will supply and install
it too, whether for a bathroom or kitchen floor. The
helpful staff will guide you through the choices
available. Marble Arch Ltd also supply granite and
limestone.

Paris Ceramics

583 Kings Rd, London SW6 2EH
tel: 0171 371 7778 • fax: 0171 371 8395
and
4 Montpellier St, Harrogate HG1 2RY
tel: 01423 523877

A huge selection of beautiful antique and new floors
from all over the world is available from this company.

The antique floors have been 'weathered' by countless
pairs of feet and the company have a range of special
services to age the newer examples. Also on offer are
terrazzo-finish composition stone floors and Romano-
British mosaics. The company also have a showroom
in Harrogate.

Stone Age

19 Filmer Rd, London SW6 7BU
tel: 0171 3857954 • fax: 0171 385 7956

Stone Age has a really vast collection of different
stones from all over the world, and specializes in
sandstone and limestone. The company can
recommend specialist tilers and give good advice on
protecting and cleaning your floor.

Stonell

Forstal House, Beltring, Paddock Wood,
Kent TN12 6PY
tel: 01892 833500 • fax: 01892 833600
and
Bockingfold, Ladham Rd, Goudhurst,
Kent TN17 1LY
tel: 01580 211167
e-mail: admin@stonell.co.uk

Stonell keeps a large stock of stone tiles so you
should avoid a long and frustrating wait once you
have chosen and ordered from their wide ranges of
limestone, slate and sandstone. Stone tiles can be
left natural for a traditional look or can be highly
polished for a more shiny finish. The tiles can also
be matched with slate or marble bouchons in order
to make quite distinctive and unusual patterns.
They do a lovely white limestone called Blanco
Classical.

Terra Firma Tiles

70 Chalk Farm Rd, London NW1 4AN
tel: 0171 485 7227 • fax: 0171 485 7203

Terracotta, slate, stone, Moroccan floor tiles, mosaics,
marble and ceramic tiles – you name the floor tile,
Terra Firma Tiles have it! A huge variety is on offer
with at least ten different colours of slates for
instance. Glass and ceramic mosaics are available and
they even have marble mosaics. Ring for more
information and an appointment to view their
showroom in Salisbury, Wiltshire.

east

Abbott Stone & Masonry
Oundle Rd, Barnwell, Peterborough,Cambs PE8 5PD
tel: 01832 274566 • fax: 01832 23293

Although this company is a manufacturer, it will supply to the customer direct. Sometimes cutting out the middleman can save you money. Limestone is quarried from sites around the country and made into floor tiles.

Terracotta Direct
Pinford End Farm, Pinford End, Bury St Edmunds, Suffolk IP29 5NU
tel: 01284 388002 • fax: 01284 388003

Purchased directly from Spain to keep costs low, these terracotta tiles can usually be delivered within seven days of ordering. Handmade terracotta tiles vary in colour, but you can ask for a shade preference.

central

Fired Earth
Twyford Mill, Oxford Rd, Adderbury, Oxon OX17 3HP
tel: 01295 812088 for stockists • fax: 01295 810832

With 'fired earth' being the literal meaning of terracotta, naturally this company has a large selection of terracotta floor tiles, but they also do natural stone including marble, limestone and slate and some Roman mosaic borders and tiles. Phone for details of your local stockist.

north west

Burlington
Cavendish House, Kirkby-in-Furness, Cumbria LA17 7UN
tel: 01229 889661 • fax: 01229 889466

Quarried from the heart of the Lake District, these stone floor tiles have names such as Elterwater and Brandy Crag to prove it! They come in two sizes and five natural tones ranging from pale green to blue/grey.

Kirkstone
Skelwith Bridge, nr Ambleside, Cumbria LA22 9NN
tel: 01539 433296 • fax: 01539 434006

The company is named after the sea-green stone Kirkstone that it sells, but it has masses of other stones in its portfolio. Travertines from Italy and Turkey are the newest introductions and these have a wide range of colourings including gold and rose. The company also has rich veins of limestones, marbles, granites and mosaics. Phone for news of their London showroom.

north east

Lapacida Ltd
2–3 Crown Place, Harrogate HG1 2RY
tel: 01423 560262 • fax: 01423 560661

A good, helpful place to go for slate that can be used for floors. *Home Front's* Neville Griffiths' went there for a large amount of slate for a salvage bathroom.

wales

Berwyn Slate Quarry
The Horse Shoe Pass, Llangollen, Denbighshire LL20 8DP
tel: 01978 861897 • fax: 01978 869292

Rich blue/black slate is quarried from this, one of the oldest quarries in the industry. The durable, deeply coloured slate makes wonderful floor tiles which you can use inside or outside your home. There are many different finishes available.

Dennis of Ruabon Ltd
Hafod Tileries, Ruabon, Wrexham LL14 6ET
tel: 01978 843484 for stockists • fax: 01978 843276

Pure Welsh clay quarry tiles that come in various shades of natural colour and also stunning heather, black and yellow, which can all be matched with decorative borders. The tiles are frost- and household chemical-resistant and you can have an anti-slip finish added.

Mandarin
Unit 1, Wonastow Rd Industrial Estate, Monmouth, Monmouthshire NP5 3JB
tel: 01600 715444 • fax: 01600 715494

If you want to see an extensive range of sandstones, limestones, marbles, slates and terracottas, this company has nearly forty variations of these natural stones. They also have a handy pocket-sized brochure for you to peruse at your leisure.

northern ireland

The Global Stone Co
Unit 1, Musgrove Park Industrial Estate, Stockmans Way, Belfast BT9 7ET
tel: 01232 381220

If you are restoring an old home and can't match, or find, the right stone floor, The Global Stone Co may be able to help you. They have a sourcing and matching service at their showroom, and they can supply new stone floors and external stone paving.

Marble Design & Installation
69 Ravenhill Rd, Belfast BT6 8DQ
tel: 01232 452000 • fax: 01232 450245

You will find a good selection of marble and granite at this showroom, mostly in sheet form, although there are some tiles. The company will also supply cladding, make fireplaces and have a full design and installation service.

Regan Tile Design
56 Glenshane Rd, Magherafelt,
Co Londonderry BT45 8RE
tel: 01648 43163 • fax: 01648 44322

There are eleven different types of stone in this company's portfolio, although if you don't find exactly what you are looking for they can source others. Most of those in stock are limestones, either new or antique. They also have marble and slate and a full design and installation service.

unusual floor coverings

Here you will find ideas for flooring that don't really fit into any other category but are certainly worth considering if you want something unique.

Bill Amberg
The Shop, 10 Chepstow Rd, London W2 5BD
tel: 0171 727 3560

Leather must be one of the most luxurious choices for floors as it's extremely expensive. However, it looks fantastic and will literally last a lifetime – ageing only makes it look better. There are still only a few suppliers in this country and Bill Amberg is famous for his winning ways with leather.

Harvey Maria
Trident Business Centre, 89 Bickersteth Rd,
London SW17 9SH
tel: 0181 516 7788 for stockists
fax: 0181 516 7789
e-mail: sales@harveymaria.co.uk

Harvey Maria attracted a lot of press attention with their funky PVC laminated cork floor tiles which brought unfashionable cork back into the spotlight. There are some really fun designs to choose from which all have a sort of photographic effect laid over cork: Meadow has wild grasses and poppies; Seashore even includes the odd crab; and Tropical Seas has fish

swimming in the bluest sea. These are just three of the designs. There is also a range of hand-painted tiles featuring Chinese rice bowls amongst other things.

HDII Design
East Workshop, 100 Lillie Rd, London SW6 7RF
tel: 0171 381 0066

If a parquet-look floor, but in leather not wood, is your heart's desire, then this company will make you one to order. Be prepared to lavish some care and attention on it once installed – it needs regular waxing (as often as once a month) but the time spent doing it will reap dividends. The bonus is, the floors improve with age.

Made of Waste
244 Gray's Inn Rd, London WC1X 8JR
tel: 0171 278 6971 for stockists • fax: 0171 833 0018

Committed to recycling, this company has a truly unique range of flooring made from plastic bottle flooring. It's not that cheap but it looks really funky and your conscience will be saved. It looks like someone has done a huge splatter painting over the floor.

ceramics

Tiling is an ever-popular solution to covering walls and floors, and responses to items about mosaic on *Home Front* – whether it's a simple tabletop, a fountain for a garden or a mosaic floor – have been phenomenal. If you're planning on using tiles on a floor, however, check first that they will be suitable. Look out for the Porcelain Enamel Institute (PEI) rating, which will indicate whether the tile is suitable for light, medium or heavy traffic. Make sure also that they are slip-resistant, particularly if you intend to tile a bathroom floor.

When buying new tiles, there is an easy way of working out how many you will need so you're not caught short. Calculate the area of the surface you intend to tile in square metres, measure the size of the individual tile, calculate the number of tiles per square metre and then multiply this figure by the area to be covered! Always add on a few – it's advisable to buy 10 per cent over and above what you need – as some are bound to get broken or snap in the tiling process. If you need to go and get more later, the colour may vary slightly from batch to batch, which will look odd if they're supposed to be a uniform colour.

Many of the companies offering ceramic tiles suitable for floors and walls also offer ones made from terracotta, marble, slate and limestone. Use chapter two's section on stone (see p.47) if these are what you are specifically looking for. The companies listed in the mosaic section of this chapter offer a variety of services so read carefully to see what they can provide. Because most are distributors we have listed them alphabetically rather than by region. You can call to find out where your nearest local stockist is.

& mosaic

key: 🏠 shows the product has appeared on
Home Front

✉ shows the company offers a mail
order service

ceramics

Ceramic tiles have been in use for thousands of years. As long ago as 5000 BC the Egyptians used them to decorate the inside of the pyramids and the way they are made today remains, in essence, largely unchanged. Tiles are made from clay and earth mixed with water and then baked under intense temperatures. It is only really the manufacturing process that has developed over the centuries.

Tiles made in this way are the perfect answer for both walls and floors. They are naturally resistant to water and heat, can withstand heavy traffic, are easy to keep clean, and come in literally any design possible. Handmade tiles are perfect if you want a unique result and, although they will have some variation in colour and thickness and may have small blemishes, this only adds to their individual quality. Machine-made tiles, on the other hand, are more uniform in size and shape and considerably cheaper. It is easy to mix the two either in patterns or by adding borders.

The upkeep of all ceramic tiles is pretty straightforward but different ones should be cleaned in different ways. To clean glazed tiles, most often found in a bathroom or kitchen, you should always use a weak solution of everyday household cleaner rather than anything abrasive, then simply mop them down with warm, clear water and leave to dry. If they're unglazed, you can scrub them with a stronger solution. If you have ingrained dirt on quarry tiles get a non-scratch scouring pad and pour a small amount of white spirit into it. Scrub the tiles and then wash off with a weakish solution of household cleaner. Rinse it off thoroughly and allow to dry naturally. If, however, they're really badly stained and the marks won't respond to this, then get some hydrochloric acid (taking extreme care and wearing gloves and goggles) and apply neat or in a strong solution. Wipe it off after just a few minutes with lots of clean water.

Alice Gibbons Handmade Tiles
4 Maplehurst Close, Hot Lane Industrial Estate,
Burslem, Stoke-on-Trent, Staffs ST6 2BY
tel: 01782 813538 • fax: 01782 813538

Mail order only, Alice Gibbons has a limited but lovely range of handmade tiles featuring classical botanical designs from the V&A Museum archive. Delicately painted ferns and flowers look incredibly lifelike, usually with one image set centrally in a creamy crackle glaze. Alice also has the exclusive licence from the Natural History Museum to use their archive paintings and drawings. The images can also be set in platinum if you want an even more contemporary look.

Bernard J Arnull & Company Ltd
1/21 Sunbeam Rd, Park Royal, London NW10 6JP
tel: 0181 965 6094 for stockists • fax: 0181 961 1585

If you need to install a hard-wearing surface, this importer has a huge range of floor and wall tiles which will do the job, in either decorative or plain finishes.

Candy Tiles

Great Western Potteries, Heathfield,
nr Newton Abbott, Devon TQ12 6RF
tel: 01626 832641 for stockists
fax: 01626 831318

Candy supply to many outlets all over the country
and, if you're after something with a Victorian feel
to it, they manufacture a range of Art Tiles that are
clever reproductions. They also do a more subdued
range in sugary pastels which have a lovely shimmery
quality.

Casbah Tiles Ltd

20 Wellington Lane, Bristol, Avon BS6 5PY
tel: 0117 942 7318 • fax: 0117 940 0037

Handmade in North Africa, these highly ornate tiles
look great when used as a border with the company's
complementary range of plain tiles. They would look
fantastic in a Moroccan-themed kitchen. Visit the shop
to see their whole range.

Ceramatizm

31 Bollo Lane, London W4 5LR
tel/fax: 0181 994 2554

This little shop has a surprisingly large range of slate,
terracotta and handmade glazed tiles which can be
given a design of your choice at a fairly reasonable
cost. They also stock vitreous glass, ceramic and
marble mosaics.

Color 1 Ceramics

404 Richmond Rd, Twickenham, Middx TW1 2EB
tel: 0181 891 0691 for showroom
fax: 0181 296 0491

A fun range of embossed tiles, including dolphins,
cows, fish and lots of seaside themed tiles – there's
even one with a prawn. If you like the hot spicy
colours of Morocco and the Mediterranean, they also
do a great range of wall tiles called Maroc Rustic which
has contrasting items called Marrakesh and Kasbah.

Colorker

Units 23/4, Cromwell Industrial Estate, Staffa Rd,
London E10 7QZ
tel: 0181 558 8399 for stockists • fax: 0181 558 8384

If you've admired the dusky red tones of floor tiles
found in Spanish farmhouses, this company has a
factory in Castellon that produces them, after which
they are distributed in this country.

Corres Mexican Tiles Ltd

Unit 1A, Station Rd, Hampton Wick,
Kingston upon Thames, Surrey KT1 4HG
tel: 0181 943 4142 for stockists • fax: 0181 943 4649

For over 130 years this company has been producing
mainly handmade tiles with a Mexican feel. They come
in all types of terracotta with painted designs in bright
colours such as blues and yellows. Recurring motifs
include flowers and birds.

Criterion Tiles

196 Wandsworth Bridge Rd, London SW6 2UF
tel: 0171 736 9610 • fax: 0171 736 0725
and
2a Englands Lane, London NW3 7EJ
tel: 0171 483 2608 • fax: 0171 483 2609

Criterion have a massive range of tiles by lots of the well-
known manufacturers in stock and are inclined towards
more handmade rather than mass-produced tiles. The
helpful staff can advise you about what you should use
where in your home and how many you will need.

CSW Tiling Ltd

22–24 Nuffield Rd, Nuffield Trading Estate, Poole,
Dorset BH17 0RB
tel: 01202 675836 • fax: 01202 668219

Importing from Italy, Spain and Germany, this
distributor does a large range of ceramic tiles suitable
for use in most settings from kitchens and bathrooms
to conservatories and patios. Ceramic tiles are great for
conservatories because they will not lift up if water is
split on them when you're watering your plants and mud
trodden in from the garden can easily be cleaned off.

Domus Tiles

33 Parkgate Rd, London SW11 2UF
tel: 0171 736 9610 • fax: 0171 924 2556
e-mail: info@domustiles.co.uk

If you want to mix and match, Domus Tiles do a
modular range that enables you to create unique
patterns by alternating different shapes with plain
colours. There is a large selection of ceramic floor
and wall tiles suitable for use in most settings, as
well as marble mosaic and other more unusual types
of marble.

Elite Tiles (London) Ltd

Elite House, The Broadway, London NW9 7BP
tel: 0181 202 1806 • fax: 0181 202 8608

A massive warehouse holds an impressive amount of stock from which you can order tiles in marble, granite, as well as hand- or screen-printed tiles. They particularly specialize in high-quality Italian tiles and have an in-house design studio for individual commissions.

Elon
66 Fulham Rd, South Kensington, London SW3 6HH
tel: 0171 460 4600 for stockists • fax: 0171 460 4601

Elon's unique range of hand-painted tiles have been much imitated but these are the real thing; and no two tiles are identical. Taking inspiration from Mexico, France and Italy, choose from hand-painted Mexican designs, Provence wall tiles, which have exquisitely painted flower designs in soft delicate colours, and floor tiles which are reminiscent of being in a Tuscan farmhouse. They also do terracotta and slate floor tiles.

Etrusca
60 Dickson House, Ridgway Rd, Hanley,
Stoke-on-Trent, Staffs ST1 3BA
tel: 01782 208549 • fax: 01782 202631

All Etrusca's tiles are made by hand, using local terracotta clay, and given a glaze. Consequently, each one is slightly different and therefore unique. They are highly decorative, taking biblical and classical images such as a reclining Adam, or heads of Bacchante and Delphi, as their inspiration. Etrusca will also work to specific commissions, producing things such as house numbers and signs.

Farmhouse Traditional Tiles Ltd
Unit 3, Park Works Park, Borough Rd,
Kingston upon Thames, Surrey KT2 6BD
tel: 0181 547 2551 for stockists
and
17 Beech Business Park, Tillington Rd, Hereford,
Herts HR4 9QJ
tel: 01432 355132 • fax: 01432 355134

As you'd expect from the name, this is a range of traditional tiles with a rustic feel. Some of them feature eaves of corn and furry doormice, and there are some plainer ones as well.

Froyle Tiles Ltd
Froyle Pottery, Lower Froyle, Alton,
Hants GU34 4LL
tel: 01420 23693 • fax: 01420 22797

These are handmade glazed tiles suitable for walls, floors and even outside, as they are made to be

frostproof. They are 1 cm thick and all plain, although they come in twenty-three different shades. The mail order service makes ordering them very easy too.

H&R Johnson Tiles Ltd
Highgate Tile Works, Tunstall,
Stoke-on-Trent, Staffs ST6 4JX
tel: 01782 575575 for stockists • fax: 01782 577377
e-mail: sales@johnson-tiles.com

Tiles with a rustic charm are the mainstay of this manufacturer's repertoire. The Country Collection of wall tiles incorporates the Cotswolds and the Chilterns ranges which, although machine-made, look as if they are handcrafted, the tiles having a deliberate colour variation and different surface textures that all adds to their appeal. There are also contrasting and co-ordinating floor tiles, and a Marbles collection.

Jones Tiles
Manor Barn, Orleton, Ludlow,
Shropshire SY8 4HR
tel: 01568 780666 for catalogue • fax: 01568 780370

All tastes are catered for here, from traditional repro blue and white Delft tiles to ones with jazzy, geometric patterns. They undertake commission work mostly and were involved in the restoration of Chatsworth House, but they will do bespoke projects for private clients.

Julie Arnall
26 Woodwaye, Watford, Herts WD1 4NW
tel/fax: 01923 228465

Julie Arnall paints original designs on to white, cream and crackle glaze tiles and the results are truly unique. Her Signs of the Zodiac, depicting clever abstract drawings of each of the twelve signs, are perfect for gifts. There are also Roman numerals, Regency urns and Classical figures set against backgrounds of rich metallic lustres and enamels.

Kenneth Clark Ceramics
The North Wing, Southover Grange,
Southover Rd, Lewes, E.Sussex BN7 1TP
tel: 01273 476761 • fax: 01273 479565

This company is a real specialist in tile design and decorates all its own tiles. Items like murals are also possible as special commissions. They operate a mail order service worldwide. Their catalogue, for which there is a charge, will give you a good idea of the vast range on offer.

Laticrete UK
133 New Haven Rd, Edinburgh EH6 4NP
tel: 0131 554 2283 for stockists • fax: 0131 553 4533

Laticrete is one of the many leading players in the ceramic tile market and has many years' worth of experience. The company have been manufacturing since 1956 and should be able to give you tried and tested advice on any aspect of tiles and tiling. They do all sorts of ceramic tiles, both patterned and plain, glazed and unglazed.

The Life Enhancing Tile Company
31 Bath Buildings, Montpelier, Bristol, Avon BS6 5PT
tel: 0117 907 7673 for stockists • fax: 0117 907 7674

This manufacturer makes a contemporary range of handmade encaustic tiles − a pattern that is made from a contrasting-coloured clay being inlaid into its surface and then fired in a kiln. They come in shades of buff, slate, grey, and terracotta and have stylized fish, stars and birds set into them. They look best if you mix them with plain tiles otherwise the effect would be overpowering. They are also available from branches of Fired Earth.

Original Style
Stovax Ltd, Falcon Rd, Sowton Industrial Estate, Exeter, Devon EX2 7LF
tel: 01392 474011 for stockists
fax: 01392 219932

Classics works of art, including Monet's *Waterlilies*, Raphael's *Galatea* and Botticelli's *Birth of Venus*, have been ingeniously and painstakingly copied on to tiles so you can gaze at a masterpiece whilst lying in the bath! They also do a range of geometric floor tiles taken from Victorian pattern books which use traditional clay colour stains.

The Original Tile Company
23a Howe St, Edinburgh EH3 6TF
tel: 0131 556 2013 • fax: 0131 558 3172

This company do a lovely range of hand-glazed terracotta tiles in many hues from the darkest orange to the pinkiest rose. They have ceramic tiles from Portugal, Brazil and Holland and hand-cut mosaics.

Out of The Fire
Unit 18, Turner Dubrell Workshop, North End, Ditchling, E.Sussex BN6 8TD
tel: 01273 841794 for commissions and mail order
fax: 01273 841813

If you're after something really personal, ceramicist Karin Bain can make it for you. Perhaps you'd like a tile with your child's handprint set into it for a special christening present, or some wonderfully detailed peacock feathers. Working from a delightful converted barn housing a community of artists, Karin can match any colour to suit your colour scheme, or do a plain border with a patterned inset. She also hand-paints china.

Paul Fricker Ltd
Well Park, Willeys Avenue, Exeter, Devon EX2 8BE
tel: 01392 278636 for stockists • fax: 01392 410508

There are hundreds of different ceramic tiles, both patterned and plain, to choose from in the Cristal range which Paul Fricker Ltd distributes. Tastefully co-ordinating borders are helpfully shown in the catalogue so that you can put your design together with ease. The company also distributes tiles by Original Style and the Spanish company Venis, amongst others.

Pavigres-Wich
Unit 154D Milton Park, Abingdon, Oxon OX14 4SD
tel: 01235 862111 for stockists • fax: 01235 862100

This is a large manufacturer that distributes its products nationwide. There are three massive factories producing everything from wall to floor tiles, both glazed and unglazed. There is a nice range of vitrified porcelain floor tiles that can be highly polished.

Pilkington's Tiles Ltd
PO Box 4, Clifton Junction, Swinton, Manchester M27 8LP
tel: 0161 727 1133 for stockists • fax: 0161 721122

Pilkington's have a huge selection of ceramic tiles for both walls and floors, including some funky metallic wall tiles and range called Vellum Prints that have an unusual pearlescent effect. They're specifically known for their swimming-pool tiles for the leisure industry but you could equally well use them at home in the bathroom.

The Reject Tile Shop
178 Wandsworth Bridge Rd, London SW6 2UQ
tel: 0171 731 6098 • fax: 0171 736 3693

As its name suggests, this shop specializes in seconds, discontinued lines and is great for bargains. It stocks tiles for walls, floors, worktops and fireplaces. It is an offshoot of Criterion Tiles (see p.55).

Stovax
Falcon Rd, Sowton Industrial Estate, Exeter,
Devon EX2 7LF
tel: 01392 474055 for stockists • fax: 01392 474011

Faithfully reproduced, classic tile designs found around hearths and fireplaces in the Victorian age. There are also Art Nouveau-style 'tube-lined and raised line tiles' where the flower motif has an embossed line drawn on to it before the coloured translucent glaze is applied.

Swedecor Ltd
Manchester St, Hull, Humberside HU3 4TX
tel: 01482 329691 for stockists • fax: 01482 212988
e-mail: info@swedecor.com

Suppliers of architectural and designer ceramics, including the Albion series, which is a collection of geometric floor tiles in traditional Victorian designs. They helpfully come in pre-mounted mesh sheets which makes them easier to lay. They also distribute the Gemini collection – a huge range of glazed wall and floor tiles.

Terra Firma Tiles
70 Chalk Farm Rd, London NW1 8AN
tel: 0171 485 7227 for stockists • fax: 0171 485 7203

Beautiful and expensive natural materials for flooring from around the world – Indian sandstone, Chinese slate and handmade terracotta from Spain. They also do regular ceramic tiles, mosaics, stone and slate.

The Tile Gallery
1 Royal Parade, 247 Dawes Rd, London SW6 7RE
tel: 0171 385 8818 • fax: 0171 381 1589

Reproduction Victorian and Edwardian wall and floor tiles are this company's speciality and their helpful staff will advise you on how to achieve either a look of genuine authenticity or a pastiche, depending on your taste. There are lots of peacocks, William De Morgan

flowers, and Art Nouveau female figures with flowing hair that are ideal for fireplace surrounds.

Tiles International
9 Tollpark Rd, Wardpark East, Cumbernauld, Glasgow G67 0LW
tel: 01236 732727 for stockists • fax: 01236 451631

Tiles International have a wide range of unusual and stylish tiles including a range called Granit90. Not as expensive as the real thing, but very like it with a speckled finish in a variety of colourways. The technical sales advice team will help you decide what you need.

Tower Ceramics
91 Parkway, London NW11 7PP
tel: 0171 485 7192 • fax: 0171 267 9571

Tower Ceramics has a huge range of ceramic tiles for every possible application and in every conceivable colourway that you can view in their London showroom. They can also order other ranges in if necessary.

Woolliscroft Tiles Ltd
Melville St, Stoke-on-Trent, Staffs ST1 3ND
tel: 01782 208082 for stockists • fax: 01782 202641
e-mail: wtiles@btinternet.com

Woolliscroft has an excellent all-round reputation when it comes to ceramic tiles. They manufacture, distribute and import them, and they tend to lean towards the harder-wearing tiles rather than more decorative ones.

World's End Tiles
Silverthorne Rd, Battersea, London SW8 3HE
tel: 0171 819 2100 • fax: 0171 627 1435

If you'd like your tiles to match your wallpaper, or just pick up one element of the design, World's End can make up a special order for you. Many of their tiles are handmade rather than mass-produced, and they are also one of the largest importers of Italian tiles in this country.

mosaic

This ancient art is enjoying the height of popularity but will always have an enduring appeal. It can be extremely satisfying and, once you have caught the bug, you will be mosaiking everything in sight! Most people think of little bits of tile for making mosaic but you can, in fact, use a whole range of 'tesserae' – meaning little bits, whether they're stone, marble, glass, smalti (opaque glass), or smashed-up glazed or encaustic ceramic tiles. However, it's best to start off with small objects before embarking on something such as a floor. Some surfaces aren't suitable either. For example, the surface of glazed ceramic tiles chip easily and will not be right for use on a floor, and glass mosaic is not really suitable in a bathroom for safety reasons.

The companies listed below offer a variety of services and it is quite important that you read what they can provide as some only stock the actual materials for making mosaic, whereas others don't stock materials at all but can provide a bespoke design service for creating everything from mosaic kitchen splashbacks to entire floors.

Alex Shaftel Mosaic Designs
Flat 9, 15–17 Clapham Common Northside,
London SW4 0RG
tel: 0171 720 6822 • fax: 0171 720 6822

Alex Shaftel makes beautiful mosaic furniture to order using stone, marble, glass, and ceramic tile. If you'd like to discuss an individual commission with him, or see examples of his work, then give him a call.

Edgar Udny & Co
314 Balham High Rd, London SW17 7AA
tel: 0181 767 8181

Edgar Udny offer a mail order service for glass and ceramic tiles, which is great if you want to have a go yourself at home. The colours on the chart aren't always very accurate representatives of the actual colours so it's best to order a couple at a time, make sure they're what you want, and then order up in quantity.

The Mosaic Studio
Unit 4, 159 Southsea Avenue, Leigh-on-Sea,
Essex SS9 2BH
tel/fax: 01702 712111

The Mosaic Studio is a decorative arts company who will design, manufacture and install mosaic of all kinds – whether it's a floor, a splashback or a piece of furniture. Examples of their work can be seen in upmarket London stores, such as Harvey Nichols and Selfridges, and throughout the country in the nationwide chains of Ravel and Wallis. Tables made by them are sold in Liberty's. They also sell all the materials you need if you do want have a go yourself plus handy starter kits which have the basic range of everything you need. They also run courses (see p.264).

The Mosaic Workshop
Unit B, 443–9 Holloway Rd, London N7 6LJ
tel: 0171 272 2446 for general enquiries
tel: 0171 263 2997 for recorded information

and
1a Princeton St, London N7 6LJ
tel: 0171 404 9249 for the store

Housed in a warehouse tucked back from the street, the Holloway Road shop sells everything you need for making mosaic. Plump glass jars house all the tiles, which look like sweets divided into colours. You simply pick what you want and weigh it on the scales and pay accordingly. There are 'sample' bags in random colours and, on sheets, gold and silver, mirror tiles, and cubes of marble and glass. All around are examples to give you inspiration. If you need materials, all the tile nippers, grout, mesh, and boards can be found here. They also run lots of mosaic courses (see p.264).

Mosaik
10 Kensington Square, London W8 5EP
tel: 0171 795 6253

A collection of hand-made mosaics – decorative panels and friezes fashioned from vitreous glass, Venetian glass, gold leaf, and available in more than 200 colours. You can fix them where you choose, like huge tiles, as long as the walls are properly prepared and the right sort of adhesive is used. It's best to use a competent tiler to do this. The shop will give you advice or recommend tilers they have used upon request. There are about thirty different designs to choose from, roughly divided into three styles – contemporary, classical and ethnic.

Paul J Marks Mosaics
56 Hilda Vale Rd, Farmborough, Orpington,
Kent BR6 7AW
tel: 01689 850285 • fax: 01689 850285
e-mail: paulmarks@virgin.net

This company has recently launched a mail order service through which you can purchase bags of tesserae or tiles on sheets, and business has really taken off. Send for a colour chart.

4

every

The kitchen has traditionally been the heart of the home. We spend most of our time in there and a *Home Front* survey revealed that, out of all the rooms in the house, most people would spend their money on a new kitchen.

You don't have to have a big kitchen for it to be the centre around which everything else revolves. In the past, *Home Front* has shown all types from traditional-style kitchens to modern, unfitted kitchens where the units move about on castors, and even a country-style kitchen with a modern twist. The programme has taken tips from top chef Antony Worrall Thompson on the best lay-out for a serious cook's kitchen, tackled storage problems in galley kitchens, given a thirties kitchen a new lease of life, and performed lots of instant face-lifts by simply changing doors and handles on units.

This chapter has been divided into a section on traditional and custom-made kitchens and a section on modern and groovy ones. Both section introductions give specific notes about what is included in each. The kitchenalia section of this chapter offers the extras like worktops, sinks, taps, etc, and appliances covers exactly what you might expect – all large things electrical (or gas) driven!

thing

including the

kitchen sink

key: **hf** shows the product has appeared on *Home Front*

✉ shows the company offers a mail order service

kitchens

Deciding on a new kitchen is one of the most difficult home improvement decisions you have to make – and probably one of the most expensive. There are all sorts of rules to be taken into consideration like the famous 'triangle rule'. This stipulates that the preparation surface, hob and sink should all be plotted at equidistant points – it's just common sense so you don't dribble hot fat from the hob to the sink, or drop the herbs you've just chopped as you carry them to the hob. Fortunately, many companies now offer a computerized design service where you can see in three dimensions exactly how your kitchen will look and you can play around to your heart's content with the layout before making a decision.

traditional & custom-made

When you say a 'traditional' kitchen most people think of farmhouse style with rustic-looking wooden cupboards and units. This look is now widely mass produced and, whether you live in the town or the country, it is enduringly popular. Available in a range of set sizes and 'off the peg', it looks best teamed with wooden racks, butcher's blocks, Belfast sinks and other traditional accessories. However, if you have a bit more money to spend, there are hundreds of skilled cabinetmakers who will make up a bespoke design to your requirements. They are also detailed here. Make sure you know exactly what a custom-made company is offering and what is included in the price. For example, some will have a collection of set designs that they alter according to the size and layout of your kitchen, whereas other more expensive companies will make a really individual kitchen in which each piece is specifically designed for you. Whatever your budget and wherever you live, use the addresses below to find a company in your region. (See p.5 if you are unsure what region to look under.)

south west

Benton
Isleport Business Pk, Highbridge, Somerset TA9 4JT
tel: 01278 789849 • fax: 01278 795855

Each Benton kitchen is unique, individually designed, and traditionally hand-built. Traditional-looking kitchens, including freestanding furniture, are suited to the architecture of the house. Benton also design other interiors including bathrooms. Ring before visiting the Highbridge showroom, so a designer is available to see you.

Bill Davies
Penny's Mill, Nunney, Frome, Somerset BA11 4NP
tel: 01373 836210 • fax: 01373 836018

Bespoke kitchens designed at this showroom along simple lines are the name of the game here. Solid wood and painted kitchens are both available and designs can be a mixture of fitted and unfitted furniture. Bill Davies has a working display kitchen at Penny's Mill or can work out an initial plan and figures from a sketch plan or drawing.

Country Kitchens of Devon
The Old Creamery, Lapford, Crediton, Devon EX17 6AE
tel/fax: 01363 83608

Individually designed furniture built by local craftsmen in the heart of Devon. This family firm offers designs ranging from traditional solid oak farmhouse styles to painted finishes, and dressers are a feature.

David Armstrong

Woodview Workshop, Pitway Lane, Farrington Gurney,
Bristol, Avon BS18 5TX
tel: 01761 453117

David Armstrong makes handmade furniture and
kitchens at prices that compare with good mass-
produced furniture. He also offers a comprehensive
kitchen design service supplying worktops, sinks and
appliances as well as furniture

Hobson's Choice

Gloucester House, Country Park, Shrivenham Rd,
Swindon, Wilts SN1 2NR
tel: 01793 490685 • fax: 01793 615982

A fun showroom for serious kitchen choice. Don't be
fazed if you come across a life-sized model of a lady
vacuuming as you search among the vast range of
different kitchen styles and prices. There's also a man
in the bath in the bathroom section upstairs! There
is a large selection of good-quality cookware, such
as Alessi, on sale and a sale area with some
good bargains.

Mark Wilkinson

Overton House, High St, Bromham, nr Chippenham,
Wilts SN15 2HA
tel: 01380 850004 for other showrooms
fax: 01380 850184

Never one to stick to convention, Mark Wilkinson
produces bespoke kitchens that are at the cutting edge
of 'traditional' design. These kitchens really do look
different from anybody else's although the earlier ones
now have their imitators. Mark produces real ground-
breaking stuff.

McFadden Cabinetmakers

Oriel House, 71 Prior Park Rd, Bath, Avon BA2 4NF
tel: 01225 310593 • fax: 01225 481558

This is a husband and wife team who design and build
bespoke furniture. Quality hardwoods are used for the
timber furniture and painted furniture can also be
supplied in a range of decorative finishes. Dressers,
tables and chairs are available as well as fitted
kitchen furniture.

Nicholas Turner

Old Well Studios, 58 High St, Shaftesbury,
Dorset SP7 8AA
tel: 01747 855044 • fax: 01747 855045

Dealing in custom designed fitted furniture, Nick
Turner can design, reproduce or restore anything fitted
or freestanding in wood. Kitchen designs include
everything from Georgian painted kitchens to high
state-of-the-art concepts. All pieces are handmade in
properly forested hardwoods.

Robinson & Cornish

Southay House, Oakwood Close, Roundswell,
Barnstaple, Devon EX31 3NJ
tel: 01271 329300 for stockists • fax: 01271 328277

Stylish bespoke kitchens with a seemingly
inexhaustible set of ideas. All the kitchens are
designed to work in harmony with the style of the
house and all are available in 'non-threatened'
woods or painted finishes. There are no standard
pieces here!

Templederry Design

Hornacott, South Petherwin, Launceston,
Cornwall PL15 7LH
tel: 01566 782461 • fax: 01566 782461

If you are looking for a flexible kitchen maker, this
could be your company. They will source any type of
kitchen desired from countrywide companies and will
visit locations and homes all over the South of England
with samples. They don't have a showroom, but say
that this just means they can achieve lower prices on
their kitchens.

Trevor Toms

Fisherton Mill, 108 Fisherton St, Salisbury,
Wilts SP2 7QY
tel: 01747 852137

Bespoke cabinetmaker Trevor Toms makes a selection
of one-off kitchens to order using a variety of woods.
Styles include freestanding and fitted furniture and a
whole host of natural, painted and distressed finishes.

Wickes

Head Office, 126–138 Station Rd, Harrow,
Middx HA1 2QB
tel: 0870 608 9001 for customer services
tel: 0500 300328 for branches

Manor House Kitchens are built exclusively for Wickes
and there are twelve designs to choose from with an
added choice of sinks, worktops and appliances. The
styles are mainly fairly traditional, but there are some
that edge towards the contemporary look.

south east

Andrew Macintosh Furniture Ltd
462–464 Chiswick High Rd, London W4 5TT
tel: 0181 995 8333 • fax: 0181 995 8999

Andrew Macintosh specializes in painted kitchens in Shaker, Mackintosh or English Country designs. The emphasis is on an unfitted or less fitted look and the use of natural materials. All the kitchens are hand-painted in the paint shop before they are delivered and a wide range of colours is available. Andrew Macintosh also designs bedrooms. Call the London store to arrange a visit to their High Wycombe showroom.

Bonham & Blackman
23 Priory St, Hastings, E.Sussex TN34 1EA
tel: 01424 712179 • fax: 01424 719269

Terry Bonham and Martin Blackman form a team which combines traditional skills and modern manufacturing trends to produce kitchen and other fitted furniture. All the timbers used are from sustainable sources and there is a choice of six finishes. They are often commissioned to design and make one-off pieces.

Crabtree Kitchens
The Twickenham Centre, Norcutt Rd, Twickenham, Middx TW2 6SR
tel: 0181 755 1121 for stockists
fax: 0181 755 4133

Handcrafted kitchens using traditional joinery techniques and quality hardwoods. There is also a hand-painting service that can match any shade or special finish. Designs include a Mackintosh-style kitchen, a Georgian kitchen, a Shaker kitchen and a Provençal kitchen. Other bespoke designs are also available.

Evergreen Kitchens
38 Albert Rd North, Reigate, Surrey RH2 9EG
tel: 01737 226863 • fax: 01737 224708

If you want to see the workmanship that will go into your kitchen, this company allows you to visit the on-site workshop and check the bespoke quality of these reclaimed pine kitchens. They can offer the whole job from design to fitting, or if you are looking for a cheaper option, they will just supply you with the furniture.

Harvey Jones
137–139 Essex Rd, Islington, London N1 2NR
tel: 0171 354 9933 • fax: 0171 354 1006

Simple and Shaker-style painted furniture in a small range of classic designs is on offer at this showroom. Handmade kitchen furniture, primed for painting is also available. Extra deep worktops are also available to match the furniture.

Hayloft Woodwork
3 Bond St, London W4 1QZ
tel: 0181 747 3510 • fax: 0181 742 1860

These kitchens are made in a simple style rather than the traditionally decorated style, and all are made to order, including fitted and some very imaginative unfitted pieces. They are available in pine, hardwood or painted finishes.

Heart of the Home
Unit 2 Brookway, Kingston Rd, Leatherhead, Surrey KT22 7NA
tel: 01372 360502 • fax: 01372 361147
e-mail: mikeheart@aol.com

If you are looking for a flexible kitchen manufacturer, this company can give you a wide scope of choice in size and colour. Their kitchens are mainly classic and traditional and they do a lot of Shaker styles. They also offer traditional oak doors in different shapes and the same in ash and maple. They can stain and lime to whatever finish or colour you want.

Hygrove
45 Fairfax Rd, London NW6 4EL
tel: 0171 624 6616 for stockists • fax: 0171 372 0600

These handmade kitchens are custom made to the highest standards in very traditional designs. The kitchens are mainly made from solid pine or oak, but they can work in any solid wood you like. With the painted furniture, the sky's the limit as their artists can create any finish and colour combination you like. They also make fitted bedroom and bathroom furniture.

Jasper & Griffith
Valdoe Studios, Goodwood, nr Chichester, W.Sussex PO18 0PJ
tel: 01243 774411

Totally bespoke, handmade kitchens using solid wood. Designs to date have included unusual features such as curved maple doors with a geometric walnut inlay,

Biedermeier-style fluted columns and early American colonial-style furniture with tiles embedded in the doors.

John Ladbury & Co

Unit 11, Alpha Business Park, Travellers Close, Welham Green, Hatfield, Herts AL9 7NT
tel: 01707 262966 • fax: 01707 265400

A family-run business with a workshop and showroom , John Ladbury & Co specialize in both traditional and contemporary bespoke kitchens and offers a full design and installation service. They're also a member of the Kitchen Specialists' Association. Finishes are either natural wood or painted, often in heritage colours. (This is a general term for colours that imitate period style colours such as Georgian or Victorian ones.)

John Lewis of Hungerford   hf

Park St, Hungerford, Berks RG17 0EF
tel: 01488 682066 for stockists • fax: 01488 686660

Designs include Artisan kitchens that offer traditional styling and quality at affordable prices. It features two main door styles and all cabinetry is painted on the outside in a choice of thirteen finishes. You can also buy it ready primed so you can paint it yourself. There is a choice of various country-style handles and an extensive range of cabinet sizes. The company has other outlets around the country, but shouldn't be confused with the John Lewis department stores. When *Home Front* was following the renovation of 300-year-old Mill Cottage in Northamptonshire, one of these kitchens was chosen.

Kitchen Design Company

22–24 Highbury Grove, London N5 2EA
tel: 0171 359 0224 • fax: 0171 359 0224

There is a wide range of styles at this showroom to suit every architectural style and price band. All the kitchens are made to order by craftsmen with twenty years of experience, in a choice of painted or hardwood finishes.

Magnet   hf

tel: 0800 192192 for your nearest showroom

Although they cater for the mass market, Magnet have a huge collection of different kitchen styles on offer, offering something for most tastes. The designs vary from the most traditional of looks to a hi-tech stainless steel kitchen with metal drawer fronts.

Millside Cabinet Makers

The Moor, Melbourne, Royston, Herts SG8 6ED
tel: 01763 261870 • fax: 01763 261673

Stylishly simple, traditional kitchens in a variety of designs with the flexibility that being cabinetmakers brings. The fitted kitchens are either made in a selection of solid timbers or they can be painted. They are all made along traditional lines with mortice and tenon or dovetail joints.

Moneyhill Interiors

1 Moneyhill Parade, Uxbridge Rd, Rickmansworth, Herts WD3 2BQ
tel: 01923 773906 • fax: 011732 844238

As well as selling their own range of very traditional English-looking, custom-built kitchen furniture, retailer Moneyhill also feature Zeyko kitchens. These are right at the other end of the scale. The Old English woodwork is custom-made traditional style, while the Zeyko kitchens are chic, contemporary styles, so you will find a bit of everything here.

Naturally Wood

Twyford Rd, Bishops Stortford, Herts CM23 3JL
tel: 01279 755501 for stockists • fax: 01279 657435

All woods used for these traditional-style kitchens come from the Appalachian regions of N.America and traditional methods without toxic chemicals are used to lime them. The bespoke kitchens are made with dovetailed drawers and hand-turned knobs. Painted kitchens are primed, delivered and painted on site. Designs include an unusual sycamore kitchen with strong Art Deco roots.

Organ & Pearce

The Old Forge, Arnewood Bridge Rd, Sway, Lymington, Hants SO41 6DA
tel: 01590 683225 • fax: 01590 683629

These are bespoke kitchens designed with no holds barred on sizes, colours or styles. Ash, pine and painted finishes feature heavily in this showroom, as do simple, uncluttered traditional kitchen styles.

The Painted Kitchen Co

Lynton Lodge, 354 Upper Richmond Rd, Putney, London SW15 6TL
tel: 0181 780 2311 • fax: 0181 780 2311

A partnership between expert in paint finishes, Robert Malston, and cabinetmaker, Barrie Higginson, this company will provide you with tailor-made kitchen furniture and they will handle everything from the initial consultation to the final design and installation.

The Pastoral Collection

Unit 10, Hampton Farm Industrial Estate, Hampton Rd West, Hanworth, Middx TW13 6DB
tel: 0181 8984781 for stockists • fax: 0181 898 0268

Although these are German kitchens, they are designed along traditional English lines. All the carcasses are constructed from solid pine and the kitchens feature framed doors, mitred mouldings and dovetailing. They come in a choice of natural pine, colourwashed pine or painted finishes and there are freestanding pieces like dressers as well.

Potts Ltd

Kiln Barn Rd, East Malling, Maidstone, Kent ME19 6BQ
tel: 01732 848444 • fax: 01732 844238

This showroom is definitely worth tracking down in its rural location. It is an enormous converted warehouse with a huge range of kitchens on display including unusual appliances such as round fridges and built-in steamers.

Rhode Design

65 Cross St, London N1 2BB
tel: 0171 354 9933 • fax: 0171 354 1006

These MDF (medium density fibreboard) painted kitchens have a strong Shaker feeling about them, although they are not restricted to this style by any means. They have a mixture of fitted and unfitted pieces at this showroom and are happy to provide a bespoke service if needs be. They can also make furniture in pine or unpainted, so you can provide your own finish.

Romsey Cabinetmakers

Greatbridge Business Park, Budds Lane, Romsey, Hants SO51 0HA
tel: 01794 522626 • fax: 01794 522451

This company offers a good collection of simple and stylish designs in a new generation of traditional-style kitchens. Solid woods include oak, cherry, and ash and the designs include unusual features such as half-circle ends to peninsula cabinets. Many of the doors have side frames giving the cabinets an unusually solid,

classic look. Painted kitchens are also a speciality as is fitted furniture for bathrooms and bedrooms.

Roundel Design

Flishinghurst Orchards, Chalk Lane, Cranbrook, Kent TN17 2QA
tel: 01580 712666 • fax: 01580 713564

Roundel Design specializes in kitchens made from reclaimed pine, oak, maple and ash, which can be contrasted with the various painted finishes. The cabinetry is manufactured by specialist craftsmen and a lot of attention is paid to detail, including hand carving. They also make bespoke items of furniture from television and video cabinets to desks and grandfather clocks.

Roundhouse Design

25 Chalk Farm Rd, Camden Lock, London NW1 8AG
tel: 0171 428 9955 • fax: 0171 267 1035

You will find several standard ranges of stylish and simple, traditional-style kitchens at this London showroom, but they can also make individually designed items to your specifications. The kitchens are wood or painted wood and are a mixture of Classic designs, Shaker designs and the Wright range in sycamore, maple or cherry.

Smallbone of Devizes

105–109 Fulham Rd, London SW3 6RL
tel: 0171 589 5998 for stockists • fax: 0171 581 9415

One of the original inspirations behind the traditional look in kitchens, Smallbone has now moved on to many other designs such as the Classical kitchen, which uses the food larder of the fifties as a starting point, as well as retaining some old favourites. There is also an Unfitted kitchen and the Inlay range in sycamore, which has a geometric inlay. There are also Smallbone showrooms in other parts of the country.

Turner & Foye

114–116 High St, Esher, Surrey KT10 9QJ
tel: 01372 470800 • fax: 01372 469412

There are no such things as standard ranges, styles or sizes at retailer Turner & Foye – everything is totally bespoke. The range of timbers used includes sweet chestnut, oak, yew, ash, sycamore, English cherry, tulip and walnut. Designs range from the truly traditional to classic, bordering on the contemporary.

Underwood Kitchens
Lawn Farm Business Centre, Grendon Underwood,
Bucks HP18 0QX
tel: 01296 770043 for other branches
fax: 01296 770412

These handcrafted, solid wood kitchens are functional
and affordable as bespoke kitchens go. Painted
finishes are a speciality, alongside limed oak,
European beech and other woods. Freestanding
dressers are custom built in a mixture of painted
finishes and woods. Customers are welcome to look
round the factory and see how the kitchens are made,
no appointments necessary.

Woodstock Furniture Ltd
4 William St, Knightsbridge, London SW1X 9HL
tel: 0171 245 9989 • fax: 0171 245 9981

This company offers hardwood and painted bespoke
fitted kitchens made by craftsmen from sustainable
woods. Designs include some unusual ones such as an
Art Deco-inspired kitchen, a curved maple kitchen, a
Gothic style and a kitchen complete with a marquetry
iris motif. Fitted bedrooms, libraries, bathrooms and
panelling are also on offer. Ring for details of their
showroom outside Basingstoke too.

Yesteryear
The Clock House, 43 London Rd, Sawbridgeworth,
Herts CM21 9JH
tel: 01279 868800 for stockists • fax: 01279 868802

As the name suggests, this is a selection of traditional
wooden kitchens in Shaker, Boston or Old English
styles and in a selection of antique, lacquered or
distressed woods. Distressed and 'rubbed' painted
kitchens are also available.

east

Clive Brown Kitchens
82–84 Victoria Rd, Cambridge, Cambs CB4 3DU
tel/fax: 01223 460437

This company designs and manufactures bespoke
kitchens, with much of their work being in hardwoods
such as ash, maple and cherry. They also make at least
50 per cent of their kitchens with painted doors that
have hardwood frames and MDF centre panels. The
cabinets are made in the traditional way and they
don't use any melamine, chipboard or plastics.

Grafham
5 Forge Close, Little End Rd, Eaton Scoton,
Cambs PE19 3TP
tel: 01480 470470 • fax: 01480 219123

Visit Grafham's showroom to experience traditional
wood kitchens with a difference. Although the
designs sit happily in any period or home, they are
not slavish copies of old furniture, but strive to
combine the best of traditional and more modern
design. Designed with quality and function in mind,
these are individual bespoke kitchens that avoid any
kind of fussiness.

Grun Swift
Incon House, Stilebrook Rd, Olney, Bucks MK46 5EA
tel: 01234 711044 • fax: 01234 711060

You can save up to 50 per cent on a bespoke kitchen
from this company if you are prepared to let it be used
as a show kitchen for other prospective buyers for a
period of three months. There is a range of over 400
different styles to choose from.

Henry Gordon Jones Furniture
The Furniture Workshops, Chapel Rd, Rendham,
Saxmundham, Suffolk IP17 2AT
tel: 01728 663717 • fax: 01728 663370

This company's showroom offers handmade, well-
proportioned kitchen furniture that has a
quintessentially traditional look. Furniture is painted
in subtle colours or made from different timbers and
many of the kitchens mix the two.

Keith Gray & Co
Great Priory Farm, Panfield, Braintree, Essex CM7 5BQ
tel: 01376 324590 • fax: 01376 328540

This showroom offers a whole range of innovative,
traditional styles. Keith Gray is particularly known for
original pieces such as unusually shaped and coloured
dressers. The furniture is all made from wood with the
painted furniture made from poplar and the plain
woods from oak, ash and maple. Keith Gray also offers
innovative designs for bedrooms and bathrooms,
including some freestanding pieces.

New From Old
The Engine House, Little Ouse, Ely, Cambs CB7 4TG
tel: 01353 676227 • fax: 01353 676313

If you are looking for really mellow wood, this
company designs and makes kitchens and freestanding

furniture from reclaimed solid woods and from sustainable hardwoods. The styles are mainly traditional or country, but there are also some contemporary pieces among this bespoke repertoire. Welsh dressers are a speciality.

The Norwich Kitchen Centre
1 Market Place, Loddon, Norfolk NR14 6EY
tel: 01508 528196 • fax: 01508 520560

This showroom, generally stocking traditional styles of kitchen, is in a character-packed cottage location overlooking the village churchyard. However, appearances can be deceptive and this Tardis-like operation has a larger warehouse showroom nearby as a back-up for those who want to see more – call the number above to get details for this.

Orwell Pine Co
Halifax Mill, 427 Wherstead Rd, Ipswich, Suffolk IP2 8LH
tel: 01473 680091 • fax: 01473 691542

This is a centuries-old whaling station that now has another role – selling reasonably priced bespoke kitchens. There is plenty of space to look around and you will find three floors of showrooms and workshops, all of which you are welcome to inspect to see the quality of workmanship.

Plain English
The Tannery, Combs, Stowmarket, Suffolk IP14 2EN
tel: 01449 774028 • fax: 01449 613519

Stylishly simple designs of kitchen furniture, made using traditional materials and methods. Cupboards are finished in a variety of subtle colours taken from the Farrow & Ball collection (see p.14). All the cupboards are made to order and freestanding pieces such as Bread & Cheese cupboards are available at this showroom.

William Ball
Gumley Rd, Grays, Essex RM20 4WB
tel: 01375 375151 for stockists
fax: 01375 386462

The Ultimate Collection is a selection of different kitchens with a lot of traditional wood designs and some more contemporary vinyl doors including a high gloss range. There is also a Shaker-look kitchen in ivory. Phone for details of your local stockist.

Willowbrook

49 Main St, Woodnewton, nr Oundle, Northants PE8 5PL
tel/fax: 01780 470066

Hand-built by Peter Farrell, these kitchens are traditionally built in solid wood, but every design is totally unique – made to the customers' own specifications. If you prefer a painted finish, this is possible too.

Winchmore Premium Kitchens
Unit 5, Northgate St Business Pk, Bury St Edmunds, Suffolk IP33 1HP
tel: 01284 724207 for stockists • fax: 01284 724197

This company's reputation was founded on traditional styles and it still offers a whole selection of solid wood and painted kitchens. Shaker kitchens come in a range of nine painted colours and there is a collection of freestanding furniture.

central

Affordable Kitchens
Saxon Pk, Hanbury Rd, Stoke Prior, Bromsgrove, W.Midlands B60 4AE
tel/fax: 01926 855044

This kitchen retailer has two brick-built warehouses packed with affordable kitchens of all kinds. They also have a host of money-saving promotions at various times during the year.

Bell Kitchens
Kingsthorpe Rd, Kingsthorpe, Northants NN2 6LT
tel: 01604 712505 • fax: 01604 721028

This well-established family firm is a kitchen retailer selling British and German styles from an old 1920s converted fireplace factory. On the appliance side, Agas and Rayburns are a speciality. They also offer a full planning and fitting service.

The Bronte Furniture Co
The Old Granary, Home Farm Yard, Castle Ashby, Northants NN7 1LF
tel: 01604 696772 • fax: 01604 696759

This furniture company – and the emphasis is on furniture – makes some wonderful freestanding pieces as well as traditional fitted kitchens. There are some interesting ideas such as designing eclectically styled freestanding pieces around a fitted kitchen and painting them all in different but complementary colours. The company also make bedroom, bathroom and other types of furniture, many of which are on show at the showroom.

Cotteswood

Station Rd, Chipping Norton, Oxon OX7 5HN
tel: 01608 641858 • fax: 01608 646464
and
14 Hill Avenue, Amersham-on-the-Hill, Bucks HP6 5BW
tel: 01494 434200 for the showroom

Cotteswood offer a variety of traditional designs including Victorian, Edwardian and Classic. The company also makes freestanding and unfitted kitchens. All kitchens are available in a choice of maple, oak, cherry or pine and in natural, painted or limed finishes.

Geoff Chater Furniture Workshops

Station St, Leek, Staffs ST13 8BP
tel: 01538 387502 • fax: 01538 386146

Hand-built fitted kitchens, designed in Victorian styles but with all the conveniences available in a modern kitchen. No corners are cut, with solid wood being used as much as possible and all the timber is obtained from managed and replanted sources. Geoff Chater also offers fitted furniture for bedrooms, bathrooms, studies and other rooms.

Hatt Kitchens

Hartlebury Trading Estate, Hartlebury, Kidderminster, Worcs DY10 4JB
tel: 01299 251320 for stockists • fax: 01299 251579

Hatt Kitchens offer a fairly wide collection of predominantly traditional-style kitchens such as Shaker and wooden farmhouse designs. They do also have some more contemporary-looking kitchen ranges and can offer round or rectangular tables and chairs to match the wooden kitchens.

Joinwood Furniture

Unit 6, Radley Rd Industrial Estate,
Abingdon-on-Thames, Oxon OX14 3RY
tel/fax: 01235 520235

This specialist has several ranges of different kinds of kitchen furniture and, although veering slightly towards the traditional side, there are plenty of

contemporary designs as well. They also offer a whole range of exciting appliances including a lot of colour, stainless steel and tasteful Italian design.

Melton Interiors

107 Waterloo St, Burton-on-Trent, Staffs DE14 2ND
tel: 01283 543482 • fax: 01283 546195

Manufacturers of fitted kitchens, bedroom and bathrooms, Melton Interiors have eighteen kitchen displays in their showroom. Designs range from melamine or laminate finishes through to timber, which can be finished as natural wood, stained, limed or hand-painted. Plans are made with a computer-aided system and you will get a quotation in three different price ranges.

Nottingham Trade Interiors

Unit 112, Queens Rd East, Beeston, Notts NG9 2FD
tel: 0115 9221122 • fax: 0115 9251111

If you are looking for a kitchen bargain, you might pick one up at this retailer. Nottingham Trade Interiors sell at direct-from-manufacturer prices, catering to most budgets. They have about 500 different designs and offer a full fitting service.

P Hooper Designs of Worcestershire

Buckholt Business Centre, Buckholt Drive, Warndon, Worcs WR4 9ND
tel: 01905 457858 • fax: 01905 757477

This is a totally bespoke kitchen-making service, enabling you to have a great deal of input into the design of your kitchen. All the kitchens are handmade in traditional styles in painted or solid wood and with full frames.

Prentice Furniture

Felsar Rd, Sandy Way, Amington Industrial Estate, Tamworth, Staffs B77 4DP
tel: 01827 313700 • fax: 01827 313701

Offers a mixture of different timber styles including designs that would fit well in traditional or more contemporary kitchens. Colours are introduced through washes and liming, with some imaginative designs using both timber and some coloured pieces.

Scottwood

Dabell Avenue, Blenheim Industrial Estate, Bulwell, Nottingham, Notts NG6 8WA
tel: 01159 770877 for stockists • fax: 01159 770367

Designs range from the furniture of the reign of George III, through Shaker furniture to a distinctive 1950s range, which is painted in pastel colours and features chrome legs. You can see Scottwood kitchens, bedrooms and bathrooms at design centres throughout the country – phone for your local stockist.

Shortland
Coachgap Lane, Langar, Notts NG13 9HP
tel: 01949 860121 • fax: 01949 861142

If you want a whole hassle-free project undertaken, family business Shortland can not only take care of the building work but, if you want them to, also furnish the finished room with accessories. Designs include more unusual choices such as the Nouveau kitchen which takes its inspiration from the 1920s. Traditional pieces of freestanding furniture, such as the Gun Dresser, are also available.

Thomas Chippendale
Foxhills, Scunthorpe, N.Lincs DN15 8QW
tel: 01724 292060 for stockists • fax: 01724 292188

Inspiration for these kitchens comes from traditional English oak and pine furniture, and from Shaker and Arts & Crafts styles. Freestanding and fully fitted wood furniture is finished to enhance the natural grain or add colour. There are some unusual touches such as chicken wire doors and medieval gargoyle head handles.

Upgrade
10 Chapel Gate, Retford, Notts DN22 6BR
tel/fax: 01777 701314

If you have an imperial-sized kitchen, rather than a metric one, and you want to keep the existing carcasses and replace the doors, you may have problems finding the right size, which is where Upgrade comes in. They can offer a large range of imperial-sized doors and fit them locally. If you don't live locally you can get them mail order.

Watts & Wright
Bentley Rd North, Walsall, W.Midlands WAS2 0DF
tel: 01922 622247 • fax: 01922 648100

Traditional-style cabinetmakers follow through each commission from the raw, uncut timber to installation. There are some unusual designs including the ornate Victora with acanthus scrolls and the Millennium which is a mixture of olive wood and ash and steel. They also make fitted bedroom furniture.

north west

Cheshire Furniture Company
Oak Farm, Chester Rd, Aldford, Chester, Cheshire CH3 6HJ
tel: 01244 620323

These are custom-made kitchens in traditional and classic styles such as Shaker and a Cook's kitchen (a generic term, based on a straightforward traditional, Edwardian style). The kitchens are made from solid wood with mfc (melamine-faced chipboard) carcasses, and some of them are available painted in dragged or washed finishes. They also make fitted bedroom and bathroom furniture here.

Christians
1 Pillory St, Nantwich, Cheshire CW5 5BZ
tel: 01270 623333 for stockists
fax: 01270 623336

This is a company with a countrywide network of very smart and upmarket showrooms. The beautifully made furniture is all of traditional style, handmade and of a consistently high quality. Their designs have become something of a benchmark for the traditional side of the kitchen industry. They also do fitted bedroom, bathroom and study furniture. Phone for details of your local showroom.

Classic by Capricorn
Capricorn House, Birchall St, Liverpool, Merseyside L20 8PD
tel: 0151 933 9633 for stockists
fax: 0151 922 3650

This kitchen furniture has traditional-style exteriors that hide up-to-the-minute interiors for the working cook. A variety of French and English styles feature prominently in woods or painted finishes.

Great Britten Interiors
6 Minshull St, Knutsford, Cheshire WA16 6HG
tel: 01565 650090 • fax: 01565 650097

This showroom has traditionally made kitchen furniture in traditional styles with framed doors and brass butt hinges. You will find Gothic styles and maple kitchens and some inlaid work amongst the different styles. They can also make full libraries and other traditional furniture.

Kitchenalia

The Old Bakery, 36 Inglewhite Rd, Longridge,
Lancs PR3 3JS
tel: 01772 785411

This is a gold mine if you are looking for unfitted kitchen pieces. There are masses of freestanding pieces of kitchen furniture made from old pine and a whole collection of old butlers' sinks, taps and accessories. You will probably find this is a good option if you are on a budget and don't want a fitted kitchen.

London Road Handmade Kitchens

17 London Rd South, Poynton, Cheshire SK12 1LA
tel: 01625 877117 • fax: 01625 859133

These handmade kitchens have solid pine carcasses and doors in a range of hardwoods, pine, and painted finishes. They are all bespoke, not with a fussy farmhouse look but slightly more contemporary than that – a classic style with simple uncluttered lines.

Martin Moore & Co

36 Church St, Altrincham, Cheshire WA14 4DW
tel: 0161 928 2643 for stockists • fax: 0161 929 1595

Individually designed and handmade kitchens in a variety of hardwoods such as oak, maple, ash and cherry. Antique yellow pine is also available. There is also a range of painted kitchens from Shaker styles to the more decorative Victorian ones. The range includes several unfitted pieces, including tables and chairs.

The Old Pine Store

Coxons Yard, Ashbourne, Derbyshire DE6 1FG
tel/fax: 01335 344112

Freestanding kitchen furniture or fully fitted kitchens made from solid wood using antique pine, reclaimed floorboards. Every item in this showroom is handmade to individual sizes and along traditional lines using mortice and tenon joints and solid brass butt hinges.

Plain & Simple Kitchens

332 Deansgate, Manchester M3 4LY
tel: 0161 839 8983 for stockists • fax: 0161 834 8107

This company offers a kaleidoscope of painted kitchens with the emphasis on simple, uncluttered design including Shaker style. The painted kitchens can be coloured and finished to individual requirements. There are also a couple of contemporary designs on offer. Ring the number above for details of your nearest stockists.

north east

Brookmans Design Group

22 Wilkinson St, Sheffield, S.Yorks S10 2GB
tel: 01142 521700 for John Lewis stockists
fax: 01142 521701
e-mail: design@brookmans-design.co.uk

Available only from John Lewis stores, these are unusual ranges of hand-built kitchen furniture. Designs include the Bradfield Parish, which is partly based on a local cricket pavilion and features etched-glass wall cupboards. Finishes include stripped pine, lime wash and a variety of traditional painted colours.

The Callerton Kitchen & Bedroom Co

Callerton House, The Village Green, Ryhope, Sunderland, Tyne & Wear SR2 0NH
tel: 0191 523 6663 for stockists
fax: 0191 523 6399

A whole range of different classic-style kitchens is on offer here in timber and colourwashed woods. The company's designers also specialize in mixing woods and colourwashes to create a very different look. The company has more than thirty outlets around the country.

Croft Interiors

78 Swanland Rd, Hessle, Humberside HU13 0NJ
tel: 01482 648107

This retailer works from home and offers handmade kitchens in antiqued finishes as well as ranges from other manufacturers. You can also get a more contemporary kitchen from here and they are very happy to show you samples, although they do not have a showroom.

Landau

Landau House, Bontoft Ave, Hull, Humberside HU5 4HF
tel: 01482 440680 for stockists
fax: 01482 440683

Landau make a wide selection of wood kitchens in a variety of woods which are either left natural or finished in a choice of paint effects. They also offer some unusual designs, such as Juniper, which is a solid maple frame with coloured panel. Phone for details of your local stockist.

The Newcastle Furniture Co
4 Green Lane Buildings, Pelaw, Gateshead,
Tyne & Wear NE10 0UW
tel: 0191 438 1342 for stockists • fax: 0191 438 4698

The simplest lines of the English and American
traditions are employed in the designs of this kitchen
furniture company. The kitchens are available hand-
painted or in natural wood and fitted or freestanding.
Phone for details of your local showroom.

Normic Interiors
Normic House, Pym St, Leeds, W.Yorks LS10 1PG
tel: 01132 429515 • fax: 01132 429262

Solid wood kitchens in a selection of seven different
timbers, with other finishes available. Dining,
bedroom, bathroom and home office furniture is also
available. You can also go and look round the
manufacturing unit to see the quality of work.

wales & the isle of man

British Kitchen Systems
Swansea West Industrial Estate, Fforestfach, Swansea,
Glam SA5 4DL
tel: 01792 586000 for stockists • fax: 01792 586001

German, Italian, French and British expertise and
design all go into this range of kitchens. The styles are
predominately traditional, with some of them being
suitable for contemporary kitchens. Most of the range
is wood, although there are other choices as well.

Caerleon Kitchen & Bedroom Centre
The Old Malthouse, High St, Caerlon, Newport,
S.Wales NP6 1AE
tel: 01633 423434

This family-run retailer prides itself on offering
personal service along with its value-for-money fitted
kitchens, which are displayed in a large, stone, historic
building. They also offer fitted bedroom furniture.

Manx Furnishers
24 West Quay, Ramsey, Isle of Man IM8 1DL
tel: 01624 815489

This compact showroom has an interesting quayside
setting and is packed with ideas for your kitchen.
Whether you are looking in the budget or the top end
of the market, they can help you.

Sigma 3
Lower Dock St, Newport, Gwent NP9 1EN
tel: 01633 252187 • fax: 01633 252190

The largest manufacturer of kitchens in Wales, this
company offers a whole range of traditional-style
kitchens in solid wood, wood veneer or wood effect
finishes. They also make painted and Shaker-style
kitchens and some hi-tech styles. There are four
showrooms throughout Wales.

scotland

Ashley Ann
19 Ormlie Industrial Estate, Thurso,
Caithness KW14 7QU
tel: 01847 894514 for branches
fax: 01847 893145

This company makes bespoke kitchens with a
reasonable price tag and it is even more reasonable if
you opt to fit them yourself. If you don't feel up to
this, they do have a fitting service. Phone for more
details of branches throughout the Highlands.

Crannog Fitted Furniture
Freepost, Lorimer Workshops, Briglands, Rumbling
Bridge, Kinross-shire KY13 7PS
tel: 01577 840461 • fax: 01577 840652
e-mail: kav97@dial.pipex.com

Crannog design and manufacture all of their solid
wood kitchens in the heart of the Scottish countryside,
using only timber from managed forests. Very
traditional designs are created in a selection of oak,
maple, ash, cherry, pine and red alder. They also offer
painted kitchens.

Echobank Joinery
Easterbowhouse, Maddison, Falkirk FK2 0BS
tel/fax: 01324 711111

This manufacturer can offer you various brands of
traditional and slightly more modern kitchen furniture.
Most of them are wood kitchens and they employ their
own kitchen fitters and installers to translate the
designs into your home.

Linton Country Furniture
Fenton Barns, Dirleton, nr Berwick,
E.Lothian EH39 5BW
tel: 01620 850488 • fax: 01620 850372

If you are after freestanding, custom-made pine furniture for the kitchen, take a look at this company. They cater for made-to-measure kitchens and make items such as tables, dressers, sideboards and sink units – in fact any kind of freestanding unit.

northern ireland

The Bespoke Kitchen Co

Hill Farm, 29 Whiterock Rd, Killinchy,
Co Down BT23 6PT
tel: 01238 541549

Nigel McGowan designs individual kitchens in any style, which are then hand built by a small team of local craftsmen. You can choose between French oak, maple, waxed pine or the company's very own pickled pine which involves bleaching, waxing and polishing. Hand-painted kitchens are also available.

Richardson Cardy

44a–48 Railway St, Lisburn, Co Antrim BT28 1XP
tel: 01846 678884 for stockists • fax: 01846 663509

Although this manufacturer makes both traditional and contemporary styles, the emphasis is more on the traditional. Most of the designs are made from solid wood, with oak and maple being the best sellers. They also offer pines, ash, alder and cherrywood and some vinyl-wrapped doors. Phone for details of your local stockist.

modern & groovy

Modern and groovy, for the purposes of this directory, encompasses a huge range of styles leaning towards the hi-tech and minimalist look. Materials favoured are stainless steel and granite, coloured plastics and laminates, melamine, but also pale and painted wood, particularly birch. 'Modern', however, does not necessarily mean fitted. Recently there has been a trend back towards having freestanding units, often with moveable islands, to meet changing needs and lifestyles.

There is obviously some overlap between companies who make both 'traditional' and contemporary kitchens. For instance, Shaker-style kitchens are technically traditional but are enjoying a revival and suit all styles of homes. So, even if you are thinking of a traditional

kitchen, it is worth browsing through the addresses below to see if anything catches your eye. As many of these companies are manufacturers we have chosen not to list them by region. You should call to find out your nearest stockist.

Allmilmo

80 Mersey Way, Thatcham, Berks RG18 3DL
tel: 01635 868181 for stockists • fax: 01635 860064

Manufacturer of garde kitchens featuring a whole host of colours and interesting shapes including prism-shaped cabinets and complementary chrome, shaped legs. This could be a good choice if you are looking for something really different, but also good quality. Phone for details of your nearest stockist.

Alternative Plans

9 Hester Rd, London SW11 4AN
tel: 0171 228 6460 • fax: 0171 924 1164

These are truly contemporary and good-quality kitchens, right on the cutting edge of design. This specialist sells a lot of Italian Boffi and German Allmilmo kitchens, both of which are very creative with their designs. Their range of appliances is all modern, exciting designs and they can offer you granite, marble, limestone and stainless steel for worktops.

Blackheath Design Studios

135 Lee Rd, Blackheath, London SE3 9DS
tel: 0181 297 8063

A Eurocentre for kitchen designs from all over the Continent including Italian, French, British and German styles. You will find something to suit most budgets and they also offer a full all-in design and fitting service.

Bulthaup

3 Wigmore St, London W1H 9LD
tel: 0171 495 3663 for stockists • fax: 0171 495 0139

If you want to see contemporary kitchen design at its best make time to call in here. These kitchens are minimalist and hi-tech and clearly based around the best in ergonomic design. The cutting edge of kitchen design.

Camargue

Townsend Farm Rd, Houghton Regis, Beds LU5 5BA
tel: 01582 699122 for stockists • fax: 01582 609361
e-mail: camargue@btinternet.com

This is a creative range of contemporary furniture that is produced in the UK. The designers combine natural woods with glass, stainless steel and matt laminates to produce some quite unusual designs. Phone for details of your local stockist.

Cameron Interiors
458–462 Crow Rd, Glasgow G11 7DR
tel: 0141 334 9532 • fax: 0141 357 3869

This retailer specializes in hi-tech Poggenpohl and Goldreif kitchen furniture and traditional Rivendell kitchen, bedroom and bathroom furniture. They also offer a free, no obligation design service and their own installation team. Most of the staff are actually interior designers as well as kitchen designers, so you can get a very thorough and inspirational service here.

Connaught Kitchens
2 Porchester Place, London W2 2BS
tel: 0171 706 2210 • fax: 0171 706 2209

Retailers selling hi-tech German Leicht and Rational kitchens which are renowned for their engineering and quality. They also have their own Italian-influenced range called Connaught Colours, and their Scottwood and Wycliffe ranges, which are bespoke English products. These are backed by a strong line-up of appliance manufacturers.

Cuisines Arthur Bonnet
Sofiseb, 142–144 High St, Orpington, Kent BR6 0JS
tel: 01689 878513 for stockists
fax: 01689 830427

These are modern French kitchens with an emphasis on colour and style and a contemporary mixing of colour and pale woods. Don't expect to find a totally modern look though, as they also have some real French traditional ranges and even a very English-looking collection. Phone for details of your local stockist.

Four Seasons Kitchens
Silburn House, Great Bank Rd, Westhoughton,
Bolton BL5 3XU
tel: 01942 840840 for stockists • fax: 01942 840084

If you are looking for a collection of mildly contemporary kitchens and some more traditional styles, this range could answer your needs. Styles range from a Shaker lookalike to high gloss doors and to the French farmhouse look.

Francis Quinn Ltd
58 The Broadway, Thatcham, Berks RG19 3HP
tel/fax: 01635 874700 for stockists

Vast range of contemporary fitted kitchen furniture designs and some which would look good in more traditional settings. Freestanding chairs and tables are also available in matching stains or colours. The company also offers fitted bathroom furniture.

Fulham Kitchens
19 Carnwath Rd, London SW6 3HR
tel: 0171 736 6458 • fax: 0171 371 9289

Fulham Kitchens place the emphasis on one-off kitchens that must work to professional cooking standards as one of the partners is a trained chef. Styles range from a reclaimed wood and etched glass kitchen to a hi-tech island designed for a loft apartment, but they make good use of specialist materials and all the kitchens are streamlined.

Goldreif
2nd Floor, Silbury Court, 368 Silbury Boulevard,
Milton Keynes, Bucks MK9 2AF
tel: 01908 247600 for stockists
fax: 01908 606958

These are good-quality, German-built kitchens that have a strong contemporary flair without being at the real cutting edge. Some of them, in fact, wouldn't look out of place in a Victorian house. The storage inside the cabinets is fabulous and all the ranges have been incredibly well planned.

Guy Mallinson Furniture
7 The Coachworks, 80 Parson's Green Lane, Fulham,
London SW6 4HU
tel: 0171 371 9190 • fax: 0171 371 5099
e-mail: info@mallinson.co.uk

Contemporary kitchen islands and butchers' blocks are made after a consultation period with clients. You can also get them to replace the doors on your existing kitchen cabinets with exquisitely matched veneers, so you get a new-looking kitchen without the upheaval.

Habitat
196 Tottenham Court Rd, London W1P 9LD
tel: 0171 255 2545
tel: 0645 334433 for branches

If you are looking for well-designed and well-made kitchen furniture, which takes in the latest trends without being too avant garde, you would do well to look here. Most of the furniture is freestanding and there is a whole host of interesting and attractive accessories to go with it.

Homebase

Head Office, Beddington House, Wallington,
Surrey SM6 0HB
tel: 0645 801800 for enquiries and branches

Wrighton is an old and distinguished name in British kitchens and now the company makes kitchens for Homebase. The kitchens are generally quite contemporary designs with pale woods such as maple, birch and lime-wood-stained cherry to the fore.

IKEA

Brent Park, 2 Drury Way, North Circular Rd,
London NW10 0TH
tel: 0181 208 5600 for enquiries and branches

These are real value budget kitchens set out in room sets with plenty of space so you can really see them properly. There is a large range of styles from trendy to slightly more traditional, all available with design and fitting service if you want – but it is even cheaper if you fit them yourself.

In Toto

Wakefield Rd, Leeds W.Yorks LS27 7JZ
tel: 0113 252 4131 for franchises
fax: 0113 252 0154

A franchise operation, you can find the German In Toto built in kitchen furniture throughout the country. Styles are mostly contemporary with a mixture of woods, veneers and coloured laminates, but there are also some more classic looks.

JS Geddes

10–12 West Netherton St, Kilmarnock,
Ayrshire KA1 4BU
tel: 01563 530838 • fax: 01563 570470

If you are at a loss about where to start in planning your kitchen, this could be a good place to go. The staff at this kitchen showroom will help you with the whole project right down to the choice of fabrics. Set in an old shoe factory, this is a showroom packed with interesting working kitchens and cookery demonstrations are a speciality.

Keller Kitchens

338/340 Manchester Rd, West Timperley, Altrincham,
Cheshire WA14 5NH
tel: 0161 962 6939 for stockists

Keller offers a choice of 1500 paint colours, more than twenty-five different designs and twelve carcass colours. These Dutch kitchens are contemporary without being avant garde and have quite a few traditional-style designs thrown in.

Kugenmeister Kitchens

29 Crwys Rd, Cardiff, South Glamorgan CF2 4NB
tel: 01222 394803 • fax: 01222 341054

If you are looking for middle to upmarket kitchens, this retailer has a good selection of British, French and German makes on offer. They have fifteen displays, which include a fine selection of cooking ranges. They also sell some traditional, handmade kitchens.

Leicht

106 Culverden Down, Tunbridge Wells,
Kent TN4 9SW
tel: 01892 519383 for stockists • fax: 01892 519383

Hi-tech German kitchens that are planned with ergonomics in mind. For instance, work stations are adapted to the height of the individual user. Designs offer myriad different heights, shapes, colours and concepts. Wood, laminates, glass and steel are all extensively used.

Miele

Fairacres, Marcham Rd, Abingdon, Oxon OX14 1TW
tel: 01235 554455 for stockists
fax: 01235 554477

This is contemporary German furniture that is built to last for ages! This must be some of the best engineered contemporary kitchen furniture on the market. Phone for details of your local stockist.

Nolte

The Clock House, 43 London Rd, Sawbridgeworth,
Herts CM21 9JH
tel: 01279 868800 for stockists • fax: 01277 868802

This German company offers a very wide range of contemporary designs including pale woods, coloured units, frosted glass and chrome handles. Choose from a huge selection of units in different styles and sizes, all with fully fitted interiors. Tables and chairs are also available. Contact Nolte for your nearest outlet.

NoName by Capricorn

Capricorn House, Birchall St, Liverpool,
Merseyside L20 8PD
tel: 0151 933 9633 for stockists
fax: 0151 922 3650

This is contemporary British fitted kitchen furniture with sleek doors and feature handles. Door fronts are a mixture of high-grade wood finishes including unusual ones such as Swiss pear and fiddleback sycamore, and coloured panels in a choice of six colours. Brushed aluminium shelves, architraves and skirtings are hard-wearing and stylish.

Poggenpohl

2nd Floor, Silbury Court, 368 Silbury Boulevard,
Milton Keynes, Bucks MK9 2AF
tel: 01908 247600 for stockists
fax: 01908 606958

Poggenpohl has been at the cutting edge of kitchen design for three decades. Stylish, up-to-the-minute designs are available in a mixture of woods and laminates. These kitchens are not just a collection of cabinets but often inspire a whole new kitchen design direction. They are very hot on ergonomics.

Rational

24–28 Crossway House, High St, Bracknell,
Berks RG12 1DA
tel: 01344 455800 for stockists
fax: 01344 455811
e-mail: rational.uk@mcmail.com

These German manufacturers make a mixture of contemporary and more traditional styles in a vast range of designs. Contemporary styles feature plain door fronts with stylish handles in a mixture of wood and coloured laminates. The company have retailers throughout the country so phone for details.

Robinson Interiors

10 Boucher Way, Belfast BT10 6RE
tel: 01232 683838 • fax: 01232 666643

This is a fairly upmarket showroom that offers well-spaced, top-end displays. The staff here can undertake everything to do with your kitchen project even down to special lighting design.

SieMatic

Osprey House, Rookery Court, Primett Rd, Stevenage,
Herts SG1 3EE
tel: 01438 369327 for stockists
fax: 01438 368920

This company has been at the forefront of German kitchen design for many years and you will find high-quality, contemporary kitchens that explore new designs. Many of their kitchens are particularly well suited to British taste with clean lines and pale wood-framed doors. Some of them would look equally at home in a period-type house.

Thomas Design

129 High St, Holywood, County Down BT18 9LG
tel: 01232 428842

This specialist will undertake the whole project of your new kitchen including design, the kitchen cabinets, plumbing, flooring and building work. You can buy anything here from a new saucepan to the whole kitchen.

Wellmann

Shaw Cross Court, Shaw Cross Business Park,
Dewsbury, W.Yorks WF12 7RF
tel: 01924 487900 for stockists
fax: 01924 437305

These are middle-market German kitchens that offer some pretty contemporary designs, but also a whole selection that would suit the most middle of the road tastes. Like all German kitchens they are very well made.

Zeyko

Business Design Centre, 52 Upper St,
London N1 0QH
tel: 0171 288 6123 for stockists
fax: 0171 288 6122

All the hallmarks of good-quality, contemporary German kitchen furniture with some extras such as the new Mobilo system thrown in. Mobilo is a mixture of wood, chrome and glass units, in a combination of open and closed units, worktops and drawers that swivel out to create more space, and mobile units on wheels.

kitchenalia

Once the bare bones of your kitchen have been installed, choosing all the finishing touches can be the most pleasurable bit. Although many people have the same kitchen units, you can stamp your own mark on them and the kitchen will look completely different.

Worktops don't, as a rule, come included in the price of a kitchen and, although the showroom display normally shows one, you don't have to stick with this if it's not to your taste. The most important thing to remember about worktops is to use something that will be suitable for the purpose and, if necessary, vary the surface according to where it is in the kitchen. For instance, the surface on either side of the oven needs to be heat-resistant so stainless steel, granite or terrazzo would all fit the bill. However, chopping vegetables on brushed stainless steel is likely to leave scratch marks. Wood is really the surface you want for food preparation although something cool like marble or ceramic is best for pastry! Rather than have a patchwork of lots of different materials which might look rather odd, you need to work out what surfaces you will be using for what and reach a compromise. Your budget will also be a contributing factor. Freestanding butcher's blocks can solve the problem as can lots of separate chopping boards in a variety of materials.

In this section you will also find all sorts of sinks, from the latest hi-tech ones to the traditional Belfast sink, as well as taps and period kitchenware.

Aero ✉

Unit 8, Glenville Mews, Kimber Rd,
London SW8 4NJ
tel: 0181 971 0022 • fax: 0181 971 0033

This company has an amazing mail order brochure with several trendy kitchen products. On the larger side it has the Linus table which you can move around your kitchen. Simply lock the wheels in place when you and your guests have decided where you would like to eat! They have shops in Notting Hill and the Kings Rd. Ring the above number for details.

Alessi

tel: 01433 650882 for stockists

Alessi is one of the cutting-edge names in kitchenware, with their beautiful and often witty Italian designs. The kettles have become a trademark of the well-dressed kitchen, but there is much, much more than this. Their products range up to the pale beech trolley, which has a practical metal top, and down to teaspoons. Everything has the Alessi hallmark of distinctive design.

Armitage Shanks

Armitage, Rugeley, Staffs WS15 4BT
tel: 01543 490253 for stockists • fax: 01543 413619

If you thought Armitage Shanks only made bathrooms you would be wrong as they also make Belfast-style fireclay sinks. They are produced at Europe's most advanced fireclay plant and are very good quality.

Astracast Sinks

PO Box 20, Spring Ram Business Park, Birstall,
W.Yorks WF17 9XD
tel: 01924 477466 for stockists • fax: 01924 475801

This company has a large range of sinks in man-made materials as well as some ceramic and stainless steel models. Man-made materials can range from plastic-based to a kind of reconstituted stone, and man-made sinks come in a variety of different colours and finishes including granite-looking finishes and a satin effect. Colours include Jade Green, Topaz Blue and Lava Black.

Atriflo
Orwell Close, Fairview Industrial Park, Manor Way, Rainham, Essex RM13 8UB
tel: 01708 526361 for stockists • fax: 01708 550220

You will find very stylish kitchen taps in this company's portfolio with thousands of combinations of colours and finishes to choose from. Many different materials are used for these taps including brass, porcelain, Corian and Avonite (these last two are a kind of reconstituted stone made partly from stone/quartz, etc, and partly from acrylics – it is very strong, hygienic and can be moulded into different shapes). There are both traditional and contemporary styles.

B&P Wynn
60 Queenstown Rd, London SW8 3RY
tel: 0171 498 4345 • fax: 0171 498 4346

If you fancy something really unusual, such as a copper, brass or nickel kitchen sink, this could be one of the places to come. The sinks are French as are the distinctive single lever, pump-style kitchen taps which also come in a variety of finishes.

Below Stairs
103 High St, Hungerford, Berks RG17 0NB
tel/fax: 01488 682317

This shop specializes in the unusual and the kitchen bits and pieces that our ancestors used. Most of the pieces are nineteenth century and there is certainly nothing under fifty years old. There are loads of old kitchen gadgets, roasting spits and good copper. There is also a small amount of stoneware and some unusual storage items.

Berwyn Slate Quarry
The Horse Shoe Pass, Llangollen, Denbighshire LL20 8DP
tel: 01978 861897 • fax: 01978 869292

Slate worktops are becoming increasingly popular, and at this quarry they are cut from a particularly rich vein

that makes them very durable and a clear blue/black colour. They can be cut to any specification with different edge profiles, drainer grooves and plinths available on request.

Billy-Joe Homewares
63 Longfields, Ely, Cambs CB6 3DN
tel: 01353 661997 • fax: 01353 661960

The kitchen sink need never be the same again! These kitchen strainers and plugs are topped with little lead-free pewter figures and motifs such as frogs, flowers, starfish, teapots, octopuses and carrots. They will fit any standard kitchen sink and they really are fun.

Blanco
Oxgate Lane, Cricklewood, London NW2 7JN
tel: 0181 450 9100 for stockists • fax: 0181 452 3399

A highly sophisticated collection of sinks, taps and waste disposal systems from one of Germany's leading manufacturers. All these products have been designed with the latest ergonomic thinking in mind and they are also very attractive and particularly suited to the semi-professional type kitchen.

Boffi at Alternative Plans
9 Hester Rd, London SW11 4AN
tel: 0171 228 6460 • fax: 0171 924 1164

Boffi manufacture an amazing mobile oven called the Boffi B95. You can take the oven anywhere you like in the kitchen, even to the table if you want to serve straight from it! You can see it at this specialist.

Bragman Flett
Unit 4, 193 Garth Rd, Morden, Surrey SM4 4LZ
tel: 0181 337 1934

This is a stainless steel and metalwork company that works with aluminium, copper, brass, zinc and rigidized metals. They can cut, notch and bend any of these materials for you but the really practical one for worktops, which they can fabricate for you, is stainless steel.

Brass & Traditional Sinks
Devauden Green, Chepstow, Monmouthshire NP6 6PL
tel: 01291 650738 for stockists • fax: 01291 650827
e-mail: sales@sinks.co.uk

If you're after either a traditional-style fireclay sink or a more unusual brass number this should be one of your first stops. The fireclay sinks come in a range of styles including Belfast and French Farmhouse and many other configurations. Solid brass sinks are joined by solid brass taps.

Builders Iron & Zincwork
Millmarsh Lane, Brimsdown, Enfield, Middx EN3 7QA
tel: 0181 443 3300

If you want an unusual worktop, visit this company which supplies zinc and stainless steel sheets. They will cut your piece to size and they also have fabrication facilities to make you a made-to-measure worktop.

The Cotswold Co
High St, Bourton on the Water, Glos GL54 2ZZ
tel: 0990 502233 • fax: 01276 609102

This company offers the Cucina storage system – a hanging rail system to which you can attach anything from a specially designed clock to storage jars. They also have myriad other accessories in wicker, wood and chrome and larger items such as mobile butchers' blocks. Visit the shop in the Cotswolds or order from the mail order catalogue.

Divertimenti
PO Box (Mail Order) Limited, PO Box 6611,
London SW15 2WG
tel: 0181 246 4300 • fax: 0181 246 4330

Professional and amateur cooks alike beat a path to the Divertimenti mail order catalogue that contains a huge selection of practical and stylish kitchenware. Items are sourced from all over the world and you can often find elusive cooking gems you've been after for ages. Divertimenti also have shops in Wigmore St and Fulham Rd, London.

Elon
66 Fulham Rd, South Kensington, London SW3 6HH
tel: 0171 460 4600 • fax: 0171 460 4601
tel: 0181 932 3000 for stockists

Elon makes the Landsdowne range of kitchen sinks and taps. The sink is a fine fireclay ceramic kitchen sink, calling to mind sturdy, old-fashioned sinks, it resists stains and scratches and is easy to clean.

Formica
Coast Rd, North Shields, Tyne & Wear NE29 8RE
tel: 0191 259 3000 for stockists
fax: 0191 258 2719

Forget the Formica-topped tables you once knew, this company now offers an enormous range of colours and designs in the most modern of laminate work surfaces. Alongside more traditional designs there are some really funky ones such as Cheetah, Safari and Boomerang! They also have designs that look like metal in all kinds of finishes and solid surface materials.

Franke
East Park, Manchester International Office Centre,
Styal Rd, Manchester M22 5WB
tel: 0161 436 6280 for stockists • fax: 0161 436 2180

Franke is one of the big names in sinks and has a huge selection to offer. The sinks are made from stainless steel, man-made (from plastic-based to a kind of reconstituted stone) or ceramic materials and they come in an almost endless range of shapes, sizes and colours. They also have a huge range of taps and a water purification system called Triflow.

GEC Anderson Ltd
Oakengrove, Shire Lane, Halstoe, Herts HP23 6LY
tel: 01442 826999 for stockists • fax: 01442 825999
e-mail: gec@ndirect.co.uk

If you are looking for a fashionable and practical stainless steel worktop or sink, this is one of the manufacturers to look at. They also make cabinets, drawers and shelving for the semi-professional look.

Granitops
West Dean Rd, West Tytherley, Salisbury SP5 1QG
tel: 01980 862253 • fax: 01980 863073

This company specializes in granite and marble for kitchens and provides the complete service to installation and finishing. Both their granites and marbles range through a wide spectrum of patterns and colours and you can choose from various edge profiles for your worktops.

The Hambledon Gallery
42 Salisbury St, Blandford, Dorset DT11 7PR
tel: 01258 454884 • fax: 01258 454225

Their House mail order brochure has a select collection of kitchen accessories such as storage baskets, plate racks, trays and china. Most are in simple designs that would look good in most kitchens and are more traditional than contemporary. Phone for mail order details.

The Holding Company

241–245 Kings Rd, London SW3 5EL
tel: 0171 352 1600
and
41 Spring Gardens, Manchester M2 2BJ
tel: 0161 834 3400
tel: 0171 610 9160 for mail order nationwide
fax: 0171 610 9166 for mail order nationwide

This company offers a small, but very useful, selection of kitchen accessories including small wicker baskets, drawer organizers, a fruit bowl with different-sized dips for different-sized fruit, trendy storage jars and some professional-style chrome racking. You can either visit their stores or order all of this by mail.

Homebase Cookshop

tel: 0645 801800 for branches

From small storage solutions to culinary gift ideas, the Homebase Cookshop is packed with kitchen accessories. They have selections of Madhur Jaffrey, Ken Hom and Italian cookware, wine coolers and electronic scales. Alongside this there are hanging storage racks, stainless steel pans and a selection of more than 200 cooking gadgets and utensils. Homebase Cookshops are located within some of the Homebase stores, so call to find out where your nearest one is.

ICTC

3 Caley Close, Sweet Briar Rd, Norwich NR3 2BU
tel: 01603 488019 for stockists • fax: 01603 488020
e-mail: admin.ictc@dial.pipex.com

ICTC have collected together much of Europe's best in terms of cookware, china, glassware and cutlery. Everything you could ever want on the baking and cooking side can be found here and many things you never even dreamed of!

IKEA

Brent Park, 2 Drury Way, North Circular Rd,
London NW10 0TH
tel: 0181 208 5600 for enquiries and branches

If you are looking for a vast selection of inspirational and handy kitchen accessories, IKEA may just fit the bill. All very cheap, with amazing savings on run-of-the-mill items that cost a fortune in many places, it's great for cheap glasses, utensils and wooden chopping boards.

Indian Ocean Trading Co

155–163 Balham Hill, London SW12 9DJ
tel: 0181 675 4808 for other branches

Although this company generally make garden furniture, they also do a very useful Butler Drinks Trolley, which is excellent when a barbecue is in the offing. If you want to do your chopping and preparation in the open air, you can wheel it out into the garden. There are two other branches – in Hampstead and Cheshire.

Jacob Delafon

Unit 1, Churchward, Southmead Park, Didcot,
Oxon OX11 7HB
tel: 01235 510511 for stockists • fax: 01235 510481

Kitchen sinks are now designer items and these stylish ones from Jacob Delafon are no exception. Choose from ceramic, granite look, stainless steel, polished brass or brushed nickel finishes and from a variety of sizes and shapes.

Junckers Ltd

Wheaton Court Commercial Centre, Wheaton Rd,
Witham, Essex CM8 3UJ
tel: 01376 517512 for stockists • fax: 01376 514401

Famous for their wooden flooring, Junckers also make wooden worktops from solid wooden staves in either beech or oak. Before they leave the factory, the tops are treated with deep penetrating oil and then given some finishing coats once they are *in situ*. This makes them hygienic and easier to keep clean.

Kirkstone

Skelwith Bridge, nr Ambleside, Cumbria LA22 9NN
tel: 01539 433296 • fax: 01539 434006

This company is well known for its own Kirkstone, a sea-green stone of volcanic origin but they have many other worktop possibilities. These include slates, granites, marbles and limestones, many of them in unusual colours. Phone for details of the London showroom.

Kitchen Bygones

c/o Alfies Antiques Market, 13–25 Church St,
London NW8 8DT
tel: 0171 258 3405

You will find a gold mine of kitchen accessories from the 1920s and 1930s at this shop. Specialities include cream and green enamelware of that era, utility china, saucepans, kettles, graters and jelly moulds. There is also a small selection of kitchen accessories from the 1940s and 1950s and some Victorian pieces.

Leisure

Meadow Lane, Long Eaton, Nottingham,
Notts NG10 2AT
tel: 01159 464000 for stockists
fax: 01159 736602

Leisure have an enormous range of different sinks
in both stainless steel and composite materials.
They have recently introduced Neostone, which is
impregnated with Bio-shield for anti-bacterial
protection in the kitchen. They also have the
designer Impressions collection of sinks and
Rangemaster in green, blue and red to match the
developing trend for these colours in kitchen
appliances.

Maaz

29 Camden Square, London NW1 9XA
tel: 0171 482 2443 • fax: 0171 482 2443

As well as making wonderfully different cabinet
handles, this company makes some really innovative
resin worktops that will set your kitchen quite apart
from others. Choose a colour or even a design with
bits and pieces of your choice moulded into the
worktop itself.

Magpies

152 Wandsworth Bridge Rd, London SW6 2UH.
tel: 0171 736 3738

Kitchen accessories from more than half a century are
on sale here – from the 1900s to the 1960s. The
kitchenware includes enamel bread bins, blue and
white storage jars, jelly moulds and herb
choppers. There is also quite a large selection of
bone-handled cutlery.

MCP

Units 1–5, Pyfi Valley Yard, Commins Coch,
Powys SY20 8LG
tel: 01650 511889 for stockists

This company sells a whole range of wooden butchers'
blocks including an all-singing, all-dancing chef's
trolley with glass rack. This has additional chopping
boards, a knife rack, a storage drawer, towel rail, glass
store and wine rack.

Millennium Worksurfaces

Linear Business Pk, Valley Rd, Cinderford,
Glos GL14 3HE
tel: 01594 824555 • fax: 01594 824451

Choose from a selection of twenty different colours
of solid work surfaces, at this showroom, which are
all provided with a ten-year warranty. The colours
include a plain white and a plain cream and eighteen
different speckled patterns ranging from ruby to
lavender.

Ocean

Freepost LON811, London SW8 4BR
tel: 0800 132985 • fax: 0171 498 8898

If you want to order kitchen accessories from the
comfort of your own home, Ocean have an impressive
array available mail order. These range through
colourful plastic bowls, gadgets and bins to more
serious kitchen utensils but all with a distinctive
design flair. Alessi ranges feature highly and this
mail order catalogue is well worth a look if you are
searching for fun objects or the design classics of
the future.

Old Colonial

56 St John's Rd, Tunbridge Wells, Kent TN4 9NY
tel: 01892 533993

Buying from France, this shop sells the classic blue and
white enamelware. You can buy a set of storage tins in
graded heights. They sell both new and old storage
tins and there are also jugs and salt tins.

Orama Fabrications

Azalea Close, Clover Nook Industrial Estate,
Somercotes, Derbyshire DE55 4FR
tel: 01773 520560 for stockists • fax: 01773 520319

This company makes a whole range of different types
of worktops including: Cygnature, which is a solid-
surface work surface (a composite worktop made of
various materials); Harmony, which is a combination of
laminate and solid surface in a choice of finishes; and
Decorama Total Edge, a work surface with a seamless
edge for a smoother, continuous finish. If you can't
visualize these, phone for details of your local stockist
and go and take a look.

Pavilion Antiques

Freshford Hall, Freshford, Bath, Avon BA3 6EJ
tel: 01225 722522

This is a by-appointment-only shop. It sells French
nineteenth-century kitchenware ranging from little
bits and bobs, like enamel flour jars, to much larger
items such as lovely old French enamel stoves.

Period House Shop

141 Corve St, Ludlow, Shropshire SY8 2PG
tel: 01584 877944 • fax: 01584 875411

Among other kitchen goodies you will find sycamore and beech draining boards here and Belfast sinks. They also sell the cast-iron legs for Belfast sinks. You can obtain your goods by post – phone for further details.

Perstorp Warerite

Aycliffe Industrial Pk, Newton Aycliffe,
Co Durham DL5 6EF
tel: 01325 315141 for stockists • fax: 01325 319634

High-quality decorative laminate worktops, including granite, terrazzo and abstract patterns, join ranks with some stunning coloured worktops in the Axiom range. Colours range from Salmon to Pistachio and from turquoise to banana yellow.

Pfleiderer Industrie

131 St Peter's Court, Chalfont St Peter, Gerrards Cross, Bucks SL9 9QJ
tel: 01753 886557 for stockists • fax: 01753 889233

This company supplies the famous Duropal laminate worktops, which come in a selection of over fifty natural patterns such as granite, wood and terrazzo patterns. Phone for details of your nearest stockist or for samples.

Polished Metal Products

Devauden Green, Chepstow, Monmouthshire NP6 6PL
tel: 01291 650455 for stockists • fax: 01291 650827
e-mail: sales@sinks.co.uk

A collection of stainless steel undermounted sinks and taps. The sinks are all designed to have practical bowl sizes and are made from sturdy heavy gauge stainless steel. The tap designs range from very English and restrained taps to funkier mixer taps from great international designers such as Philippe Starck.

Purves & Purves

80–81 & 83 Tottenham Court Rd,
London W1P 9HD
tel: 0171 580 8223 • fax: 0171 580 8244

This shop has a showroom and does mail order. It specializes in the kind of professional cookware which is difficult to find elsewhere apart from in catering outlets. So, if you are a really serious cook, it's

definitely worth taking a look. They also have a big range of brightly coloured plastic accessories.

Quality Marble

Fountayne House, Fountayne Rd, London N15 4QL
tel: 0181 808 1110 • fax: 0181 885 2455

In spite of the name, this company deals mainly with granite although it does offer marble and slate tops as well at this showroom. It offers hundreds of different types of the three materials and can advise on which would suit your kitchen best. They will fabricate your worktops for you.

Regan Tile Design

56 Glenshane Rd, Magherafelt,
Co Londonderry BT45 8RE
tel: 01648 43163 • fax: 01648 44322

If you are looking for a Pyrolave worktop in Northern Ireland, come to this shop as they have exclusivity. If you don't know what it is, come and see! It is an enamelled lavastone in bright and translucent colours with a delicate crazing. It is hard-wearing and durable and comes in an amazing range of colours.

Roundel Design

Flishinghurst Orchards, Chalk Lane, Cranbrook,
Kent TN17 2QA
tel: 01580 712666 • fax: 01580 713564

This company makes the most wonderful butcher's block. It has a huge, hard-wearing chopping surface, a drawer, towel rails and adjustable shelves. It also has lockable castors so, although you can move it around, you can also make it totally stable.

Scotts of Stow

The Square, Stow-on-the-Wold, Glos GL4 1SS
tel: 0990 449111 • fax: 0990 449800
e-mail: sales@scottsofstow.demon.co.uk

You can either visit the shop at the above address or, if that is too far to go, take advantage of their very varied mail order brochure. The products range from foldaway knives to quite large items of kitchen furniture such as French farmhouse tables and chairs. They also have a huge selection of all kinds of tableware, cookware, crockery and cutlery.

Sinks & Things

Unit 17, Shield Rd, Ashford, Middx TW15 1AU
tel: 01784 247494 for stockists • fax: 01784 242834

As the name suggests, this company has a portfolio of all kinds of sink products and some appliances. They have taps, waste disposal units, water purification systems and, of course, sinks from a variety of different companies – here you will find everything from the simplest product to the very upmarket.

Summerhill & Bishop
100 Portland Rd, London W11 4LN
tel: 0171 221 4566 • fax: 0171 727 1322

If you are a Francophile, don't miss visiting this shop. It is packed with French kitchenware, and you will find both old and new pieces here. A lot of the stock is pottery and there are some cutting boards, knives and kettles as well.

T&G Woodware
Old Mill Rd, Portishead, Bristol, Avon BS20 9BX
tel: 01275 841841 for stockists • fax: 01275 841800

A large selection of wood, marble and melamine kitchenware is just part of T&G's portfolio. They also sell an extensive range of wooden kitchen trolleys, including a very trendy ice-cream cone-shaped one if you want a talking point in your kitchen!

Trans-Form
Unit 1, The Fairways, New River Trading Estate, Cheshunt, Herts EN8 0NJ
tel: 01342 410444 • fax: 01342 410555

Changing your kitchen can be a massive upheaval but this company offers face-lifts for kitchens where the carcasses stay *in situ* and the doors are replaced to give a new lease of life. They can also add new units, appliances and worktops and reckon you will save up to 50 per cent on the cost of a completely new kitchen.

UK Marble
21 Burcott Rd, Hereford, Herefordshire HR4 9LW
tel: 01432 352178 • fax: 01432 352112

This company manufactures and fits marble, granite and stone work surfaces and cladding. The choice the offer at this showroom is almost limitless as they can source stone from all over the UK and Europe within a reasonable time frame. They will also offer you valuable advice as to which stone works best in which place.

Villeroy & Boch
Building Ceramics Division, 267 Merton Rd, London SW18 5JS
tel: 0181 871 4028 for stockists
fax: 0181 870 3720

Villeroy & Boch may be better known for their bathroom pieces, but don't miss out on seeing their wonderful range of kitchen sinks. These come in a range of colours, materials and designs, some of which are very unusual.

appliances

When it comes to appliances, it seems size matters. British designers of everything from washing machines to fridges are either obsessed with making everything smaller and more compact, or as giant as possible. The trend for huge American-style refrigerators, in particular, is still on the up. You can really inject some colour into your kitchen by having one of the bright ones around today, although they will set you back a good few 'dollars'. But the trend also reflects our changing lifestyles – as we tend to buy more and more fresh food that is perishable, rather than living out of tins, the big fridge is a positive bonus.

Cookers, too, including built-in hobs, ovens, and ranges, also seem to be getting bigger. It's open to debate, though, as to whether it's because we are becoming a nation of semi-professional cooks or if they're just for show as we eat out more often. Whatever the reason, there are some beautifully designed, stainless steel and sleek models around which you would hardly want to dirty with a pan.

Appliances like these deserve to be on show but the trend is also towards hiding away the more mundane ones such as dishwashers and washing machines. Concealing and integrating machines behind the kitchen furniture doors is a good way of streamlining your kitchen.

We have concentrated on large items here rather than smaller pieces of equipment like kettles and blenders. In this section you will find some of the best and newest appliances around but as most of these companies stock appliances to other outlets, phone first for details of your nearest stockist.

AEG
Cornwall House, 55–77 High St, Slough,
Berks SL11 1DZ
tel: 01753 872500 for stockists
fax: 01753 872403

Even before it was really trendy, AEG were working to make their upmarket appliances as environmentally friendly as possible and they are still among the leaders in this field. German manufacturers, they offer the full range of quality built-in and freestanding appliances.

Aga
PO Box 30, Ketley, Telford, Shropshire TF1 4DD
tel: 0345 125207 for stockists

The Aga hardly needs any introduction but you may be surprised to know that it is now available in a wide range of colours and with added options such as conventional ovens that are designed to look like the Aga range and sit well beside it.

Alpha Cookers
89 New Greenham Park, Greenham, Thatcham,
Berks RG19 6HW
tel: 01635 582068 for stockists • fax: 01635 37870

This company offers a collection of range-style cookers with traditional cast-iron components and in a selection of different colours. They will not only do the cooking but also control your central heating system.

The American Appliance Centre
52 Larkshall Rd, Chingford, London E4 6PD
tel: 0181 529 9665 • fax: 0181 529 9666

As the name suggests this company offers a wide range of American appliances including the Thermador Professional Series of cooking professional ranges for the home. They also offer the kind of cooker hoods needed for cooking with these ranges. They have an extensive range of other American products, notably some of the most famous names in large American refrigerators.

The Appliance Warehouse
Unit 2, Bunny Trading Estate, Bunny, Nottingham,
Notts NG11 6QJ
tel: 01159 844357 • fax: 01159 456001

If you want to find cheap kitchen appliances it is worth a look here. They have a stock of up to 30 000 appliances at any one time so you will probably be able to find what you want and have it delivered immediately. Because they buy in bulk the prices are very competitive and they have appliances from most brands.

Ariston
3 Cowley Business Park, High St, Cowley, Uxbridge,
Middx UB8 2AD
tel: 01895 858200 for stockists
fax: 01895 858270

As well as all the normal, middle-market built-in and freestanding appliances, Ariston have some stunning stainless steel ovens and 90cm-wide hobs. Their wacky fridge freezers, however, are really something. You can buy these in a range of colours or decorated with pictures ranging from the New York skyline, through cut limes to giant-sized strawberries.

Asko

Bradshaw Appliances, Kenn Rd, Clevedon, Bristol,
Avon BS21 6LH
tel: 01275 343000 for stockists • fax: 01275 343454

Asko specialize in dishwashers, washing machines and
tumble dryers that are sturdily built and intended to
stand the test of time. Some of the models are
electronically controlled to make life easier and the
company is very conscious of ecological issues and the
amount of noise their appliances make. See entry for
Viking, another part of Bradshaw Appliances,
specialising in products imported from America.

Atag

19 Hither Green, Clevedon, Somerset BS21 6XU
tel: 01275 877301 for stockists • fax: 01275 871371

When other companies were making appliances in
white or brown, Atag broke the mould and offered
them in a huge rainbow of colours. They have now
extended their range of actual products to include
three sectors, one for people on a limited budget, a
complete range of built-in appliances, and one of
really special appliances for the hobby cook.

Bauknecht

PO Box 45, 209 Purley Way, Croydon, Surrey CR9 4RY
tel: 0181 649 5000 for stockists • fax: 0181 649 5060

Bauknecht offer an impressive line-up of
contemporary-style kitchen appliances, with an
emphasis on cooking and cooling. Their appliances are
built in and they have some interesting products such
as 90 cm wide ovens and hobs and side by side fridges
and freezers which will fit under the worktop.

Baumatic

Baumatic House, 3 Elgar Industrial Estate, Preston Rd,
Reading, Berks RG2 0BE
tel: 0118 931 0055 for stockists • fax: 0118 931 0035

This is a range of Italian-designed appliances which, as
you would expect, have all the usual design flair of
that country. The range includes some quite unusual-
looking products, some sleek designs and quite a bit of
stainless steel and colour.

Belling Appliances

Talbot Rd, Mexborough, S.Yorks S64 8AJ
tel: 01709 579900 for stockists • fax: 01709 579964

If the name Belling makes you think immediately of
the Baby of the family, you might be surprised to see

what else they now have on offer – a whole range of
built-in and slot-in cooking appliances as well as the
Farmhouse range-style cooker in blue, green and red.

Bonk & Co

8 Harbour Rd, Inverness IV1 1SY
tel: 01463 233968

You're unlikely to forget this name in a hurry – or what
they offer here. This retailer is a centre of excellence
for Rayburns, re-conditioned cast-iron traditional
cookers, and French ranges. They have more than fifty
examples of traditional and modern range cookers.

Bosch

Grand Union House, Old Wolverton Rd, Old Wolverton,
Milton Keynes, Bucks MK12 5ZR
tel: 01908 328200 for stockists

Bosch offer a sturdy mid-market range of appliances
for both freestanding and built-in options. They are
German made and good quality for often quite
surprisingly reasonable prices.

Buyers and Sellers

120–122 Ladbroke Grove, London W10 5NE
tel: 0171 229 1947 • fax: 0171 221 4113

This shop has some of the keenest prices on every type
of kitchen appliance and, if you buy three or more
appliances at once, you will get them all at trade
prices. They stock at least sixty different brand names
and offer every kind of appliance at every price level.
There is also a rapid nationwide delivery service.

Candy

New Chester Rd, Bromborough, Wirral,
Merseyside L62 3PE
tel: 0151 334 2781 for stockists • fax: 0151 334 0185

Manufacturer Candy offers a good middle-of-the-road
selection of cooking, cooling, laundry and dishwashing
appliances. Choose between built-in or freestanding
appliances. Lately, they have introduced some pretty
trendy designs such as the Convex built-in ovens,
which have a bowed front.

Cannon

Morley Way, Peterborough, Cambs PE2 9JB
tel: 01782 385500 for stockists • fax: 01782 385544

More than a century of experience has gone into this
range of slide-in cookers, which are available in
various sizes and shapes including range-style cookers.

The Classic American Fridge Company
Two Gate Cottages, Chorleywood Common,
Chorleywood, Herts WD3 5LW
tel/fax: 01923 490303

If you are a fifties freak you will love this place. It is
full of fully restored, original fifties fridges. They have
all been completely stripped and re-made, and you can
have one sprayed in any colour you like. The company
also offers a restoration service for an old family fridge
that may be very dear to your heart!

Country Cookers
Thorncliffe Industrial Estate, Chapeltown, Sheffield,
S.Yorks S35 2PZ
tel: 0114 257 2300 for stockists
fax: 0114 245 3021

The Nobel is the main product from this company and
it is a traditional heat storage cooker, which looks like
a range. It has some unusual features such as an
electric element in the simmering oven to boost the
temperature on demand. It is available in three
finishes and five colours.

Creda
Grindley Lane, Blythe Bridge, Staffs ST11 9LJ
tel: 01782 388388 for stockists • fax: 01782 394599

Creda have a full range of laundry, cooking,
dishwashing and refrigeration products in both
freestanding and built-in models. The built-in models
include some integrated appliances that are hidden
behind a furniture door.

Crosslee
Lightcliffe Factory, Hipperholme, Halifax,
W.Yorks HX3 8DE
tel: 01422 203555 for stockists • fax: 01422 206304

Crosslee make the famous White Knight tumble dryers
in a whole range of specifications. The tumble dryers
are available in primary, natural and pastel colours,
some fully coloured, some with just the fascia panel
coloured.

De Dietrich
Intec Four, Wade Rd, Basingstoke RG24 8NE
tel: 01256 843485 for stockists • fax: 01256 843024

There is always something new and exciting in this
huge collection of French appliances. Their ovens have
special self-cleaning systems such as the Pyro-Turbo,
which cleans itself at 500 degrees Centigrade, so all

you have to do is sweep out some fine ash. There is
probably every kind of oven you could wish for
including steam ovens and compact ovens. There is
also a huge range of other built-in appliances, many
with the same kind of unusual features.

Electrolux
55–77 High St, Slough, Berks SL1 1DZ
tel: 08705 805805 for stockists
fax: 01753 872499

A well-known name, but have you seen their latest
offering? It includes coloured appliances and fully
integrated appliances – those are the ones which are
hidden behind a furniture door so you can't see the
appliance at all. Their built-in range includes cooking,
cooling, washing and dishwashing appliances.

Elica/DR Cooker Hoods
Elica House, 10 Invincible Rd, Farnborough,
Hants GU14 7QU
tel: 01252 515355 for stockists • fax: 01252 540194

Don't be fooled into thinking a cooker hood is
unnecessary and unglamorous. DR Cooker Hoods have
some wonderful shaped, even funky hoods which can
be at the centre of a kitchen design. They also have all
the expertise to set up an extraction system that is
really necessary in a steamy kitchen.

Flavel-Leisure
Clarence St, Royal Leamington Spa, Warks CV31 2AD
tel: 01926 427027 for stockists
fax: 01926 450526

The Rangemaster is the flagship of the collection – a
range-style cooker that will wave goodbye to all your
catering problems with its two full-size ovens, separate
grill, griddle, electric warming plate and storage
drawer. Leisure also make the Victoriana, a collection
of ovens with period looks.

Fourneaux de France
62 Westbourne Grove, London W2 5SH
tel: 0171 792 0991 for stockists
fax: 0171 229 6417

Stylish French semi-professional stoves offer some
secrets of the trade such as a powerful burner in the
hob. The company has now also added semi-
professional fridges and freezers and semi-professional
cooker hoods that are designed to complement range
cookers.

Gaggenau

Grand Union House, Old Wolverton Rd, Old Wolverton,
Milton Keynes, Bucks MK12 5ZR
tel: 01908 328360 for stockists

If you are looking for some really design-led
appliances, Gaggenau have had that reputation for
some years now. Their appliances are not cheap but
they are at the design forefront and technologically
superior.

Godin

Unit 6a, Bruce Grove, Shotgate Industrial Estate,
Shotgate, Essex SS11 8QN
tel: 01268 572232 for stockists • fax: 01268 560271

If you want a traditional-style range cooker, this is
definitely one of the collections you should look at.
The Godin ranges come in a whole selection of sizes
and colours and can be fuelled by wood, coal, gas or
electricity. There are smaller versions, extensions such
as a deep-fat fryer and cooker hoods to match.

Hoover

Dragonparc, Abercanaid, Merthyr Tydfil,
Mid Glamorgan CF48 1PQ
tel: 01685 721222 for stockists • fax: 01685 382946

Much more than just vacuum cleaners – Hoover also
do a whole range of kitchen appliances including
refrigeration, washing and cooking and have some
really good machines with interesting features.

Hot & Cold

13 Golbourne Rd, London W10 5NY
tel: 0181 960 1200

If you are trying to save money on your kitchen
appliances, this shop is a good place to look. They
have a vast range of different appliances from
practically every manufacturer, but many are end-of-
line bargains and models that are no longer available.
They also have a range of built-in appliances.

Hotpoint

Morley Way, Peterborough, Cambs PE2 9JB
tel: 01733 568989 for stockists • fax: 01733 341783

One of the leading British appliance manufacturers,
Hotpoint make cookers, fridges, dishwasher and
laundry appliances and have both freestanding and
built-in ranges. Their Casatta range has fascia panels
in a selection of ice-cream colours.

Imperial

Fairacres, Abingdon, Oxon OX14 1TW
tel: 01235 554455 for stockists • fax: 01235 554477

These are German-made, designer-led appliances
which look good in the most upmarket, avant garde
kitchen. They are often way ahead of their time, like
the built-in steam cooker that has been in the range
for some years, but is still unmatched by anything
else.

Indesit

Merloni House, 3 Cowley Business Park, High St,
Cowley, Uxbridge, Middx UB8 2AD
tel: 01895 858200 for stockists • fax: 01895 858270

Indesit manufacture a select range of value-for-money
built-in and freestanding appliances in quite a diverse
range of designs including modern and more
traditional. Ovens, dishwashers, laundry appliances
and refrigeration all feature strongly.

Kuppersbusch

Unit 238, Cocker Rd, Walton Summit Centre, Bamber
Bridge, Preston, Lancs PR5 8AL
tel: 01772 321333 for stockists • fax: 01772 698855

Smart German kitchen appliances that major on
cooking rather than cooling appliances. If you are
looking for advanced technology and some really
stylish design, take a look at this company.

LEC Refrigeration

Bognor Regis, W.Sussex PO22 9NQ
tel: 01243 863161 for stockists • fax: 01243 868052

LEC have a wide range of Softline 25 models of fridges
and freezers to choose from including giant-sized
fridges and upright and chest freezers. They also have
'side by side' fridge freezers, designed to fit under a
worktop.

Miele

Fairacres, Marcham Rd, Abingdon, Oxon OX14 1TW
tel: 01235 554455 for stockists • fax: 01235 554477

The quality of the appliances from this German
company is really hard to beat which is why they may
seem expensive at first, but they often last a lifetime.
They have all kinds of interesting electronic abilities
including a chip that means many of them can be
frequently updated with new programmes as
technology develops.

Neff
Grand Union House, Old Wolverton Rd, Wolverton,
Milton Keynes, Bucks MK12 5TP
tel: 01908 328300 for stockists • fax: 01908 328399

German company Neff has been a leading specialist in
the built-in appliance market for some years now and
the range offers a wide choice of both gas and electric
appliances. They are probably particularly well known
for their cooking appliances.

New World
New World House, Thelwall Lane, Warrington,
Cheshire WA4 1NL
tel: 01925 627627 for stockists

New World's reputation is largely built on highly
successful cooking appliances, particularly the Image
1000 range cooker, which is a modern-style range
cooker that can be powered by gas or electric. It
has two huge ovens, a grill, a hob and a large
storage compartment.

Norcool
PO Box 1049, Doncaster, S.Yorks DN11 8XB
tel: 01302 751223 for stockists • fax: 01302 751233

A leading manufacturer of cooling appliances, Norcool
specialize in enormous walk-in larder fridges. You can
use these to store all your food and drink from
cornflakes to cream cakes and you can even keep
flowers fresh in there. The walk-in larder fridges are
available freestanding or integrated and Norcool also
offer other cooling products.

NRC Refrigeration
Vaux Rd, Finedon Industrial Estate, Wellingborough,
Northants NN8 4TG
tel: 01933 272222 for stockists • fax: 01933 279638

If you want one of those gigantic American fridge
freezers this company has an impressive collection
within the Amana range. They also offer smaller
fridges and blue, green, red and yellow ones. Many of
the enormous ones have ice dispensers on the outside.

Ocean
Intec 4, Wade Rd, Basingstoke, Hants RG24 8NE
tel: 01256 843485 for stockists • fax: 01256 843024

This range incorporates affordable appliances such as
fridge freezers, chest freezers, home laundry and
dishwashers. There is no great attempt at fashionable

design, but the prices are good and you will be covered
by nationwide after-sales service.

Power Warehouse
59 Lingfield Rd, East Grinstead, W.Sussex RH19 2EU
tel: 01342 410444

You can get first-rate bargain appliances here and save
yourself up to 30 per cent on the cost of built-in. They
mainly operate on a mail order basis but there is a
small showroom if you want to visit. They claim to
stock almost every make on the market and have
good warranties.

Rayburn
PO Box 30, Ketley, Telford, Shropshire TF1 4DD
tel: 0345 626147 for stockists

This company offers traditional range cookers which
can also supply all your hot water and run the central
heating as well. They come in a selection of sizes and
colours.

Rosières
New Chester Rd, Bromborough, Wirral,
Merseyside L62 3PE
tel: 0151 334 2781 for stockists • fax: 0151 334 0185

This French manufacturer, which is a subsidiary of
Candy (see p.85) has an interesting collection of built-
in appliances, including a host of advanced cooking
appliances. They also make refrigeration, home
laundry and dishwashing models for the middle to
upper end of the market. Their cooking line-up
includes the Bocuse cooker – a semi-professional type
of cooker.

Siemens
Grand Union House, Old Wolverton Rd, Old Wolverton,
Milton Keynes, Bucks MK12 5ZR
tel: 01908 328400 for stockists

Design and function come together in this range of
German-made appliances. The range is vast with some
quite hi-tech technological features, while the designs
are also very modern with a great deal of stainless
steel on offer.

Smeg
Corinthian Court, 80 Milton Pk, Abingdon,
Oxon OX14 4RY
tel: 01235 861090 for stockists • fax: 01235 861120
e-mail: smeg@miltonpark.co.uk

Very smart Italian appliances, including range cookers, which would look good in modern or period kitchens, 1950s-style fridges and dishwashers that have a special design to make them more efficient.

Stanley Cookers
Abbey Rd, Wrexham Industrial Estate, Wrexham, Clwyd LL13 9RF
tel: 01978 664555 for stockists • fax: 01978 664567

Choose from a selection of classically styled cast-iron range cookers that can either be just cooker units or can also act as a boiler supporting your central heating system. They are available in oil, gas or solid fuel versions and in a large choice of colours.

Stoves
Stoney Lane, Prescot, Merseyside L35 2XW
tel: 0151 426 6551 for stockists • fax: 0151 426 3261

Stoves have an interesting collection of cooking appliances including some in unusual pastel colours and both contemporary and more traditional designs. They also have modern range cookers in various designs and colours, and a small collection of other built-in appliances.

Teka
Teka House, 117 Milton Park, Milton, Abingdon, Oxon OX14 4SE
tel: 01235 861916 for stockists • fax: 01235 831237

Teka used to make professional appliances and have brought their experience into domestic appliances. These are German built-in appliances including ovens, refrigeration, and washing machines in designs ranging from traditional to trendy.

Trembath
C71 Barwell Business Pk, Leatherhead Rd, Chessington, Surrey KT9 2NY
tel: 0181 410 0170 for stockists • fax: 0181 410 0155

If you're looking for American appliances contact this company as they import a few different brand names. The enormous American fridges come from Maytag who also do large domestic washing machines. They also sell large range cookers from Five Star.

Tricity Bendix
55–57 High St, Slough, Berks SL1 1DJ
tel: 0990 805805 for stockists • fax: 01753 872499

A full range of middle-market built-in and freestanding appliances, with some integrated (hidden behind furniture doors) products as well. The products come in a small range of colours with either modern or more traditional styling. They also offer slimline appliances if you have a small kitchen.

Viking
Bradshaw Appliances, Kenn Rd, Clevedon, Bristol, Avon BS21 6LH
tel: 01275 343000 for stockists

Bradshaw Appliances stock Viking professional-style appliances imported from America. These chunky, stainless steel stoves, ovens, hobs and dishwashers have all been based on professional appliances, so take a look if you are a serious cook. Phone for details of your local stockist. See entry for Asko, another part of Bradshaw Appliances, specializing in products imported from Finland.

Whirlpool
PO Box 45, 209 Purley Way, Croydon, Surrey CR9 4RY
tel: 0181 649 5013 for stockists

This American company offers a huge variety of middle-range European-style appliances from cooking appliances to laundry, dishwashing and refrigeration. They have both built-in and freestanding appliances for every type of kitchen.

Zanussi
PO Box 530, 55–77 High St, Slough, Berks SL1 1BE
tel: 0990 140140 for stockists • fax: 01753 872350

From sleek stainless steel to classic retro styling, and from vibrant colours to time-saving features, the Zanussi range of built-in appliances has a good deal to offer. If you are after freestanding appliances they have some exciting products, such as the Oz fridge, which has a rolling door and an enormous capacity.

5

bath

Bathroom makeovers are very popular on *Home Front*. It seems that everyone is stuck with something they don't like – whether it is a suite in an outmoded colour, grotty tiles that you can't afford to change, or a bath that has become scratched and worn. Over the years we have shown bathrooms being transformed on all types of budgets – from instant face-lifts achieved by simply painting over the tiles and replacing the taps and blinds, to a state-of-the art wetroom designed by Anne McKevitt.

Once you have decided on whether you buy a whole new suite or just jazz up the old one, there are hundreds of other things to decide upon. Bathroom sinks no longer just come in avocado or white and nowadays you can get freestanding ones, wooden ones, stainless steel ones, even glass ones. This chapter will guide you through the maze of choices whether your taste is traditional or modern. It will also tell you where to go if your bath is scratched and needs re-enamelling. The accessories section at the end of the chapter deals with the final details, like unusual shower curtains, taps and toilet seats that will really finish your bathroom off in style.

time

key: 🔲 shows the product has appeared on *Home Front*

✉ shows the company offers a mail order service

bathrooms

The traditional bathrooms section below covers a wide range of styles – historical and new – but fundamentally deals with bathroom furniture made from ceramics, enamels and plastics, including fittings. The modern and groovy section covers hi-tech materials such as glass and steel. Read each introduction to get a better idea of exactly what each section offers. Many of these companies stock other outlets, so call first to find out your nearest stockist.

traditional

We have come a long way since the days when huge tin baths were laboriously filled with water heated up over a fire. You'd do your ablutions, which would certainly not be daily, in a room (probably the kitchen), and would leave your dirty water for the next member of the family to use. It was not until the middle half of the nineteenth century that purpose-built bathrooms began to be installed and that was only if you were lucky enough to be wealthy. Bathrooms were styled to mirror the rest of the house with separate items of 'furniture'; the sink, for example, would be housed in an ornate pedestal washstand, probably skirted with flounces of fabric, and the bath would be in the centre of the room. Eventually, people decided that fabrics and furnishings in the bathroom were probably not a good idea, hygiene-wise, and bathroom furniture very gradually evolved into the fitted coloured suites we know today.

Traditional-shaped baths, such as the 'slipper bath' (so called because one end slopes upwards like a shoe) with its roll top and claw feet, have recently become highly sought after. If you would like the traditional look, there are many companies still producing similar style baths and pedestal sinks. However, sometimes it is nonsensical to try to achieve a look of authenticity if it outstrips the practicality. A typical Victorian WC, for example, would have had a high-level cistern, with the flush chain up quite high. If you are considering having one of these installed, think whether your walls are high enough of the water pressure to work sufficiently well to flush properly, and whether small children will be able to reach the flush chain by themselves. Consider aesthetics, too, when deciding on style – a Victorian bath doesn't necessarily sit well with an ultra-modern power shower.

In this section, the word 'traditional' has been taken to encompass a wide range of styles. Here you will find bathroom fittings (baths, sinks, taps, etc) mostly in ceramics, enamels and plastics.

south west

Antique Baths of Ivybridge
Erme Bridge Works, Ermington Rd, Ivybridge, Devon PL21 9DE
tel: 0800 685156

This place is well worth a visit if you are looking for that special period piece. They have a huge collection of old baths and sanitary ware that they restore to their original standard, and it is all set in a seventeenth-century stone mill.

Bathcare
21 Prideaux Close, Tamar View Industrial Estate, Saltash, Cornwall PL12 6LD
tel: 01752 849563

If you are a rolltop bath enthusiast it is worth contacting these people, especially if you have one that is in bad condition. They re-enamel, restore and sell old rolltop baths and Victorian and Edwardian sanitary ware and you can get a discount if you buy the whole lot from them.

Christies Fitted Bathrooms

First Avenue, Royal Portbury Dock Estate, Portbury, Bristol, Avon BS20 9XP
tel: 01275 378000 for stockists • fax: 01275 378090

This company offer an ensemble of fitted bathrooms including furniture manufactured by themselves, Ideal Standard sanitary ware, and Pilkington's tiles. Christies will undertake the whole installation including all the plumbing and tiling, down to the last accessory.

Heritage Bathrooms

Heritage House, 1a Princess St, Bedminster, Bristol, Avon BS3 4AG
tel: 0117 963 9762 for stockists • fax: 0117 923 1078

Heritage Bathrooms offer a huge range of traditional-style sanitary ware, furniture, baths, brassware, accessories and tiles. There is a truly comprehensive collection on offer here.

south east

Aston Matthews

141–147a Essex Rd, Islington, London N1 2SN
tel: 0171 226 7220 • fax: 0171 354 5951

Aston Matthews stocks over twenty-five models of baths in sixteen sizes ranging from the traditional rolltop to contemporary hi-tech designs. These are joined by a massive selection of basins, bidets, WCs, shower screens and ceramic shower trays. There are also taps and accessories in various finishes.

Barber Wilsons

Crawley Rd, Westbury Ave, Wood Green, London N22 6AH
tel: 0181 888 3461 • fax: 0181 888 2041

Ask your local bathroom specialist about this company if you are on the lookout for authentic-looking, period-style taps. Each design is manufactured to the original design from a portfolio which dates back to 1905 when the company was first founded. Inside, however, the taps have all mod cons to ensure they are more efficient than at the turn of the century.

Bath Doctor

Prospect House, Canterbury Rd, Chollock, Ashford, Kent TN25 4BB
tel: 01233 740532 • fax: 01233 740830

If you have an old and ailing cast-iron bath, this company could be able to help. They restore antique baths of all descriptions to return them to their former glory. *Home Front* took an old bath Neville Griffiths had found in a salvage yard there to be restored. You are welcome to go and view the standard of work before you make your decision. They can also restore other pieces of sanitary ware.

Bathroom Discount Centre

297 Munster Rd, London SW6 6BW
tel: 0171 381 4222

You can get up to 25 per cent off famous bathroom names at this showroom. They have every conceivable type of bathroom equipment, but you will have to find your own plumber as they offer no fitting service. They do have a list of plumbers they can recommend. Open seven days a week.

Czech & Speake

39c Jermyn St, London SW1Y 6DN
tel: 0171 439 0216 for stockists • fax: 0171 734 8587

This company offers everything for the truly traditional bathroom from the Czech and Speake bath with claw feet, to taps and shower heads and a small range of sanitary ware. They also offer accessories, mirrors and heated towel rails. All these very traditional designs are made from high-quality materials.

HM James

736 Romford Rd, Manor Park, London E12 6BT
tel: 0181 553 1521

If you want to match that lilac loo from the sixties and can't find anything, this could be the place for you. They have an enormous range of well-priced, discontinued pieces in stock here, including every colour ever known to bathroom sanitary ware. They also have a showroom with contemporary designs as well.

Max Pike Bathrooms

4 Eccleston St, London SW1W 9LN
tel: 0171 7307216 • fax: 0171 7303789

Their helpful brochure, which gives you tips on how to choose your bathroom, shows that they really know their stuff here. They sell designs that range from very traditional to more contemporary, and every conceivable type of bathroom product, including their own style of baths.

Miscellania
Crossways, Churt, Surrey GU10 2JA
tel: 01428 714014 for showrooms
fax: 01428 712946

One of the luminaries of the bathroom showroom scene, this outlet has sixteen rooms covered from floor to ceiling with old and new bathrooms in every conceivable style, colour and size. They also have seven acres of stock to draw on and five other showrooms around the country – phone for further details.

Swadling Furniture
Unit 8, Lowesden Works, Lambourn Woodlands, Hungerford, Berks RG17 7RU
tel: 01488 72037

This is handcrafted bathroom furniture in a wide choice of traditional designs. If you can't find what you want in their standard range of fixtures and fittings they also offer a bespoke service. You can select from a wide choice of timbers, which can be left natural, limed in a variety of colours, or white-primed for you to paint.

Ware Bathroom Centre
4 Star St, Ware, Herts SG12 7AA
tel: 01920 468664 • fax: 01920 411321

This retailer offers a vast range of bathroom products from a host of different companies. Styles are generally on the traditional side, but there are some more contemporary products as well. Ware Bathroom Centre has a large, well-appointed showroom, they are members of The Bathroom Showroom Association and have been established for eighteen years.

The Water Monopoly
16/18 Lonsdale Rd, London NW6 6RD
tel: 0171 624 2636 • fax: 0171 624 2631

If you want fine English or French antique sanitary ware, this showroom is one of the first places you should look. Specialists in Georgian, Victorian, Edwardian, French Empire, Art Nouveau and Deco bathroom fittings, most of their pieces come from salvage yards, auctions, private houses and public buildings. All the pieces are fully restored with specialist equipment.

east

Aylsham Bath & Door Centre
Burgh, Aylsham, Norwich, Norfolk NR11 6AR
tel: 01263 735396 • fax: 01263 734800

This is a huge retailer with more than seventy displays of bathroom suites in five different showrooms. You will find everything you need for your bathroom in a massive range of different styles, most of which are competitively priced.

Montrose Furniture
10 Waltham Road Industrial Estate, Boreham, Chelmsford, Essex CM3 3AW
tel: 01245 450405 for stockists • fax: 01245 450406

If you want fitted bathroom furniture to maximize the space in your bathroom, this company offers ten ranges of mainly traditional styles in vinyl or wood.

Old Fashioned Bathrooms
Little London Hill, Debenham, Stowmarket, Suffolk IP14 6PW
tel: 01728 860926 • fax: 01728 860446

The showroom carries a comprehensive range of Victorian and Edwardian baths, taps, showers and fittings, original basins, WCs and towel rails. The Tubby Bath resurfacing kit is also on sale.

Perrin & Rowe
Orwell Close, Fairview Industrial Park, Manor Way, Rainham, Essex RM13 8UB
tel: 01708 526361 for stockists
fax: 01708 550220

This company offers a whole range of traditional-style showers and controls but with all the advantages of modern technology hidden away inside.

Stiffkey Bathrooms
14 Wells Rd, Stiffkey, Wells-next-the-Sea, Norfolk NR23 1AJ
tel: 01328 830460

This is a traditional bathroom lover's paradise. An old Methodist chapel is packed with the original and the unique as well as high-quality reproductions. All the old pieces are fully re-conditioned and you will get some top expert advice if you need it.

central

The Alscot Bathroom Co
The Stable Yard, Alscot Park, Stratford Upon Avon,
Warks CV37 8BL
tel: 01789 450861

Set in the grounds of a stately home, you can only visit
by appointment. It is worth making the effort as they
have a gigantic stock of original sanitary ware, which
covers about a quarter of an acre. Everything is fully
refurbished and well set out.

BC Sanitan
Silverdale Rd, Newcastle Under Lyme, Staffs ST5 6EL
tel: 01782 717175 for stockists • fax: 01782 717166

One of the famous names that made traditional-style
bathrooms trendy again, the company now has a fairly
wide range of styles including Victorian, Edwardian
and Elizabethan. They also offer taps, heated towel
rails, vanity units, baths and accessories.

The Deva Tap Company
10 Melbourne House, Corby Gate Business Park,
Priors Haw Rd, Corby, Northants NN17 5JG
tel: 01536 205949 for stockists • fax: 01536 205361

Modern thermostatic showers are encased in
traditional-style bodies for those who want to mix the
best of past and present. If you are a fan of the old-
fashioned large rose shower heads there are some
examples in this range. The company also make
traditional-style taps.

Dolphin Fitted Bathrooms
Bromwich Rd, Worcester, Worcs WR2 4BD
tel: 01905 748500 for stockists • fax: 01905 429034

A nationwide chain of showrooms is backed up by a
home design service. The products cover quite a wide
range of styles including showers and tiles.

The Imperial Bathroom Co
Unit 2, Stag Industrial Estate, Oxford St, Bilston,
W.Midlands WV14 7HZ
tel: 01902 404111 for stockists • fax: 01902 401700

This company makes a wide range of traditional style
sanitary ware and is one of the few still to do a lot of
decorated ware in the traditional manner. They also
offer brassware and a range of accessories to match all
their suites.

Lefroy Brooks
Moorfield Rd, Off Upper Villiers St, Wolverhampton,
W.Midlands WV2 4PG
tel: 01902 21922 for stockists • fax: 01902 27109

Manufacturers of traditional British brassware all made
by hand from solid brass. Designs are based on period-
style taps with modern components. Accessories,
radiators and towel rails and lavatory chinaware are
also on offer as is the Casteron Bath, a traditional
rolltop design made from a man-made material which
is light, strong and keeps the water warmer than
cast iron.

Watershed
The Stable Yard, Hillend, Hogshaw, Buckingham,
Bucks MK18 3JY
tel: 01296 670182 • fax: 01296 670179

A mail order operation that will supply you with a
variety of traditional-style taps and showers. The
brassware comes in a selection of chrome or gold
finishes and is designed to combine old-fashioned
looks with the latest technology. Phone for mail
order details.

north west

Cabuchon Bathrooms
Whitegate, Lancaster, Lancs LA3 3BT
tel: 01524 66022 for stockists • fax: 01524 844927
e-mail: designandform@msn.com

You will find this company offers a whole range of
exciting bath shapes and sizes made from Ficore, a
strong and versatile man-made material. Designs
include the freestanding Osbourne, which can be
primed for painting, and the soaking baths which
cradle the user like an armchair.

Chatsworth Bathrooms
10 & 12 Seddon Place, Stanley Industrial Estate,
Stanley, Skelmersdale, Lancs WN8 8EB
tel: 01695 559874 for stockists • fax: 01695 556549

Chatsworth offers a huge range of bathroom styles
from Art Nouveau, through Gothic to Antique,
including such gems as the Nautilus, which was
adapted from an 1890s design and more recently was
specified by Elvis Presley for his master bathroom
at Gracelands.

Manhattan Showers

Marsden Mill, Brunswick St, Nelson, Lancs BB9 0LY
tel: 01282 605000 for stockists • fax: 01282 604762

Although there are some more modern-looking shower enclosures in this collection, most have profiles or glass patterns that would better suit traditional-style bathrooms. All kinds of shapes, sizes and colours are topped by the Roosevelt, which has an unusual arched top to the enclosure and is available in three different configurations.

north east

Airbath International

International House, Swinnow Lane, Leeds,
W.Yorks LS13 4TY
tel: 0113 255 6666 for stockists • fax: 0113 239 3406

What about a massage bath which pump warm air into the bath water through hundreds of air jets for an all-over body massage? Airbath offers a huge range of bath designs including a round bath, a rose-shaped one, a rolltop and a slipper bath.

The Mantaleda Bathroom Co Ltd

Church View Industrial Estate, Brompton,
Northallerton, N.Yorks DL6 2UP
tel: 01609 771211 for stockists • fax: 01609 760100

This company offers several unusual baths such as compact tub baths, which save space, rolltop baths and luxury baths including two round baths, one in a gold metallic finish and another in a mother-of-pearl finish.

Shires Ltd

Beckside Rd, Bradford, W.Yorks BD7 2JE
tel: 01274 521199 for stockists • fax: 01274 521583

This is one of Britain's largest bathroom manufacturers, making a wide range of classic styles. The designs range from traditional cottage suites, to period styles and even Continental looks without ever being too stylized. The company offers everything from baths and sanitary ware to taps, showers and accessories.

Victorian Bathrooms

Unit 2, 3 & 4 Ings Mill, Dale St, Ossett,
W.Yorks WF5 9HQ
tel: 01924 267736

This is a large showroom in a converted mill with about thirty displays of mainly traditional bathroom ware. You can get some really good bargains here if you are on a budget but you must be prepared to pay cash or a cheque on delivery.

Victorian Original Waterworks

103 Poppleton Rd, York, N.Yorks YO2 4UN
tel: 01904 780330

This is a tiny shop but don't be deceived. It is backed by a large stock in storage which can always be called upon, to the extent that the owner says he can get practically anything from the traditional right through to the more modern.

wales

TW Thomas

Unit 6B, Lion Way, Swansea Industrial Park,
Llansamlet, Swansea SA7 9FB
tel: 01792 700500 • fax: 01792 700900

You will receive the fruits of years of bathroom experience if you buy your bathroom here. The staff here are ready to problem solve while you choose from more than forty-five suites on display in spacious, modern surroundings.

scotland

Countryside

The Courtyard, Allanton, Duns, Berwickshire TD11 3PY
tel: 01890 818888 • fax: 01890 818431

If you're lucky you may spot the resident ghost in this rural, courtyard setting. Otherwise, there is plenty to see including an impressive range of traditional-style bathrooms, kitchens and tiles. There is also a good design and fitting service on offer.

northern ireland

Beggs & Partners

Great Patrick St, Belfast BT1 2NX
tel: 01232 235791 • fax: 01232 233273

This is a huge purpose-built showroom with masses of displays, some of which are working models. It is a meeting point for plumbers in the know, but also a good place for consumers. It has a once a year sale when you can get really good bargains.

John Dickson Home Improvement Centre
200B Moira Rd, Lisburn, Co Antrim BT28 2SN
tel: 01846 674376 • fax: 01846 663849

You can buy everything for the bathroom including tiles in this large showroom. If you want choice, there are nearly twenty-five suites on show covering many styles and a whole range of prices from budget upwards.

modern & groovy

Walk into some bathrooms – especially those in whichever newly designed hotel is currently flavour of the month – and it can be quite confusing as to what is what. Everything from how you operate the taps to where the flush mechanism is, can be a potential source of embarrassment. But you can also marvel at the ingeniousness of the designer and it is not all about art for art's sake. The innovative design of bathrooms is also being led by a very worthwhile concern – the need for water conservation. This has particularly effected the evolution of the shape of WCs, which are now increasingly wall, rather than floor, mounted and have shallower bowls.

Once, in the seventies, the thought of a chocolate brown or avocado-coloured suite was considered the very height of fashion. Today we balk at the idea. White, white and nothing but white is the order of the day and estate agents state that prospective owners are much more likely to put in an offer to buy if there's a white, rather than a coloured, bathroom suite in the property. If you long for hi-tech minimalism, then the companies listed below will be able to help whether you're looking for a glass basin, a stainless steel toilet or streamlined chrome taps. Be wary of making your bathroom look too cold and clinical unless that's really what you want.

As the majority of the companies listed here stock other outlets around the UK, we have chosen not to divide the section into region as you can call to find out your nearest stockist.

Adamsez
766 Upper Newtownards Rd, Dundonald,
Co Down BT16 0TQ
tel: 01232 480465 for stockists • fax: 01232 480485

Adamsez manufactures sleek, modern-looking baths, some completely plain and some with a touch of decoration. The baths are made from a high-quality man-made material and they can all be fitted with one of the company's whirlpool or spa systems if you are looking for that extra bit of luxury.

Alstone Shower Rooms
Unit 7, Shirethorn, Wiltshire Rd, Hull,
E.Yorks HU4 6PA
tel: 01482 572061 for stockists • fax: 01482 504972

This company makes a whole range of shower room ideas including interesting-shaped shower enclosures and shower trays in a variety of colours, shapes and sizes. They also have different glass designs and products for people with restricted mobility.

Alternative Plans
9 Hester Rd, London SW11 4AN
tel: 0171 228 6460 • fax: 0171 924 1164

If you are a fan of contemporary design, a visit to this specialist is something of an experience. Right on the cutting edge of bathroom design, their products include many Italian names and some German ones. They have an enormous range of the best-designed basins in the world, matched by some wonderful taps. They even have stainless steel loos.

Aqualisa
The Flyer's Way, Westerham, Kent TN16 1DE
tel: 01959 560000 for stockists • fax: 01959 560030
e-mail: Marketing@Aqualisa.e-mail.com

High-performance showers for a really thorough blast. Many of the showers are fitted with a thermostatic mixer valve, which means your shower is always the temperature you want it. If you prefer a different type of shower, they manufacture quite a selection. The ultimate luxury of body jets is also an option.

The Bathroom Centre
194 High Rd, Woodford Green, Essex IG8 9EF
tel: 0181 504 1765 for stockists
fax: 0181 504 5471

This retailer specializes in bathrooms for the mid-upmarket sector and does all kinds of styles ranging from the traditional and modern to the outrageous. They also offer their own fitted furniture and will do the total job for you from supply through to the complete fit.

Bathroom City
Amington Rd, Tyseley, Birmingham,
W.Midlands B25 8ET
tel: 0121 708 0111 • fax: 0121 706 6561

This mega showroom has over a hundred bathroom displays and, as many of them are working models, you can try them out before you buy. They buy unusual products direct from Germany and Italy, so you may get something that isn't readily available elsewhere in the UK.

The Bathroom Studio
103–105 Gilesgate, Durham DH1 1JA
tel: 0191 386 8868

This award-winning bathroom studio has over thirty-five working bathroom displays set out on two floors. The staff are very experienced and willing to provide you with as much advice as you need. They will handle the complete job from planning to polishing the final installation.

Burg
Unit 16, First Quarter, Blenheim Rd, Epsom,
Surrey KT19 9QN
tel: 01372 726116 for stockists • fax: 01372 743773

The Germans have been fans of fitted bathroom furniture for much longer than the British and it shows when you see a highly sophisticated range such as this. Contemporary fitted furniture for every situation in a large selection of colours, finishes and designs.

Caradon Mira Ltd
Cromwell Rd, Cheltenham, Glos GL52 5EP
tel: 01242 221221 for stockists • fax: 01242 221925

Mira have been producing showers for more than seventy years and now offer a wide range of electric, mixer and power showers with a lot of attention devoted to quality and safety. Their brochure is very helpful on how to choose the best shower for you (sometimes a confusing minefield!) and they can provide you with details of your local stockist.

Classic Marble Showers
31 Garvaghey Bridge Rd, Ballygawley,
Co Tyrone BT70 2EW
tel: 016625 68081 for stockists • fax: 016625 68082

There are over a hundred different colours in the range of shower trays this company manufactures. They are all made from resinstone and there are also about twenty different sizes and shapes.

Colourwash
165 Chamberlayne Rd, London NW10 3NU
tel: 0181 459 8918 • fax: 0181 459 4280

The three Colourwash shops in Kensal Rise, Fulham High St and Sunningdale are the ideal place to browse for bathroom ideas as they display a huge amount of products, but in a very accessible way. The styles range enormously, but perhaps the emphasis is more on contemporary than traditional, although you will find a bit of everything here. Great efforts are made to keep prices down as well.

CP Hart
Newnham Terrace, Hercules Rd, London SE1 7DR
tel: 0171 902 1000 • fax: 0171 902 1001

A feast of contemporary bathrooms in this vast showroom including many designed by the legendary Philippe Starck. If you are looking for something a little less daring, there is also a whole range of modern classics and some traditional suites. Taps, baths and accessories are also on offer as well as sanitary ware.

Dansani
RSJ Associates, Unit 5, Greenfield Farm Industrial Estate, Greenfield Rd, off Back Lane, Congleton, Cheshire CW12 4TR
tel: 01260 276188 for stockists • fax: 01260 280889

A whole range of contemporary-style, but not avant garde, fitted bathroom furniture, mainly available in laminates with a few wood finishes. The Dansani range is very versatile and features washbasins made from cast marble in a range of seven different finishes. Phone RSJ Associates for details of your local stockist.

Daryl
Alfred Rd, Wallasey, Wirral, Merseyside L44 7HY
tel: 0151 606 5000 for stockists
fax: 0151 638 0303

A complete range of original designs of shower enclosures, doors and bath screens in a variety of finishes. They have also developed the unique Hydrasenta, which is a showering system incorporating an overhead shower, handheld shower, mid-body shower and foot shower and is discreetly tucked away in one corner of the shower enclosure.

Dornbracht
Locky's Orchard, Broadmead Lane, Norton sub Hamdon, Somerset TA14 6SS
tel: 01935 881418 for stockists • fax: 01935 881404

If you are in the market for stylish tap designs, do not miss out on this company. Many of the designs are the brainchildren of famous designer Dieter Sieger.

Gainsborough Bathrooms
Premier House, Hewell Rd, Enfield, Redditch, Worcs B97 6BW
tel: 01527 594204 for stockists • fax: 01527 594227

These baths are generally contemporary in design, but they are handmade. A whole range of designs are on offer in almost any colour whether new or old. If you don't have much room, soaking tubs that you sit in, totally immersed, are a good option.

Granitops
West Dean Rd, West Tytherley, Salisbury SP5 1QG
tel: 01980 862253 • fax: 01980 863073

If you are looking for a special piece of marble or granite for your bathroom countertops, this company has a wide portfolio of patterns and colours to choose from. They can also provide an expert installation and finishing service.

Hans Grohe
Units D1/D2 Sandown Park Trading Estate, Royal Mills, Esher, Surrey KT10 8BL
tel: 01372 465655 for stockists • fax: 01372 470670
e-mail: Sales@Hansgrohe.Telme.Com

Definitely up with the élite trendsetters in taps and showers, German company Hans Grohe has some of the most exciting designs, some by Philippe Starck. They are also high quality and high performance. The Pharo Shower Temple is aptly named – combining overhead, hand and body showers and even steam for a showering experience worth worshipping!

Homerite
Unit D3, Westpoint Industrial Estate, Penarth Rd, Cardiff CF1 7JQ
tel: 01222 711001 • fax: 01222 228200

You will find everything for the bathroom here right down to towels and accessories and right up to large displays of sanitary ware, showers and baths. They also offer advice and a full fitting service.

Huppe
RSJ Associates, Unit 5, Greenfield Farm Industrial Estate, Greenfield Rd, off Back Lane, Congleton, Cheshire CW12 4TR
tel: 01260 276188 for stockists • fax: 01260 280889

Stylish, contemporary shapes are the hallmark of Huppe's shower enclosures, which have slim profiles (the metal bit) and big modern expanses of plain glass. There are many curved enclosures and a large selection of bath screens to choose from. The enclosures are high quality and they also have a very good-value range. Call RSJ Associates for details of your local stockist.

Hydra-Spa
Unit D2, Crossgate Drive, Queens Drive Industrial Estate, Nottingham, Notts NG2 1LW
tel: 0115 986 6444 for stockists
fax: 0115 986 6440

If you are after total relaxation in your bathroom, Hydra-Spa are suppliers of whirlpool and airspa bathing systems and Aqua-Mist steam cabins and generators. Masters in the art of supplying total luxury, Hydra-Spa have retailers throughout the country.

Ideal Standard
The Bathroom Works, National Avenue, Hull, E.Yorks HU5 4HS
tel: 01482 346461 for stockists • fax: 01482 445886

A huge range of designs from one of the best-known bathroom companies in Britain. Most of the designs are bordering on the contemporary, although you will find some traditional ones as well. Unusual designs include Contrasts, where the sanitary ware interior is white and the exterior a choice of green or blue, and Kyomi, which has frosted glass handles on the taps.

Jacob Delafon
Unit 1 Churchward, Southmead Park, Didcot, Oxon OX11 7HB
tel: 01235 510511 for stockists • fax: 01235 510481

You will find good-looking French bathrooms within this range. The styles vary from the ultra-modern Trocadero and Fleur through to the neo-classical Revival. There is probably a style to suit everyone here and they also have the full range of baths, showers and accessories.

Jacuzzi UK

17 Mount St, Mayfair, London W1Y 5RA
tel: 0171 409 1776 for stockists • fax: 0171 495 2353

The name that has become synonomous with luxury hydramassage bathing. Jacuzzi offer a wide variety of exciting-shaped baths to go with the system as well as units that combine showers with whirlpool units, and mind-blowing units which offer hydramassage cascades, turbomassage and steam baths. They really have to be seen to be believed.

Kermi

Unit A, Marconi Courtyard, Brunel Rd, Earlstrees Industrial Estate, Corby, Northants NN17 4LT
tel: 01536 400004 for stockists • fax: 01536 203774

This is a range of very stylish German shower enclosures. Many of them use curved glass in special designs which have as little frame as possible to give an even sleeker appearance. There is a wide choice of colours and other finishes. The design emphasis is on wide expanses of safety glass with the profiles and decoraton kept to a minimum. Kermi also make towel radiators in a whole rainbow of colours.

Keuco

Berkhamsted House, 121 High St, Berkhamsted, Herts HP4 2DJ
tel/fax: 01442 865260 for stockists

You will find a huge range of contemporary, high-quality furniture and accessories from this German company. The furniture is very stylish, almost avant garde, and has some nice, unusual features such as tambour doors. If you don't want to go the whole hog on fully fitted furniture, there is also a very good range of simple, clean-lined mirrored cabinets.

Kubex

Francis St, Hull, E.Yorks HU2 8DT
tel: 01482 211421 • fax: 01482 323975

If you want to avoid the installation and tiling of a traditional shower cubicle, Kubex offer the option of one-piece shower cubicles that are self-contained and delivered fully sealed and ready to be installed. They come in five different styles.

The Majestic Shower Company

1 North Place, Edinburgh Way, Harlow, Essex CM20 2SL
tel: 01279 443644 for stockists • fax: 01279 635074

If you need an awkward-shaped shower door these could be the people to come to. They also make standard size doors and enclosures in clean-cut designs with a choice of different-coloured glass and different frame finishes. Bath screens are also a feature.

Mary Rose Young Bathrooms

Oak House, Arthur's Folly, Parkend, Lydney, Glos GL15 4JQ
tel: 01594 563425 • fax: 01594 564544

This is a collection of really wacky rose-covered sanitary ware from this designer. You can have loos or basins strewn with stylized modern roses in bright colours or abstract designs in all the colours of the rainbow. See it to believe it!

Matki

Churchward Rd, Yate, Bristol, Avon BS37 5PL
tel: 01454 322888 for stockists • fax: 01454 315284
e-mail: helpline@matki.co.uk

This company offers designer shower enclosures, shower trays and bath screens. Styles are simple and stylish with interesting shapes and showering solutions. They also have the full range of shower trays and accessories.

Oggetti da Bagno

145 Kew Rd, Richmond, Surrey TW9 2PN
tel: 0181 940 0804 for stockists • fax: 0181 948 8200

Offer a very contemporary and stylish range of Fantini taps, Sicart basins and Agape basins and furniture. These are all Italian makes with some exciting shapes, colours and materials.

Original Bathrooms

143–145 Kew Rd, Richmond, Surrey TW9 2PN
tel: 0181 940 7554 • fax: 0181 948 8200

You will get some of the best bathroom advice anywhere from this retailer as the family who run the business have been big in bathrooms for generations. They will also be able to show you a wonderful mix of modern and traditional Italian bathrooms with some from Germany thrown in for good measure.

Poggenpohl

2nd Floor, Silbury Court, 368 Silbury Boulevard, Milton Keynes, Bucks MK9 2AP
tel: 01908 247600 for stockists • fax: 01908 606958

Poggenpohl is world famous for its stylish contemporary kitchens, but this German company also makes a collection of equally chic bathroom furniture. The emphasis is on clean lines and a minimalist look and you can either have a whole fitted bathroom, or one or two pieces.

Regal Showers

The Airfield Estate, Hixon, Staffs ST18 0PF
tel: 0889 270989 for stockists • fax: 0889 270734

Simple shower doors designed to suit all the popular sizes of shower tray and in a range of seven different shapes. They also have full- or half-framed bath screens and a more traditional Victoriana shower enclosure.

Ripples

18 & 20 Regent St, Clifton Village, Bristol,
Avon BS8 4HH
tel: 0117 973 1144 for branches
fax: 0117 973 2728

This is a very stylish bathroom showroom set in an old bank and showing some of the best contemporary products on the market. They also have some traditional pieces and three other similar branches in the South West.

Roca

Samson Rd, Hermitage Industrial Estate, Coalville,
Leics LE67 3FP
tel: 01530 830080 for stockists • fax: 01530 830010

You will find everything you need for the complete contemporary bathroom in this manufacturer's portfolio. From hydrosaunas to sanitary ware and from vanity basins to mirrors, the range is extensive. The sanitary ware is available in seven different colours and three special matt satin finishes. Back-to-wall, wall-hung sanitary ware and large basins are all features of the range.

Satana

Wyndford Industrial Estate, Higher Halstock, Leigh,
Yeovil, Somerset BA22 9QX
tel: 01935 891888 for stockists • fax: 01935 891819

Fed up with the mirror misting up? Satana could have the answer with their heated mirrors, which are water- and steam-proof and keep your reflection as clear as day. Satana can make any size mirror to suit any specification and have a large range of styles.

Showeristic

Unit 10, Manor Industrial Estate, Flint,
Clwyd CH6 5UY
tel: 01352 735381 • fax: 01352 763388

If you have a sloping ceiling or are looking for a shower enclosure to squeeze into limited space, Showeristic can provide solutions to most standard and non-standard shower enclosure situations with their made-to-measure service. The actual designs are mostly contemporary with some traditional ones as well.

Showerlux

Sibree Rd, Coventry, W.Midlands CV3 4EL
tel: 01203 639400 for stockists • fax: 01203 301528
e-mail: custserv@showerlux.co.uk

Looking for innovative bathroom design? You may just find it among the offerings from this company. From the snail-shaped Europa enclosure to the fish-shaped Portofino freestanding bath there's nothing dull here.

Sottini

The Bathroom Works, National Avenue, Hull,
E.Yorks HU5 4HS
tel: 01482 449513 for stockists • fax: 01482 445886

Upmarket bathroom designs, including such jewels as the Belvedere with its extravagant, sweeping shape and contemporary washstands. Classic and traditional styles are also on offer.

Teuco

Suite 314, Business Design Centre, 52 Upper St,
London N1 0QH
tel: 0171 7042190 for stockists • fax: 0171 7049756

Enter the world of luxury with these Space Age whirlpool baths, multifunction showers, hydrosteams and hydroshowers. Some of these systems have to be seen to be believed with showers, whirlpools, and five-climate sauna systems that are electronically controlled. Move over James Bond.

Triton

Shepperton Park, Caldwell Rd, Nuneaton,
Warks CV11 4NR
tel: 01203 344441 • fax: 01203 349828
tel: 01203 324543 for stockists

Electric showers, mixer showers and power showers, Triton makes a shower to suit everyone from the economical to the luxury. They also have an extensive range of bathroom accessories under the Metlex brand.

Twyfords

Lawton Rd, Alsager, Stoke-on-Trent,
Staffs ST7 2DF
tel: 01270 879777 for stockists
fax: 01270 873864

Twyfords has been making bathrooms since the middle of the last century but they offer plenty of modern styles today. Clean lines and simple shapes are the hallmark of their modern suites and they have a limited range of wall-hung styles. They also offer taps, baths and accessories and are one of Britain's leading bathroom manufacturers.

Ucosan

Melville, Bowden House Lane, Wilmslow,
Cheshire SK9 2BU
tel: 01625 525202 for stockists • fax: 01625 531979

Beautifully designed baths in a choice of unusual shapes that have been ergonomically designed to fit the shape of the human body perfectly. They also offer simple and stylish shower enclosures and trays and can fit aqua and air systems to their baths.

Utopia Furniture

Patrick Gregory Rd, Wednesfield, Wolverhampton,
W.Midlands WV11 3ED
tel: 01902 305453 for stockists
fax: 01902 728994

Utopia offers fitted bathroom furniture in a selection of exciting styles. These include unusual designs such as a Shaker-style range in Pearwood and Driftwood with newly designed door handles and accessories. They also have a collection of simpler styles in a range of different finishes and solid surface countertops for the bathroom.

Vernon Tutbury

Silverdale Rd, Newcastle-under-Lyme,
Staffs ST5 6EL
tel: 01782 717175 for stockists • fax: 01782 717166

If you are looking for contemporary bathrooms which are not too way out, this is a good company to look at. They major on stylish, well-designed sanitary ware including gems such as the Novello bath which has a curved protrusion at the shower end, so you have more room to shower. The collection also includes some trendy accessories.

Victor Paris

178 Dundee St, Edinburgh EH11 1DQ
tel: 0131 228 4000 • fax: 0131 228 5570

This specialist has more than a hundred displays with many unusual pieces sourced and imported direct from Europe. It is all set in two storeys of an easy-access, city-centre shop and you will get very friendly service here.

Villeroy & Boch

267 Merton Rd, London SW18 5JS
tel: 0181 871 4028 for stockists • fax: 0181 870 3720

A range of innovative bathroom sanitary ware and fitted furniture is added to a huge selection of tiles. Sanitary ware designs include Amadea, which can be aggressively trendy or very classic. There is a very wide range of designs on offer.

Visions

Beckside Rd, Bradford, W.Yorkshire BD7 2JE
tel: 01274 521199 for stockists • fax: 01274 521583

This is one of Britain's largest bathroom companies with designs that range from classic to contemporary, but which would happily suit most British bathrooms. They have some unusual designs on offer.

Vitra

121 Milton Park, Abingdon, Oxon OX14 4SA
tel: 01235 820400 for stockists • fax: 01235 820404

Manufacturers of subtly contemporary designs with a couple of more traditional-looking suites thrown in. They offer quite a lot of modern back-to-wall (where sanitary ware butts up to the wall with no pipework showing) and wall-hung options and some wonderful large basins. Taps and accessories are mostly stylish, modern designs.

Vola

Unit 12, Ampthill Business Park, Ampthill,
Beds MK45 2QW
tel: 01525 841155 for stockists • fax: 01525 841177

The man behind Vola is the famous Danish architect Arne Jacobsen and the designs of these taps and accessories certainly reflect a masterful touch at work. If you are looking for purity of form and stylish simplicity these will knock your socks off!

accessories

Adding the final details to your bathroom can make all the difference. They can change the room from being just a place to have a quick wash and brush up, with neither character nor charm, to being somewhere that reflects your taste as much as the other rooms in your home. The accessories you choose – things like shower curtains, toilet seats and even loo roll holders – can pull the whole room together and enable you to create a theme of your choice. It only seems a few years ago that if you wanted a shower curtain you had the choice of half a dozen rather bland colours. Today there are all sorts of funky designs, from metallics and ones which look like bubble wrap, to ones with pockets in for everything from soap to plastic flowers. The humble toilet seat no longer just comes in wood or plastic, now it is decorated with fish, leopard print and (photocopied) barbed wire! Whatever look you want to create, there is something for everyone and the companies listed below are a good source of unusual bathroom accessories to help you.

Aero
Unit 8, Glenville Mews, Kimber Rd,
London SW18 4NJ
tel: 0181 971 0022 • fax: 0181 971 0033

Trendy bathroom accessories available mail order. Many of them, such as the Excalibur Toilet Brush are designed by famous designers for Aero, but all are chic in a mixture of pale wood, matt chrome and matt plastic.

After Noah
121 Upper St, London N1 1QP
tel: 0171 359 4281
and
261 Kings Rd, London SW3 5EL
tel: 0171 351 2610
e-mail: mailorder@afternoah.demon.co.uk

If you want a shower curtain with a difference, After Noah sell transparent ones covered in luminous orange goldfish or ones covered in green grass. These are one of their most successful mail order products.

Billy-Joe Homewares
63 Longfields, Ely, Cambs CB6 3DN
tel: 01353 661997 • fax: 01353 661960

You will never have trouble getting kids in the bath again with this wonderful range of bathroom plugs topped with pewter figures such as dolphins, turtles and ducks. They also have a range of hand-painted enamel plugs with designs including hearts, cats, pigs and cows.

Bisca Design
Shaw Moor Farm, Harome, York, N.Yorks YO6 5HZ
tel: 01439 771702 for stockists • fax: 01439 771002
e-mail: bisca@easynet.co.uk

This is a collection of very contemporary-looking accessories in forged stainless steel. Organic shapes are used for the collection of towel rail, soap dish, toothbrush holder, loo roll holder, hooks and towel ring.

Black Country Heritage
Britannia House, Mill St, Brierley Hill, Worcs DY5 2TH
tel: 01384 480810 for stockists • fax: 01384 482866

The name of this company gives away the fact that they are drawing on a long tradition of local metal-working skills to make these fine-quality, solid bathroom accessories. The designs are mostly classic or traditional and they also make towel warmers.

BoBo Designs

10 Southampton St, Brighton, E.Sussex BN2 2UT
tel: 01273 684753 • fax: 01273 279160

This company is run by design duo Nick Gant and Tanya Dean who specialize in creating dynamic contemporary furniture and accessories out of plastic. They have appeared on *Home Front* several times with their unique designs, but are perhaps best known for their 'seats of desire' – a range of acrylic toilet seats in funky colours and designs.

The Cotswold Co

High St, Bourton on the Water, Glos GL54 2ZZ
tel: 0990 502233 • fax: 01276 609102

You can either visit the shop in the Cotswolds or order mail order with this company. They have a good range of bathroom accessories including boat-shaped wicker items and others in chrome and frosted plastic. They also offer a few wooden accessories.

Eurobath

Eurobath House, Wedmore Rd, Cheddar,
Somerset BS27 3EB
tel: 01934 744466 for stockists • fax: 01934 744345

Eurobath has an extensive range of contemporary-style taps, showers and accessories. All the designs are in metal and a good many of them are in designs that team a gold finish and chrome together.

Habitat

196 Tottenham Court Rd, London W1P 9LD
tel: 0171 255 2545
tel: 0645 334433 for branches

New products are introduced bi-annually, but you are almost guaranteed to find something you like at any time. They are best at simple things and there are usually some classic, unfussy, stainless-steel bathroom cabinets, wooden slatted bath mats and chrome and glass accessories. They also have a small stock of funky shower curtains.

The Hambledon Gallery

42 Salisbury St, Blandford, Dorset DT11 7PR
tel: 01258 454884 • fax: 01258 454225

Their House mail order catalogue has some unusual accessories, such as an enamel pitcher and basin in a very simple Victorian design. It also offers a variety of wicker baskets and an attractive distressed whitewash bathroom cabinet. Phone for mail order details.

The Holding Company

241–245 Kings Rd, London SW3 5EL
tel: 0171 352 1600
and
41 Spring Gardens, Manchester M2 2BJ
tel: 0161 834 3400
tel: 0171 610 9160 for mail order nationwide
fax: 0171 610 9166 for mail order nationwide

This company is totally devoted to storage ideas and has some unusual accessories for the bathroom. These include stylish plastic holders which grip the wall by means of suction pads and which can hold all your bathroom bits and bobs and can be moved around. They also have a range of perspex organizers and subtly coloured plastic accessories plus wooden accessories and small cupboards.

IKEA

Brent Park, 2 Drury Way, North Circular Rd,
London NW10 0TH
tel: 0181 208 5600 for enquiries and branches

IKEA has a good selection of contemporary-style bathroom cabinets in all shapes and sizes and a limited selection of accessories, all of which are very reasonably priced and usually well designed. They also have a good selection of towels.

Junction Eighteen

Stephens Way, Bath Rd, Warminster,
Wilts BA12 8PE
tel: 01985 847774 for stockists • fax: 01985 846414
e-mail: junction18@btinternet.com

Small but select range of bathroom accessories that includes nautical style cupboards, funky wirework soap and tumbler holders with smiley faces, and an octopus-shaped contraption for hanging things on. Many of the larger accessories combine chrome and rattan.

McCord

Universal House, Devonshire St,
Manchester M60 6EL
tel: 0990 535455 • fax: 01793 487002

All kinds of things are packed into this mail order catalogue, but there is a healthy selection of bathroom accessories including chrome storage stands, wooden frame laundry bags and starfish chrome accessories.

Next Home

tel: 0345 100500 for mail order

You will find quite a range of bathroom accessories in this catalogue including woodwork washed in a choice of colours, and chrome and black accessories. They also have some very trendy shower curtains and blinds.

Ocean

Freepost LON811, London SW8 4BR
tel: 0800 132 985 • fax: 0171 498 8898

If you want to order highly stylish bathroom accessories but can't be bothered to traipse around the shops, this mail order company offers a wide range from classic chrome designs to funky matt plastic containers and accessories. They also have very chic stainless-steel mirrored cabinets and stainless-steel basins.

Purves & Purves

80–81 & 83 Tottenham Court Rd,
London W1P 9HD
tel: 0171 580 8223 • fax: 0171 580 8244

Accessories here range from the sedate lines of the Samuel Heath range, through some Philippe Starck creations, to frankly fun, brightly coloured plastic scrubbing brushes. They also have quite a selection of trendy shower curtains.

Samuel Heath
Leopold St, Birmingham, W.Midlands B12 0UJ
tel: 0121 772 2303 for stockists • fax: 0121 772 3334
e-mail: mail@samuel-heath.com

Well-crafted, high-quality bathroom accessories are the name of the game with this company. They make a few ranges of traditional and classically styled accessories, which could also be used in contemporary settings without being way out. They also make towel warmers and showers.

Turnstyle Designs
Village St, Bishops Tawton, Barnstaple,
Devon EX32 0DG
tel: 01271 325325 • fax: 01271 328248
e-mail: turnstyle@mcmail.com

Contemporary accessories some of which have 'bone' and maple bases with polished and weathered pewter discs. The Inset bathroom range is available with bright- and satin-finish chrome fittings and back plates. There is also a Natural Bathroom Collection which includes hand print, fish, ammonite or frog-shaped bases.

W Adams & Sons
Westfield Works, Spon Lane, West Bromwich,
W.Midlands B70 6BH
tel: 0121 553 2161 for stockists
fax: 0121 500 6145

This company has been working with brass for over sixty years and produces well-crafted, traditional-style showers, taps and accessories. Styles include Georgian, Edwardian and Antique ranges.

Water Front
9 The Burwood Centre, Station Rd, Thatcham,
Berks RG19 4YA
tel: 01635 872500 for stockists • fax: 01635 872200

Water Front's accessories have been designed to work really well, not just look good. A lot of thought has gone into making them practical, but they are also very attractive classic pieces made from solid brass. There are several finishes available for their accessories including Antique Gold, Chrome, Bright Nickel, Satin Nickel and Polished Brass.

6

let there be

Lighting is one of the most important aspects of interior design but, ironically, it is also one of the things that gets most frequently overlooked. Getting it right can make all the difference to the atmosphere of your home. Each room usually has an all-purpose overhead pendant light. But why not consider using an uplighter, either mounted on the wall or a free-standing one? If the light source bounces off the ceiling, it won't cast unsightly and gloomy shadows in the corners of your room. Decide what specific lighting you need by breaking down each room, in turn, into different areas and pinpointing what you do in each one. For instance, in a kitchen you'll probably need a good overhead light, not necessarily central, but perhaps over the dining area that can be pulled up or down, or fitted with a dimmer. Elsewhere in the kitchen you will need good 'task' lighting to cook and prepare food by, such as small strip lights placed under the units. Fluorescent strips are effective in a kitchen if positioned to throw the light upwards making sure that it is not too harsh.

In any room that you use for reading or computer work, you will need directional light that you can use to focus on the page or VDU screen without causing glare. Anglepoise and desk lamps, as well as spotlights and uplighters, can all do the trick and prevent tired eyes and headaches. Bathroom lighting is slightly trickier as fewer manufacturers seem to cater for this area. Ensure the light you buy is suitable for use in a bathroom and get a qualified electrician to fit the switches outside or operate them from a pull-switch. 'Bowl' type uplighters can work wonders in a dingy hall and a light placed at the top rather than the bottom of a flight of stairs should ensure an accident-free zone.

Don't forget that lighting can also be fun and not necessarily just for practical, mundane purposes. You can use it to highlight a favourite picture or plant and create a striking silhouette. Purely decorative lighting can be wonderfully indulgent and some of this type of lighting on the market today is a work of art in its own right.

light!

key: 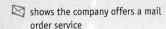 shows the product has appeared on *Home Front*

✉ shows the company offers a mail order service

lighting

Sometimes, improving the lighting in your home can be as simple as making sure you have the right light bulb in your appliance. Bulbs that have a silver reflector on one side can create a much warmer glow than a normal one. Tungsten-halogen bulbs will give off a 'whiter', purer light than ordinary filament ones, and will last longer. Low-voltage or low-energy light systems mean that the bulbs are more energy-efficient than normal ones and, again, will last longer. However, at a certain voltage some may need a transformer fitted. Always check with your lighting supplier. Think of good lighting as a series of building blocks. Create a basic foundation with good, general or 'ambient' lighting, and then build on it steadily until you achieve a lighting design that works for you. Use the beauty of natural light to work in your favour and don't forget the endless fascination of light from a real fire and candles.

This chapter – which has been divided into two sections – a traditional one and a modern and groovy one – will help you find what you are looking for whether it's a reproduction chandelier or a hi-tech industrial tracking system. Some companies supply both of course so there is necessarily some overlap and, anyway, the two are not mutually exclusive within the home. At the end of the chapter, you will also find a list of the most unusual and best light switches around.

traditional

In this section you will find everything from cut-glass and crystal chandeliers to wrought-iron wall sconces and candlesticks. If you are looking for something particular such as a wonderful Tiffany lampshade with its opalescent colours painstakingly leaded into beautiful designs, or a medieval Gothic look, you will find it here. The retail outlets and suppliers are listed alphabetically by region so that you can easily find the nearest outlet to you.

south west

Camborne Forge
Trevu Rd, Camborne, Cornwall TR14 8SR
tel: 01209 719911 • fax: 01209 719911

This forge makes a range of pretty iron chandeliers and wall sconces alongside floorstanding and table candlesticks. They are also very happy to accept commissions, so you can have your own original, one-off design.

Lucy Cope Designs
Fox Hill House, Allington, Chippenham, Wilts SN14 6LL
tel: 01249 650446 • fax: 01249 444936

This specialist sells a selection of antique and period-style lighting, but there is also another side to the business. Lucy Cope is a specialist lampshade maker, which is very useful if you are looking for something extra special. She will also restore antique lamps and lampshades.

Newton Forge
Stalbridge Lane, Sturminster Newton, Dorset DT10 2JQ
tel: 01258 472407 • fax: 01258 471111

Handmade wrought-iron light fittings that are fashioned in a traditional forge. You can choose from electric wall sconces or from a variety of candleholders which are floorstanding, table-standing or chandeliers. They are all available in various styles.

Stuart Interiors
Barrington Court, Ilminster, Somerset TA19 0NQ
tel: 01460 240349 for stockists • fax: 01460 242069

Stuart Interiors specialize in interesting iron design lighting – from a substantial iron chandelier to a simple two-arm wood and iron wall light. There are also a couple of pewter designs and a fabulous floorstanding candletree.

south east

Albert Bartram
177 Hivings Hill, Chesham, Bucks HP5 2PN
tel: 01494 783271 • fax: 01494 783271

If pewter is your thing, Albert Bartram makes beautiful chandeliers and wall sconces in this metal and by the same methods as the pewterers of old. The pieces, which can be made to take candles or light bulbs, are finished in either an Antique or Polished finish.

Beaumont & Fletcher
The Old Imperial Laundry, 71 Warriner Gardens, London SW11 4XW
tel: 0171 498 2642 • fax: 0171 498 2644

You will find a small but exquisite selection of lighting here with styles ranging from Adam-style giltwood and metal wall lights to a fabulous Regency-style wall light in black and gold with eagle cresting!

British Home Stores
Marylebone House, 129–137 Marylebone Rd, London NW1 5QD
tel: 0171 262 3288
tel: 0990 247000 for catalogue and mail order

British Home Stores has long been known for having a good lighting department, but now you can enjoy it mail order. They offer plenty of period-style lights in different styles, including chandeliers, uplighters and ironwork. They also have a small, specialist collection of different switches and bulbs.

Chandelier Cleaning & Restoration Services
Guppy Mead, Fyfield, Essex CM5 0RB
tel: 01277 899444

This company will make a traditional chandelier for you to order. They also will restore your own one, rewiring, polishing and lacquering as necessary.

Christopher Wray Lighting Emporium
591 Kings Rd, London SW6 2YW
tel: 0171 736 8434 for branches
fax: 0171 731 3507
e-mail: christopher-wray@ dial.pipex.com

The largest lighting store in the UK, it has three floors brimming with British, European and North American lighting accessories. Lights from every period are represented including a huge collection of Tiffany lamps, chandeliers of every description and some one-offs such as the Charles Rennie Mackintosh lantern. If you don't want to wander around for hours, try ordering the catalogue before you visit the shop and narrow your field of exploration a bit! Phone for details of other countrywide branches.

Contessa Furnishings
4 Lower Sydenham Industrial Estate, Kangley Bridge Rd, London SE26 5BA
tel: 0181 778 9166 for stockists • fax: 0181 659 9527

This company has more than 250 stockists nationwide, selling period-style lighting such as the Blenheim and the Dorchester ranges. The Blenheim is a range of chandeliers, wall lights, standard lamps and table lamps in a mixture of antique silver finish and traditional gold plating, while the Dorchester is is a collection of ornate luminaires with peacock figures cast in solid brass and then plated in 22 carat gold or pure silver. The glass fantails are the light shades.

Elite Lighting
7 Goodwood Parade, Upper Elmers Rd, Beckenham, Kent BR3 3QZ
tel: 0181 639 0050 • fax: 0181 639 0051

You can get fine-quality crystal chandeliers mail order from this manufacturer. They also have polished brass and ceramic light fittings, wall brackets and table lamps on offer. Many of the fittings are 24-carat-gold-plated frames, dressed in high-quality Swarovski Strass Crystal. Call for mail order details.

Elstead Lighting Ltd

Mill Lane, Alton, Hants GU34 2QG
tel: 01420 82377 for stockists • fax: 01420 89261

If you're into the Gothic look, this company has a whole range of lighting that draws its inspiration from medieval influences. The hand-finished iron light fittings are made using traditional methods and are available in three colour options as standard.

Emily Readett-Bayley

St Lukes Old Rectory, 107 Grange Rd,
London SE1 3BW
tel: 0171 231 3939 for stockists • fax: 0171 231 4499
e-mail: contact@emily-readett-b.demon.co.uk

If you are looking for something unusual, this designer offers some wonderful bamboo lampstands and shades. Much of the bamboo is distinctively marked or there are some plainer designs if you prefer. She also offers classic black and gold lamp bases and some heavy candlesticks.

The Façade

196 Westbourne Grove, London W11 2RH
tel: 0171 727 2189 • fax: 0171 727 2890

This is a shop full of lights from the 1920s, 1930s and 1940s. They include chandeliers and wall lights from France and Italy and all are originals. Most of them are made from glass and/or iron and the shop also has a collection of old French mirrors.

Fantasia

The Flyers Way, Westerham, Kent TN16 1DE
tel: 01959 564440 for stockists • fax: 01959 564829

If you are after a ceiling fan with combination light, this is the place to come. You can choose between Tiffany, crystal and frosted shades or ones with Regency-shaped shades – and of course they all come with ceiling fan attached.

The Grace Collection

PO Box 86, Fleet, Hants GU13 0TN
tel: 01252 851413 for stockists • fax: 01252 626103

The Grace Collection has a whole selection of reproduction antique Chinese table lamps with the traditional blue and white ceramic bases. Many of them are hand-painted and modelled on designs from the fifteenth-century Ming period.

Hermitage Antiques

97 Pimlico Rd, London SW1W 8PH
tel: 0171 730 1973

Proprietor Bernard Vieux-Pernon travels the world in search of interesting antique lights and has amassed a wonderful collection of some really interesting examples, which you may not find in other antique shops or lighting centres.

Le Paul Bert

198 Westbourne Grove, London W11 2RH
tel: 0171 727 8708

Nick Haywood sells antique lighting with a difference at this shop. For lovers of the American fifties style, there are lots of original table lamps from this era, some of which are quite wacky. There are also some 1940s original Belgian lamps and a small amount of Art Deco reproductions.

Light Innovation

362 Kingston Rd, Ewell, Epsom, Surrey KT19 0DT
tel: 0181 873 1582 • fax: 0181 224 8949

This company offers a largish range of metal period-style lights including chandeliers, wall lights, ceiling lights and picture lights. The styles include a Gothic range and an Edwardian-style range. Choose from a variety of colours and distressed finishes and glass or parchment shades.

Lights on Broadway

17 Jerdan Place, Fulham Broadway, London SW6 1BE
tel: 0171 385 8614

If you are an Art Nouveau freak you will definitely find a gem to suit you here. Modelled on lamps produced from the late Victorian era to the mid-1920s these are all hand built in solid brass and finished with a dark patina to make them look more like originals.

Magic Lanterns at By George

23 George St, St Albans, Herts AL3 4ES
tel: 01727 865680

Josie Marsden is a lighting consultant who sells a fascinating selection of mostly antique, but some reproduction lights. Her original lights are all fully restored and cover a wide-ranging collection of lights from many ages in floorstanding, wall-hanging, ceiling-hanging and table-standing options.

Marks & Spencer
tel: 0345 902902 for your local home store or
mail order

Not the first place you may think of looking for period-style lighting, but a glance at their mail order catalogue may surprise you. They actually have quite a vast selection in black and verdigris iron, ceramics and brass. You can get everything from standard lamps and chandeliers to uplighters, wall brackets and table lamps.

McCloud & Co Ltd
269 Wandsworth Bridge Rd, London SW6 2TX
tel: 0171 371 7151 • fax: 0171 371 7186

Lighting expert Kevin McCloud says his company manufactures 'nigh on everything' in the lighting field and it is all made by British craftspeople. It is no idle boast as there is an enormous selection of designs and a whole catalogue of different variations of finish. All the lights come with a choice of different candle fittings and lengths, chandeliers with optional hanging tassels and blown glass balls.

Period Brass Lights
9a Thurloe Place, Brompton Rd, London SW7 2RZ
tel: 0171 589 8305 • fax: 0171 589 8305

This shop sells a large selection of all kinds of lights, some of which are originals and some reproductions. They have a good selection of chandeliers in crystal, brass and wrought iron, and also table lamps, wall brackets and picture lights.

Renwick & Clarke
190 Ebury St, Mozart Terrace, London SW1W 8UP
tel: 0171 730 8913 for stockists • fax: 0171 730 4508

This company offers a fabulously varied range of lamp bases and shades. Styles range from highly decorative porcelain to very restrained fluted Deco mirrored lampbases. Shades are beaded, pleated silk, devore velvet and many more.

Smithbrook Ltd
Smithbrook, nr Cranleigh, Surrey GU6 8LH
tel: 01483 272744 for stockists • fax: 01483 267863

If you're looking for iron lighting, you could well find what you want in this varied range with styles from the sturdy Elizabethan look to intricate and delicate chandeliers and simple wall sconces. All are available in a variety of finishes.

Sugg Lighting Ltd
Sussex Manor Business Park, Gatwick Rd, Crawley,
W.Sussex RH10 2GD
tel: 01293 540111 • fax: 01293 540114

Buckingham Palace has been lit by Sugg lamps since 1910 and they were the first people to bring gas lighting to London. Today they make traditional wall brackets, pedestals, plinths etc, mainly for outside lighting.

Turn On Lighting
116–118 Islington High St, Camden Passage,
London N1 8EG
tel: 0171 359 7616 • fax: 0171 359 7616

These one-off original lights are generally from the century between 1840 and 1940. The shop specializes in English lights from this period, mainly in metal and for every conceivable place in the home. The owner is very particular about matching the right shade to the right base, in keeping with the style of the time.

W Sitch & Co Ltd
48 Berwick St, Oxford St, London W1V 4JD
tel: 0171 437 3776 • fax: 0171 437 5707

A simply fascinating shop packed full of period lights. The business itself dates back to the 1770s and the wealth of centuries of experience makes it a great place to find your lights. There is a host of electrical fittings and the company also undertakes repairs, gilding, plating, lacquering and restorations.

Wilkinson & Son
1 Grafton St, London W1X 3LB
tel: 0171 495 2477 • fax: 0171 491 1737

If you have a photograph of a favourite lamp, this company can make a replica of it. They also rewire chandeliers and offer a general restoration service.

east

The Antique Lighting Co
The Old Rectory, Kennett, Newmarket, Suffolk CB8 7QL
tel: 01638 751354

You will find a large collection of antique lighting here and a huge amount of expertise. The lighting styles range from the nineteenth century to Art Deco with a glorious amount of variety on offer. There is also a full restoration service.

Bella Figura
Decoy Farm, Old Church Rd, Melton, Suffolk IP13 6DH
tel: 01394 461111 • fax: 01394 461199

A mixture of plain and more ornate period lighting including ceramic lamp bases, wall lights, chandeliers, standard lamps and candelabras at this store. They also have a wide range of different types of lampshade.

Jim Lawrence
Scotland Hall Farm, Stoke by Nayland, Colchester, Essex CO6 4QG
tel: 01206 263459 • fax: 01206 262166

Jim Lawrence makes all kinds of ironwork in a traditional-style forge and one of his métiers is candelabras and floorstanding candleholders. These come in a variety of designs and finishes including verdigris.

The Stiffkey Lampshop
14 Wells Rd, Stiffkey, Wells-next-the-Sea, Norfolk NR23 1AJ
tel: 01328 830460

This shop is a complete delight for anyone who is looking for genuine period pieces. The lamps range from thirties library lamps and Moorish lanterns to lacemakers' candlesticks and ornate candelabra. Most of them are originals but some are faithful reproductions and they also offer quite a few accessories such as light switches.

Woolpit Interiors
The Street, Woolpit, Bury St Edmunds, Suffolk IP30 9SA
tel: 01359 240895 • fax: 01359 242282

This company designs and makes decorative lamps, table lamps, wall lights and chandeliers that are often based on traditional styles. They do tea-cannister and Gothic lamps, and hand-painted items that they colour match to your interiors, and they'll do commissions.

central

Best & Lloyd
Cambray Works, William St West, Smethwick, W.Midlands B66 2NX
tel: 0121 558 1191 for stockists • fax: 0121 565 3547

This is a handcrafted range of period-style lighting. For over 150 years this company have been designing and manufacturing beautiful brass and, more recently, crystal lighting. Today they have an extensive pattern library covering Renaissance, Georgian, Rococo and Colonial styles. You will be in distinguished company if you buy from here as they have worked on projects in Windsor Castle and Buckingham Palace.

Fritz Fryer
12 Brookend St, Ross-on-Wye, Herefordshire HR9 7EG
tel: 01989 567416

Choose from over 500 examples of antique lights which are displayed in the showroom at any one time. If you are looking for lighting of a particular style or period, you can discuss what you are after and the staff will send you photographs of any current stock that could fit the bill.

Isis Ceramics
The Old Toffee Factory, 120a Marlborough Rd, Oxford, Oxon OX1 4LS
tel: 01865 722729 for stockists • fax: 01865 727521

Isis Lamps are available in a variety of colours and patterns and most are supplied on mahogany bases. Designs include a Teacaddie Lamp, a Wigstand Lamp, a Candlestick Lamp and a Large Jar Lamp. There is a variety of different style shades.

Stuart Buglass
Clifford Mill House Workshop, Little Houghton, Northampton, Northants NN7 1AL
tel: 01604 890366 • fax: 01604 890372

Visit the company's gallery and coffee shop and choose between metal chandeliers and electric lighting and a large variety of iron candleholders. All the products are handmade and finished by local craftspeople.

Thomas Blakemore Ltd
Atlas Works, Sandwell St, Walsall, W.Midlands WAS1 3DR
tel: 01922 625951 • fax: 01922 611330

If you are looking for an antique style but don't want to pay the price for the real thing, this company makes hand-cast reproductions of antique lamps. They use a chemical composite and specialist, hand-painting techniques to make this look like brass, wood or marble. Their lamps are available in Harrods, House of Fraser, John Lewis and other department stores.

West Midlands Lighting
10–12 York Rd, Erdington, Birmingham,
W.Midlands B23 6TE
tel: 0121 350 1999 for stockists
fax: 0121 377 7490

This company manufactures a vast selection of period-style lighting including lamps with beaded shades, intricate glass chandeliers, and Chinese hand-painted porcelain bases.

north east

Period Lamp & Lighting Co
80 Hough Lane, Wombwell, nr Barnsley,
S.Yorks S73 0EF
tel: 01226 375595

You will find a whole selection of antique lights at this shop which specializes in Victorian, Edwardian and 1920s lights. All of them are completely renovated and they do offer a renovation service for your own antique lights as well. The collection includes chandeliers, wall lights, floor lights and table lamps.

north west

Chelsom Ltd
Heritage House, Clifton Rd, Blackpool, Lancs FY4 4QA
tel: 01253 831444 for stockists
fax: 01253 791341

Get yourself ready for a vast selection of period-style lights here, ranging from the simple to the most intricate chandelier. The company is also heavily involved in the restoration and repair of period light fittings – they can even manufacture new components for missing pieces.

wales

Laura Ashley
PO Box 19, Newtown, Powys SY16 1DZ
tel: 0990 622116 for mail order and branches
tel: 0800 868100 for their Home Furnishing Catalogue

Laura Ashley have a surprisingly varied range of period-style lighting ranging from formal table lamps in brass, nickel and verdigris finish to the more flamboyant crystal drop metal wall lights. They also do a range of more country-style ceramic or wood bases and simple checked, gingham, striped or plain shades.

scotland

R&S Robertson
36 Bankhead Drive, Edinburgh E11 4EQ
tel: 0131 442 1700 for stockists
fax: 0131 442 4356
e-mail: re-robertson@rs-robertson.co.uk

This company manufactures a simply enormous range of period-style decorative lighting, from the most exquisitely elaborate chandeliers to simple fisherman-style lamps. There are some contemporary styles amongst their repertoire as well.

northern ireland

Arches Lighting
16–20 Queen's Place, Lurgan BT66 8BY
tel/fax: 01762 322322

A window full of chandeliers will alert you to the fact that this is one of the big specialities in this lighting shop! They also have a good range of handmade lampshades and can make them to order to match your interior colours.

modern & groovy

Modern and contemporary lighting encompasses a huge range of styles from Low-voltage Tungsten Halogen systems (LVTH in the trade) to recessed 'spots' which can be set into the ceiling or the floor if you like your lighting to be effective but unobtrusive. Some designers have played on traditional lighting shapes, such as the chandelier, and created beautiful objects replacing the glass with metal or plastic drops. Steel and chrome are the mainstays of modern lighting, although moulded plastic is also a great favourite. In this section, you will find all sorts of weird and wonderful innovative creations from fluffy pom-pom lights to lava lamps.

south east

Aero
96 Westbourne Grove, London W2 5RT
tel: 0171 221 1950 • fax: 0171 221 2555

Lots of chrome and glass can be found in this emporium of style. They have a good range of spot and wall lights as well as larger pendant and floor lights, including some funky uplighters.

After Noah
121 Upper St, London N1 1QP
tel: 0171 359 4281
and
261 Kings Rd, London SW3 5EL
tel: 0171 351 2610
e-mail: mailorder@afternoah.demon.co.uk

If you are hunting for an original 1930s anglepoise lamp, the workshop connected to this eclectic shop salvages them, then rewires, chromes and polishes them until they are gleaming. There are also new lights, such as modern Italian lamps. After Noah was one of the first shops to sell chilli-pepper lights – a fun variation on traditional Christmas fairy lights.

Aktiva Systems Ltd
10b Spring Place, London NW5 3BH
tel: 0171 428 9325 • fax: 0171 428 9882

If you want the industrial feel, Aktiva have lots of great searchlights, uplighters, low-voltage spotlights on tracks, as well as simple and stylish wall lights. The Filo range has bendy stems for easy directional use and the conical wrap-round shades come in vibrant colours . They also do a very unusual range of lights, called Ikon, which have a screen-printed shade made from polycarbonate set in an anodized aluminium frame.

Alternative Light
257 Kennington Lane, London SE11 5QU
tel/fax: 0171 582 2676

Alternative Light, run by designer Sophie Chandler, is committed to contemporary lighting design and is a showcase for some lovely wacky ideas. Recurring materials include recycled plastic (which has rainbow patterns), glass bottles suspended on a bicycle wheel for an unusual chandelier, and lots of coloured cable. The Litebowl is a bowl of light bulbs which can all light up at once – simple but effective. Sophie herself has appeared on *Home*

Front showing how to make some of her lights. The designs are made to order, on a commission basis. Phone first for an appointment.

Alva Lighting
4 Ella Mews, Cressy Rd, London NW3 2NH
tel: 0171 267 5705 for stockists • fax: 0171 267 7086
and
7 Linenhall St, Belfast BT2 8AA
tel: 01232 233296 for stockists • fax: 01232 249252
e-mail: alva@isides.demon.co.uk

Out of their Belfast-based factory, Alva produces a range of modern lights that are all variations on a theme – namely simple designs with white or coloured polypropylene shades wrapped round to form cones, spheres and other shapes, and then visibly studded together. Giving off a soft diffused light, they are fashioned into table, pendant and floorstanding lamps and given great three-letter names such as Yam, Boo and Moo.

Aram Designs
3 Kean St, London WC2B 4AT
tel: 0171 240 3933 • fax: 0171 240 3697

Top-of-the-range classics here with names such as Arteluce, Artemide, Flos and Ingo Maurer. It's more like an art gallery than a shop and is not always open at weekends so ring to check first.

Brats
281 Kings Rd, London SW3 5EW
tel: 0171 351 7674 • fax: 0171 349 8644
and
624c Fulham Rd, London SW6 5RS
tel: 0171 731 6915

Brats sells all sorts of quirky off-beat things including a small range of fun lights. Strings of fairy lights have characters from Disney or The Simpsons hanging from them instead of the more usual stamen-shaped bulbs. They also do great mirror balls for making your room into an instant disco.

British Home Stores
Marylebone House, 129–137 Marylebone Rd,
London NW1 5QD
tel: 0171 262 3288
tel: 0990 247000 for catalogue and mail order

British Home Stores has become renowned in the last few years for offering a very stylish range of lights at extremely reasonable prices. There is something to suit all tastes from beaded-twist shades, anglepoise lamps, star lanterns, and lovely cylindrical hanging silk shades in delicious colours.

Candell Lighting

20–22 Avenue Mews, London N10 3NP
tel: 0181 444 9004 for stockists • fax: 0181 444 5232

Candell are the sole agents in this country for Luce, an Italian range (not to be confused with Luceplan) and Blux, a Spanish range. In addition, they can re-create items from photographs, undertake restoration and source spare parts for all sorts of lights.

Catalytico

25 Montpelier St, London SW7 1HF
tel: 0171 225 1720 • fax: 0171 225 3740
e-mail: catalyt@dircon.co.uk

Catalytico are one of the main agents for lighting such as Foscarini, Flos and Luceplan and can source these beautiful objects for you – works of art in their own right. All three companies make a large range of lights but special mentions must be made of Foscarini's Orbital freestanding light, which looks like an artist's palette, and Luceplan's Blow – a ceiling fan with propellors in clear or coloured plastic which look stunning in action.

Concord Lighting Ltd

174 High Holborn, London WC1V 7AA
tel: 0171 497 1400 • fax: 0171 497 1404

Very good for low-energy spotlights and low-voltage halogen lighting in hi-tech designs. Their downlighters are good to place in recesses, and they also have spotlights you can conceal neatly under the floor.

Eccentrics

3–5 Fortis Green Rd, London N10 3HP
tel: 0181 883 8030 • fax: 0181 883 5030
and
21 Market Place, Hampstead Garden Suburb,
London NW11 6JY
tel: 0181 458 9697

Fun and funky is the name of the game here with lampshades covered in fake fur and velvet, two-tone plastic table lights with patterns of bubbles, hearts or flowers, and lots of shades made from scrunched up paper with metal rivets. Visit the stores or use their mail order service.

EncapSulite

Youngs Trading Estate, Stanbridge Rd,
Leighton Buzzard, Beds LU7 8QF
tel: 01525 376974 • fax: 01525 850306

Fluorescent lighting need never be dull again with this company's highly coloured sleeves. Recommended for use with their tubes, you simply slip them over the tube to give an effect like neon lighting. There are twenty-five colours to choose from.

Extralite

26 Northways Parade, College Crescent,
London NW3 5DN
tel: 0171 722 7480

A good range to suit the average pocket is available here; sturdy tracking systems, low voltage lights and up and downlighters.

Flos

31 Lisson Grove, London NW1 6UB
tel: 0171 258 0600 • fax: 0171 723 7005

Here you will find classics by top-name designers – Philippe Starck, Achille Castiglioni and Jasper Morrison to name but three. They are real objects of desire and will no doubt become an investment in years to come.

The Furniture Union

46 Beak St, London W1R 3DA
tel: 0171 287 3424 • fax: 0171 287 3424

The Furniture Union acts as a showcase for the best of young British talent and if you've seen a particular name at one of the trade fairs, such as Decorex and 100% Design, they will usually find their way here.

Habitat

196 Tottenham Court Rd, London W1P 9LD
tel: 0171 255 2545
tel: 0645 334433 for branches

A trip to Habitat for lighting can always be relied on to produce the goods if you're looking for something modern and contemporary and not prohibitively expensive. Most of the lights are chrome and glass, although they usually have anglepoise lamps in funky colours, and break out into colours for bases. A good place to go for the perennially popular paper shades in white and parchment. Try and buy the bulbs at the same time because some of the lights only seem to take Habitat bulbs.

Haus
23–25 Mortimer St, London W1N 8AB
tel: 0171 255 2557 • fax: 0171 255 1331
e-mail: info@haus.co.uk

Extremely classy top-of-the-range lighting is housed in this massive space. Keep your eyes open for the likes of works by Ingo Maurer which are masterpieces in their own right.

IKEA
Brent Park, 2 Drury Way, North Circular Rd,
London NW10 0TH
tel: 0181 208 5600 for enquiries and branches

You can pick up some real bargains at IKEA in their large lighting department. They are particualrly good on low voltage and halogen lights, and there are always some very reasonably priced standard and table lamps with paper and aluminium shades. The only drawback is that they quickly sell out of particular models so phone for stock availability before trekking all the way there.

Inflate
3rd Floor, 5 Old St, London EC1V 9HL
tel: 0171 251 5453 • fax: 0171 250 0311

You'll need to have plenty of puff when you visit here – all the lights are blown up and secured with a plastic popper just like a rubber ring. There are hanging ones in great colours which look like giant UFOs as well as little table lamps. Simply let the air down when you want to pack them away – although why would you?

John Cullen Lighting
585 Kings Rd, London SW6 2EH
tel: 0171 371 5400 • fax: 0171 371 7799

If you want to see for yourself how different lighting effects would look, John Cullen has a useful demonstration studio in which to try things out. As well as this, there is a wide range of lights on offer. (See also Outdoor Lighting, p.246.)

The Light Store
11 Clifton Rd, London W9 1SZ
tel: 0171 286 0233 • fax: 0171 266 2009

A wide range of modern lighting can be found here. Choose from ceiling lights with frosted glass diffusers, steel hanging lamps, aluminium wall lights, and some

strange desk lights in anthracite that would look at home in a sci-fi movie.

London Lighting Co
135 Fulham Rd, London SW3 6RT
tel: 0171 589 3612

Uplighters, downlighters, recessed spots and halogen lights can all be found here. They stock lights by Best & Lloyd and some of the top Italian names.

Mathmos
179 Drury Lane, London WC2B 5QF
tel: 0171 404 6605

This small, but well-stocked, shop in the heart of London's Covent Garden, tucked away behind the New London Theatre, is dedicated to the sale of lava lamps which come in every rainbow hue. Shaped like torpedoes and mini rockets, you'll be unable to make up your mind which one you want. They've been making lamps since 1963.

MOG Contemporary Lighting
127 Peperharrow Rd, Godalming, Surrey GU7 2PW
tel: 01483 419515 • fax: 01483 419515

Wooden bases with paper shades in subtle colours are this company's trademark and they have become a favourite with the style magazines. They have a wonderful range of chocolate and duck-egg blue lamps, and an Hourglass lamp with undulating curves picked out in contrasting shades.

Mr Light
275 Fulham Rd, London SW10 9PZ
tel: 0171 352 7525 • fax: 0171 376 8034
and
279 Kings Rd, London SW3 5EW
tel: 0171 352 8398 • fax: 0171 351 3484

Mr Light is particularly good if you're after unobtrusive and discreet lighting – for instance, their Micron Halogen spotlight is great for throwing light onto a favourite painting or object. They are also one of the few outlets to stock nice bathroom lights – look out for the Anais, which comes in chrome and opalized glass, and the Cadiz, which is Deco influenced.

Ochre
151a Sydney St, London SW3 6NT
tel: 0171 565 8888 • fax: 0171 565 8889

These are elegant lights which are both innovative and clever. Taking traditional forms, they are then imbued with a quirky touch. For example, a beautifully carved wooden base is topped off with a wire and paper shade, which looks like a billowing cloud or a suspended plume of smoke.

Oliver Bonas

80 Fulham Rd, London SW6 5HE
tel: 0171 736 8435 for the store
tel: 0171 627 4747 for enquiries and branches
fax: 0171 622 3629

A small but stylish range of lighting including hanging beaded and silk shades, miniature beaded table lamps, and wrought iron bases with plain shades. They have five other London shops, in Chiswick, Clapham Common, Richmond, Shepherd's Bush and Twickenham.

Optelma Lighting

14 Napier Court, The Science Park, Abingdon, Oxon OX14 3NB
tel: 01235 553769 • fax: 01235 523005

Some truly weird and wonderful designs can be found here by Atelier Sedap, a French lighting company, whose trademark is white plaster. Look out for giant leaf shapes, one that looks like a flying comet by designer Neil Poulton, and some novel uplighters.

Optime Lighting

156 Ladbroke Grove, London W10 5NA
tel: 0181 964 9711 • fax: 0181 969 3026

If you need lighting track to go round bends or even zig zags, Optime have the solution with their range of modular track lighting. There are also low halogen spotlights suspended from wires to look like mini-trapezes, and some truly spectacular chandeliers that take the traditional aspects of a chandelier and use halogens and metallized discs instead of glass drops.

Pira

Pira Ltd, Sayesbury Manor, Bell St, Sawbridgeworth, Herts CM21 9AW
tel: 01279 600620 • fax: 01279 600608

This company concentrates on aluminium clip-on lights in very simple but effective designs – there's one that looks like a wok hanging upside down. They also stock Lumibar's lights in the shape of teddy bears that glow in the dark and are popular with adults as well as children.

Places & Spaces

30 Old Town, Clapham, London SW4 0LB
tel: 0171 498 0998

Frequented by the trendy set, this shop sells top-of-the-range lights by top names such as Ifimu Noguchi. Look out for a beautiful floor light which looks like a block of glass.

Prolumena

Unit 4, Barley Shotts Busniess Park,
246 Acklam Rd, London W10 5YG
tel: 0181 968 2130 for stockists • fax: 0181 986 1488

This company designs and manufactures a range of uplighters and display lighting used in stores but which is also available for domestic use. If you want to cover a wall evenly with light but don't want the light source to show, their wallwashers are shallow enough to fit into ceiling voids.

Purple Pom Pom

Dunfield House, Dunfield, nr Fairford, Glos GL7 4HE
tel: 01285 810659 • fax: 01285 810692

Kitsch and colourful designs, which are definitely different, are this mail order company's speciality. The Pom Pom electric light is a pink fluffy ball sat atop black tripod legs. They also have very strange light bulbs with rubber spikes, like a Mohican hair cut, plugged into bendy lamp bases. Truly wacky.

Purves & Purves

80–81 & 83 Tottenham Court Rd,
London W1P 9HD
tel: 0171 580 8223 • fax: 0171 580 8244

Lots of lighting ideas from top, mostly European, designers with some at the more mid-range price bracket. Take a flexi lamp from Spain, which is a great little versatile anglepoise, or a cute Italian Bullo Lamp in a choice of five colours, which is one complete mould. The whole lamp lights up when on.

Ruth Aram Shop

65 Heath St, London NW3 6UG
tel: 0171 431 4008 • fax: 0171 431 6755

Most of the top Italian names are represented here as well as up and coming and established British designers such as Tom Dixon and Patrick Quigly. Look for moulded sculptural shapes which sit on the floor and hanging mobiles.

Ryness

Head Office, 34 White Lion St, London N1 9PQ
tel: 0171 437 8833 for branches

Ryness has dozens of branches and is good for
sturdy, well-made items such as recessed 'eyeballs'
which can swivel round for directional light from the
ceiling, low halogen spotlights and the odd strange
thing such as lights in the shape of yellow plastic
tulips.

SKK

34 Lexington St, London W1R 3HR
tel: 0171 434 4095 • fax: 0171 278 0168
e-mail: skk@easynet.co.uk

SKK stands for Shiu-Kay Kan the designer. There is a
wide range of state-of-the-art chrome uplighters and
floor-mounted spotlights. If you like your lights as
unobtrusive as possible, try their simple glass panel
which is back-lit – perfect for minimalist living. In
addition, there are some really weird and wacky
things. The Lucellino lamp, for example, designed by
Ingo Maurer, is just a bare bulb with two feathery
wings attached. It looks like a bird or an angel with
a sky-high price to match.

Viaduct

1–10 Summers St, London EC1R 5BD
tel: 0171 278 8456

If you're looking for something by a particular
designer, Viaduct can attempt to source products for
you. They are agents for the designers Artemide,
Arteluce, Flos, Foscarini and Ingo Maurer.

east

Quip
71 Tenison Rd, Cambridge, Cambs CB1 2DG
tel: 01222 394131 • fax: 01222 394131

Quip are dealers for Flos, Arteluce, Artemide and
Luceplan. If you want something really special made,
they will also undertake commissions for chandeliers
and designer lights.

central

Central
33–35 Little Clarendon St, Oxford OX1 2HU
tel: 01865 311141 • fax: 01865 511700

Amongst a large selection of furniture, glassware and
plastics, you will find lights by Flos, Foscarini and Aero.
Oxford's answer to The Conran Shop or Heals'.

Insitu
35 Friar St, Worcester, Worcs WR1 2NA
tel: 01905 613515 • fax: 01905 724141

Insitu has a good range of Italian lighting, representing
names such as Artemide and Luceplan. They also sell less
expensive lines and lights made by art students.

north west

Howe Sutton
Marbury House Farm, Higher Whitley, Warrington,
Cheshire WA4 4QW
tel: 01925 730050

Although they say there's not a huge call for it in their
neck of the woods, if you're looking for Italian lighting
this company can source it for you. Some of the lights
are truly inspirational; simple shapes which are
classically beautiful.

Lloyd Davies Modern Living
14 John Dalton St, Manchester M2 6JR
tel: 0161 832 3700 • fax: 0161 832 5141

In this huge space which occupies around 10 000
square feet, you will find lots of top-quality, classy
lighting from the likes of Artemide, Flos and Arteluce.
They are one of the main stockists for B&B Italia.

north east

Bisca Design

Shaw Moor Farm, Harome, York, N.Yorks YO6 5HZ
tel: 01439 771702 • fax: 01439 771002
e-mail: bisca@easynet.co.uk

Traditional lights with a twist – literally. Their
standard lamps have a knot in the base, topped with a
parchment shade. Their K lights are up- or downlighters
with a wavy tapering to a point with a zinc or black finish.

David Village Light Associates
285 Ecclesall Rd, Sheffield S11 8NX
tel: 0114 2683501 • fax: 0114 266 9088

If you want to get your hands on some lights made by the top Italian names such as Artemide and Flos, David Village is one of the main stockists in the north west of England and will source lights for you.

The Home
Salts Mill, Victoria Rd, Saltaire, Bradford BD18 3LB
tel: 01274 530770 • fax: 01274 530839

Set in an old wool mill, this shop sprawls over two huge neighbouring sites. They have stuff from all over the world and you will find names like Philippe Starck stocked here.

wales

Richard Beere Contracts
111–117 Woodville Rd, Cardiff CF2 4DY
tel: 01222 394 131 • fax: 01222 394148

This company offers a complete interior design service and their showroom at Woodville Road has examples on display, in fully designed room sets.

scotland

Inhouse
28 Howe St, Edinburgh EH3 6TG
tel: 0131 225 2888
and
24–26 Wilson St, Glasgow G1 1SS
tel: 0141 552 5902

Inhouse is Scotland's design emporium brimming with modern and largely European names, with Artemide and Starck to name a few. A sleek and stylish setting here shows the lights off to their best advantage.

Tony Walker Interiors
Whithall Court, 14 Telford Rd, Edinburgh EH4 2BD
tel: 0131 343 6151

An elegant backdrop for top-of-the-range, mostly European, lighting is provided by the furniture from Knoll, Vitra and Eames. If you're looking for a lighting design classic, this is a good place to start. They are agents for Luceplan.

northern ireland

Alana Lighting
30–32 Queen's Place, Lurgan, Craigavon BT66 8BY
tel: 01762 322322 • fax: 01762 321248

This shop offers a bit of everything – both modern and traditional. You will find everything from Tiffany lamps and crystal chandeliers to modern shapes in wrought iron.

Bangor Lighting Centre
121a High Street, Bangor, Co Down BT20 5BD
tel: 01247 270606

A broad range of traditional styles can be found here from desk lamps to crystal chandeliers. Focusing mainly on decorative lighting, there should be something to suit all tastes.

Beechmount Iron Craft
23 Moygannon Lane, Donaghacloney,
Co Down BT66 7ND
tel/fax: 01762 881162

As the name suggests, all the lights made here are forged in iron. There are lights for both interior and exterior use.

Lighting Design Supplies
118 Duncrue St, Belfast BT3 9AR
tel: 01232 351435 • fax: 01232 3513482

As well as operating a consultancy service for both business and domestic clients, this company sells some ultra-modern and fun lights with products ranging from quirky table lamps to recessed halogen spots.

The Natural Interior
51 Dublin Rd, Belfast BT2 7HE
tel: 01232 242656

Lights by Babylon Design – hanging lampshades in silk or cotton in gorgeous magenta, deep blue or sea green plus coloured paper shades and other lights made by SKK.

Off The Wall Lighting
6 Plantation St, Killyleagh, Co Down BT30 9QW
tel/fax: 01396 821168
e-mail: jmcccrum@unite.net

This retail outlet has a good range of wall lights made from recycled paper; patterns have been cut into the paper to give an unusual effect. They also have some nice table lamps made out of driftwood.

lighting accessories

Attention to detail can make all the difference when planning the design of your house. If you live in a period house and have decorated it in keeping with that style, a standard or ultra modern light switch can sometimes look out of place. There are now companies who will reproduce period light fittings – switches and sockets – for you in everything from Bakelite to brass, depending on what is appropriate. However, if you want your switches to remain as unobtrusive as possible, there are also clear backplates available where the light switch virtually disappears into the wallpaper or paint. If, on the other hand, you really want to make a feature of your switches there are some original and wacky styles available in rainbow plastics and strange mutant shapes that will jump out of the wall. Below you will find the best around – many of them do a mail order service.

A Touch of Brass
210 Fulham Rd, London SW10 9PJ
tel: 0171 351 2255 • fax: 0171 352 4682

If you want to get away from white plastic light switches and sockets, A Touch of Brass make them in brass and in a range of styles including Tudor, Georgian and Regency styles. They also offer black and chrome ones.

Brass Tack Fittings Ltd
177 Bilton Rd, Perivale, Greenford, Middx UB6 7HG
tel: 0181 566 9669 • fax: 0181 566 9339

If you have a period room and want everything to be in keeping, this company does a range of light switches and fittings in period styles – from Regency, Georgian and Victorian to black iron.

Bromleighs of Bergholt
68 Chapel Rd, West Bergholt, CO6 3JA
tel: 01206 241434

Hand-finished wooden switchplates in selected hardwoods and with plain or chamfered edges. There is a choice of nine different finishes and a full selection of switches, dimmers, sockets and accessories. There is also a range of brass and chrome pullswitches and light fittings.

Forbes & Lomax
205a St John's Hill, London SW11 1TH
tel: 0171 738 0202 • fax: 0171 738 9224

This company does an unusual range of transparent acrylic plate sockets and light switches which are unobtrusive on your favourite wallpaper. From a slight distance all you see is the actual switch. They come in either square or round shapes.

House of Brass
45–47 Milton St, Nottingham, Notts NG1 3EZ
tel: 0115 947 5430

A selection of nearly fifty different brass sockets and light switches, some of which are modern and some traditional. They include every conceivable type of switch or socket you might have such as TV points.

JD Beardmore & Co
17 Pall Mall, London SW1Y 5LU
tel: 0171 637 7041 • fax: 0171 436 9222

This company has a significant range of brass light switches and sockets. There is quite a variety of designs from the very traditional style to the more classic and many in between. If you can't make up your mind from the mail order catalogue, they now have a showroom where you can see them in the flesh.

Olivers Lighting Co
6 The Broadway, Crockenhill, Swanley, Kent BR8 8JH
tel: 01322 614224 • fax: 01322 614224

For the period lighting freak, these are the light
switches to match. Made from antique mahogany, oak
or natural oak, the backplates sport brass switches in a
choice of designs. There are also sockets to match.

Period House Shop
141 Corve St, Ludlow, Shropshire SY8 2PG
tel: 01584 877944 • fax: 01584 875411

This is a small mine of lighting extras including jelly
mould and brown dolly light switches, cotton-covered
flex, replacement oil lamp shades and other period-
style glass shades.

R Hamilton & Co
Quarry Industrial Estate, Mere, Wilts BA12 6LA
tel: 01747 860088 for stockists • fax: 01747 861032

An extensive range of wooden, metal and period-style
light switches and sockets. The wooden ones come in a
range of eight different finishes and there is also
another range of coloured switches.

Sussex Brassware
Napier Rd, Castleham Industrial Estate,
St Leonards on Sea, Sussex TN38 9NY
tel: 01424 440734 • fax: 01424 853862

A whole rainbow of different coloured switches and
sockets including ten different metal finishes and
fourteen different colours including turquoise and
sunshine yellow. All the paint finishes are available in
British Standard or RAL colours. (RAL is a German
system of ranking colours, which has an incredibly
wide range.)

Switch to Wood
Unit 4B, Firsland Pk Estate, Henfield Rd, Albourne,
W.Sussex BN6 9JJ
tel: 01273 495999

A whole range of wooden light switches and sockets,
which are made by hand in a choice of three timbers —
dark 'mahogany', medium oak and light ash. The
accessories fit directly into standard wall boxes and
can be ordered with either black or white inserts.

Tin Shed
Brook House, Meadow Vale, Haslemere,
Surrey GU27 1DH
tel/fax: 01428 641845

If you fancy something a little bit different from
square or round light switches, this company do a
range of six different switch plates which look exactly
like their names — Splat, Drip, Flower — all with a
stainless steel toggle. Choose from seven funky
colours — blue, purple, orange, lime-green, red, blue
and aluminium.

7

sofas

Choosing a bed and a sofa are probably two of the most important decisions you will make when it comes to furnishing your home. Both are quite large investments and so you have to be sure you get it right. It's not just a question of money either – comfort is of prime importance for both but especially with beds, as we spend one third of our lives asleep!

Before you order your sofa or bed, and this may sound obvious, do check first that it is actually going to fit through not only your front door but also any internal doors on the way to where it's going, and that it can negotiate any immovable obstacles. Everyone knows a horror story of someone who has shelled out for their dream sofa, only either to have to virtually dismantle the house to get it in or, worse still, take it back to the shop shamefaced – and that's if they'll let you. So take measurements of the space and the door frames before you go shopping. Some sofa stores will helpfully give you a card with the measurements on, when you place an order, and then give you a few days to cancel if there's no way it'll fit.

When you first spot a sofa or bed you like, it's quite difficult to imagine what it will look like, in a spatial sense, back in your room. *Home Front* designer Anne McKevitt has a good tip – go home and mark the dimensions out on the floor either with tape or lay down newspaper. This will visually remind you of the size as well as giving you a good idea of how much space you will have left to walk around. That way it won't be so much of a shock when it's delivered and suddenly dwarfs your room!

& beds

key: **hf** shows the product has appeared on
           Home Front

      ✉ shows the company offers a mail
         order service

sofas

The average sum most people spend on a sofa is a lot of money to waste if you realize you've made a ghastly mistake. When choosing a sofa, consider some easy questions first. Do you want somewhere to lounge around on, sprawled in front of the telly? Do you want to be able to lie out flat on it – and with more than one of you on there at once? Does it have to take the brunt of children bouncing on it, animals climbing all over it, and will you be happy to let guests sit on it with a glass of red wine without having to cover it in polythene sheeting first? Would an unexpected guest, or someone closer to home who was in the doghouse, be able to sleep the night on it? The answers to all these questions will dictate what sort of sofa you buy – or whether indeed you decide on a sofa bed. They will also determine what fabrics you choose and whether, very importantly, the covers come off and are machine washable.

When you have found a sofa you like, don't be shy about testing it out in the store. If you can feel the springs poking through, then it's a no-no, and neither should you be able to feel the frame. A squishy sofa is great for sinking into but it should still support your back properly. Remember, also, that if you've been traipsing around different stores all day, anything is bound to feel comfortable! Tip it upside-down and see if there are lots of staples on the underside – that indicates it's not very well made. If it has been properly secured and looks professional, you have passed one hurdle.

traditional

In this section you will find a varied selection of 'traditional' sofas – fairly classical shapes, such as Chesterfields, which normally have a wooden frame construction, are upholstered with fabric, and have proper arms. Listed here are manufacturers who make designs that have been around for years and still look good gracing both period and contemporary-style homes.

south west

John Alan Designs
120–122 Walcot St, Bath, Avon BA1 5BG
tel: 01225 466963 • fax: 01225 448838

You will fnd a whole collection of traditional-style sofas and sofa beds at this showroom, with each piece individually made for each customer at quite a reasonable rate. They have accounts with most of the fabric houses or you can provide your own, and they have a free design service to help you find the fabric you are looking for.

Leather Chairs of Bath
11 Bartlett St, Bath, Avon BA1 2QZ
tel: 01225 447920 • fax: 01225 462525

Much more than just leather at this showroom, although they do make a couple of traditional leather Chesterfields and a Queen Anne two seater. In addition they have upholstered camelbacks, Knoles and a wonderfully ornate chaise as well as many other styles.

William Sheppee
Old Sarum Airfield, Salisbury, Wilts SP4 6BJ
tel: 01722 334454 for stockists • fax: 01722 337754

A collection of five different colonial-style sofas includes two settles, an opulent, caned Raj sofa and a stylish Raffles bergère two-seater sofa. They also have a wooden Maharaja sofa on offer for those who like to lord it a bit.

south east

A Barn Full of Sofas and Chairs
Furnace Mill, Lamberhurst, Kent TN3 8LH
tel: 01892 890285 • fax: 01892 890988

Sally Symmons literally has a barn full of old sofas and chairs but she also has a brochure of reproductions of many of the pieces that have passed through her hands over the years. All are made in the traditional manner with great attention to detail. Some, such as the Curly Chesterfield which can seat nine, are simply irresistible.

Beaumont & Fletcher
The Old Imperial Laundry, 71 Warriner Gardens, London SW11 4XW
tel: 0171 498 2642 for stockists • fax: 0171 498 2644

If you are looking for traditional looks to die for, Beaumont & Fletcher have gems like their Regency day bed and their Alexandra sofa which would bring an authentic period touch to any room. The furniture is made in a rigorously traditional way and many of the fabrics are based on original patterns dating from the eighteenth and nineteenth centuries.

Bevan Funnell
Reprodux House, Norton Rd, Newhaven, E.Sussex BN9 0BP
tel: 01273 513762 for stockists • fax: 01273 516735

Traditional leather sofas in a range of designs including different styles of Chesterfields. There is also a very ornate chaise longue, a Georgian-style upholstered sofa and a bergère.

Cintique
43 Andrews Rd, Cambridge Heath, London E8 4RN
tel: 0171 254 1262 for stockists • fax: 0171 254 6774

Cintique make quite a few ranges of very traditional and cottage-style sofas. Their styles are nothing outrageously different, but they would look right in the cosy type of traditional living room.

David Salmon
555 Kings Rd, London SW6 2EB
tel: 0171 384 2223 • fax: 0171 371 0532

Dedicated to making pieces that have all the characteristics of the golden age of furniture making, David Salmon has some simply stunning period designs including a Georgian-style sofa, a Regency Sabre Leg sofa and a subtle Regency mahogany sofa at this showroom.

Ducal
Andover, Hants, SP10 5AZ
tel: 01264 333666 for stockists
fax: 01264 334046

Pine lovers should investigate the Ducal collection of sofas. They have their fair share of wood, but are also specially sprung and upholstered to give a very comfortable place to sit or lounge. They are available in a variety of sizes and designs.

Ercol Furniture
Ercol Buildings, London Rd, High Wycombe, Bucks HP13 7AE
tel: 01494 464488 for stockists
fax: 01494 462467
e-mail: sales@ercol.com

Ercol's sofas cover a small range of different styles. Some of them have very obvious wooden frames with upholstered cushions while others are a bergère style with caned sides. They all have matching chairs and come in a range of sizes.

George Smith
587–589 Kings Rd, London SW6 2EH
tel: 0171 384 1004 • fax: 0171 731 4451

Quite simply some of the most interesting and unusual period pieces you will find without buying originals. Really special designs at this showroom include the Dog Kennel Bed, the Conversation Piece, which has four seats all pointing in different directions, and the George Smith chaise, which is like an armchair with an elongated seat.

Highly Sprung
310 Battersea Park Rd, London SW11 3B
tel: 0171 924 1124 • fax: 0171 924 1150
and
185–186 Tottenham Court Rd, London W1P 9LE
tel: 0171 631 1424 • fax: 0171 636 7987

This company makes fifteen different models of sofas, which are all available as two-seaters, two-and-a-half-seaters or three-seaters – sizes with great names such as Couch Potato and Hangover. The frames are made from traditional beech or seasoned hardwood and they will make it up in your own fabric if you can't find a fabric you like in the shop. If the material doesn't comply with fire regulations, they will even interline the sofa for you at a small extra charge.

Hodsoll McKenzie
52 Pimlico Rd, London SW1W 8LP
tel: 0171 730 2877 for stockists • fax: 0171 823 4939

Classical and restrained traditional designs include a stylishly simple three-seater sofa, two fully buttoned Chesterfields and a small button-back sofa. All are available in a range of different fabrics.

Marks & Spencer

tel: 0345 902902 for your local home store
or mail order

Marks & Spencer has a surprisingly large offering on the sofa front including a leather Chesterfield. Most of the other shapes are safe and classic and they all come in two sizes and some as sofa beds.

Nordic Style
109 Lots Rd, London SW10 0RN
tel: 0171 351 1755

If you are into the restrained elegance of traditional Scandinavian furniture, you could do no better than treat yourself to a sofa from this showroom. All their furniture uses models from eighteenth-century Swedish country houses as inspiration. They have some delightful cot sofas, which are available in wood or a painted finish.

Peter Guild
84–92 College St, Kempston, Bedford, Beds MK42 8LU
tel: 01234 273372 for stockists • fax: 01234 270838

Traditional manufacturing skills are backed up by a ten-year guarantee on these sofas. They also offer a fabric collection which include chenilles, prints,

tapestries, weaves and velvets. Most of the designs are safely traditional but the huge camel-back Henley offers luxury which is out of the ordinary. There are matching armchairs and footstools and the famous Clutterbox which is a footstool that opens to reveal storage space.

Pier Fagan
132 Bermondsey St, London Bridge, London SE1 3TX
tel: 0171 403 5585

These are the sofas with hidden talents. This company has several drop-end sofas that can have one arm lowered for practical purposes, such as putting someone up for the night. All Pier Fagan's sofas are handmade and in sizes to suit your requirements.

Recline & Sprawl
604 Kings Rd, London SW6 2DX
tel: 0171 371 8982 • fax: 0171 371 8984

Recline & Sprawl aim to offer traditional bespoke sofas at exceptional prices at this showroom and you can also supply your own fabric to cover them with if you wish. Styles include a Knole, a Chesterfield, chaise longues and a couple of unusual sledge stools. They also make upholstered chairs.

Scandecor
20 Castle St, Brighton, Sussex BN1 2HD
tel/fax: 01273 820208

If you are looking for an unusual Art Deco-style sofa you could find your dreams come true here! There are also some more traditional designs such as a chaise longue with turned mahogany legs, Victorian styles and fully buttoned leather Chesterfields.

Sofa Workshop

Boxall House, East St, Petworth, W.Sussex GU28 0AB
tel: 01798 343400 for branches
fax: 01798 345321

A very wide range of sofa shapes which includes classic and very traditional ones. They have some value-for-money sofas or they can custom-build the perfect sofa for your needs if you can't find what you want. There is a network of stores countrywide, so ring for details of your nearest one.

Sofas & Sofa Beds
82 Tottenham Court Rd, London W1P 9HD
tel: 0171 813 1490 for branches

Choose from a range of over thirty different styles here and an enormous range of different fabrics. Although they are in the heart of London they really do offer quite reasonable prices and most designs are available as either sofas or sofa beds and in four sizes with matching armchairs. They also have two other London branches and one in Glasgow.

Wesley-Barrell
Park St, Charlbury, Oxford, Oxon OX7 3PT
tel: 01608 810481 for stockists • fax: 01608 811319

Your sofa will be handcrafted to your specifications here including the size, style and amount of support. Styles are very traditional but include a caned sofa and an impressive Knole.

east

Arthur Brett & Sons
Hellesdon Park Rd, Drayton High Rd, Norwich, Norfolk NR6 5DR
tel: 01603 486633 for stockists • fax: 01603 788984
e.mail:enquiries@arthur-brett.com

Fine reproductions of eighteenth-century furniture is this company's speciality and they make some beautiful sofas including a Regency-style chaise and a mahogany love seat in the Sheraton style. They are also happy to accept commissions.

James Adam
24 Church St, Woodbridge, Suffolk IP12 1DH
tel: 01394 384471 • fax: 01394 384520

James Adam have a small, select range at this showroom of very beautiful sofas including a Louis XVI, a Regency and a Directoire Parisienne style. They also have a Louis XV sofa bed and other styles of put-up beds.

Lloyd Loom of Spalding
Wardentree Lane, Pinchbeck, Spalding, Lincs PE11 3SY
tel: 01775 712111 for stockists • fax: 01775 710571

You may not think of having such a large item as a sofa made from paper-based materials, but the test of time has shown how sturdy Lloyd Loom is. They make a wonderful colonial-style Orient sofa, which is just made for sipping Singapore Slings on, and comes in a range of colours and upholstery.

The Slipcover and Furnishings House
PO Box 1206, Ilford, Essex IG1 4EH
tel: 0870 603 0220

This is not strictly a sofa company, but it is a useful ally to anyone who has an ailing sofa or chair and doesn't want to splash out on a new one. They make one-piece slipcovers to rejuvenate worn upholstered furniture and give them a new lease of life.

central

Brights of Nettlebed
Kingston House, Nettlebed, nr Henley on Thames, Oxon RG9 5DD
tel: 01491 641115 for branches • fax: 01491 641864

Choose from a range of very traditional sofas and upholstered chairs in a variety of fabrics. More unusual sofas include a Knole sofa model and several caned examples with matching chairs.

Duresta Upholstery Ltd
Fields Farm Rd, Long Eaton, Nottingham, Notts NG10 3FZ
tel: 0115 973 2246 for stockists • fax: 0115 946 1028

Duresta have been making their handmade upholstery for over sixty years and now have a wide collection of traditional styles. Along with a range that varies from the sumptuous to the more modest, the company also has an exclusive agreement with The National Trust to reproduce a collection of sofas and chairs from its historic houses, including Chartwell and Lanhydrock House.

Parker Knoll
London Rd, Chipping Norton, Oxon OX7 5AX
tel: 01608 642141 for stockists

One of the best-known names in the business, Parker Knoll offer much more than their recliners. Their sofas include traditional and cottage styles, as well as some slightly more contemporary shapes. All of them are part of a suite except for the sofa beds.

Richard Kimbell
Rockingham Rd, Market Harborough, Leics LE16 7QE
tel: 01858 433444 for stockists

This company's main business is furniture but it does have one sofa which is so attractive and such good value that it is worth tracking it down. It is a stylish day bed that is made from Quebec pine with two canvas cushions. Reminiscent of the traditional Swedish look, it is a very solid piece of furniture.

The Ross Collection
The Old Mill, Brookend St, Ross on Wye, Herefordshire HR9 7EG
tel: 01989 564520 for stockists • fax: 01989 768145

This is a company that makes a small selection of traditional and classic-style sofas and armchairs in a variety of different upholstery fabrics and sizes.

Stag Furniture
Haydn Rd, Nottingham, Notts NG5 1DU
tel: 0115 960 7121 for stockists • fax: 0115 969 1399

Stag's sofas are in the classical traditional mould and range from the simple lines of Charlotte to the twin-skirted Claudia. You can choose from a range of over a hundred different fabrics including damasks, stripes and natural weaves.

Wychwood Design
Viscount Court, Brize Norton, Oxon OX18 3QQ
tel: 01993 851435 • fax: 01993 851594

Wychwood make an unusual and stunning collection of sofas and chaise longues in several different period styles. These range from a Louis XVI chaise longue, through a bamboo two-seater sofa, to a wonderfully stylized Empire-style two-seater. They also have a range of more commonly seen styles such as the Chesterfield and a Knole sofa.

north west

Derwent Upholstery
Greenhill Industrial Estate, Greenhill Lane, Riddings, Derbyshire DE55 4BR
tel: 01773 604121 for stockists • fax: 01773 540084

A well-known name with a host of traditional styles on offer. Most of the sofas have chairs, and often foot-stools, designed specifically to go with them and the sofas may also come in two or three different sizes.

Kiani
Kiani House, Kitling Rd, Knowsley, Prescot, Merseyside L34 9HN
tel: 0151 549 0101 for stockists • fax: 0151 549 0830

Wicker and rattan sofas have successfully made it out of the conservatory and into the living room and Kiani has quite a collection on offer from the simple to the highly decorative. They also have the ultra-modern German Schutz of living-room furniture, which combines innovative rattan sofas with contemporary prints and materials.

The Odd Chair Co
70–72 Blackbull Lane, Fulwood, Preston, Lancs PR2 3JX
tel: 01772 787990

You will find over 400 antique sofas and chairs at this store, which they totally restore to calico so you can choose your own upholstery fabric. They hand copy a few original sofas as well, using traditional materials and methods. You can really find something unusual among their stock.

Tetrad
Hartford Mill, Swan St, Preston, Lancs PR1 5PQ
tel: 01772 792936 for stockists
fax: 01772 798319

Opulent leather Chesterfields and enormous squashy sofas are just some of the styles offered by this company. Many have chairs to match and some have removable covers.

north east

The Iron Design Co
Summer Carr Farm, Thornton Le Moor, Northallerton, N.Yorks DL6 3SG
tel: 01609 778143

The iron sofas that this company makes are really designed for conservatories but there is nothing to stop you using them in a living room. They have good, crisp designs including a Gothic style and the company will always make to commission if you don't find what you want in their catalogue.

wales

Berkeley House
Unit 6, Penllyne Way, Vale Business Park, nr Cowbridge, Vale of Glamorgan CF71 7PF
tel: 01446 772900 • fax: 01446 774282

If you are looking for classic-style sofas, which would live quite happily in traditional or modern houses, this company has a good selection. There is nothing outrageous, but some elegant styles that won't date too quickly. They are all delivered to your home through a mail order service, which also makes them quite good value.

Classic Choice
Brynmenyn Industrial Estate, Bridgend,
Mid Glamorgan CF32 9TD
tel: 01656 725111 • fax: 01656 725404

This company specializes in direct sales of sofas in classic styles including two styles of leather Chesterfield. Brand-name fabrics like Crowson, Dovedale and Ross are used in the upholstery and your finished sofa should be delivered to you within four to six weeks.

Enigma
Lanelay Rd, Talbot Green, Pontyclun,
Mid Glamorgan CF7 8YE
tel: 01443 238585 • fax: 01443 238355

You will find a good selection of sofa beds on offer from this company at reasonable prices. They offer quite a diverse selection of styles, although nothing too mind-blowing. They have a very efficient delivery service.

Laura Ashley
PO Box 19, Newtown, Powys SY16 1DZ
tel: 0990 622116 for mail order and branches
tel: 0800 868100 for their Home Furnishing Catalogue

Choose from a smallish range of about eight different sofas in classic shapes. Most of them come in at least two sizes, some of them in five sizes, and there is an elegantly shaped chaise longue. There is also a range of chairs to complement them including two leather ones.

scotland

Camerons of Perth
26/34 George St, Perth, Perthshire PH1 5JP
tel: 01738 622261 • fax: 01738 633359

You will get a good selection of big brand names such as Parker Knoll, Cintique and Ercol from the thirty-five

sofas on display at this store. The styles are generally fairly traditional, with a few that edge a little closer to modern. They also have a massive range of upholstery fabrics to choose from.

Martin & Frost
138 MacDonald Rd, Edinburgh EH7 4NN
tel: 0131 557 8787 • fax: 0131 557 8045

There are over 200 sofas on display in this store, usually as part of suites. Many of the big brand names are here such as Parker Knoll and Ercol. Most of the styles are traditional and come in two-, two-and-a-half and three-seater versions.

northern ireland

Carpenter & McAllister
Yorkgate Shopping Centre, York St,
Belfast BT15 1AQ
tel: 01232 351425 • fax: 01232 351537

There is a huge selection of sofas at this retail outlet with a choice of over forty different brand names. They have examples of most types of styles including both traditional and mildly contemporary. A huge and busy showroom.

Comfort in Style
310 Newtownards Rd, Belfast BT4 1HE
tel: 01232 731419 • fax: 01232 731419

If you are long in the leg, or don't fit normal-sized sofas, or if you just want a special-sized sofa to fit the dimensions of your room, this company can help. They custom make sofas to non-standard depths and any size you want. They have a range of styles at this showroom, but you can adapt the styles if you want to. If you are on a budget, they can also help.

Orior By Design
Unit 12, Greenbank Industrial Estate, Newry,
Co Down BT34 2QU
tel: 01693 62620 for stockists • fax: 01693 63810

Classic designs are mixed with more contemporary styles in this thirty strong portfolio of different styles. All the sofas, however, are made in a traditional style using hand-tied spring units. They come in two- and three-seaters, with co-ordinating chairs.

modern & groovy

When it comes to modern and groovy sofas, anything goes. As long as they meet standard fire regulations, designers have been given a free rein to create weird and wonderful shapes – perhaps you'd like a sofa shaped like a giant pair of lips, or one with fake fur in zebra stripes? On the whole, contemporary design has made the sofa larger and you could almost get lost in some of them! Sometimes a plain, boxy shape in a block of one colour can look wonderful and become the focal point of your room. Whatever your taste, you are bound to find something you like in the companies listed below.

Albrissi
1 Sloane Square, London SW1W 8EE
tel: 0171 730 6119 • fax: 0171 259 9113

Although these are ultra-modern designs for sofas they are made in a traditional way with springs and horsehair so you get the best of both worlds. They have two to three ranges of sofas in stock at this shop but can make to order in any size within a range of designs. You can choose from their own fabrics or supply your own.

Aram Designs
3 Kean St, Covent Garden, London WC2B 4AT
tel: 0171 240 3933 • fax: 0171 240 3697

See some really up-to-the-minute design here including sofas, chairs and other furniture. The showroom has links with a vast number of designers, so there will always be something new and exciting. You can also have special designs manufactured to order.

The Conran Collection Shop
12 Conduit St, London W1R 9TG
tel: 0171 399 0710

Contemporary-style sofas are a part of this complete range, which has all been designed in house by Conran's own designers. The shapes are modern and the colours are very neutral and soft with some ethnic influences.

Contour Upholstery
Llwynypia, Tonypandy, Mid Glamorgan CF40 2JP
tel: 01443 438303 for stockists • fax: 01443 430146

If you are worried that your sofa will look grimy within a few months, this company offers the Buffalo wipe-

clean fabric which does not pill, resists abrasions and is soft to touch. The sofas also come in a variety of other fabrics and a whole host of shapes and sizes. All of them have matching chairs and footstools.

Design America
1 Knockhundred Row, Midhurst, W.Sussex GU29 9DQ
tel: 01730 817722 for stockists • fax: 01730 817744

Funky-shaped sofas from Florida with matching chairs. The sofas can be upholstered in either leather or a choice of fabrics and there are also some very contemporary footstools, occasional tables and other furniture.

Designer's Guild
267–271 & 275–277 Kings Rd, London SW3 5EN
tel: 0171 243 7300 for stockists • fax: 0171 243 7710

Modern and stylish pieces of furniture that you can order in a Designer's Guild fabric of your choice. There are always a few on display, which rotate regularly, and they always look stunning. They look best in large expanses of a vivid solid colour and are perfect for loft-style rooms.

Domain
83 Rusper Rd, Horsham, W.Sussex RH12 4BJ
tel: 01403 257201 for stockists • fax: 01403 262002

Simple sofas in contemporary shapes with the added excitement of some really unique pieces at the cutting edge of design. Most are Italian designs and there are even some contemporary interpretations of the traditional chaise longue.

Habitat
196 Tottenham Court Rd, London W1P 9LD
tel: 0171 255 2545
tel: 0645 334433 for branches

Habitat always have a very cool collection of understated contemporary sofas in a good range of sizes including the enormous! The shapes are designed to stand the test of time and even become classics of the future rather than be too avant garde.

IKEA
Brent Park, 2 Drury Way, North Circular Rd,
London NW10 0TH
tel: 0181 208 5600 for enquiries and branches

If you are on a budget, this is an excellent place to buy contemporary-style sofas, which they have in an abundance of styles and fabrics. They have particularly reasonable leather sofas at a fraction of prices you will pay elsewhere.

Intermura
27 Chalk Farm Rd, London NW1 8AG
tel: 0171 485 6638 • fax: 0171 284 4564
e-mail: intermura@mcmail.com

These are truly sensuous sofas with undulating curves and an imaginative use of colours and fabrics. All made in the company's factory in Hackney, the designs are contemporary yet classic, and are all dreamt up by husband-and-wife team Christopher and Ann Hymers (who are a furniture designer and former fashion and textile designer respectively). The whole range is on display at their London showroom.

Next Home
tel: 0345 100500 for mail order

This mail order catalogue offers a small range of restrained modern designs in a variety of shapes and sizes. They also have sofa beds and armchairs and a collection of different fabrics.

Purves & Purves
80–81 & 83 Tottenham Court Rd,
London W1P 9HD
tel: 0171 580 8223 • fax: 0171 580 8244

Purves & Purves specialize in stylish contemporary sofas at this store with a few wacky ideas thrown in. They have a good selection of chic Italian sofas and chunkier British ones and a wonderful Grand Piano Chaise in shocking pink.

Roset
95 High St, Great Missenden, Bucks HP16 0AL
tel: 01494 865001 for stockists
fax: 01494 866883

An exciting range of different-looking sofas including enormous corner configurations and ones where you and a companion can sit facing in opposite directions! Some are squashy, some are pert but all are original.

Sofa Solutions Direct
Unit 6, Penllyne Way, Vale Business Park,
nr Cowbridge, Vale of Glamorgan CF71 7PF
tel: 01446 772900 • fax: 01446 774282

Bright checks and tartans are a hallmark of this collection of furniture, which includes sofas in different shapes and sizes, all with matching armchairs and footstools. Many of the sofas also have a sofa bed option. The shapes are simple and clean and you can order all of these from the comfort of your own home by mail order.

Suzanne Ruggles Ltd
436 Kings Rd, London SW10 0LJ
tel: 0171 351 6565 • fax: 0171 351 7007

Amongst a whole wealth of contemporary wrought iron furniture, you will find some exotic day beds and sofas, also in wrought iron. There is a standard range of work at this showroom, or you can commission exactly what you want and there is plenty of choice due to collaboration with other artists and furniture designers.

Viaduct
1–10 Summer's St, London EC1R 5BD
tel: 0171 278 8456 • fax: 0171 278 2844

Don't miss these exquisitely shaped sofas which are the work of top designers such as Philippe Starck. Shapes at this shop range from an S-shape to an almost banana-shaped sofa with metal legs. They really are worth a look!

World of Leather
Unit C, New Mersey Retail Park, Speke Rd, Liverpool, Merseyside L24 8RZ
tel: 0990 604060 for stockists

Choose from a large collection of leather sofas including a knock-out lipstick red number with crossover chrome legs. Many of the sofas, chairs, sofa beds and recliners are contemporary, although there are a couple of more traditional ones including an Art Deco model. They have thirty-four shops nationwide so phone for details of your local stockist.

beds

With beds, the most important thing is the mattress. The frame is largely decorative. Try not to skimp on the mattress as it really is the thing which will give you a good night's sleep, good posture and limit future back problems. Ideally you should buy the mattress and bedframe at the same time as the mattress will feel different depending on the frame.

Don't forget that the genuine antique bed you've got your eye on might not fit the size of the mattresses manufactured today. If it doesn't, you can get one of specific size made to order but it's quite costly. As the mattress is the most important thing about your bed, it could even be worth considering altering the size of the bed frame instead.

Think too about how comfortable it will be when you're sitting in bed reading, watching television or eating breakfast. Iron beds, for example, can look great but some of them have ornate bedheads which might dig into your back even through a pillow. Having said that, iron beds are versatile – they can suit the period chintz look just as well as modern minimalism.

When you're hunting for the perfect bed, try to ignore whether the shop calls it a single, double, queen or king size. Terms vary from store to store and it's the actual size that really matters, so take along a tape measure.

traditional

In this section you will find all sorts of beds from four posters to genuine period wrought-iron beds, as well as new wrought-iron beds that have been cleverly produced to imitate old-style ones. There are beds fashioned from beautiful woods such as rose- and cherrywood, Art Deco-style beds, Regency and Queen Anne style, and Parisian-style ones. The companies are listed alphabetically by region. Sweet dreams!

south west

The Colonial Bedstead Co
Pymore Mills, Bridport, Dorset DT6 5PJ
tel: 01308 458066 for stockists • fax: 01308 424002

Period-style metal frame beds in a selection of finishes and with slatted wooden bases. Styles include the Saxon, the Medici and a day bed that opens out into a double sofa bed.

Dorset Antique Beds
Upstairs, The Antique Centre, 25–27 London Rd, Dorchester, Dorset DT1 1NF
tel/fax: 01305 250723

Choose from sixty restored antique beds or another 600 that are waiting their turn at this shop. The beds are a mixture of brass, iron and wooden pieces and are either English or Continental. They are predominately Victorian and Edwardian and include half tester and four posters.

The Feather Bed Co
Crosslands House, Ash Thomas, Tiverton, Devon EX16 4NU
tel: 01884 821331 • fax: 01884 821328

Traditional feather beds are not a thing of the past. They are sold as a second 'mattress' to go on top of a modern mattress – that way you get the support of a modern mattress and the real luxury and perfect heat of the old, traditional feather bed.

Millside Forge
Gospel Ash Farmhouse, Milborne Port, nr Sherborne,
Dorset DT9 5DU
tel/fax: 01963 251555

As expected from a traditional forge, these beds are
solid iron and very sturdy. They are all individually
hand-crafted by skilled smiths using century-old
methods. There are traditional and contemporary styles
on offer and all designs can be made into four posters.

Morpheus
Elgin House, 1 New Church St, Tetbury, Glos GL8 8DS
tel: 01666 504068 for stockists • fax: 01666 503352

A whole mixture here of genuine antique beds in brass,
iron or wood alongside a range of handcrafted English
beds, which are manufactured by the company. The
latter include *lits bateaux*, colonial four posters and
Victorian mahogany beds.

Simon Poyntz
Kennel Lodge Rd, Bower Ashton, Bristol, Avon BS3 2JT
tel: 0117 963 2563 • fax: 0117 963 2563

Simon Poyntz served his apprenticeship with an
eminent Italian cabinetmaker and is now a member of
the Guild of Master Craftsmen, making classic beds.
Every one is based on an authentic, original four
poster or a French bed. Because they are totally
bespoke you can choose the wood, finish, carving
style, shape and size of your bed.

south east

After Noah
121 Upper St, London N1 1QP
tel: 0171 359 4281
and
261 Kings Rd, London SW3 5EL
tel: 0171 351 2610
e-mail: mailorder@afternoah.demon.co.uk

Frequent trips to Ireland and France ensure that this
shop always has a good stock of antique beds. The
workshop sets to work, getting rid of the ancient
layers of rust and paint by dipping and then
sandblasting the frame. Then the beds are polished up
to a silvery metal finish before they are put on display
in the shop. Because both shops are small, there are
more beds to see in the workshop – phone for an
appointment. They also sell contemporary beds.

Amazing Emporium
249 Cricklewood Broadway, Edgware Rd,
London NW2 6NX
tel: 0181 208 1616 • fax: 0181 450 4511

Specialists for French sleigh beds or *lits bateaux*, this
company also stocks pine and iron beds, sofa beds,
mattresses and divan sets. The *lits bateaux* come in
various styles from the cherrywood Louis Philippe to
the Provençal in cherrywood, oak, mahogany, beech
or pine.

And So To Bed
638–640 Kings Rd, London SW6 2DU
tel: 0171 731 3593 for branches • fax: 0171 371 5272

This company really knows its stuff when it comes to
beds. Their knowledge about antique beds means they
make sumptuous reproductions that look every bit as
good as the originals. Their designs include some
elegant caned beds and many, many others.

Beaudesert
Old Imperial Laundry, 71 Warriner Gardens,
London SW11 4XW
tel: 0171 720 4977 • fax: 0171 720 4970

If you have set your heart on a hand-carved wooden
bed, this is one of the places you must visit. There are
some set styles, but if these aren't exactly what you
are looking for, you can have a design made to order.
Four posters are a speciality and, like the other beds,
can be painted or gilded.

David Salmon
555 Kings Rd, London SW6 2EB
tel: 0171 384 2223

David Salmon is a master at making fine furniture
which takes its inspiration from the past and his beds
bear testimony to this. At this shop he specializes in
four poster beds that can be hand-painted to match
the fabrics you plan to use to dress the bed.

Deptich Designs
7 College Fields, Prince George's Rd,
London SW19 2PT
tel: 0181 687 0867 for stockists • fax: 0181 648 6515

Deptich do a wide-reaching range of period-style beds
and have three different catalogues for wooden, cast
and hand-forged metal and brass bedsteads. All are
newly made and, although they may not be exact
reproductions, they are inspired by period styles.

Elizabeth Eaton

85 Bourne St, London SW1W 8HF
tel: 0171 730 2262 • fax: 0171 730 7294

This shop has a small selection of headboards, some of which are simulated bamboo and can be painted to your own colour choice. They also have upholstered headboards, pine headboards and an interesting copy of an eighteenth-century design with a curtain suspended from a brass rail.

Harriet Ann Sleigh Beds

Parkfield, Standen St, Iden Green, nr Cranbrook, Kent TN17 4HR
tel: 01580 243005 for stockists

In spite of the name, this company has all kinds of wooden beds as well as sleigh beds. They are all available in a natural wood finish or in a painted finish which costs extra. They also make children's beds.

House of Steel

400 Caledonian Rd, London N1 1DN
tel/fax: 0171 607 5889

If you are after a metal bed, you are bound to find something to suit here. As well as stocking original Victorian beds, they can also make reproductions in steel, steel and brass, or brass. They can make to order in any style and size and it is a fascinating place to visit as they have 5000 square feet of all kinds of metalware.

Hypnos

Station RD, Princes Risborough, Bucks HP27 9DN
tel: 01844 342233 for stockists • fax: 01844 346112

This family-run company has been producing handmade beds for more than four generations and hold two Royal Warrants. They offer a choice of mattresses and divan bases to suit any kind of bed from a four poster to a sleigh bed. They also have The Cotton Rich Collection, which is made from the totally natural fibres of wool, cotton and silk. The Orthos Collection has firmer beds if that is your preference.

The Iron Bed Co

Southfield Pk, Delling Lane, Old Bosham, Chichester, W.Sussex PO18 8NN
tel/fax: 01243 574049 for stockists

Inspired by the past, yet designed for today, these iron beds range from the most ornate Baroque design to

traditional-shaped metal beds in sherbet yellow, pink, orange and turquoise. They also offer a range of pure cotton bed linen in checks, stripes and plaids.

Judy Greenwood Antiques

657 Fulham Rd, London SW6 5PY
tel: 0171 736 6037 • fax: 0171 736 1941

Judy Greenwood has a large selection of nineteenth- and early-twentieth-century French beds and day beds on offer at this showroom. You will find Louis XV and Louis XVI styles here, all made from wood and some painted and gilded.

Marilyn Garrow

6 The Broadway, White Hart Lane, London SW13 0NY
tel/fax: 0181 392 1655

Antique French beds often offer far more romantic and elaborate styles than their British counterparts, so if you are looking for something quite decorative Marilyn Garrow has an excellent selection of French beds including some Louis XV and Empire models at this shop.

Marks & Spencer

tel: 0345 902902 your local home store
or mail order

Marks & Spencer sells quite a vast range of beds including iron, steel and brass in simple and ornate shapes and divans. If you are looking for ways to put up occasional overnight visitors, they also have hideaway beds where a spare bed is stored under a single bed, ready to swing up for use.

Nordic Style

109 Lots Rd, London SW1 0RN
tel: 0171 351 1755

If you are looking to give a plain divan a stylish period look, this company make some very attractive headboards in various designs. They are all based on the traditional-style Scandanavian furniture which they excel in and some of them can be caned or upholstered.

The Old Forge & Foundry

Unit 7, The Looe, Reigate Rd, Ewell, Epsom, Surrey KT17 3DB
tel: 0181 287 2965 • fax: 0181 287 2965

There are iron beds in a variety of designs at this showroom including the very intricate Gothic, to the more simple. Some of the beds have built-in candle holders at each corner for the ultimate in romance, and there is also a four poster.

Once Upon A Time
The Green, Ripley, Surrey GU23 6AL
tel: 01483 211330

Callers are welcome to browse among the 400 or so antique beds that are kept in stock at any one time here. You can choose from the already restored beds in the showroom, or pick out your own from those waiting for treatment. The beds are Victorian iron and brass and, although most of them were only made to double size, owner Michael Cripps can make them into queen size or larger.

The Pier

200 Tottenham Court Rd, London W1P 0AD
tel: 0171 637 7001 • fax: 0171 637 3332
tel: 0171 814 5004 for stockist and mail order
tel: 0171 814 5020 for branches

This may not be the first place you might have thought of looking in for a traditional-style bed, but they do sell a couple of lovely wicker bedheads with matching bedroom furniture. Vermont is painted white and looks very romantic, while Kenya is in a natural antique finish. Phone for details of your local stockist and for mail order details.

Simon Horn Furniture
117–121 Wandsworth Bridge Rd, London SW6 2TP
tel: 0171 731 1279 for stockists
fax: 0171 736 3522

Simon Horn reintroduced the French *lit bateau* bed to Britain in the early 1980s and has never looked back. Now you will find all kinds of other beautifully made, traditional styles in his repertoire. They are all solid wood and all handmade. There are over sixty different designs ranging from the simple Empire to the carved splendours of the Marie Antoinette. Many of the beds can be caned or upholstered and you can choose from a variety of woods.

Sleeping Beauty
579–581 Kings Rd, London SW6 2DY
tel: 0171 471 4711

Sleeping Beauty claims to be the largest antique bed dealer in London and the South East with more than 900 beds and fifty bedroom suites in stock. The beds,

which are wooden, brass or iron, are all fully restored in workshops in Hove where they also have another showroom. If you are looking for something big, they are specialists in king-sized antique beds.

Tim Wood Furniture
93 Mallinson Rd, London SW11 1BL
tel: 0171 924 1511

Each piece of furniture that Tim Wood makes is totally bespoke, designed and crafted to meet your individual requirements and the beds are no exceptions. Part of his repertoire are sleek, lined mahogany sleigh beds, but he has many other styles up his sleeve.

The Victorian Brass Bedstead Co
Hoe Copse, Cocking, nr Midhurst,
W.Sussex GU29 0HL
tel: 01730 812287

Take your pick from more than 2000 iron and brass bedsteads dating from 1870 to 1925, all stored in farm buildings, and have it restored by owner and expert David Woolley. The bedsteads are sorted into eight different styles although each one is original and unique. You can have your find finished in one of a full range of colours and finishes.

east

A Barn Full of Brass Beds
Abbey House, Eastfield Rd, Louth, Lincs LN11 7HJ
tel: 01507 603173

This is a good place to find a whole collection of antique English, French, Portuguese and Spanish beds as they have five barns full of them. All the beds are Victorian, Edwardian, Art Nouveau or Art Deco and range from singles to doubles. Although you can visit every day, including Bank Holidays, you will have to make an appointment first.

Antique Bed Shop
Napier House, Head St, Halstead, Essex CO9 2BT
tel: 01787 477346 • fax: 01787 478757

You will find antique beds here sourced from Portugal, Spain, Italy and France. Most of the beds were made before the turn of the century and all are wooden, although none of them is pine. They are all one-offs and fully restored.

Bed Bazaar
The Old Station, Station Rd, Framlingham,
Woodbridge, Suffolk IP13 9EE
tel: 01728 723756 • fax: 01728 724626

Over 2000 genuine antique metal bedsteads are on
offer here in a choice of styles, periods and sizes. Beds
are restored using the most up-to-date stove-
enamelling process, polishing and lacquering, or they
can be kept close to their original condition with only
a sympathetic cleaning job done.

James Adam Furniture
24 Church St, Woodbridge, Suffolk IP12 2QF
tel: 01394 384471

This is a truly significant collection of beds in several
period styles, many of them faithfully reproduced from
the originals. There are *directoires*, *lit bateaux*, four
posters including a Jacobean style, bergères and
American period-style beds. Most of the beds are
available in any size and there is a variety of
wood finishes.

Lovelace
Broad Piece, Soham, Cambridge, Cambs CB7 5EL
tel: 01353 721339 for stockists • fax: 01353 723257

Lovelace's pine beds are made from good-quality
Redwood timber and designed to last for many
generations. They have a simple range of beds
including a clean-lined four poster, and a spindle bed,
as well as beds with drawers underneath.

central

Brass & Iron Bedsteads
Manor Farm Antiques, Standlake, nr Witney,
Oxon OX8 7RL
tel: 01865 300303

This is a well-established business which has been
dealing with antique beds for nearly thirty-five years.
They offer mostly English beds which were made in
Birmingham in the 1880s and exported all over the
world. Now they have come back home and are being
sold here. There are about twenty at this showroom
that have been restored and another 200 waiting.
They can be finished in black, white, cream or green.
They also have some turn-of-the-century wooden
French beds.

Bylaw
The Old Mill, Brookend St, Ross-on-Wye,
Herefordshire HR9 7EG
tel: 01989 562356 for stockists
fax: 01989 768145

These four poster beds are inspired by original designs
from the early seventeenth century and have
intricately panelled canopies distinctive of the period.
They are, however, made to accept a modern divan
base and mattress and can be made to any size.

Stag Furniture
Haydn Rd, Nottingham, Notts NG5 1DU
tel: 0115 9607121 for stockists
fax: 0115 9691399

Stag's beds are traditional without being based on any
kind of historical design. There is a choice of full beds,
including a sleigh bed, or headboards and most of
them have a complete range of bedroom furniture
designed to go with them.

north east

The Iron Design Co
Summer Carr Farm, Thornton Le Moor,
Northallerton, N.Yorks DL6 3SG
tel: 01609 778143

The Iron Design Co take their inspiration from
Italianate, Rococo and Gothic designs and make
all their beds by hand in a traditional forge. You
can choose from a selection in the brochure or
commission adaptations and one-offs. The finishes
can also be from a standard range, or made to
special order. A mail order service makes the prices
particularly good.

Works of Iron
Crowtrees, 15 Leeds Rd, Rawdon, W.Yorks LS19 6HQ
tel: 0113 250 0150

Carefully restored antique beds that retain the existing
character wherever possible. There is truly a wide
range from simple iron beds to sumptuous wooden and
caned bergères. All prices include a UK mainland
doorstep delivery.

north west

Brass Knight
Cumeragh House, Cumeragh Lane, Whittingham,
Preston, Lancs PR3 2AL
tel/fax: 01772 786666

You will find warehouses full of old Victorian beds
when you visit here. You can either pick one that has
already been restored, or you can choose from those
that are waiting and have it restored for you. All the
beds are 100 per cent genuine and made from either
iron or brass.

Dico
Constantine St, Oldham, Lancs OL4 3AD
tel: 0161 665 1445 for stockists • fax: 0161 627 2948

This company makes a huge selection of period-style
metal beds, some of which are intricately decorated.
They also have a range of pine beds with some quite
unusual styles on offer including a four poster.

wales

Diploma Beds
Bruce Rd, Swansea Industrial Estate, Fforestfach,
Swansea SA5 4HY
tel/fax: 01792 560100 for stockists

If you are besieged by occasional visitors, sleepovers
or just need more storage, take a look at the Diploma
range of ottoman storage and visitors' beds. The
storage beds come in many shapes and sizes including
the celebrated Gullwing, where both sides of the bed
can lift up to reveal storage underneath. The visitors'
beds have an additional bed that swings out from
under the normal bed, to make a single into a double.

Seventh Heaven
Chirk Mill, Chirk, Wrexham County Borough LL14 5BU
tel: 01691 777622 • fax: 01691 777313
e-mail: requests@seventh-heaven.co.uk

This is a family-run major source of antique beds
mostly from 1840–1910. These beds are brought to
Britain from around the Mediterranean, Africa and
elsewhere. Both metal and wooden beds are fully
restored. The showrooms are in three floors of an old
mill and they also house a collection of other
bedroom furniture.

scotland

Martin & Frost
138 MacDonald Rd, Edinburgh EH7 4NN
tel: 0131 557 8787 • fax: 0131 557 8045

With a vast collection of different brand-name beds,
this store has a good selection of divans, iron beds and
pine beds. Brand names such as Vi-Spring, Millbrook,
Dunlopillo and Deptich are well represented. They also
have Belgian Ergo orthopaedic beds and a computer
system which gives you a personal reading so the bed
can be minutely adjusted to suit the needs of your back.

northern ireland

French Antique Beds
The French Warehouse, 72 Dunmore Rd, Spa,
Ballynahinch, Co Down BT24 8PR
tel: 01238 561774

Here's a good selection of antique French provincial
beds, which date from between 1800 and 1900. They're
made from woods such as wild cherry, oak and walnut
and are very decorative. Having been fully restored,
most of them will take king-sized bases and mattresses.

modern & groovy

Futons, fold-away and wall-sprung beds, and simple
frames made from wood and metal can all be classified
as modern and groovy beds and there is something here
to suit all events and practicalities.

south west

Vi-Spring Ltd
Ernesettle Lane, Ernesettle, Plymouth, Devon PL5 2TT
tel: 01752 366311 for stockists • fax: 01752 355109

The first company to manufacture pocketed spring
mattresses. Nowadays each Vi-Spring is highly sensitive,
giving an increased level of support and comfort. Pure
cashmere, lambswool, horsehair and cotton felt from all
over the world are used to increase the comfort and
divans come with a variety of headboards.

south east

After Noah

121 Upper St, London N1 1QP
tel: 0171 359 4281
and
261 Kings Rd, London SW3 5EL
tel: 0171 351 2610
e-mail: mailorder@afternoah.demon.co.uk

As well as selling antique beds (see p.133), After Noah offers two contemporary beds in two different models and three different sizes – double, queen and king. Both wrought from mild steel, their so-called Wavy Bed is billed as a 'timeless classic' with its elegant yet modern lines, whereas the Odeon Bed, with its geometric design, has a thirties feel. All the beds are handmade to order so you have to allow four to eight weeks for delivery.

Art In Iron
New Factory Showroom, Unit F, Bridges Wharf, Bridges Court, off York Rd, Battersea, London SW11 3AD
tel: 0171 924 2332

This showroom has contemporary iron beds, including a modern interpretation of the good old four poster. These are complemented by matching bedside tables, iron curtain rods, mirrors, mattresses and bed linen. All the ironwork can be finished in a choice of four different finishes.

Charles Page
61 Fairfax Rd, Swiss Cottage, London NW6 4EE
tel: 0171 328 9851 • fax: 0171 328 7240

The Italian Molteni beds at this showroom are made along 'healthy sleeping' lines, limiting the number of metal pieces (less metal = fewer ions, and the fewer ions the better!) to make these bio-compatible beds. Bed linens are all made from natural fabrics. The wide range of styles brings the best of Italian contemporary design to the bedroom.

The Conran Shop
Michelin House, 81 Fulham Rd, London SW3 6RD
tel: 0171 589 7401 • fax: 0171 823 7015
and
55 Marylebone High St, London W1M 4HS
tel: 0171 723 2223

You will find quite a selection of very stylish beds here from the contemporary through to the quite traditional. Some have been designed in house and some are from outside designers. Others have developed over a number of years into design classics.

Habitat

196 Tottenham Court Rd, London W1P 9LD
tel: 0171 255 2545
tel: 0645 334433 for branches

Habitat always has a range of well-designed, fashion-conscious beds for children and adults alike. Usually they are nothing outrageous, but easy-to-live-with designs that could well become the classics of the future. They also have slightly more unusual pieces such as their simple rattan beds in single and double sizes.

Heals'
196 Tottenham Court Rd, London W18 9LD
tel: 0171 636 1666 for branches
and
234 Kings Rd, London SW3 5UA
tel: 0171 349 8411
and
Tunsgate, Guildford, Surrey GU1 3QU
tel: 01483 576715

No bed search would ever be complete without a look at what this world-famous furniture emporium has to offer. The beds you will find here are nearly all contemporary and there is a very good selection with some stunning bedroom furniture and accessories to match.

Hulsta
22 Bruton St, London W1X 7DA
tel: 0171 629 4881 for stockists
fax: 0171 409 2417

Contemporary beds in a range of different styles, many of which are matched to built-in bedroom furniture. Different shapes and finishes means there should be something to suit everybody.

IKEA
Brent Park, 2 Drury Way, North Circular Rd, London NW10 0TH
tel: 0181 208 5600 for enquiries and branches

You will find contemporary-style beds here that are a fraction of prices in many other places. You can choose from a range of mattresses and even match your bed with complementary bedroom furniture. However, be warned, their bedding doesn't seem to fit normal British duvets and neither do their pillowcases. Unless you buy their Swedish-sized quilts and pillows, you will be joining the returns queue.

Interlubke
239 Greenwich High Rd, London SE10 8NB
tel: 0171 207 4710 for stockists

Comfort, style and ergonomics are all combined in these contemporary-style German beds. Designs come upholstered or in a choice of veneers, lacquers and colours. One highlight is the Tatami bed which can be moved along the headboard to produce a double or two single beds. The headboard can also be used as an important storage area.

The Iron Bed Company
Terminus Rd, Chichester, W.Sussex PO19 2ZZ
tel: 01243 778999 for stockists
fax: 01243 778123
e-mail: info@ironbed.co.uk

Beds, mattresses, bed linen, accessories and furniture – it's all available from this company. The beds are a mixture of simple and intricate iron styles and one or two wooden ones. If you have a football fan in the family they also offer a bed that can be decorated with footballers wearing their team's colours.

Moriarti's Workshop
High Halden, nr Ashford, Kent TN26 3LY
tel: 01233 850214 for stockists • fax: 01233 850524

This business started when Ian de Fresnes (alias Mr Moriarti) made his own bed. This grew into a range of twenty-two beds, available in seven sizes. All are made from solid pine and styles include bunks, study and storage beds as well as more straightforward doubles and singles. One highlight is a copy of Churchill's Campaign Bed, which makes a useful and attractive sofa bed.

Moss Brothers Metal Designs
26 Sunbury Workshops, Swanfield St, London E2 7LF
tel/fax: 0171 739 2361

Alex and Oliver Moss are both trained and experienced in furniture design and now specialize in contemporary wrought iron designs, many of which are beds. The bed designs at this shop are split between chic minimalism and more flamboyant and decorative styles.

Planet Ironworks
Kings Cross Factory Shop, 23–27 Pancras Rd, London NW1 2QB
tel: 0171 833 3945 • fax: 0171 833 8199

Designed by Cameron Souze, the contemporary metal beds at this showroom include a wide variety of interesting shapes. They also have sofa beds, a chaise longue and a limited amount of living-room furniture.

Purves & Purves
80–81 & 83 Tottenham Court Rd, London W1P 9HD
tel: 0171 580 8223 • fax: 0171 580 8244

Be ready to have your socks knocked off by the beds at this shop including the Italian Domino corner unit, which can be converted from a two-seater sofa, to two single beds, to one double bed. There are also some very simple and very contemporary Italian cherrywood beds and other Italian and Danish designs.

Roset
95 High St, Great Missenden, Bucks HP16 0AL
tel: 01494 865001 for stockists • fax: 01494 866883

This is a collection of imaginative and stylish French designs with attached lighting, removable revolving side tables and exciting shapes. All are designed by contemporary designers.

Sleepeezee
61 Morden Rd, London SW19 3XP
tel: 0181 540 9171 for stockists • fax: 0181 542 0547

One of Britain's most famous bed manufacturers, with the world's best-selling pocketed spring system. Styles include divans with headboards and the Adjustable Collection where either side of the bed can be raised independently for reading, watching TV or eating breakfast in bed. One of the styles also has variable-speed massage motors at foot and head that switch themselves off after you have gone to sleep.

Sterling Wrought Ironworks
Unit 8, Angerstein Business Park, Horn Lane, Greenwich, London SE10 0RT
tel/fax: 0181 305 1874

Handcrafted contemporary wrought iron beds with wooden bases at this outlet. Designs include a modern four poster and up-to-date colonial-style four posters. The company also make matching bedside tables to complement all the styles.

Viaduct
1-10 Summer's St, London EC1R 5BD
tel: 0171 278 8456 • fax: 0171 278 2844

Stunning contemporary Italian beds in pale woods or metal frames including a very modern four poster are on offer at this shop. The wooden beds are in a variety of wonderful shapes and some have fabric headboards. The bases have been designed to accommodate both European and British mattress sizes.

Yakamoto Futon Co
339b Finchley Rd, London NW3 6EP
tel: 0171 794 8034 • fax: 0171 435 4545

If you are into futons you will find a large selection of different types here in addition to futon covers, cushions, beanbags and bolsters. They also have traditional-style mattresses, coloured mattresses in a choice of twenty colours and a futon in a bag, available in a choice of colours.

east

Geoffrey Drayton
104 High St, Epping, Essex CM16 4AF
tel: 01992 573929 • fax: 01992 560818

An exciting selection of contemporary beds including French and Italian designs at this retailer, some of which are dreamed up by design guru Philippe Starck. You will also find a good selection of bed linen, accessories and complementary bedroom furniture.

central

Adrian Reynolds
The Old Chapel, Church Rd, Coalbrookdale,
Shropshire TF8 7NS
tel: 01952 433222 • fax: 01952 433623

You will not see beds like this anywhere else. Contemporary meets fairytale in wonderful concoctions of iron. There is the Crystal Ball Bed which has decorative glass marbles as part of its design, the Curly Four Poster Bed and the Fleur de Lys Scroll Bed. They are all made to order in king, queen and double sizes and accompanied by a small amount of equally inspirational bedroom furniture.

north east

The Futon Shop
168-170 Devonshire St, Sheffield, S.Yorks S3 7SG
tel: 0114 272 1984 • fax: 0114 278 0369
e-mail: sales@futonshop.co.uk

An inspiring mix of futon sofa beds and dramatic contemporary-style beds at this shop. Most of the beds are made from Scandinavian pine, but they also use ash, tulipwood and maple. These can be smooth sanded for a natural look or clear lacquered or stained.

Rest Assured
Mill Forest Way, Grange Rd, Batley,
W.Yorks WF17 6RA
tel: 01924 474477 for stockists • fax: 01924 472736

Modern divans with the Advanced Comfort System. The Comfort Zzone (sic) is found at the core of every Crown bed which supports your body wherever you, and your partner, choose to sleep in the bed. So you shouldn't get that irritating 'roll together' phenomenon, which is the source of so many arguments!

north west

Silentnight
PO Box 9, Barnoldswick, Colne, Lancs BB8 6BL
tel: 01282 850107 for stockists • fax: 01282 813051

Famous for their Hippo and Duck advertising to illustrate the idea that these are beds in which two very different people can sleep and not roll together and squash one another. Their unique continuous coil spring system allows you to sleep right up to the edge of the bed and stops you rolling into the middle.

Slumberland
Salmon Fields, Oldham, Lancs OL2 6SB
tel: 0161 628 2898 for stockists
fax: 0161 628 2895

Slumberland's Posture Springing offers up to seven times more springs than an ordinary bed, which they say gives you a better night's sleep. They have a whole range of products, including adjustable beds, and have just introduced a system where you can change your new bed after forty nights if you feel you have made the wrong choice.

northern ireland

Carpenter & McAllister
Yorkgate Shopping Centre, York St, Belfast BT15 1AQ
tel: 01232 351425 • fax: 01232 351537

An enormous showroom with a huge bed section. Look around and you will find nearly every kind of divan you could ever want with lots of different brand names on offer. There is a price to suit everyone.

Deep Sleep
85 Fyfin Rd, Victoria Bridge, Ftrabame,
Co Tyrone BT82 9JJ
tel: 016626 58006

You will find a large selection of different types of beds here, mostly along the traditional line. Choose from divans, metal, pine or bunk beds. They also have orthopaedic beds for those with back problems.

specialist

Specialist beds, here, are those designed to flip up, fold away, convert into something else – usually in the name of space-saving. If you live in a studio flat, cramped bedsit or simply have a lot of visitors, this could be the answer. We've also slipped in the odd waterbed company!

British Waterbed Co
228 Withycombe Village Rd, Exmouth, Devon EX8 3BD
tel: 01395 268866 for stockists • fax: 01395 267967

This leading waterbed manufacturer makes them in all shapes and sizes including designs with up to eight drawers underneath. The waterbeds are heated and the amount of fluid can be varied to make the bed softer or harder. If you have an asthma sufferer in the family, it is worth remembering that the beds are also allergy free.

The Dormy House
Stirling Park, East Portway Industrial Estate
Andover, Hants SP10 3TZ
tel: 01264 365808 • fax: 01264 366359
e-mail: dormyhouse@compuserve.com

The Dormy House has a headboard upholstering service. The headboards are available in four shapes and covered in thick flame-retardant foam. You can either have them covered in a calico or your own choice of fabric.

Hideaway Beds
Unit 17, Bell Pk, Bell Close, Plympton, Plymouth,
Devon PL7 4JH
tel: 01752 341111 for stockists • fax: 01752 341190

The Swingaway bed is a wallbed designed to be swung into a wall unit when not in use. It is easy to fit and can be installed in an hour. The company also offer BaKare beds, which are touch control, height adjustable.

The London Wallbed Co
430 Chiswick High Rd, Chiswick, London W4 5TF
tel: 0181 742 8200 • fax: 0181 742 8008

Beds which simply fold up into the wall when you need the extra space! As such, they are ideal for studies, TV rooms, spare rooms or playrooms and can be in modern or classical designs. They come in over forty different finishes in all standard mattress sizes and they easily fold away, complete with bedding, so you don't have to remake the bed every time you use it.

The London Waterbed Co
99 Crawford St, London W1H 1AN
tel: 0171 935 1111

Choose from a range of waterbed styles including contemporary Scandanavian models, divans and pine beds complete with head- and footboards. All the beds have a thermostatically controlled heating system.

The Odd Mattress Factory
Cumeragh House, Cumeragh Lane, Whittingham,
Preston, Lancs PR3 2AL
tel/fax: 01772 786666

If you have an awkward-sized bed, this company can make a mattress to fit it. Many of the mattresses go to bed owners who have bought an antique bed which was made in the days before the sizes were regulated, or to people who have an antique foreign bed.

Wallbeds Direct
Suite 622, Linen Hall, 162–168 Regent St,
London W1R 5TB
tel: 0171 434 2066 • fax: 0171 287 2329

Make the most of your space at home by folding the bed into the wall during the day. These beds have 8-inch deep interior sprung mattresses and all-steel mechanisms. You can have off-the-peg or bespoke sizes to suit the dimensions of your particular room. *Home Front*'s Anne McKevitt chose one of their beds to help create more room in a cramped studio flat.

furni

Today's style is all about blending old with new, antique with modern and, if done well, the results can look stunning. Collecting antique or period furniture can be very rewarding if each piece tells a story – family heirlooms, pieces bought at auction, and things picked up in junk shops can all add to the individual nature of your home. No one likes having a house full of mass-produced pieces that look the same as everyone else's.

If you do want to mix styles, follow a few simple rules such as making sure the pieces are of a comparable scale. A massive oak chest of drawers stretching to the ceiling, for example, will dwarf a modern glass and steel nest of tables. If you live in a relatively small house, disproportionately large-scale items can look out of place and it is better to opt for smaller ones. Conversely, large-scale houses and lofts can take impressively sized furniture and will look strange if filled with lots of little bits. If you move from one size of house to another, you will often find that your furniture just doesn't look right. Not many people have the means, yet alone the desire to chuck it all out and start again, so wise choices are a must when building up a capsule of furniture.

ture

key: **hf** shows the product has appeared on
             Home Front

     ✉ shows the company offers a mail
           order service

furniture

Sofas and beds have been covered in the chapter on p.122 so, in this section, you will find all types of other furniture from unfitted bedroom furniture to dining room pieces, occasional tables, chairs, tables, and some conservatory furniture. Materials range from wood and metal to plastic and even paper and we have loosely divided it into a section covering traditional and reproduction furniture, and a modern and groovy section covering contemporary furniture. At the end of the chapter you will find a section on furniture you paint yourself – what is known in the trade as 'blanks'. This is a growing industry which allows you to have some creative input into your own furniture.

traditional & repro

The term 'traditional' when applied to furniture covers a huge range of styles, united by the fact they are usually handcrafted and not mass produced. In this section you will find genuine antique pieces, as well as replicas – replicas being defined as fine copies of old styles of furniture, which are painstakingly accurate in most details. Given the amount of crafts-manship involved, you can expect to pay quite a lot for this level of expertise. On the other hand, 'reproduction' or 'repro' is used to denote items that draw on the look of a particular period without necessarily being accurate in any way. When you are considering buying a piece of furniture, you should always establish what it is you are buying – the price will not always be an indication. A genuine antique may not always be more expensive than a repro pieces as prices vary wildly according to what the item is. Companies offering all the above types of traditional furniture are listed here by region.

south west

Charlie Roe
1 Firs Glen Rd, Talbot Pk, Bournemouth,
Dorset BH9 2LW
tel/fax: 01202 546043
e-mail: charlieroe@clara.net

Viking to Voysey, Burges to Bloomsbury, and Scandanavian to Santa Fe – take your pick from this exciting collection of design and craftsmanship. Whether you want something unusual for the dining room, living room or bedroom, you will definitely have plenty of scope. Gothic, Arts & Crafts and eighteenth-century Norwegian are just some of the styles on offer, or you could buy a replica of the furniture from Van Gogh's bedroom!

The Cotswold Collection
Hangar No 1, Babdown Airfield, Beverston, nr Tetbury,
Glos GL8 8TT
tel: 01666 503555 • fax: 01666 502959

This classic pine furniture includes living room, bedroom and kitchen styles. Their pine dresser can be quite a stunner as there is a choice of a hand-ragged finish in either terracotta, fir green, elderberry or daffodil. The whole range includes over 200 styles of tables and chairs, seven bedroom ranges and other furniture, all available in forty natural wood finishes plus colours.

David & Audrey Martin (Furniture Makers)
Old Chapel Workshop, Woodview, Blakeney Hill,
Blakeney, Glos GL15 4BS
tel: 01594 510514

This couple specializes in exquisitely made rolltop desks of the kind which were so popular in the nineteenth century. The desks are made from North

American hardwoods from sustainable forests and are very solid and heavy, and extremely attractive.

DC Stuart Antiques
34–40 Poole Hill, Bournemouth, Dorset BH2 5PS
tel: 01202 555544 • fax: 01202 295333

This shop specializes in handmade copies of antique furniture in solid mahogany. There is a huge range of different styles of bureaux, desks, chaise longues, chairs and many more items. They even do heavily carved mirrors and towel rails if you are looking for something smaller.

Finds
The Old Gasworks, Chuley Rd, Ashburton,
Devon TQ13 7DH
tel/fax: 01364 654270
e-mail: steve.bradshaw1@virgin.net

The moment you walk into this shop you are offered a cup of good coffee to help you browse around an eclectic mixture of old and repro pine furniture, pots, lamps and South American models. Much of the repro furniture is made from reclaimed wood and some is made in Zimbabwe, some in Slovenia, but all by people using traditional country woodworking skills.

Gentle & Boon
6 St Gluvias St, Penryn, Cornwall TR10 8BL
tel: 01326 377325 for stockists
fax: 01326 378317

This company specializes in handcrafted and hand-painted furniture in the old country styles. The inspiration for their pieces comes from the Cornish-climate weathering they find in their surroundings. The furniture is designed for interiors from cottage to country house and if you don't see something you like in the catalogue they are happy to make bespoke pieces to your requirements.

John Edmonds Cabinet Maker
Buscott Farm, Ashcott, Bridgwater, Somerset TA7 9QP
tel: 01458 210359 • fax: 01458 210096

Britain's first skateboard maker has since turned cabinetmaker and produces everything in wood from fine furniture to traditional four posters, from wooden panelling to farm carts. He supervises from the felled log to the finished product.

Leather Chairs of Bath
11 Bartlett St, Bath, Avon BA1 2QZ
tel: 01225 447920 • fax: 01225 462525

The name is a bit misleading as this shop now offers a selection of desks, tables and chests of drawers in very traditional styles and in a choice of many different timbers including yew, burr elm and mahogany. They also do larger pieces like bookcases and dining tables.

Mark Wilkinson Furniture
Overton House, Bromham, Wilts SN15 2HA
tel: 01380 850004 • fax: 01380 850184

Mark is well known for his unusual kitchen and furniture design, but there is another side to his talent and that is producing one-off pieces of furniture covering a wide range of subjects. A good example of his skill is the carved Cloak Chair where the cloak that hangs over the back of the chair is carved as well as the chair itself.

The Original Book Works Ltd
1 Wilkinson Rd, Cirencester, Glos GL7 1YT
tel: 01285 641664 • fax: 01285 641705

If you like the comforting look of leather-bound books you'll love this range where they 'turn into' clocks, music and video storage boxes, magazine tidies, bedside cabinets and even false doors! These faux books are just part of a long tradition of which even the British Library in London is a part.

The Repro Shop
108 Walcot St, Bath, Avon BA1 5BG
tel: 01225 444404 • fax: 01225 448163

In spite of the name, this shop has a mixture of old and repro furniture. You will find dressers, oak refectory tables, chairs and pine tables. They also have a constant supply of old pews and church chairs.

Rooths
18 Market St, Bradford-on-Avon, Wilts BA15 1LL
tel: 01225 864191

Julia Fleming-Williams specializes in the restoration and gilding of picture frames here, but she also heads a whole network of specialists who restore old furniture. They say that they can restore practically anything you walk through the door with. They have done a good deal of work for the National Trust.

Shabby Chateau

Unit 11, College Farm Buildings, Tetbury Rd,
Cirencester, Glos GL7 6PY
tel: 0836 659208

Pick your way through a large barn full of antique
French country furniture made from European
hardwoods such as ash, oak, beech and chestnut.
There is also some furniture from Spain and many
of the pieces are suitable for use in a kitchen or
dining room.

The Somerset Willow Co

The Wireworks Estate, Bristol Rd, Bridgwater,
Somerset TA6 4AP
tel: 01278 424003 • fax: 01278 446415

If you want some really traditional willow
furniture this is the place to come as they have
been cultivating willow here since the Bronze Age.
Nowadays, this company offers ranges of tables,
chairs, armchairs, log baskets and picnic hampers.
Some of the furniture is made from metal and
willow combined.

Stuart

Barrington Court, Barrington, Ilminster,
Somerset TA19 0NQ
tel: 01460 240349 for stockists • fax: 01460 242069

These copies of the solid oak and walnut furniture
from medieval times to the eighteenth century are
rich in carving and craftmanship. The designs are
reproduced from original surviving pieces,
contemporary paintings, illuminations and drawings,
with some new designs that are particularly suited to
modern living.

William Sheppee

Old Sarum Airfield, Salisbury, Wilts SP4 6BJ
tel/fax: 01722 334454 for stockists

This company offers an eclectic mix of furniture from
different countries and cultures. Indian thakat
furniture rubs elbows with an Ottoman collection,
some European styles and colonial furniture. There is
also a selection of smart, military-style Campaign
furniture.

south east

Adam Richwood

5 Garden Walk, London EC2A 3EQ
tel: 0171 729 0976 • fax: 0171 729 7296

These are fine reproductions of bureaux, bookcases
and desks and the styles include Georgian, Regency
and Colonial. If you work at home but want traditional
furniture in your office, they also make period-style
filing cabinets.

Altfield

Unit 2/22, Chelsea Harbour Design Centre,
Chelsea Harbour, London SW10 0XE
tel: 0171 351 5893 • fax: 0171 376 5667

Among the varied products which Altfield offers at this
shop is a goodly range of reproduction furniture on the
more unusual side. They do quite a selection of faux
bamboo (wood made to look like bamboo), French
styles and a large collection of Japanese-style screens.

Ann May

80 Wandsworth Bridge Rd, Fulham, London SW6 2TF
tel: 0171 731 0862

The owners admit that this is not a smart shop but you
will find treasures, such as original French armoires
and decorative pine mirrors.

Artichoke Interiors

D1, The Old Imperial Laundry, 71–73 Warriner Gardens,
London SW11 4XW
tel: 0171 730 2262 • fax: 0171 978 2457

This company offers a fascinating collection of
nineteenth-century Chinese furniture alongside
porcelain and rugs. They have quite a few bamboo
pieces on show as well as some more exotic furniture.

The Arts & Crafts Furniture Co

49 Sheen Lane, London SW14 8AB
tel: 0181 876 6544

As the name suggests this is where you will find
totally original and beautifully restored pieces of
furniture from famous designers who worked during
the Arts & Crafts period. As well as exquisite pieces,
you will also find a huge wealth of knowledge about
the period.

Ben Norris Cabinetmakers

Knowl Hill Farm, Knowl Hill, Newbury, Berks RG20 4NY
tel: 01635 297950

Ben Norris is a cabinetmaker and restorer of fine antique furniture. He produces totally bespoke pieces, often for kitchens, with unusual colour combinations and designs.

Bevan Funnell

Reprodux House, Norton Rd, Newhaven,
E.Sussex BN9 0BZ
tel: 01273 513762 for stockists • fax: 01273 516735
e-mail: enquiries@bevan-funnell.co.uk

Reproduction furniture made in the traditional manner with an enormous amount of attention to detail, and with the idea that it will be able to sit beside genuine antiques and not look out of place. The pieces are made in a huge variety of woods and styles.

Bombay Duck

16 Malton Rd, London W10 5UP
tel: 0181 964 8881 • fax: 0181 964 8883

Inspired by French designs, this range of iron furniture and accessories is available mail order. The style is ornate and the pieces include occasional tables, chairs, shelves and storage units.

British Antique Replicas

M06 School Close, Queen Elizabeth Avenue,
Burgess Hill, W.Sussex RH15 9RX
tel: 01444 245577 for stockists

If you are looking for something that looks like an antique piece of furniture, but you don't want to pay enormous prices, this company makes replicas of old pieces of furniture. They copy every detail and all the pieces are made by master craftsmen.

Cane Connection

57 Wimbledon Hill Rd, Wimbledon, London SW19 7QW
tel: 0181 947 9152 for stockists • fax: 0181 947 4291

As you would expect from the company name, cane furniture is the name of the game here with pieces suitable for throughout the house, from dining sets to planters. The items come in various styles, colours and finishes.

Chiswick Country Pine

158 Chiswick High Rd, London W4 1PR
tel: 0181 747 0734

This company makes pine furniture but renders it out of the ordinary by specializing in traditional finishes with painted variations which are on show at the shop. More recently they have introduced a whole range of French oak furniture in a rustic style. This also comes in different finishes.

Colin Blythe-Holmes

11 West Way, High Salvington, Worthing,
W.Sussex BN13 3AX
tel: 01903 690639

If you are looking for something really different, this designer/craftsman could provide it for you. He specializes in unique designs which are inspired by the Art Deco and Art Nouveau movements, but also investigates contemporary and futuristic ideas. He can also make faithful replicas of period pieces if this is what you want. If you commission a piece, you can be as involved in the design as you like.

Country Desks

78 High St, Berkhamsted, Herts HP4 2BW
tel: 01442 866446

Home office furniture doesn't have to be modern or contemporary and you can always try to retain a period look in keeping with your other decor if you'd like to. You will find a whole host of traditional-style desks and other home furniture here in a variety of designs and finishes.

David Linley Furniture

60 Pimlico Rd, London SW1W 8LP
tel: 0171 730 7300 • fax: 0171 730 8869

Furniture with the royal touch. If you buy from this company you are involved right from the start in all the initial design discussions. The inspiration for the pieces is drawn from the great cabinetmakers of the past and gives rise to some truly stunning, yet original, pieces.

David Salmon Furniture

555 Kings Rd, London SW6 2EB
tel: 0171 384 2223 • fax: 0171 371 0532

Some of this furniture at this showroom is copied from originals and some is based on features of the period, but all is made to a very high standard including expert craftsmanship such as water gilding and marquetry. Styles range from a copy of Napoleon's Campaign Chair to Sheraton, Queen Anne and Gothic styles, to name a few.

Deacon & Sandys
Hillcrest Farm Oast, Hawkhurst Rd, Cranbrook,
Kent TN17 3QD
tel: 01580 713775 • fax: 01580 714056

If you are into seventeenth- and eighteenth-century
English furniture, this company does some good
reproductions. The pieces range from dressers to
chairs and are mostly made from oak. Deacon &
Sandys can also do wood panelling and individual
commissions.

The Dining Room Shop
63–64 White Hart Lane, Barnes,
London SW13 0PZ
tel: 0181 878 1020 • fax: 0181 876 2367

This specialist stocks all kinds of furniture for the
room where you eat. From country to formal styles,
from pricey antiques to modest pieces and from
Regency antiques through bespoke, modern and
repro, they really do have examples of everything.
They also have a wide range of silver, glass, china,
napkins and all sorts of tableware to deck your dining
room out in style.

The Dorking Desk Shop
41 West St, Dorking, Surrey RH4 1BU
tel: 01306 883327 • fax: 01306 875363

If you are looking for an antique desk, this shop is well
worth travelling to. They stock more than one hundred
old desks and other specialized writing furniture from
small knee-hole jobs to huge, impressive partner's
desks. You will also find roll-tops, secretaires and
bureaux here.

The Dormy House
Stirling Pk, East Portway Industrial Estate,
Andover, Hants SP10 3TZ
tel: 01264 365808 • fax: 01264 366359
e-mail: EI12@aol.com

Traditional furniture by post with this mail order
catalogue. Screens, occasional tables, storage cabinets
and small chairs are all on offer as well as some lovely
painted and plain, traditional Swedish-style tables,
cupboards and shelves.

Ducal Ltd
Andover, Hants SP10 5AZ
tel: 01264 333666 for stockists • fax: 01264 334046

Traditional pine furniture in a range of designs and
finishes, with a host of different pieces available.
They also do a Riverdale collection, which is finished
in subtle, ivory tones and designed along quite
simple lines.

Eighty Eight Antiques
88 Golborne Rd, London W10 5PS
tel: 0181 960 0827

This shop has a large amount of Victorian stripped
pine, especially pieces for kitchens and bedrooms.
Most of their furniture is original but they do offer
some reproduction and made-up pieces. They also
make kitchens, mainly in the painted Shaker style.

Emily Readett-Bayley
St Lukes Old Rectory, 107 Grange Rd, London SE1 3BW
tel: 0171 231 3939 for stockists • fax: 0171 231 4499
e-mail: contact@emily-readett-b.demon.co.uk

An exciting designer who produces furniture and
accessories in bamboo, reclaimed teak, shell,
palmwood and mother of pearl. She has workshops in
Indonesia and her work is heavily influenced by the
materials and designs from this part of the world.

Ercol Furniture
London Rd, High Wycombe, Bucks HP13 7AE
tel: 01494 521261 for stockists • fax: 01494 462467
e-mail: sales@ercol.com

Ercol offers solid wood furniture in a huge variety of
different pieces and traditional designs, which are not
period pieces. The furniture is available in four
different finishes and the pieces range from full dining
suites to small items of occasional furniture.

Fens Restoration & Sales
46 Lots Rd, London SW10 0QF
tel: 0171 352 9883

If you have furniture that needs restoring, this shop
specializes in it. They will restore all kinds of furniture
and can strip and sandblast, French polish, or apply
different finishes to bring it back to its original
condition. They also restore old ironwork and sell
restored furniture as well as being able to make pieces
to order from old wood.

Freud Ltd
198 Shaftesbury Ave, London WC2H 8JL
tel: 0171 831 1071 • fax: 0171 831 3062
e-mail: fanmail@freudlemos.com

You must take a look at this showroom if you are a Mackintosh fan. They have a range of Mackintosh-style chairs from stock and tables are made to order. They will give you a 10 per cent discount on the table price if you also buy six chairs.

Frost's
205 West End Lane, London NW6 1XF
tel: 0171 372 5788

Diana Frost is an antique dealer who specializes in cane, bamboo and wicker and has a wealth of knowledge in this field. She has some wonderful pieces on offer at any one time including originals from the Victorian era through to the 1930s. If you are looking for something unique, this could well be the place you will find it.

The General Trading Co
144 Sloane St, London SW1X 9BL
tel: 0171 730 0411 • fax: 0171 823 4624

This shop is quite an experience as it occupies four Victorian townhouses and is full of furniture, gifts, accessories and even a restaurant. On the furniture side you will find fine British furniture including Georgian and Victorian antique pieces and non-period furniture made by leading craftsmen to traditional designs.

Grand Illusions
2–4 Crown Rd, St Margarets, Twickenham, Middx TW1 3EE
tel: 0181 744 1046

A whole collection of country-style furniture in French and New England styles is on offer from this showroom. Paint finishes in lovely muted colours are a feature and there is a whole selection of accessories, including lighting, pottery and wooden utensils, to go with them.

John Elbert Furniture Workshops
Royal Victoria Patriotic Building, Trinity Rd, London SW18 3SX
tel: 0181 874 3361

Each cabinetmaker who works here carries every individual project through from beginning to end and they rarely make the same piece twice. They use traditional English timbers and sustainable exotic timbers coupled with the latest laminates and finishing techniques to create unique pieces. Every item is made and finished by hand.

Jon Mills at Tin Star Studios
38 Cheltenham Place, Brighton, Sussex BN1 4AB
tel: 01273 621822

Jon Mills makes highly unusual pieces of furniture. He works almost completely in steel to produce fantastical items that are real works of art. He is happy to be commissioned and is open to discussing your ideas.

Julian Chichester Designs
Unit 12, 33 Parsons Green Lane, London SW6 4HH
tel: 0171 371 9055 • fax: 0171 371 9066

These are truly beautiful and unusual traditional designs, many of which are highly decorated. Several of the pieces are copies from the Regency era in Britain but there is also a wealth of designs from other periods and countries. The majority are gilded, but not all.

Kingshill Designs
Kitchener Works, Kitchener Rd, High Wycombe, Bucks HP11 2SJ
tel: 01494 463910 • fax: 01494 451555

This is traditional Swedish furniture copied from the great country houses of Sweden. All the pieces are made in the traditional manner with hand-carved details. The furniture consists mainly of bedroom and dining room pieces.

Mark Furse Design
Hulkes Lane, 351 High St, Rochester, Kent ME1 1EE
tel/fax: 01634 830401

Provide this company with a space, however large or small, tell them your ideas and your budget and they will be happy to discuss with you what kind of bespoke furniture they can offer. They will advise on a wide variety of timbers and how to combine these with other materials such as glass, metals, plastics and stone. They can even make their own handles and hinges.

Marks & Spencer

tel: 0345 902902 for your local home store
or mail order

If you have never been to a Marks & Spencer home store, you might not have thought of buying your furniture here, but their mail order catalogue shows that they have quite an extensive range of wooden and metal collections for all parts of the house.

Millside Cabinet Makers
The Moor, Melbourn, Royston, Herts SG8 6ED
tel: 01763 261870 • fax: 01763 261673

Each individual piece is handmade in English oak or English cherry and many are based on early sixteenth- and seventeenth-century designs. The furniture is made as a one-off piece to your own specifications.

Nordic Style

109 Lots Rd, London SW10 0RN
tel: 0171 351 1755 • fax: 0171 351 4966

The popular traditional Swedish look is available from this company who import and manufacture Swedish painted furniture, simple fabrics and decorative Swedish accessories. At this showroom choose from a range of beds, tables, chairs, desks and others.

The Old Forge & Foundry
Unit 7, The Looe, Reigate Rd, Ewell, Epsom, Surrey KT17 3DB
tel/fax: 0181 287 2965

On show here is wrought iron furniture that would look good in either period or more modern interiors. The individually handmade and finished pieces range through dining tables, coffee tables, sofas and chairs, wine racks and curtain rods.

Out of the Wood
Rowan Cottage, Gascoigne Lane, Ropley, Alresford, Hants SO24 0BT
tel/fax: 01962 773353

Strong, traditional-style furniture that is designed to be functional and unique. All the pieces are made from MDF and can be finished in a wide variety of colours and finishes. The designers generally work to commission and can take their starting point from colour samples of your curtains, carpets or existing furniture.

Paperchase

213 Tottenham Court Rd, London W1P 9AF
tel: 0171 580 8496 for branches

This may seem a surprising place to buy furniture if you are used to getting your stationery here. But if you look on the second floor they have a small but very attractive selection of bamboo furniture including chairs and screens.

Parsons Table Company
362 Fulham Rd, London SW10 9UU
tel: 0171 352 7444

French and English furniture is the speciality of the house at this shop. All the furniture is copied from original designs dating from the period between 1670 and 1840.

Phelps
133–135 St Margarets Rd, East Twickenham, Middx TW1 1RG
tel: 0181 892 1778 • fax: 0181 892 3661

If you are looking for a genuine original piece of furniture from the Victorian age up to the 1920s, this shop is definitely one of the 'finds' you should not miss. An antique dealer with a great portfolio and you don't necessarily have to spend mega-bucks here.

The Pier

200 Tottenham Court Rd, London W1P 0AD
tel: 0171 637 7001 • fax: 0171 637 3332
tel: 0171 814 5004 for stockist and mail order
tel: 0171 814 5020 for branches

This is just one of a range of nationwide shops that are all backed by a mail order brochure. Along with accessories they do plenty of furniture in mostly classic styles. These include rattan, iron, and the two combined. There is also the Santa Fe range which is a collection of chunky distressed pine which is given an extra rustic look by the addition of hand-forged iron handles.

R&D Davidson
Romsey House, 51 Maltravers St, Arundel, W.Sussex BN18 9BQ
tel: 01903 883141 for stockists • fax: 01903 883914
e-mail: rddavidson@btinternet.com

The brochure shows over 110 standard models of fine furniture, but special commissions are also an important part of the company's work. The pieces are copies of designs ranging from the eighteenth century, through Regency and Biedermeier styles, to the more recent Art Deco period.

Restall, Brown & Clennell

120 Queensbridge Rd, London E2 8PD
tel: 0171 739 6626 • fax: 0171 739 6123

This family business has been making fine English traditional furniture for four generations and can offer furniture in practically every traditional style. They do concentrate on Sheraton-style satinwood decorated furniture, and mahogany and walnut pieces from the Queen Anne and Georgian periods. They also have a superb Art Deco collection. Examples of their work can also be seen at Harrods.

Romanesque

258 Archway Rd, Highgate, London N6 5AX
tel: 0181 245 9414

Danielle Romer specializes in designing furniture to be hand-painted and gilded by herself in wonderful, romantic designs. She also restores antique furniture to sell alongside her own creations at this showroom.

Shaker

322 Kings Rd, London SW3 5UH
tel: 0171 352 3918
and
25 Harcourt St, London W1H 1DT
tel: 0171 724 7672

Pure Shaker styles include cabinets, bureaux, dressers and wardrobes at this shop. The distinctive Shaker hanging shelves are also included in the range and most of the pieces are either made in cherry or maple. They also have chairs, large and small tables and, of course, the distinctive Shaker boxes and Shaker-style rocking chairs.

Tim Wood Furniture

93 Mallinson Rd, London SW11 1BL
tel: 0171 924 1511 • fax: 0171 924 1522

All Tim Wood's freestanding furniture is custom built to exacting standards. Each piece is uniquely designed and crafted from the first drawing to suit individual requirements. The designs use clean lines and beautiful woods.

Trading Boundaries

Lady Cross Farm, Hollow Lane, Dormansland, nr Lingfield, Surrey RH7 6PB
tel: 01342 870010 • fax: 01342 811483

A half-and-half mixture of antique and reproduction Indian furniture, the collection at this showroom is imported directly from the sub-continent, which helps to keep the prices very reasonable. You will find everything from coffee tables to dining suites in tropical woods, and brass and ironware. They also do some beautifully painted Indian furniture.

Trevor Lawrence Classic Oak Furniture

105–107 Station Rd East, Oxted, Surrey RH8 0AX
tel/fax: 01883 730300

Trevor Lawrence provides a very broad cabinetmaking operation here from classic oak tables and desks in the traditional style to kitchens. They also undertake commissions for furniture and panelling and restore and repair antiques. In fact, there seems to be little they don't do – they also provide a soft furnishing service.

Villa Garnelo

26 Pimlico Rd, London SW1W 8LJ
tel: 0171 730 0110 • fax: 0171 730 0220

The fine, hand-finished furniture at this shop is made by experienced craftsmen in Valencia and uses high-quality woods and veneers including cherry, mahogany, Spanish walnut, olive and sycamore. Carlos Gil, the inspiration behind the company, says they strive to look at the past and refresh it for the present.

Villiers Brothers

Fyfield Hall, Fyfield, Essex CM5 0SA
tel: 01277 899680 • fax: 01277 899008

Beautifully designed and original pieces of furniture, each one inspired by tradition but with a twist, are this company's hallmark. Console tables with wrought iron or cast bronze bases and tops in a choice of maple, limestone or fumed oak are a particular speciality. There are highly ornate chairs like mini-thrones, along with ones fashioned of a simple sweep of birch ply, which looks extremely comforable. The company is led by brothers Tim and Harry Villiers and if you would like something in particular made, they can also provide drawings and make up prototypes before the piece is commissioned.

The West Sussex Antique Timber Co

Reliance Works, Newpound, Wisborough Green,
W.Sussex RH14 0AZ
tel: 01403 700139 • fax: 01403 700936

The best of reclaimed timbers are used to make a wide range of traditional-style furniture. From kitchens to dining tables, to bookcases – any piece is possible. It will be made by craftsmen to your own individual specifications. They also offer flooring, joinery services and barn interiors here.

Wildwood Antiques

Yard Farm, Bradsholt, nr Blackmoor, Liss,
Hants GU33 6DE
tel: 01420 489303

This company specializes in antique French country furniture mainly from the mid-eighteenth to the mid-nineteenth centuries. Much of this timber furniture is made from cherrywood and walnut and is fully restored in the workshops on the premises.

William Bartlett & Son

Sheraton Works, PO Box 41, Grafton St,
High Wycombe, Bucks HP12 3AL
tel: 01494 526491 for stockists

If you are looking for furniture that is made in the traditional Regency style, don't miss seeing this company's offerings. They tend to work in a choice of mahogany or yew finishes on fine pieces of furniture.

Wood Bros

Marsh Lane, London Rd, Ware, Herts SG12 9QH
tel: 01920 469241 for stockists • fax: 01920 464388
e-mail: enquiries@oldcharm.co.uk

The Old Charm collection is based on Tudor and Elizabethan designs with their full decorative carvings. No two pieces are ever identical as they are all hand-carved with great attention to detail. Oak is used throughout and there are many pieces like video cabinets that are more suited to modern homes than Tudor ones!

east

Arthur Brett & Sons

Hellesdon Park Rd, Drayton High Rd, Norwich NR6 5DR
tel: 01603 486633 for stockists • fax: 01603 788984
e-mail: enquiries@arthur-brett.com

Five generations of the Brett family have been involved in making fine English furniture, the inspiration of which comes from 'The Golden Age' of British furniture design – the eighteenth century. Arthur Brett now has a core range of over 200 pieces, but they will also undertake special commissions. They have showrooms in London and Norwich and produce a very comprehensive catalogue.

The Cane Collection

70 Fred Dannatt Rd, Mildenhall, Suffolk IP28 7RD
tel: 01638 714832 for stockists • fax: 01638 510840

This cane furniture is largely for conservatories but there is also quite a choice of dining sets and armchairs. The styles vary a good deal from sturdy frames of heavily twisted cane with delicate weaving on the chair backs to the simpler styles.

Country & Eastern

8 Redwell St, Norwich, Norfolk NR2 4SN
tel: 01603 623107 • fax: 01603 758108

If you are looking for robust cane furniture to use in your conservatory, living room or kitchen, it is a speciality of this company. Their furniture is made from tough pulut cane and has a natural scrubbed finish, rather than the shiny, varnished version. Because the furniture is imported directly the prices are good too. They also have a branch in Kensington, London.

Dickson of Ipswich

Baird Close, Hadleigh Rd Industrial Estate, Ipswich,
Suffolk IP2 0HB
tel: 01473 252121 • fax: 01473 212941

As a maker of exclusive reproduction furniture, Dickson has an enormous range with some real stunners, such as an oak card table covered in antique leather and inlaid dining tables. All the furniture is handmade and French-polished by hand. They also accept commissions.

James Murdoch Smith

New Barns, St Neots Rd, Abbotsley, St Neots,
Huntingdon, Cambs PE19 4UU
tel: 01767 677748

This is an exciting designer who takes much of his inspiration from the Arts & Crafts, Mackintosh and Art Deco movements. However, these are not slavish copies, but contain a lot of the designer's own creative impulses. They are mostly made in pine and other softwoods, and painted, distressed or waxed.

Lloyd Loom of Spalding
Wardentree Lane, Pinchbeck, Spalding,
Lincs PE11 3SY
tel: 01775 712111 for stockists • fax: 01775 761255

Famous worldwide, this woven furniture is made from paper yarn but is surprisingly hardwearing. Chairs, desks and beds are all part of the line-up and there is now a choice of twenty different colours. Although most of the styles are traditional, they have also introduced a small range of designer, contemporary items that are well worth a look.

Lovelace
Broad Piece, Soham, Cambridge, Cambs CB7 5EL
tel: 01353 721339 for stockists • fax: 01353 723257

Lovelace make fine Redwood furniture in the traditional way, with the idea that it is going to last many generations. They only buy timber from professionally managed pine forests in Northern Scandinavia. The whole range is large and includes dining, bedroom and occasional furniture.

Titchmarsh & Goodwin
Back Hamlet, Ipswich, Suffolk IP3 8AL
tel: 01473 252158 • fax: 01473 210948
e-mail: Teeangee@BTInternet.com

Woodturners, carvers, cabinetmakers, glaziers and gilders all work under one roof in the workshops here to produce fine, handmade furniture in mahogany, oak, yew, birch and walnut. They also have a range of chinoiserie. Each piece is polished by hand and goes through eighteen polishing processes. There is now a London showroom at Chelsea Harbour.

central

Andrew Varah
Little Walton, nr Pailton, Rugby, Warks CV23 0QL
tel: 01788 833000 • fax: 01788 832527
e-mail: varah@quartet.co.uk

Andrew Varah and other cabinetmakers specialize in designing one-off pieces of furniture in Biedermeier, Art Deco and Art Nouveau styles, along with many other periods, using the same materials and details that would have been used on furniture from that time. Andrew makes contemporary furniture as well which is also on show here.

Brights of Nettlebed
Kingston House, Nettlebed, nr Henley on Thames,
Oxon RG9 5DD
tel: 01491 641115 for branches • fax: 01491 641864

Antique replica and reproduction furniture that includes a variety of oak, cherry, walnut and mahogany pieces as well as traditional upholstery and office furniture. Cabinetmakers are able to reproduce virtually any piece of furniture in a period style and to your own specifications.

Bylaw
The Old Mill, Brookend St, Ross on Wye,
Herefordshire HR9 7EG
tel: 01989 562356 for stockists • fax: 01989 768145

If you are looking for seventeenth- and eighteenth-century-style furniture, Bylaw draws all its inspirations from these periods. The main style is based on the country furniture makers of that time who worked in solid oak and fruitwoods. They offer a choice of timber, size, colour and finish.

Charmwood Furniture
Cannon Business Park, Gough Rd, Cosely,
W.Midlands WV14 8XR
tel: 01902 565554 for stockists

This company offers a selection of casual dining sets made from rubber wood and carrying tiled tops. They are available in a variety of finishes including blue and green. They have traditional and some more contemporary styles that are sourced from around the world.

The Cotswold Co
High St, Bourton on the Water, Glos GL54 2ZZ
tel/fax: 0990 502 233

This is a mainly mail order company although they do have a shop in the Cotswolds if you are local. Otherwise their mail order catalogue has quite a diverse range of country-style furniture including rattan and wood, rattan and iron, and Mexican rustic wood furniture.

Grange
PO Box 18, Stamford, Lincs PE9 2FY
tel: 01780 54721 for stockists • fax: 01780 54718

Grange offers an eclectic range of traditional French furniture from nineteenth-century-style French cherrywood, to rattan and some ironwork.

Haselbech Interiors
Haselbech Hill, Northants NN6 9LL
tel: 0604 685360

These fine antique replicas are handmade in mahogany, yew, walnut and solid oak to original seventeenth- and eighteenth-century designs. Each piece is individually made and, because they are replicas rather than reproduction, they will offer you the look of an antique at a fraction of the price.

Parker Knoll
London Rd, Chipping Norton, Oxon OX7 5AX
tel: 01494 557850 for stockists

A whole range of fitted and unfitted living, dining and bedroom furniture in generally traditional styles. There is also some home office furniture. A variety of woods and finishes is used for a choice of styles.

Pukka Palace

The Market Hall, Craven Arms,
Shropshire SY7 9NY
tel: 0345 666660

You will find a wealth of mail order furniture and accessories here, often with colonial overtones. There are Gothic styles, Empire-style furniture and wonderful canvas screens to name but a few. The catalogue is fun too and a good read!

Richard Kimbell
Rockingham Rd, Market Harborough, Leics LE16 7QE
tel: 01858 433444 for stockists

This company offers solid pine furniture for home offices, living rooms, bedrooms and kitchens. They do a Gothic range for kitchens and an attractive wooden sofa.

Robin Clarke Furniture
Keepers House, Brockmanton, nr Leominster,
Herefordshire HR6 0QU
tel: 01568 760272

Traditional rocking chairs, side chairs and kitchen chairs are joined by some more unusual designs, such as the writing chair with an integral table and drawer. Robin Clarke also makes narrow-backed Arts & Crafts-style chairs from locally grown oak or elm and cherry. He can also make tables and other items in the same style.

Stag Furniture
Haydn Rd, Nottingham, Notts NG5 1DU
tel: 0115 960 7121 for stockists • fax: 0115 969 1399

Stag offers a full range of living and dining furniture, occasional furniture and bedroom furniture in timber finishes from light beech to rich cherry. The styles are traditional without being based on any particular historical period.

The Village Idiot
12 Hewell Rd, Barnt Green, Worcs B45 8NE
tel/fax: 0121 447 7237

Don't be put off by the name, these farmhouse tables are craftsman-made in a traditional style. The tops are chunky and made from genuine nineteenth-century timber and the bases are painted in a choice of twelve colours created by paint effect specialist Annie Sloan to give an authentic period look. There is also a range of colour-matched chairs.

William Bartlett & Son
Sheraton Works, Grafton St, High Wycombe,
Bucks HP12 3AL
tel: 01494 526491 for stockists • fax: 01494 451021

The Strongbow Collection of mahogany and yew traditional furniture has been made for five generations and reflects styles from the eighteenth century and Regency periods.

Wychwood Design
Viscount Court, Brize Norton, Oxon OX18 3QQ
tel: 01993 851435 • fax: 01993 851575

Wychwood have a very stylish collection of period-style pieces of furniture including Louis XV tables and armchairs, bamboo and Chinese styles, and Empire styles. They also make enormous dining room tables and some bedroom furniture. If you don't see what you like here in the set range, they can always make a one-off piece for you.

north east

Jarabosky
Old Station Yard, Exley Lane, Elland, W.Yorks HX5 0SW
tel: 01422 311922 for stockists • fax: 01422 374053

What has happened to all those redundant wooden railway sleepers that were put down in Colonial Africa?

Jarabosky is now using them to make unusual furniture. The timbers used were Australian and Asian woods and have been well seasoned under the African sun. They make interesting tables, desks and storage furniture.

Tansu
Skopos Mills, Bradford Rd, Batley, W.Yorks, WF17 5LZ
tel: 01924 422391 • fax: 01924 443856
e-mail: tansu@tansu.co.uk

If you like Japanese design you are going to love this place. They claim to have the largest collection of antique Japanese furniture in the world outside Japan. They have more than 10 000 square feet of display space and 700–800 pieces of furniture mostly from the Edu (1603–1868) and the Meiji (1868–1912) periods.

north west

Cape Country Furniture
114 Foregate St, Chester, Cheshire CH1 1HB
tel: 01535 600483 for stockists

Handcrafted in South Africa, this is very English-style, traditional pine furniture. Freestanding kitchen pieces are joined by a bedroom range, a living room range and a collection of furniture made from railway sleepers.

Downes Furniture Co
Criftin House, Wentnor, Bishop's Castle,
Shropshire SY9 5ED
tel/fax: 01588 650270

Mr Downes is a skilled cabinetmaker who makes fine English furniture in the English country house tradition. He is able to take on any ideas you may have, such as the design, timber, colour and finish, and produces pieces like George III mahogany dining chairs, Hepplewhite benches and Sheraton-style dining tables.

Kiani
Kiani House, Kitling Rd, Knowsley, Prescot,
Merseyside L34 9HN
tel: 0151 549 0101 for stockists • fax: 0151 549 0830

Kiani are generally involved with making rattan and wicker furniture but they do have some metal designs as well. Much of their repertoire is fairly traditional

but they do have an ultra-modern German Schutz collection of living and dining furniture.

The Old Pine Store
Coxons Yard, Ashbourne, Derbyshire DE6 1FG
tel/fax: 01335 344112

Traditional pine furniture made from reclaimed wood. Most pieces can be made to individual sizes and to suit your requirements. Furniture can also be made to your own design if you are feeling creative. Designs on show here include dressers, bedroom furniture, tables and chairs.

Traditional Living Collection
The Coach House, 114 Barlow Moor Rd, Didsbury,
Manchester M20 2PN
tel: 0161 446 2022 • fax: 0161 445 3460

The copies of sturdy eighteenth-century country furniture on show here are made from MDF and then painted in Shaker blue, dark green or dark red. Designs include some really unusual pieces such as a hooded Lambing Chair (to keep draughts away from sick lambs being nursed by the fire), a spectacular Gothic Armchair and a child's rocking chair which can be personalized with a name.

wales

Home Workshop Direct
Coed Cae Lane, Pontyclun CF7 9DX
tel: 01443 239444

You will find mail order furniture in two styles here. The Mediterranean collection is a range of country-style furniture in solid wood with escutcheon plates, handles and hinges all in heavy iron, while the Celtic Collection is along simpler, lighter lines but still in solid wood.

Laura Ashley
PO Box 19, Newtown, Powys SY16 1DZ
tel: 0990 622116 for mail order and branches
tel: 0800 868100 for their Home Furnishing Catalogue

Laura Ashley offers a small, but attractive, selection of handcrafted casual country furniture in three styles: painted in ivory, painted and pine, or natural antiqued pine. The pieces include a dresser, tables, chairs, bookcases and trunks. They also have two gilt mirrors.

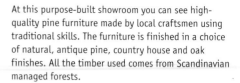

scotland

Jonathan Avery Design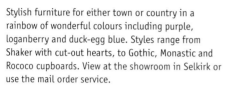
The Old Joinery, Selkirk TD7 5LU
tel: 01750 22377 • fax: 01750 22377

Stylish furniture for either town or country in a
rainbow of wonderful colours including purple,
loganberry and duck-egg blue. Styles range from
Shaker with cut-out hearts, to Gothic, Monastic and
Rococo cupboards. View at the showroom in Selkirk or
use the mail order service.

The Morris Furniture Co
147 Drakemire Drive, Glasgow G45 9SS
tel: 0141 634 9000 for stockists • fax: 0141 634 4044

Traditional styles combine with traditional methods
of furniture making here to produce a range of dining
room, living room and occasional furniture. This is
available in a variety of veneers and it is the company's
policy only to buy from sustainable sources.

northern ireland

Carpenter & McAllister
Yorkgate Shopping Centre, York St, Belfast BT15 1AQ
tel: 01232 351425 • fax: 01232 351537

You will find a huge selection of traditional-style
furniture in this busy retail outlet, as well as some
contemporary lines. The pieces include dining room
sets, traditional bedroom furniture as well as other
kinds of furniture.

Country Furnisher
Mill House, 66 Carsonstown Rd, Saintfield,
Ballynahinch BT24 7EB
tel: 01238 510398

You will find an enchanting mix of traditional Irish
country and French provincial furniture at this shop.
All the pieces are genuine originals but have been fully
restored. The Irish pieces are pine dressers, farmhouse
tables and corner cupboards, some painted and some
stripped. The French pieces are made from woods such
as cherrywood.

Pinewood Furniture
5–7 Fountain Place, Ballymena BT43 6DX
tel: 01266 46111

At this purpose-built showroom you can see high-
quality pine furniture made by local craftsmen using
traditional skills. The furniture is finished in a choice
of natural, antique pine, country house and oak
finishes. All the timber used comes from Scandinavian
managed forests.

modern & groovy

We are lucky in this country that the cutting edge of
modern design is quickly filtered down to the high-street
stores and available for all, rather than remaining the
exclusive preserve of the rich. Modern furniture is a huge
term, which spans the breadth of anything that plays
around with form and function, from stacking chairs to
collapsible tables, using materials as diverse as plastic,
resins and paper.

The ingenious design of some objects may even at
first obscure their actual purpose – is it a chair, is it a
table? Modern designers often revel in play as well
as practicality. In this section, you will find everything
from cult design classics, particularly European ones,
which have withstood the test of time – from Arne
Jacobsen and Charles Eames designs to works by new,
barely known designers who may themselves become
household names. Perhaps rather inevitably, the shops
do tend to congregate around London and become
sparser in other regions – so we have listed the outlets
alphabetically rather than by region.

About Face
22 Princess Victoria St, Clifton Village, Bristol,
Avon BS8 4BU
tel: 0117 923 7405

Inflatable furniture in day-glo colours brightens up
this shop. This sort of furniture was first seen in the
1960s and has since sprung up everywhere on every
market stall. This is good quality and unlikely to spring
a leak on the first sitting.

Aram Designs
3 Kean St, London WC2B 4AT
tel: 0171 240 3933

Wander in off the street and you might not be quite
sure whether you're in a shop or someone's very
stylish pad. There are some very exclusive items here,
such as sofas by Charles Eames and Eileen Gray.

Ben Huggins Ltd

Pound Corner, Whitestone, Exeter EX4 2HP
tel: 01647 61191 • fax: 01647 61134

Ben Huggins's furniture designs are innovative and
often ingenious, yet functional. He employs a variety
of materials from marine birch ply to recycled plastic,
as well as more expensive materials. All his furniture
can be made to order. He's definitely a name
to watch.

Bisca Design

Shaw Moor Farm, Harome, York,
N.Yorks YO6 5HZ
tel: 01439 771 702 • fax: 01439 771002
e-mail: bisca@easynet.co.uk

Mail order only, Bisca have an unusual range of
steel-framed, zinc-plated furniture. The chairs are
available with laminate, mesh or upholstered
seats and, for tables, choose from beech, ash or
toughened glass tops. All the furniture is classically
elegant but is distinguished by some quirky
details – perhaps with chunky legs that splay at the
bottom. Many of the chairs have the company's
trademark wavy curls and gradually flaring uprights.
The prices aren't cheap but they are beautifully
hand-forged pieces.

Cargo Homeshop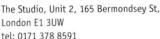

JW Carpenter Ltd, Dormer Rd,
10 Park Industrial Estate, Thame, Oxon OX9 3HD
tel: 01844 261800 for branches

Don't overlook this shop for stylish design – it has a
version of the Paloma chair in beech which is
considerably cheaper than anyone else's.

Century

68 Marylebone High St, London NW1 3AQ
tel: 0171 487 5100

This tiny shop is packed with pieces of post-war
American furniture that have become design classics.
They sometimes have originals of the Arne Jacobsen
'Ant' chair, which gained its notoriety from having
Christine Keeler sit provocatively astride it.

Chairs Designs Ltd

George House, 10b George Rd, Guildford,
Surrey GU1 4NP
tel: 01483 304648 • fax: 01483 440019
e-mail: sales@chairs-designs.co.uk

Weird and wonderful one-offs can be found here as
well as a small standard range. There are sofas made
to look like a huge pair of red lips and chairs kitted
out in leopard skin. Popular with interior designers
and architects.

The Coast Collection

The Studio, Unit 2, 165 Bermondsey St,
London E1 3UW
tel: 0171 378 8591

This small company has produced a stylish and simple
range of furniture, lamps and mirrors. It is run by
partners David Coote and Atlanta Bartlett who use
mostly birch marine ply to create 1950s-inspired
sideboards and coffee tables. They deliberately keep
to a limited range of colours – Lilac, Pistachio,
Sky Blue and Rosewood. Their Ark Sideboard has
appeared in virtually every style magazine. The
prices aren't cheap but you do get a beautiful piece
of furniture.

Coexistence

288 Upper St, London N1 2TZ
tel: 0171 354 8817 • fax: 0171 354 9610

A small shop that looks like someone's storage bunk –
with pieces all put in randomly together. On closer
inspection, design classics by the likes of Alvar Aalto
can be found. The shop deals mostly in contract work
but it will source pieces for you.

The Conran Shop

Michelin House, 81 Fulham Rd, London SW3 6RD
tel: 0171 589 7401 for branches • fax: 0171 823 7015

It is always a pleasure to visit The Conran Shop as it is
full of beautifully designed pieces that are highly
covetable. Not as cutting edge perhaps as it once was,
but still at the forefront of modern design.

Designer's Guild

267–271 & 275–277 Kings Rd, London SW3 5EN
tel: 0171 243 7300 • fax: 0171 243 7710
tel: 0171 351 5775 for general enquiries

As well as their sofas, Designer's Guild have quirky
things dreamt up by the leading lights of British
design, such as a chest of drawers fashioned from tuna
cans. It's mostly very stylish including lots of Phoenix
chairs in bright colours down in the basement.

Geoffrey Drayton
85 Hampstead Rd, London NW1 2PL
tel: 0171 387 5840

A very classy shop which is a pleasure to wander round – even if you're just looking. All the greats are here including B&B Italia and Ingo Maurer.

Habitat
196 Tottenham Court Rd, London W1P 9LD
tel: 0171 255 2545
tel: 0645 334433 for branches

Habitat can always be relied on for its simple, clean lines and versatile shapes. There are always well-designed, reasonably priced chairs, tables, cabinets and shelving in stock that can form the main staples of any home.

Haus
23–25 Mortimer St, London W1N 7RJ
tel: 0171 255 2557 • fax: 0171 255 1331
e-mail: info@haus.co.uk

Committed to 'displaying the best of Modernism', the 3000-square-feet space is full of design classics from names such as Florence Knoll, Ingo Maurer, de Sede to name but three. Haus has the exclusive rights in Central London on the Studio range of US design company Knoll. If the names mean anything to you, you'll be in seventh heaven, if not it's still worth a visit. But beware of the rather aloof sales assistants.

Heals'
196 Tottenham Court Rd, London W1P 9LD
tel: 0171 636 1666
and
234 King's Rd, London SW3 5UA
tel: 0171 349 8411
and
Tunsgate, Guildford, Surrey GU1 3QU
tel: 01483 576715

Heals' is a delight to wander round in. It has everything from wrought iron tables with beautiful mosaic tops to tables, chairs, sofas and beds. (See also p.138.)

Inhouse
28 Howe St, Edinburgh EH3 6TG
tel: 0131 225 2888 • fax: 0131 220 6632
and
24–26 Wilson St, Glasgow G1 1SS
tel: 0141 339 9520 • fax: 0141 552 5929

Inhouse is Scotland's largest outlet for European design classics. Here you will find examples by husband-and-wife team Charles and Ray Eames, Cassina, Molteni and other Italian and Spanish designer names.

Interiors bis
60 Sloane Avenue, London SW3 3DD
tel: 0171 838 1104

Some truly sumptuous leather furniture is on sale here – a leather desk for a huge price but that is beautifully crafted and will last a lifetime. There are also leather stools and leather cushions.

MDW Design
Studio J, 105/6 Tower Bridge Business Complex,
100 Clements Rd, London SE16 4RJ
tel/fax: 0171 394 2882 to view and for retail outlets

Distinctly different designs are the name of the game for this company, who mostly sell to interior designers and architects. The furniture, principally designed by Mike Walker, has an anthropomorphic quality with crab-like legs, but even tiny items such as ashtrays and candle holders have been as carefully designed as the larger items.

Muji
187 Oxford St, London W1R 1AJ
tel: 0171 437 7503

Very simple yet elegant furniture in boxy shapes. There are low coffee and side tables on castors in laminated beech or aluminium, MDF veneer units, and shelving systems. Muji has four branches in London – Oxford St being the largest. Not all of them stock all the furniture so it's best to ring first.

Next Directory
Freepost 2, Leicester, Leics LE5 5DZ
tel: 0345 400 444

Don't forget about Next for furniture. They always have simple, well-designed things in their range and, using their catalogue, you can order it direct from the comfort of your own armchair.

Nice House
The Italian Centre, Courtyard, Ingram St,
Glasgow G1 1DA
tel: 0141 553 1377

This three-storey shop has a good range of contemporary furniture, including example pieces by B&B Italia, and Phillippe Starck. Nice House also design and manufacture their own collection of furniture.

Places & Spaces
30 Old Town, London SW4 0LB
tel: 0171 498 0998

Judging by the fact that this shop always seems to be busy with browsing shoppers, the owners have got it right with their mix of the best of modern contemporary design with a few twentieth century greats thrown in, such as Eames and the Danish Arne Jacobsen. In a relatively small shop space, they manage to show off the pieces they stock to the very best advantage and make you want to take the entire collection home.

Purves & Purves
80–81 & 83 Tottenham Court Rd,
London W1P 9HD
tel: 0171 580 8223

If you want to see what Britain's bright young things are designing, this is the place to come. Work by established names, such as Terence Woodgate, Tom Dixon and Martin Ryan, abounds. There are huge sofas and lots of examples of the Phoenix chair in every conceivable colour.

Retro Home
20 Pembridge Rd, London W11 3HL
tel: 0171 221 2055

This shop is such a good idea, it's surprising no one else thought of it first. With the boom in demand for twentieth-century design, this shop has taken the initiative and buys examples of good design from members of the public and sells them on to others. If you have a really excellent example of something in top condition, they might be interested but try not to flood them, particularly at weekends. It's best to ring first to establish interest to save you carting it all the way there.

Same
The Bridge, 146 Brick Lane, London E1 6RU
tel: 0171 247 9992 • fax: 0171 247 9993

This funky new shop opened in June 1998 and has quickly become the talk of the town, appearing in all the glossy style magazines. It is a showcase for the best of European design with companies from countries like Sweden, Holland and Finland represented. Look out for established designer names such as Ingo Maurer alongside new talent, which the owners are consciously trying to promote. There are also exhibitions held in this great space on the site of the old Trumans Brewery. Visiting here is a truly global experience.

SCP
135–139 Curtain Rd, London EC2A 3BX
tel: 0171 739 1869 for stockists
fax: 0171 729 4224

It can be slightly intimidating walking into SCP as everything looks so expensive and like it has been placed 'just so'. But there's nothing to be frightened of here – there's no pressure from the sales assistants even if you're just looking, and it's definitely worth a visit. Pieces from the classic European designers are much in evidence – and Le Corbusier seems to feature particularly. They also do their own range of contemporary furniture which is distributed to some other outlets around the country.

Space
214 Westbourne Grove, London W11 2RH
tel: 0171 229 6533

A beautifully laid out shop with lots of space – as you might expect from its name! Everything is here in its own right, from the carefully chosen sculptural candles to the furniture in fluid and sensual shapes by the latest names (for example British designers Michael Young and Alison Cooke of sleeper beanbag fame).

Viaduct
1–10 Summers St, London EC1R 5BD
tel: 0171 278 8456

If you're a Philippe Starck devotee you're in luck, you will find lots of his work here including the sculptural 'Lord Yo' chair made out of subtly-hued plastic. In this huge loft-type space, you will also see the work of lots of other top European names such as the Dutch group Montis, Kartell & Driade.

furniture you paint yourself

If you enjoy having a go at making things yourself, there are a growing number of companies who are now making unpainted, unadorned items of furniture that you can decorate yourself. Known as 'blanks', they are usually made from Medium Density Fibreboard (MDF) which can take a whole host of different types of paint and paint effects. So far, most companies seem to be supplying smaller items such as chests, blanket boxes, ottomans, and screens although some have branched out into larger pieces. Often operating by mail order, the companies listed below give you the chance to create something really personal and pleasurable, especially if you can't find anything to your liking elsewhere.

The Dormy House

Stirling Park, East Portway Industrial Estate,
Andover, Hants SP10 3TZ
tel: 01264 365808 • fax: 01264 366359
e-mail: dormyhouse@compuserve.com

Mail order only, the Dorny House supply MDF blanks in various models – blanket boxes and ottomans, scalloped and console tables. Particularly useful are their folding screens, which can be used to divide off rooms or cover up unsightly messes!

Harvey Baker Design Ltd

Unit 1, Rodgers Industrial Estate,
Yalberton Rd, Paignton, Devon TQ4 7PJ
tel/fax: 01803 521515
e-mail: info@harvey-baker-design.co.uk

There are lots of fun shapes here for you to paint yourself including mirrors,wardrobes, pine cabinets, beds, chests of drawers and CD cabinets. They do some lovely designs for children, such as a fairytale bed. All available by mail order only.

Heart of the Country

Home Farm, Swinfen, nr Lichfield,
Staffs WS14 9QR
tel: 01543 480669 for stockists • fax: 01543 481684

Blank trays, toy chests, screens and small items of furniture all ready to paint yourself, ideally using their own range of Heritage Village Colour Paints from America. Alternatively, the in-house painters will do it for you to your own requirements.

IKEA

Brent Park, 2 Drury Way, North Circular Rd,
London NW10 0TH
tel: 0181 208 5600 for enquiries and branches

Ikea is excellent for small and large items of furniture in pale birch wood that you can paint and customize yourself. There are often examples dotted around the store to give weary shoppers inspiration. As well as their little wooden boxes which you can paint all colours under the sun, the Swedish superstore has a good range of other bits and bobs which could all be used for special paint effects, from key cabinets to occasional tables.

Moriarti's Workshop

High Halden, Kent TN26 3LY
tel: 01233 850214 • fax: 01233 850524

If you want to try out your newly acquired skills at paint effects, Moriarti's supplies all sorts of furniture, which has been left untreated, but sanded, ready for you to get painting on. It would be rather costly if you haven't first tried out the techniques on smaller items, as these are mostly dressers and wardrobes. The range is called In The Raw and, if you're ordering by mail, you deduct 10% off the price of the same items that have been stained or lacquered. The staff are very helpful if you're not sure of anything.

Paint Creative

17 Holywell Hill, St Albans,
Herts AL1 1EZ
tel: 01727 859898 for branches and mail order
fax: 01727 875872

Folding screens, magazine racks, cachepots and planters as well as larger items, such as bookshelves and tables, all make up a range called The Unpainted Finish which can be ordered by post or purchased from any branch of Paint Creative. All the items are made out of MDF, and are ready to be painted, scumble- or crackle-glazed and waxed. They also sell the materials for achieving all of these paint effects.

Scumble Goosie

Lewiston Mill, Toadsmoor Rd, Stroud,
Glos GL5 2TB
tel: 01453 731305 • fax: 01453 731500

Using high-quality MDF, this company manufactures 'blanks' or what they call 'The Naked Collection', which you then paint yourself. Choose from large items – such as bookcases, drop-leaf tables, and folding screens – or rococo-style mirror frames, peg rails and trugs (baskets). Visit their showroom in the delightful setting of the Cotswolds.

first

Keeping the exterior of your house in good order is always important but perhaps especially if you are trying to sell it. A newly painted front door can make all the difference in giving the impression that you care about your house. Estate agents claim that a house with a blue door is more likely to sell than any other colour. Whatever your choice, if your door is looking decidedly scruffy, there's no doubt that sanding it down, repairing any cracks or dents with filler, and giving it a coat of primer followed by a couple of coats of an oil-based paint, can give it an instant new lease of life. Replacing the battered door furniture with new models can also help and needn't necessarily cost the earth. This chapter tells you where to start looking.

One of the most popular items on *Home Front* was when Graham and Maxine Walsh had a beautiful stained glass front door fitted in their Yorkshire Victorian terrace. This chapter gives you details about some of the best craftspeople we know of working in the stained glass field, as well as where to go to get the materials if you want to try doing it for yourself.

Keeping your windows in good order is another important aspect of creating a good first impression of a house, but it's one that is frequently overlooked. We have not included here all the double glazing and UPVC companies that abound. Instead we have included the more exciting first impressions for windows, such as what curtain poles and fittings are on the market, where to go if you want to have blind specially made or see a good range of ready-made ones. Alternatively if you've always wanted to have shutters on your windows you'll be able to find out where to go to have them custom-made.

impressions

key: 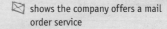 shows the product has appeared on *Home Front*

       ✉ shows the company offers a mail order service

doors

The style of your front door is a good starting point for dating the house. If you are lucky enough to have a genuine period door, it is almost always best to try and keep it rather than buy a new one. This is because doors were made much more sturdily then, and were often braced, with cross-rails, and framed. Even the wood itself was more solid and hard-wearing. If your period door has seen better days, but is not beyond hope, it is better to try and get a qualified carpenter, who will understand the precise way it has been constructed, to repair it for you. It will work out cheaper than having a reproduction door made for you from scratch, although this is an alternative if your door is really past repair and poses a security risk. New doors on period properties almost always stick out like sore thumbs, although there are some good reproduction ones around.

Another alternative is to scavenge round salvage yards for old doors that could be restored but do check that they aren't warped before you buy. If you want to make sure it will be in keeping with the date of your property, try having a look at neighbouring houses built at a similar time. They can vary wildly, but it should give you some idea of what would be appropriate. If – and it's a big if – you are sure, from having first taken very accurate measurements, that it will fit, the cost of restoration will again be considerably cheaper than buying a brand-new door. Remember, you can have a few centimetres planed off the top or bottom but any more and you're likely to ruin the proportions of the door. This chapter tells you where to start hunting for both old and new doors, as well as listing craftsmen who can make reproductions. It will also tell you where to go for the best door furniture and stained glass.

old doors

If you're searching for an original period door to fit the style of your house, try looking in these salvage companies – all of which have stocks of old doors. They are listed by region alphabetically. It is always best to ring salvage yards in advance about when they are open as they do tend to keep less-than-regular hours.

south west

The Architectural Recycling Centre
Wheal Agar Yard, Agar Rd, Pool, Redruth, Cornwall TR15 3EJ
tel: 01209 314755

This yard has lots of genuine doors in stock – mostly Victorian and Georgian. If you'd like a pine door stripped in an acid bath they will sort it out for you. Open Mon–Sat 9.30 a.m.–5.30 p.m.

Dorset Reclamation
Cow Drove, Bere Regis, Wareham, Dorset BH20 7JZ
tel: 01929 472200 • fax: 01929 472292

They don't have a huge range of doors but you might strike lucky. If you do find one, they can arrange delivery and have a useful matching and search service.

John Tyler Environmental Reclamation
The Barn, Lower Littleton Farm, Winford Rd, Chew Magna, nr Bristol BS40 8QQ
tel: 01275 333589

Recycling has been taken to its logical conclusion here and you can find new-to-you doors that have been constructed using old timber, salvaged from other items. A worthwhile place with well-constructed doors.

The Original Reclamation Trading Co
22 Elliott Rd, Love Lane Industrial Estate, Cirencester, Glos GL7 1YS
tel: 01285 653532

You should be able to find an old door to your liking at this yard which has friendly staff. They're all original, from a mixture of periods. Open Tues–Fri 9 a.m.–4 p.m.

Source
108 Walcot St, Bath, Avon BA1 3SD
tel: 01225 469200 • fax: 01225 444404

If you're prepared to root around amidst the jumble of stuff, you could just find the door you are after. With Bath's rich Georgian legacy, it could unearth a door from this era or some suitable door furniture if you're lucky.

Toby's (The Old Builder's Yard & Store)
Exminster Station, Exminster, Exeter, Devon TQ12 4PB
tel: 01392 422711

This is a good place to come for old doors that are in various states but you might have to rummage around a bit. They don't deliver, so bring transport large enough to take a door home with you!

south east

Architectural Emporium
55 St John's Rd, Tunbridge Wells, Kent TN4 9TP
tel: 01892 540368

A good place to visit if you're looking for an old door, with or without stained glass. They also sell salvage pieces of stained glass, which can look beautiful just freestanding around the home. The Emporium usually has a range of antique door fittings in stock too.

Architectural Rescue
1–3 Southampton Way, London SE5 7JH
tel: 0171 277 0315 • fax: 0171 277 0315

This company concentrates more on the internal and decorative fittings rather than on building materials. They specialize in fixtures and fittings such as doors, baths, sinks and stained glass. Much of their stock is Victorian.

In Doors
Beechin Wood Farm, Beechin Wood Lane, Platt, nr Sevenoaks, Kent TN15 8QN
tel/fax: 01732 887445

A good supply of old timber doors can be found here and, if you want them stripped, they will do that as well.

Old Door & Fireplace Company
67–69 Essex Rd, London N1 2SF
tel/fax: 0171 251 8844

A large range of old doors, which have mostly been stripped, available here and at quite reasonable prices. Ones with the original staned glass still intact are obviously considerably more expensive, but you can pick up a sturdy door for less than £100.

Original Door Specialists
298 Brockley Rd, London SE24 2RA
tel: 0181 691 7162

This is a great place to come to search for an old door – they have literally hundreds in stock at any one time suitable for exterior or interior use.

Renaissance
193–5 City Rd, London EC1 1JN
tel: 0171 251 8844

This outfit specializes in restoring old doors – particularly period ones from the Victorian and Georgian ages, and bringing them back to life. They use their own range of door furniture in keeping with the door's style if the original ones are missing or badly damaged. They will also put the door in for you – a useful service as hanging a door properly can sometimes be tricky.

Save A Tree Original Doors
93 Endwell Rd, London SE4 2NF
tel: 0171 252 8109

A great name for a company that encourages people to use old doors rather than new ones. There are quite a few in stock at any one time, and they usually have some of the original fittings as well, although not necessarily the actual ones belonging to the door you may be purchasing.

east

Stiffkey Antiques
The Chapel, Stiffkey, Wells-next-the-Sea,
Norfolk NR23 1AJ
tel: 01328 830099 • fax: 01328 830005

If the original door to your Victorian property has been replaced with a new one and you'd like to reinstate one that's in keeping, try coming here and you're almost bound to find a suitable one. Whilst you're there you may pick up some of the genuine period door furniture as well.

central

Coventry Demolition Company
Unit M, Wolstyon Business Park, Main St, Wolston,
Coventry CV8 3LL
tel: 01203 545051

The premises are open to the public from 8 a.m.–5 p.m. during the week and from 8 a.m.–3 p.m. on Saturdays but is best to call and check first. Doors rescued from sites that are about to be, or have been, demolished make their way here. It's fairly unlikely that you'll find anything really period here but other types of more modern doors are readily available.

Dickinson's Architectural Antiques
14 Corve St, Ludlow, Shropshire SY8 2PG
tel: 01584 876207

A good selection of doors are held in stock here, with the stock changing quite rapidly. Open Mon–Sat 10 a.m.–5 p.m.

The Victorian Ironmonger
The Old Garage, 70 Broad St, Brinklow, Rugby,
Warks CV23 0LN
tel: 01788 832292

As the name suggests, you're likely to pick up a door from the Victorian age here, and perhps some fittings to go with it. Open Weds–Sat 10 a.m.–5 p.m. and Sun 11 a.m.–4 p.m.

north west

Andy Thornton Arcitectural Antiques
Victoria Mills, Stainland Rd, Greetland, Halifax,
W.Yorks HX4 8AD
tel: 01422 377314

This is one of the largest salvage yards in the north of England and possibly in the country, so be prepared to have a really good root around. That perfect door may be lurking there, somewhere.

In-Situ Architectural Antiques
607 Stretford Rd, Manchester M16 0QJ
tel/fax: 0161 848 7454

If you'd like a period front door there are dozens here on display, for both internal and external use. If you can't find one that fits, they can make you a reproduction door to your required size.

north east

Borders Architectural Salvage
2 South Rd, Wooler, Northumberland NE71 6SN
tel: 01668 282475

This yard has a large range of doors of all sizes and ages. It's worth spending time looking round to find one that will suit your house.

Havenplan
The Old Station, Station Rd, Killamarsh,
Sheffield S31 8EN
tel/fax: 0114 248 9972

If you'd like an original front door complete with stained glass, Havenplan has hundreds of them in varying states of repair. Concentrating mainly on Edwardian and Victorian doors, you can also find panelled front doors in their vast stock.

wales

Cardiff Reclamation
Site 7, Tremorfa Industrial Estate, Cardiff CF2 2SD
tel: 01222 458995

There isn't a huge selection of doors on offer here as they really tend to specialise in fireplaces and sanitary ware from the Victorian age, but you might see the odd door or two if you're visiting.

Gallop & Rivers
Ty'r Ask, Brecon Rd, Crickhowell, Powys SY21 8HH
tel: 01938 555647

Gallop & Rivers has a wide range of all sorts of architectural salvage, including some doors. It's best to give them a ring first, before setting out, to check what's in stock at any time.

new doors

Sometimes only a new door will do and all the companies below will make you a brand-new door for either the front of your house or internally. Many of them can make reproduction-style doors if you live in a period house. Unlike old doors, which, being one-offs, are listed by region, we have listed new doors alphabetically by company as they are mass-manufactured. Phone the number given for details of your nearest stockist or for information about whether the company will deliver.

Cotswood Door Specialists
5 Hampden Way, London N14 5DJ
tel: 0181 368 1664 • fax: 0181 369 9635

Garage doors can be tricky to find but this company has a good selection, as well as standard size doors for both inside and out. They will take accurate measurements and install the door for you as well.

County Hardwoods
Creech Mill, Mill Lane, Creech St Michael, Taunton, Somerset TA3 5PX
tel: 01823 443760 for stockists • fax: 01823 443940

If you fancy having a go yourself, their doors come in kit form for you to assemble. Choose from softwood or hardwood.

The Designer Door Company
Bow Wharf, Grove Rd, London E3 4PE
tel: 0181 880 6739
e-mail:desdoors@aol.com

Doors are treated as pieces of furniture in their own right by this company. They will make a bespoke design for you and they can incorporate stained glass, if you wish, into their doors – both modern and traditional designs.

Grandisson
The Mill, Alansway, Ottery St Mary, Devon EX11 1NR
tel/fax: 01404 812876 for stockists

If none of their own designs suit you or their standard sizes don't fit, Grandisson will make any design to order and is good if you've got an awkward-size door. Only the best woods are used – walnut, rosewood, sturdy oak and rich mahogany. They don't offer an installation service.

Humphrey & Stretton
Pindar Industial Estate, Hoddeson, Herts EN11 0EU
tel: 01992 462965 for stockists

Although they deal mainly in contract work for offices, this company will supply doors for the domestic market in some cases – possibly not for just one-offs though. Doors with a wood veneer finish are their main staple, but they also do more unusual finishes in rubber and leather. They do not offer an installation service.

John Russell Architectural
Unit 7, Rosemary Works, Branch Place, London N1 5PH
tel: 0171 739 2241

Solid timber doors using only woods from sustainable forests are what you can expect to find here. Their friendly staff will come and measure your door to make the template for the new one and, once made, will install it for you.

The London Door Company
Unit 1–3, Wellington Rd Industrial Estate, Wellington Rd, London SW19 8ED
tel: 0181 947 7771 for stockists • fax: 0181 944 6244

If your French windows need replacing and you'd like wooden ones rather than double-glazed with UPVC, this company can help. They also do a good repro of a Victorian-style door in pine, and a Georgian-style one.

Lualdi Doors
163 Eversholt St, London NW1 1BU
tel: 0171 816 6166 for stockists
fax: 0171 388 8118
e-mail:sales@faram.demon.co.uk

A stylish Italian door could be yours if you choose this company. Using wood veneer, glass and high-gloss polyester lacquer, these doors are normally found in offices but they will supply to the domestic market.

Premdor Crosby Ltd
Stephenson Rd, Groundwell Industrial Estate,
Swindon, Wilts SN2 5BQ
tel: 01793 708200 for stockists • fax: 01793 706179

Give this manufacturer a call and they will tell you where your nearest retail outlet is for their vast range of new wooden doors. If you send for their catalogue first, it will give you some idea of the designs they do. They have over a thousand different ones!

Shadbolt International
FR Shadbolt & Sons Ltd, North Circular Rd,
South Chingford, London E4 8PZ
tel: 0181 527 6441 for stockists • fax: 0181 523 2774

Shadbolt is one of the best-known names in new doors, which they make in wood veneers and laminates. There is an endless list of door types available ranging from panelled and glazed to partitioning, acoustic and fire doors. They claim to be able to make special designs as easily as ones that are produced in mass.

door furniture

If you want to make your house the smartest in the street, look after your door furniture. The central knob or door-pull, the letterbox, bell, knocker and hinges all say something about your house and your taste. If you live in a old house and the original door furniture is still intact, it will give you a good indication of the exact period of your house. For instance, the Victorians went in for quite fussy and elaborate door furniture and put as much as possible on a door. The Georgians preferred much more simple and pared-down designs with perhaps just a brass knocker. If your door furniture is all in good order, it's probably best just to give it a really good

clean. If it's been replaced by the previous owners with items that are not in keeping with the style of the house, you could hunt in salvage yards or buy reproductions. Many of the same styles are still being produced today. If you can afford it, it's worth investing in some of the more expensive ones rather than those from the larger DIY outlets as they will stand up to the elements better in the long run.

There is nothing to say that you can't give an old door a modern makeover and *Home Front* designer Lloyd Farmar showed how by adding some stylish chrome accessories to a distinctly worn-looking old door. If you are putting in a new letterplate, make sure it will fit and that the postman won't get his fingers trapped. The correct position for a letterbox, according to the Royal Mail, is 43 inches/107 cm from the ground and it should be at least 10 inches/25 cm in width.

In this section, you will find companies that make and sell traditional reproduction door furniture as well as modern. There are also some unusual ideas for handles and knobs for internal and cupboard doors using everything from pewter to stone and glass.

A&H Brass
201–203 Edgware Rd, London W2 1ES
tel: 0171 402 1854

If you want traditional brass knobs and knockers, look no further. A&H Brass have hundreds of styles from Lion's heads to foxes, horses and period styles.

Allgood Hardware
297 Euston Rd, London NW1 3AQ
tel: 0870 609 0009 for a catalogue

Allgood have one of the largest ranges of door furniture in the country with tastes to suit all styles. If you think that the details on a door are as important as other elements of design and you're after something really swanky but restrained, why not fork out for a design by Philippe Starck or Jasper Morrison?

Architectural Components Ltd
4–8 Exhibition Rd, London SW7 2HF
tel: 0171 581 2401 • fax: 0171 589 4928
e-mail: gj@locks-and-handles.co.uk

Within this company is Locks & Handles of South Kensington who have an excellent range of all styles of door furniture. They also make enamel house numbers – with a choice of traditional blue or green and black backgrounds, with gold lettering.

Ashfield Traditional

The Cricketers, Forward Green, Stowmarket,
Suffolk IP14 5HP
tel: 01449 711273

If your period door latch is missing or has been lost
over the years, this company can make new ones, in
style, which are all hand forged.

Brass Foundry Casting

The Old Wheelwright's Shop, Brasted Forge, Brasted,
Westerham, Kent TN16 1JL
tel: 01959 563863

If you're looking for handmade door furniture rather
than mass produced, this is a good place to come. The
finishes are, as you'd expect, traditional brass and
bronze and all beautifully turned out.

Brass Tack Fittings Ltd

177 Bilton Rd, Perivale, Greenford, Middx UB6 7HG
tel: 0181 566 9669 • fax: 0181 566 9339

Brass Tacks offers a wide range of imitation period
door furniture in helpfully named groups such as
Georgian Suite, which comprises everything you need
from letter boxes to escutcheons all in a cohesive
style. They will also match original items or make you
up something particular. Visit the showroom at the
address above or send for samples on a sale or
return basis.

Bullers

Albion Works, Uttoxeter Rd, Longton,
Stoke-on-Trent, Staffs ST3 1PH
tel: 01782 599922 for stockists • fax: 01782 598037

English porcelain door handles can't be beaten for that
traditional look. This manufacturer is still making them
to a high quality using only the finest porcelain in
black, ivory or decorated with flowers.

Charles Harden

14 Chiltern St, London W1M 1PD
tel: 0171 935 2032

This long-established company will make door fittings
for you to order if you're after something particularly
unusual. It's also worth hunting through their existing
stock of unique pieces if you want something that
little bit out of the ordinary. Ceramic door knobs in
either plain colours or patterned are available. Each
one is beautifully finished to give your door that extra
bit of style.

Clayton Munroe Ltd

Kingston West Drive, Kingston, Staverton,
Totnes, Devon TQ9 6AR
tel: 01803 762626 for stockists
fax: 01803 762584
e-mail: mail@claytonmunroe.co.uk

All Clayton Munroe's products have been co-ordinated
to fit in with a design concept to ensure that every
product belongs to a 'family'. Choose from their
trademark Patine finish or black, rust, polished or
satin brass. Rough At The Edges is hand-forged and
looks very rustic. Celtic balls, fancy escutcheons, and
hooks in the shape of pears, apples, ducks and rabbits
can also be found in their catalogue.

Franchi International Ltd

Unit 2/11, Chelsea Harbour Design Centre,
Chelsea Harbour, London SW10 0XE
tel: 0171 351 4554

Sleek and stylish designs incorporating chrome and
glass make for a range of unusual door furniture.
Delightful to the touch, there are egg-shaped balls of
amber-coloured glass with shallow grooves cut into
them, mounted on top of chrome fittings.

Franco-file

PO Box 31, Tiverton, Devon EX16 4YU
tel/fax: 01884 253556

If you've admired those enamel numberplates that
adorn the doors of French houses, this company
imports them directly from France to sell here. One-
and two-digit numbers are held in stock but if your
house number is three digits or more it costs a few
pounds extra and the order may take slightly longer.
One of the only companies to do this, you can also
have the name of your house displayed on either a
vitreous blue or green enamel background. There are a
few French designs available such as 'Privé' and
'Défense de Fumer' too.

Glover & Smith Ltd

Maker's Cottage, 14 London Rd, Overton,
nr Basingstoke, Hants RG25 3NP
tel: 01256 773012 • fax: 01256 773012

A very unusual range of door and cupboard handles,
available by mail order only. Choose from the Forest
Collection, which has leaves, twigs and acorns
fashioned out of pewter, bronze or hand-gilded items,
or a seaside theme with shells, seahorses and starfish.

HAF
HAF House, Mead Lane, Hertford,
Herts SG13 7AP
tel: 01992 505655 for catalogue
fax: 01992 505705

Slick contemporary fittings in chrome and nickel plus
many other finishes, with lovely streamlined shapes
and no fussy detail, which are perfect for modern
living. They also feel really nice to touch.

Haute Deco
556 Kings Rd, London SW6 2DE
tel: 0171 736 7171

If you're bored of brass and sick of silver, this shop
sells an unusual range of knobs in colourful metals
and resins, but they're also a good supplier of the
more usual fittings.

HEWI (UK) Ltd
Scimitar Close, Gillingham Business Park, Gillingham,
Kent ME8 0RN
tel: 0800 253704 for catalogue

If you've admired those brightly coloured chunky
handles often found on trains and public lavatories,
this German company manufactures them. They would
look good in a very modern home or a child's room –
big enough for little fingers to grasp!

JD Beardmore & Co
17 Pall Mall, London SW1Y 5LU
tel: 0171 637 7041

Established more than 130 years ago, this top-quality
ironmongery company has furnished the likes of the
insides of the Orient Express, ocean liners and hundreds
of stately homes. The catalogue is well laid out with
styles of door furniture grouped together by period.
Visit the London showroom or send for a catalogue.

Looking For Ages

East Hill, Parracombe,
Devon EX31 4PF
tel/fax: 01598 763300

If you want one of those traditional door bells, which
is set on a block of wood and jangles inside when the
bell is pulled, look no further. This company is still
manufacturing the ever popular Domus Doorbell
reminiscent of the Victorian age. Everything available
by mail order only.

Merlin Glass
Barn St, Station Rd, Liskeard, Cornwall PL14 4BW
tel/fax: 01579 342399

Coloured glass knobs that look and feel beautiful are
this company's speciality.

Nice Irma's

Unit 2, Finchley Industrial Centre, 879 High Rd,
London N12 8QA
tel: 0181 343 9766 • fax: 0181 343 9590

If you fancy something a little bit different, Nice
Irma's make unusual door pulls in glass with jewel-like
colours. Chunky door handles in a pewter finish come
in the shape of fish, flowers, and shells.

Nu-Line Builders Merchants
315 Westbourne Park Rd, London W11 1EF
tel: 0171 727 7748

A brilliant trade supplier that sells all sorts of things
and has a very good range of stylish and simple door
furniture in steel if you don't want something fancy or
brass (although they do this as well). *Home Front*
designer Lloyd Farmar gave an instant update to a
tired front door with their range of door furniture.

Oliver Bonas
tel: 0171 627 4747 for enquiries and branches
fax: 0171 622 3629

Handmade drawer knobs in unusual shapes in an
aluminium finish. Mix spirals with hearts and daisies.
Available in all branches (see p.117 for shop locations).

Ornamental Arts
1–7 Chelsea Harbour Design Centre,
Chelsea Harbour, London SW10 0XE
tel: 0171 351 0541

A visit to the London showroom gives you a good idea
of what this company does. It's all fairly traditional –
brass, bronze and chrome – although some of the
ranges also come in verdigris if you want that aged look.

Romany's Architectural Ironmongers
52–56 Camden High St, London NW1 0LT
tel: 0171 387 2579 • fax: 0171 383 2377

This shop boasts a huge array of stock all displayed on
boards according to style. You should be able to find
anything you are looking for here whether you want
traditional repro or ultra-modern.

stained glass

Stained glass windows and panelled doors can transform the exterior of your home into a work of art. The glass refracts the light and will make lovely shafts of coloured light in your hall. Stained glass panels are not really any more insecure than other types of door, but you can always fit a panel of security glass behind it to be sure. A crack in a pane will weaken it and make it easier for a burglar to smash, so keep your glass in good order. If a panel has cracked or fallen out, it is quite a specialist job to replace it, but it is worth sorting out. Many of the companies listed below also undertake restoration work.

If your door is bare or has ugly glass you'd like to repace with some stained glass, you can have some made for it. Most stained glass companies can repair cracks and missing peices, or they will make new panels to fit an old door. Many workshops and companies take commissions. To get something in keeping with the period of your house, look around to see what your neighbours in your street have as it is likely all the doors and glasses were installed at the same time. Of course you needn't keep to the period, you could have something new and modern made up to your liking. If you fancy having a go at making your panel yourself, some of the companies listed here sell the materials – lead, soldering iron, etc – you will need, and all the glass. It can work out quite expensive, so be really sure you are dedicated to the project, or go on a course where the equipment is provided in tuition costs to try out the technique first. *Home Front* designer Lloyd Farmar has shown that it is possible to make a simple, relatively inexpensive, stained glass panel yourself and that, with a little patience and practice, you can have a truly original front door.

Please read the entries in this section carefully – only some of the companies sell the materials for making your own stained glass panels. Most of them work mainly on commissions and restoration work.

Anderson Studios
21 Elmtree Rd, Teddington, Middx TW11 8SJ
tel/fax: 0181 943 1657

This small workshop, run by stained glass expert Tilley Anderson-Ford, will undertake restoration work on pieces of leaded glass that may have been damaged over the years. She will also make up new designs in keeping with the character of your house – both period and contemporary. She also does gold leaf work on glass. Phone her first to discuss your requirements.

Glasshouse
20 Cross St, Hampton Hill, Middx TW1 4LZ
tel: 0181 941 7589

This company will undertake any repair or restoration work that you may need done on existing leaded glass. They also will make up designs of your choice.

Goddard & Gibbs
41–49 Kingsland Rd, London E2 8AD
tel: 0171 739 6563 • fax: 0171 739 1979

One of the most well-known companies for stained glass in London, they can offer a wide range of services on many types of glass.

Inside Art
26 Albert St, Ramsbottom, Bury, Lancs BL0 9EL
tel: 01706 823997 • fax: 01706 827910

This company does all sorts of amazing things with glass including ceiling domes and panels of laminated glass mosaic. Not really the place to go if you just want a small panel of leaded light in your door or window, although they do undertake some. But it is the place to go if you want something spectacular.

James Hetley & Co
Glasshouse Fields, Schoolhouse Lane,
London E1 9JA
tel: 0171 790 2333 • fax: 0171 790 2682

James Hetley sell all types of glass – from the machine-made to the more expensive mouthblown or 'antique' glass – in tons of different colours, plus all the materials you need to install it yourself. They also have a wide selection of books on the subject.

Karim Yasamee
27a Muspole St, Norwich, Norfolk NR3 1DJ
tel: 01603 622288

Karim is a stained glass artist who actually paints on glass, as well as using the more traditional method of leading with coloured glass. Everything is specially commissioned by the client and he works to their specifications.

Lead & Light
35a Hartland Rd, London NW1 8DB
tel: 0171 485 0997 • fax: 0171 284 2660

Even the double doors that lead into this impressive studio are made from the most stunning stained glass to give you a taste of what's inside. Upstairs is the studio where the skilled staff work on various projects, and below are racks and racks of glass, all neatly divided into types and colours. The very helpful staff will guide you on the best choice for your particular needs and they can make beautiful panels from ultra-modern to very elaborate and ornate ones. (See also Courses p.263.)

Mark Angus Stained Glass
144 North Rd, Combe Down, Bath, Avon BA2 5DL
tel: 01225 834530

Mark Angus specializes in stained glass for windows but in abstract designs rather than formal patterns based on period styles. If this sounds like more what you had in mind, and you'd like something really original, he could be the person to contact.

Parkin Cathedral Glass
6 Long Drive, Greenford, Middx UB6 8LZ
tel: 0181 575 6436

If one of your stained glass panels is cracked or missing, they will restore and repair so it is as good as new. They also do re-leading and general face lifts. Stained glass can be commissioned and they will manufacture doorlights and windows.

Paul Lucker Designs Group
Thorncliffe House, Thorncliffe St, Lindley,
Huddersfield, W.Yorks HD3 3JL
tel: 01484 644982 • fax: 01484 460143
e-mail: pld@dgd.co.uk

This is a well-established company and it undertakes many large projects, including a lot of ecclesiastical work. However, they also cater for the domestic market and are happy to discuss individual commissions.

The Stained Glass Place
3 Turnham Green Mews, London W4 1QU
tel: 0181 747 8218

Walk all the way up a rickety flight of iron stairs and you will come to the tiny studios. It's well worth a visit for inspiration alone and, although cramped, is full of wonderful examples of stained glass in process and finished pieces about to be taken to the client's home. The staff are often away on site so phone first before visiting. They don't sell any glass or materials.

The Stained Glass Studio
Workshop 4, Brewery Arts, Brewery Court, Cirencester,
Glos GL7 1JH
tel: 01285 644430

Stained-glass windows can be made to order in both modern and period styles at this small workshop run by Daniella Wilson-Dunne. She is also trained in the art of restoration if one of your own panels is damaged.

windows

It doesn't seem long ago that, if you wanted to hang a pair of curtains at your window, you had a choice of plain old curtain track or a wooden or brass pole. It seemed that more traditional tastes were being catered for but there was nothing on the market for the more modern style of home. Today designers and manufacturers have woken up to the fact that people would like more of a choice – you only have to look at the way the demand for wrought-iron curtain poles went crazy in the 1980s. Curtain poles and finials, the bits stuck at the end to stop the rings or hooks falling off, are now available in every style possible and in an exciting range of materials to suit both modern and period homes. Finials come in pewter, glass, wood, iron, plastic and in every conceivable design from daisies to ducklings. This section also covers blinds and shutters – great alternatives to curtains.

window furniture

This section covers some of the more unusual curtain poles and window furniture available today.

Artisan
Unit 4a, Union Court, 20 Union Rd,
London SW4 6JP
tel: 0171 498 6974 for stockists and mail order
fax: 0171 498 2989

Artisan was one of the first companies to launch the black wrought iron poles with curls and crooks at the end, which took off in a huge way and are still hugely popular. They are sold in large department stores like John Lewis. They are still leading the way with new ranges introduced regularly, and they seem to predict trends. Finials now come in pale wood in simple sensual shapes as well as glass ones tapered like tear drops.

Byron & Byron
4 Thane Works, Thane Villas, London N7 7NU
tel: 0171 700 0404 • fax: 0171 700 4111

This company makes curtain poles in the unusual Modern Rope collection which has pale wood poles wound round with natural rope in muted yellows, oranges and naturals. A good choice if you want your poles to be stylish yet not too noticeable as their soft colours fade into the background.

Hang Ups Accessories Ltd
Unit 2, Springfield Farm, Perrotts Brook,
Cirencester, Glos GL7 7DT
tel: 01285 831771 for stockists • fax: 01285 831881

There are several ranges of curtain poles on offer – all with matching finials. The nursery range has teddy bears, Peter Rabbits and ducklings stuck on them, whereas the Heraldic range has plaques with unicorns, lions and castles on proud parade. They are quite ornate but fun. There are also pelmets with swags and swirls, and mirrors to match the themes of the poles.

Harrison Drape
Bradford St, Birmingham, W.Midlands B12 0PE
tel: 0121 766 6111 for stockists • fax: 0121 772 0696

A wide range of curtain poles and finials in painted wood which are adorned with acorns, balls and flowers. They also do several different designs of iron curtain poles with shepherds' crooks at each end.

Jennings & Jennings
Whitmore Cross, Tillington, Hereford, HR4 8LE
tel: 01432 760034

This company makes elegant wooden poles with carved ends that would look perfectly at home in a period property. Some have a gold leaf or crackle glaze look for an 'antique' finish.

Kiosk
Studio 72, The Big Peg, 120 Vyse St,
Birmingham B18 6NF
tel: 0121 604 3200 • fax: 0121 604 3311
e-mail: bydesignkiosk@btconnect.com

Kiosk are mail order only but they have some great curtain finials that come in strange shapes – from wiggly lines to arrowheads – all in a shiny silver finish. Their designs are designed solely in the UK and are exclusive to the company.

McKinney & Co
1 Wandon Rd, London SW6 2JF
tel: 0171 384 1377 • fax: 0171 736 1196

McKinney's have a massive selection of curtain furniture and you're sure to find something you like. There are reproduction poles as well as antique ones, and the finishes include brass, metal and wood. If you want to have brass items antiqued, they can do this for you.

Nice Irma's By Post
Unit 2, Finchley Industrial Centre,
879 High Rd, London N12 8QA
tel: 0800 328 1867

An unusual mail order range of expanding iron poles, which come in either black or polished pewter with a choice of finials – daisies, paisley swirls, and bay leaves.

Rufflette
tel: 0161 998 1811 for stockists

Handy packs of clips or rings, which are ideal for hanging curtains without sewing.

blinds

Austrian, roller, ruched, vertical, Venetian – the choice is infinite. Whatever the size or shape of your window, there is a company that can make a blind to fit it.

Roller blinds, operated by a chain mechanism, come in a massive range of colours and materials and most companies now offer a custom-made service making up blinds to measure in your own choice of fabric (see also Fabrics p.176 for ideas). You can put roller blinds behind curtains to cut out light and they're good if you've got odd shaped windows and want a relatively inexpensive option.

Venetian blinds, in wood, metal, PVC and plastic, with horizontal slats, are good for controlling the amount of light. Ones with an aluminium coating on the back of each slat help reflect the light back out so you don't get too hot. Their only drawback is that they collect dust and can give the feel of an office. They best suit minimalist and hi-tech styles of home. Vertical blinds, with slats running from top to bottom, have recently enjoyed a comeback with the seventies revival and are ideal to cover large windows. Austrian blinds, with their flounces and frills, seem to have fallen out of favour but no doubt will be back. Whatever blind you favour, always consider what sort of light your room gets and how you want to control it.

Alison White

c/o Novatec, Star Lane, Margate, Kent CT9 4EF
tel: 01843 604430

Distributed through Novatec, Alison White's roller blinds are stunningly simple, yet brilliantly effective. Available in a range of contemporary colours, she cuts tiny squares, circles or eye-shaped slits into them so that the shafts of light pierce them.

Appeal Blinds

6 Vale Lane, Bedminster, Bristol, Avon BS3 5SD
tel: 0117 963 7734 • fax: 0117 966 6216
e-mail: sales@appeal-blinds.co.uk

Conservatory blinds made from pinoleum – a laminated wood. What's great about Appeal is that they will tint the blinds to match Farrow & Ball paint colours (see p.14).

Artistic Blinds

111 Staple Hill Rd, Fishponds, Bristol, Avon BS16 5AD
tel: 0117 957 1798 • fax: 0117 960 4224

This company will make up blinds in your own fabric and offer a totally made-to-measure service.

BCL Window Blinds

22 Victoria St, Burnham-on-Sea, Somerset TA8 1AL
tel: 01278 780094 • fax: 01278 785272

A manufacturer of all types of blind from roller, vertical, Venetian, louvre – even awnings for tents and caravans.

Blind Date Blinds

Red Hatch Yard, Reading Rd, Burchfield Common, Reading, Berks RG7 3BL
tel: 0118 983 1800 • fax: 0118 983 1333

This company makes lots of blinds for the film and tv industries but may undertake domestic orders as well.

Blinds Direct

4 Kingston Walk, Kingston Centre, Milton Keynes, Bucks MK10 0BA
tel: 01908 282043 • fax: 01908 282063

Remember when everyone had those vertical slatted blinds which were the epitome of seventies style? If you'd like to have new ones made, this company makes them in all sorts of colours and finishes such as PVC, metal and fabric. The staff are extremely helpful.

Cooks Blinds & Shutters Ltd

Burnet Rd, Sweet Briar Industrial Estate, Norwich, Norfolk NR3 2BS
tel: 01603 410304 • fax: 01603 405090

PVC blinds in rainbow colours are an unusual offering amongst the usual range of roller, Venetian, and vertical blinds. The blinds are manufactured by Loveless Cook Blinds – part of the company that also makes awnings, security grilles and industrial shutters.

Silent Gliss

Star Lane, Margate, Kent CT9 4EF
tel: 01843 863571

The Metropolitan is a very useful curtain track that can go round bay windows. They also do roller blinds – their Corazza is very chic although quite pricey.

The Velux Company Ltd

Woodside Way, Glenrothes East, Fife KY7 4ND
tel: 01592 772211 • fax: 01592 771839
tel: 0800 980 7180 for stockists

Velux is almost synonymous with the word windows, and most people know they make roof windows, which are most often installed in loft conversions and attics. What you may not know is that they also manufacture a wide range of blinds, specifically to fit their windows, in all different varieties (Venetian, roller, awning, pleated and roller shutters to name a few), and all in many colourways. They are sold mainly through branches of John Lewis and the larger B&Q warehouses, but phone for your nearest stockist.

shutters

Many period homes had window shutters fixed internally. They were usually solid blocks of panelling with hinges which folded back into the recess and almost disappeared from view. Sometimes they went across the whole height of the window, sometimes just the lower half. If you've got old shutter boxes on your windows, new shutters could be more easily re-installed.

Some of the companies below make new shutters to resemble period ones or perhaps you fancy something a bit more modern. If you hate curtains, can't sew or simply like the look, shutters could be the answer. Anne McKevitt makes them out of MDF and has fretwork installed. They needn't look old-fashioned – you could have a basic frame covered in felt for an unusual way to diffuse the light.

American Shutters
72 Station Rd, London SW13 0LS
tel: 0181 876 5905 • fax: 0181 878 9548

This company is the only UK distributor of the American Pinecrest shutters. Painted or stained to a colour of your choice, they can custom-make them to fit any size window, no matter how awkward the space. Phone for a quotation and technical advice.

The House of Shutters
Studio 2, The Birches Business Centre,
Selsey, nr Chichester, W.Sussex PO20 9EP
tel: 01243 603020 • fax: 01243 603069
e-mail: hos@globalnet.co.uk

This company provides an all-round service – they will custom-make shutters to your specific requirements as well as installing them. You can have adjustable louvred panels or solid panels if you want to achieve a more period feel. They come in natural pine or they will stain or paint them in a finish of your choice. They also have a London office (tel. 0171 610 4624).

Jali
Apsley House, Chartham, Canterbury,
Kent CT4 7HT
tel: 01227 831710

Jali make beautiful fretwork shutters out of MDF which look more expensive than they actually are. They offer a prompt and friendly service and make designs to order.

Lindman
Tower Lane, Warmley, Bristol, Avon BS15 2XX
tel: 0117 961 0900 for technical advice
fax: 0117 961 0901

Available in ten solid colours, these shutters have a wood-grain texture but are actually made from co-polymer resin, which means you don't need to protect them in the same way as wood and the paint will not flake off with exposure to the elements.

London's Georgian Houses Ltd
291 Goswell Rd, London EC1V 7LA
tel/fax: 0171 833 8217

Wooden shutters were often found in period homes of the eighteenth and nineteenth centuries and this company can restore your own, if they are still in existence, or make new ones in keeping with the house. They use only traditional methods and materials and are experts in all types of period woodwork whether it's doors, floors or wood panelling. Phone for an appointment and someone will come to assess your house and give you a quotation before you decide to proceed.

Plantation Shutters
131 Putney Bridge Rd, London SW15 2PA
tel: 0181 871 9333 • fax: 0181 871 9222

To give your home the tropical feel, these custom-made shutters come in basswood or poplar – both renewable resources – and known for their resistance to warping. There is a consultancy service available, depending on where you live, or you can visit the premises in south-west London.

The Shutter Shop
Queensbury House, Dilly Lane, Hartley Wintney,
Hants RG27 8EQ
tel: 01252 844575 for brochure and quotation
fax: 01252 844718

There's a choice of twenty different paint stains to finish off your custom-made shutters, all of which are manufactured in the UK using kiln-dried poplar wood. You can have them slatted or solid, or half and half, fixed or louvred. Even if your window is an odd angle or an arch, they can make shutters to fit. They offer a free measuring service within the M25 catchment area.

the soft

Fabrics and soft furnishings are usually the finishing touch to a room and can bring the whole room together. Sometimes, however, a particular piece of fabric can be the initial inspiration and spark off the whole idea for the colour scheme. Whichever way round, choosing fabrics and furnishings can be one of the most pleasurable aspects of designing your home.

Fabric plays a minor role in *Home Front* but occasionally it takes centre stage. Designer Lloyd Farmar used over 500 metres of slub muslin to decorate the interior of a town hall for one couple's wedding. Designer Nishma Chande used wonderful sari fabric to create canopies and beautiful accessories for an Indian-style bedroom in the Lewsey family's Norfolk barn, and Anne McKevitt used fake fur to cover chairs and trimmed mirrors with fluffy maribou.

To list every fabric shop in the entire United Kingdom would not have been possible, so instead we have listed (alphabetically rather than by region) the best places we have discovered where you will find particularly good bargains, and large companies who do mail order.

touch

fabric & furnishings

Although there are some colour combinations for fabrics that will forever look good together, such as blue and white or blue and yellow, there are really no hard and fast rules about which colours should be paired with each other and sometimes mixing what are conventionally thought of as 'clashing colours' can look fantastic. If you're not sure, try building up a little collection of swatches and keep mixing and matching them – trust your eye to tell you.

When it comes to pattern, try and avoid repeating a single design throughout a room if you don't want the effect to look too contrived or artful. Instead try mixing stripes with spots, checks with florals, or mix checks of varying sizes together. The smaller the pattern, the further away it seems and if you want to create a light airy feel to a room, go for small-scale designs. In a small space, you do not have to limit yourself to one design. As long as you keep some uniformity of colour, you can use as many different patterns as you like. If you have a very large room or one with high ceilings and want to make the room appear cosier, then go for richer colours with bold flourishes of pattern. Also try to juxtapose different weights and textures such as floaty voiles next to toiles. Think of texture and finish too – a chintz with a high sheen to it can brighten up a dull room but too much and you will end up climbing the walls. Conversely, too many rustic sludges and dull colours can drag a room down.

You needn't spend a fortune either. Muslin, calico, sheeting and voiles can all be picked up quite cheaply and can look stunning as window dressing if you don't want traditional curtains. Dress fabrics can also be used instead of curtain fabrics on a window and this will also save you money, although you may have to line them.

The criteria for choosing one fabric over another has much to do with its suitability for its intended purpose. There's no point covering a sofa in a dress fabric. It simply won't be tough enough. Lightweight fabrics, such as voile and muslin, unlined cotton and linen, work brilliantly for windows. Just hang them on simple curtain poles, narrow rods, or simply staple them up. Cotton sheeting can be used for making your own duvet covers – it's cheap and comes in wide widths. Tough fabrics include canvas, which you can use for blinds, deckchair slings and cushions. Calico can be found at most department stores and is cheap. It looks good in its natural cream-coloured state but can be dyed.

Anta Scotland Ltd

Fearn, Tain, Ross-shire IV20 1XW
tel: 01862 832477 for stockists • fax: 01862 832616
e-mail: antascot@acl.com
and
32 High St, Royal Mile, Edinburgh EH1 1TB
tel: 0131 557 8300

You don't need to hail from the Glens to admire these tartans and plaids. Forget the traditional kilt patterns, and think instead of contemporary colours in beautifully soft, worsted fabrics and plaids.

Beaumont & Fletcher

261 Fulham Rd, London SW3 6HY
tel: 0171 352 5553 for stockists • fax: 0171 352 3545

Visit this showroom for a wonderful selection of richly patterned fabrics including chenilles and linens. It's top-of-the-range stuff with price labels to match.

Benchmark

184 Westbourne Grove, London W11 2RH
tel: 0171 229 4179 • fax: 0171 229 4179

This is a strange but fascinating antique shop which has been included because it has a very rare source of upholstery pins which come from a French factory that closed down in the twenties. There are ones in Arts & Crafts style, ones with Egyptian hieroglyphics and they are all exquisite in their own right.

Bennett Silks

Crown Royal Park, Higher Hillgate, Stockport, Cheshire SK1 3HB
tel: 0161 477 5979 for stockists • fax: 0161 480 5385

Silks in every colour of the rainbow are produced by this company and sold at retail outlets throughout the country. Choose from plain blocks of colour, which have a gorgeous filmy transparency, or ones with subtle patterns woven in. They also do silk brocades and some velvets.

Bernard Thorp & Co

53 Chelsea Manor St, London SW3 5RZ
tel: 0171 352 5457

Imagine you find some fabric belonging to your grandmother in the attic and would love some more made up. It is possible to have fabrics copied but be prepared for it to be costly because the fabric presses

have to be set up in the same way whether you are printing a few or thousands of metres. You must also take into consideration the copyright of the fabric. This company, expert in the field, should be able to advise you.

The Berwick St Cloth Shop

15 Berwick St, London W1V 3RG
tel: 0171 287 2881

To those in the know, Berwick St in London's Soho is synonymous with cheap fabrics and this great shop is a favourite haunt of dress designers and tailors looking for materials to create their latest inspiration. There are hundreds of utility fabrics from stripy ticking to soft felts.

Blithfield & Company

68 Scarsdale Villas, London W8 6PP
tel: 0171 460 6454 • fax: 0171 460 6493

This company produces a small and exclusive range of screen-printed cottons and linens based on eighteenth- and nineteenth-century French and English 'documents' – a document being an original piece of fabric. Their best-selling fabric is a floral called Chelverton.

Borovick Fabrics

16 Berwick St, London W1V 4HP
tel: 0171 437 2180

This is billed as the oldest established theatrical supplier in London and has been in business since 1932. Supplying the film, theatre and television industries, it's great for inexpensive materials – not really furnishing fabrics but everything else from cheap lining to raw silk and brocades. As their stock is so huge, it's best to send a SAE in the first instance stating what you're looking for and they will send you some samples by return.

Brunschwig & Fils

10 The Chambers, Chelsea Harbour Drive, Chelsea Harbour, London SW10 0XF
tel: 0171 351 5797 for stockists
fax: 0171 351 2280

A large range of fabrics are on show at their Chelsea showroom, mostly in traditional styles from heavily patterned chinoiserie to French toiles and silks.

Bute Fabrics

Rothesay, Isle of Bute PA20 0DP
tel: 01700 503734 • fax: 01700 504545
tel: 0800 212064 freephone
e-mail: sales@butefabrics.co.uk

A beautiful range of really unusual fabrics suitable for upholstery and cushions. They are all made from natural materials – mostly wool – and have a gorgeous range of subtle colours from heathers to pewter greys.

The Cloth Clinic

The Old Rectory, Sheldon, nr Honiton, Devon EX14 0QU
tel/fax: 01404 841718 for stockists
e-mail: Stoyel@AOL.com

Weird and wonderful fabrics that are cut out with lasers – a revolutionary technique for fabrics which may be the way of the future. The results are stunning, with materials such as stainless steel spun as fine as gossamer but remaining stiff to the touch. You can hang sheets of it at the window if money is no option. The cost per metre is not cheap, but you expect that because of the materials used and because of the technology that has gone into making them.

The Cloth Shop

290 Portobello Rd, London W10 5TE
tel: 0181 968 6001

A day's outing to London's Portobello Market should include a visit to this shop. It's small but stuffed with bargains. They're particularly good on silks, which often form their window display to entice you in, as well as rolls of felt, fake fur, and calico and muslin.

Cotswold Fabric Warehouse

5 Tewkesbury Rd, Cheltenham, Glos GL51 9AH
tel: 01242 255959 • fax: 01242 257373

You will be overwhelmed by the choice on offer at this massive warehouse, which is crammed full of linens, checks, dress and upholstery fabrics, cheap sheeting plus a range of curtain poles and trimmings.

Cover Up Designs

The Barn, Hannington Farm, Hannington,
Hants RG26 5TZ
tel: 01635 297981 • fax: 01635 298363

If you can't sew yourself or can't find what you want in the shops, this company can produce loose and fitted covers for you, to go with their own range of furniture from dressing tables to ottomans. The furniture usually comes in a stone-white painted finish, with or without glass tops where applicable. If you like flouncy dressing tables covers, or fancy some bolsters and cushions to match an existing fabric, they can run them up for you – all to a highly professional finish. Headboards, screens, and stools are all part of their repertoire.

Designer's Guild

267–271 & 275–277 Kings Rd, London SW3 5EN
tel: 0171 243 7300 for the store • fax: 0171 243 7710
tel: 0171 351 5775 for general enquiries

The walls are awash with colour at the showroom of No. 277, which has hundreds of fabrics, arranged by colour, hanging in lines. Tricia Guild's trademark vibrant colours of turquoise and fuchsias abound with blowsy flower motifs. Pop a few doors down into the store and you can see the fabric put into use from everything from bed linen to cushions.

Donghia

Unit G/23, Chelsea Harbour Design Centre,
Chelsea Harbour, London SW10 0XE
tel: 0171 823 3456 for showroom
fax: 0171 376 5758

Donghia has some very classy and beautifully made fabrics at the top end of the market including the intriguingly named puckered chenille, moiré, silk, and lots of silk damask hand woven in India.

Fibre Naturelle

51 Poole Rd, Bournemouth, Dorset BH4 9BA
tel/fax: 01202 751750 for stockists

Supplying over 600 retail outlets, this company manufactures hand-woven Indian cottons, voiles, silks in stripes, plains and checks, chenille throws, and lots of heavy-duty upholstery material.

Hagg & Weil AB

Ever Trading Ltd, 12 Martindale, East Sheen,
London SW14 7AL
tel: 0181 878 4050 for stockists • fax: 0181 876 5717

This Swedish company have really cornered the market for strikingly youthful and fresh designs. They are very distinctive and found in all sorts of stylish retail shops. You'll recognize them by the big rosebuds, slices of orange, gerberas, raspberries, fish and seahorses all in day-glo colours.

Harlequin Fabrics & Wallcoverings
Cossington Rd, Sileby, Leics LE12 7RU
tel: 01509 813112 for stockists • fax: 01509 816003
tel: 0800 328 7084 for a brochure

Brightly coloured cottons with contrasting checks
are just one of this company's ranges. The colours
are contemporary, mixing lime-green with orange,
and great for creating timeless style in children's
rooms.

HL Linen Bazaars
Churchbridge, Oldbury, W. Midlands B69 2AS
tel: 0121 541 1918 for mail order and branches

If you've ever wondered what happens to some of
the excess stock that hotels and other establishments
over order, now you know – although don't worry,
the sheets and towels don't have the name of the
hotel on! HL Linen have fifteen shops in locations
across the country from Liverpool down to Bristol.
All sell linen for bathrooms, bedrooms and kitchens.
They receive job lots of very slight seconds as well
as perfects, and some of the stock is available by
mail order.

Ian Mankin
109 Regents Park Rd, London NW1 8UR
tel: 0171 722 0997
and
271 Wandsworth Bridge Rd, London SW6 2TX
tel: 0171 371 8825

A pioneer of the use of utility fabrics – calicos,
butcher's stripes and tickings – which are fantastic
all around the house for covering chairs, making
deckchair covers, loose covers and cheap curtains
and blinds. They have around 300 different natural
fabrics in stock. A good selection is shown in their
mail order catalogue but there are hundreds more
besides.

John Boyd Textiles Ltd
Higher Flax Mills, Castle Cary, Somerset BA7 7DY
tel: 01963 350451 for samples • fax: 01963 351078

Horsehair fabrics are this company's speciality, which
come in more patterns and designs than you would
have thought possible and are surprisingly soft to the
touch. They are suitable for upholstery from sofas to
chaise longues.

Just Fabrics
The Bridewell, Dockacre Rd, Launceston,
Cornwall PL15 8YY
tel: 01566 776279 • fax: 01566 773239

One of the biggest fabric libraries in the country
where they have recently introduced computer-
assisted room sets which means you can see how
your room would look with a certain fabric. They
stock all the leading names in interior fabrics, lush
cushions, throws and some material on the roll.

KA International
60 Sloane Avenue, London SW3 3DD
tel: 0171 584 7352 for stockists
fax: 0171 589 9534

Specializing in 100 per cent cottons in warm and
vibrant colours such as mustard yellows and reds.
Choose from floral prints or bold stripes and checks.
New collections are introduced regularly.

Knickerbean
tel: 01842 751327 for branches

If you're looking for designer name bargains, this
chain of fabric shops has a good range of stock from
Zoffany, Jane Churchill and Liberty's amongst others.
If a line has been discontinued or has been over-
ordered, you can sometimes save up to 50 per cent on
the original retail price. They have a good range of
upholstery and furnishing fabrics, can make up loose
covers, stock cushions, tie-backs and other trimmings.
There are branches in Bath, Newbury, St Albans,
Tunbridge Wells and Bury St Edmunds – call the main
number for details.

Loose Ends
Giles Green, Brinkworth, Chippenham,
Wilts SN15 5DQ
tel/fax: 01666 510685 for mail order

This is a good source of discontinued fabrics, and you
may get some real bargains. It's also good for plainish
upholstery fabrics and linings.

MacCulloch & Wallis
25–26 Dering St, London W1A 3AX
tel: 0171 409 0725 • fax: 0171 491 9578

A very good place to visit if you want to see a large
selection of fabrics from ginghams to silks and velvets.

Malabar Cotton Company

31–33 The South Bank Business Centre,
Ponton Rd, London SW8 5BL
tel: 0171 501 4200 for stockists • fax: 0171 501 4210

This company imports directly from India and specializes in hand-woven cotton which is suitable for upholstery. It's 100 per cent cotton and comes in vibrant colours like Turmeric and Paprika. You can visit the showroom and take some samples away with you but it's not a shop as such.

Melin Tregwynt

Melin Tregwynt Mill, Castlemorris,
Haverfordwest, Pembs SA62 5UX
tel: 01348 891225 • fax: 01348 891694
tel: 01348 891644 for mail order

A real fully working mill where you can see the traditional Welsh designs being made up on the looms, if you can bear the thundering noise. The blankets and throws are beautiful – choose from angora/wool throws or plaids. If you can't get there then they do a mail order service. Identical blankets are available at the Designer's Guild in London but you'll pay less if you buy them at source.

The Natural Fabric Company

Wessex Place, 127 High St, Hungerford,
Berks RG17 0DL
tel: 01488 684002 • fax: 01488 686455

This company operates from a tiny shop under an old coaching arch and demand for their fabrics was so great that they have now set up a mail order service, although you can still visit the shop. As their name indicates, natural fabrics are their speciality including hessian, linen, gingham, chambray, sheers, damask, calico, chintz, and tickings.

Nina Campbell

c/o Osborne & Little
49 Temperley Rd, London SW12 8QE
tel: 0181 675 2255 for stockists • fax: 0181 673 8254

Osborne & Little distribute Nina Campbell's designs, which are quintessentially English and of top quality. New ranges are regularly introduced – but her trademarks are stylized floral silhouettes and classical colours. There are some truly beautiful fabrics here that are timeless.

Nono Designs

Unit A, Marlborough Close, Parkgate Industrial Estate,
Knutsford, WA16 8XN for stockists
tel: 01565 757402 • fax: 01565 757405
e-mail: gill-nono@msn.com

A top-of-the-range collection of fabrics frequently seen in the style magazines and inspired by things as diverse as the 1960s, abstract flowers and decidedly Oriental influences.

The Old Loom Mill

Mulbrooks Farm, Ersham Rd, Halisham,
E. Sussex BN27 2RH
tel: 01323 848007

A good place to come for lining and large expanses of sheeting. As its name suggests, the mill's heritage is wool, which is sold by the weight. It's also a good place to come for seconds.

The Original Silver Lining Company

Workshop 29, Lenton Business Centre,
Lenton Boulevard, Nottingham NG7 2BY
tel: 0115 955 5123

Linings by the hundredweight abound here – and a good source of blackout linings for those of us who need complete darkness to sleep. Available by mail order, there are also lots of muslins and lawns, some ready-made cushions without the fillings, and lots of calico and cotton sheeting.

Pongees

28–30 Hoxton Square, London N1 6NN
tel: 0171 739 9130 • fax: 0171 739 9132

A great supplier of silk including parachute silks which can be used for creating canopies, bedspreads, curtains or wonderful cushions.

Temptation Alley

361 Portobello Rd, London W10 5SA
tel: 0181 964 2004 • fax: 0171 727 4432

An absolute treasure trove of a shop where you can root around to your heart's content. Very good for all sorts of trimmings and braids, maribou, fake fur and utility fabrics.

Turquaz
The Coach House, Bakery Place, 119 Altenburg
Gardens, London SW11 1JQ
tel: 0171 924 6894

Only natural fibres are used in this ready-made range,
blending together Egyptian and Indian cottons and
using checks and stripes and a limited palette of
colours so you can mix and match. They can look
modern and timeless. Lots of care has been taken with
the details, such as cloth-covered buttons, and the
bed linen is all hand finished with contrasting binding.

Tuscarora
31–35 Stannary St, London SE11 4AA
tel: 0171 735 8848

If your old beanbag is looking a bit saggy or you want
to make a new one from scratch, this company sells
polystyrene beads you can fill beanbags with. You will
need about eight cubic feet of beads, which are sent in
a box, to fill an average-sized bag.

Waltons Mill Shop
41 Tower St, Harrogate HG1 1HS
tel: 01423 520980
and
36 Piercy End, Kirkbymoorside, York YO6 6DF
tel: 01751 433253

Once you've chosen your colour scheme and basic
fabric, it's fun to choose all the bits and bobs that
make up the trimmings – tassels, cords and braid, to
name but three. This is a good place to come as there
are myriad colours and the prices are often particularly
low as they deal a lot in bankrupt stock.

Wolfin Textiles
64 Great Titchfield St, London W1P 7AE
tel: 0171 636 4949 • fax: 0171 580 4724

A great place to visit for bargains. They sell plain
cotton sheeting at very reasonable prices, cotton
ticking, calico, muslin, and lots of utility fabrics.

11

sort out

Lack of storage space is the bane of many people's lives and it is about this seemingly universal problem that *Home Front* receives the most letters. As more and more people work from home, the need for organized space is becoming increasingly essential. Over the last few years shops dedicated solely to storage have sprung up – a reflection of our cluttered lives and our desire for organized living as we cope with so many demands on our space.

Clutter can be overwhelming as well as time-consuming but storage solutions needn't be dull. There are hundreds of fun products around to get your life in order. Look out for old filing cabinets in second-hand office suppliers – after a good sand down, a coat of primer and a coat of car spray paint in any colour under the sun, you won't recognize it. Big catering suppliers will often have great stainless steel cabinets you can customize for use anywhere in the house. They may need some alterations, but they can look modern and funky as well as being extremely useful. Even the humble orange crate or wooden vegetable tray can make great storage – the sort you see piled up high outside markets and greengrocers for the dustmen on rubbish days. Ask your local wine merchants if they'll let you have any of their old packing crates. Check for splinters before giving them a coat of paint and you will have instant storage!

Some of the outlets listed in this chapter (alphabetically rather than by region), may seem odd at first glance but the trick is to think laterally and use your imagination. Go on, get organized!

your
space!

key: 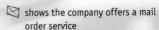 shows the product has appeared on
Home Front

✉ shows the company offers a mail
order service

Action Handling Equipment
The Maltings Industrial Estate, Station Rd,
Sawbridgeworth, Herts CM21 9JY
tel: 01279 724989 for catalogue
fax: 01279 600224
e-mail: ahandling@aol.com

The mail order only catalogue is full of pallet trucks
and fire extinguishers for industrial use, but if you can
plough your way through all this, there are some great
ideas for storage. If you remember keeping your school
plimsolls in a wire mesh locker, they are now very
fashionable and you can really use them for just about
anything – books, magazines, food – whatever takes
your fancy.

Ascott Designs
Units 4–6 Marley Way, Banbury, Oxon OX16 7RL
tel: 01295 270848 for catalogue
fax: 01295 270965

This company has decorative but sturdy baker's racks
fashioned from wrought-iron that look as good in a
kitchen as a conservatory. There are ones with either
three or four tiers, or a collapsible one which is handy
if you want to move it around.

Cleerline Storage Equipment
19 Station Way, Cheam Village, Sutton,
Surrey SM3 8SD
tel: 0181 770 7077 for brochure • fax: 0181 770 7015

This company specializes in mobile clothes rails. The
fact that they supply to the retail industry indicates
that the rails are sturdy enough not to buckle under
the weight of heavy clothes. They do various different
models, all of which slot together easily. They also
have canvas hanging systems, shoe racks,
coathangers, and modular storage systems made from
impact resistant thermoplastic resin. All items are
available by mail order only.

Country Furniture
36 London Rd, Stapeley, Nantwich,
Cheshire CW5 7JL
tel: 01270 610543 for catalogue

If you'd like one of those very useful hanging rails but
feel that a chrome one would look out of place in your
home, this company makes wooden ones. Each rail can
hold up to twenty suits or dresses, which means you
need never go rummaging at the bottom of your
wardrobe again.

Cubbins & Co
Unit 1, Rampisham Manor, Dorchester,
Dorset DT2 0PT
tel: 01935 83060 for brochure • fax: 01935 83257

If you like everything matching – from tissue boxes to
linen bins – this mail order only company will cover
anything in your own choice of fabric. The standard of
finish is very high. They will trim the edges with co-
ordinating braid, and line wastepaper bins with clear
plastic. Alternatively, you can opt for a paint finish –
with a ragged, dragged, sponged or crackle-glazed
finish from a choice of seven colours.

Cubestore
Charlwoods Rd, East Grinstead,
Sussex RH19 2HP
tel: 01342 310033 for catalogue • fax: 01342 310099

An exclusive range of storage and shelving systems are
available through the post from this company. There is
a choice of finishes – natural beech wood veneer,
lacquered finished beech wood veneer or white
melamine – and you simply choose combinations of
different modules and units to create your own
individual design. All the units are pre-drilled and
they will deliver direct to your home.

The Domestic Paraphernalia Company
Unit 15, Marine Business Centre, Dock Rd,
Lytham, Lancs FY8 5AJ
tel: 01253 736334 for brochure • fax: 01253 795191

If you've been after one of those old-fashioned clothes
airers that come down on a pulley from the ceiling,
look no further. This mail order company does one
called The Sheila Maid and it's made from wood and
iron. They also do plate racks in wood and plant
stands – not a huge range but what they do produce
is well made.

The Dormy House
Stirling Park, East Portway Industrial Estate,
Andover, Hants SP10 3TZ
tel: 01264 365808 • fax: 01264 366359
e-mail: dormyhouse@compuserve.com

Ottomans and blanket boxes are great for concealing a
whole host of things that can clutter up the place, but
good ones can be quite difficult to find. The Dormy
House makes both in decent sizes and in a choice of
finishes. The blanket box comes in plain MDF, or
painted cream or white and with a foam seat covered

in your choice of fabric. If you need to work from home, the ottoman can come with a handy hanging suspension rack to store A4 files.

The Empty Box Company
The Old Dairy, Coomb Farm Building,
Balchins Lane, Westcott, Surrey RH4 3LE
tel: 01306 740193 for brochure • fax: 01306 875430

If you need somewhere to store something precious, like a wedding dress or christening gown, this mail order only company has designed a collection of hand-made boxes just for this purpose. Rather than hanging in a cupboard or in a protective cover, a box is apparently better at protecting the delicate fabric from light and dust. They also look pretty, being handcovered with papers, lace and ribbon. Hat, CD, and toy boxes are also available, in a range of papers from traditional William Morris to brightly coloured polka dots.

Graham & Green
10 Elgin Crescent, London W11 2JA
tel/fax: 0171 727 9717

Just off London's bustling Portobello Rd, you will find the peace and tranquillity of Graham & Green. Everything is beautifully displayed and you could happily pass a few hours browsing amongst the wares. They carry lots of stuff by top design names that you can find elsewhere, such as wavy CD racks, wire racks, and some useful folding shelves, but it's such a pleasure to shop here.

Grand Illusions
2–4 Crown Rd, St Margarets, Twickenham,
Middx TW1 3EE
tel: 0181 744 1046 • fax: 0181 744 2017

The company celebrated its tenth anniversary in 1998. Its philosophy is how to achieve 'purer style'. They have two shops and operate a mail order service. The mail order catalogue (£2.50 but worth it) is called *Maison* and is beautifully presented with the sort of styled photographs more often seen in a coffee-table book. It is full of things you thought you could only get from antique shops or from spending years hunting round French brocantes – linen chests, wooden plan chests, galvanized storage jars, willow laundry baskets, simple cream jugs and bowls, and little cabinets with chicken mesh fronts. Truly classy storage ideas.

Habitat
196 Tottenham Court Rd, London W1P 9LD
tel: 0171 255 2545
tel: 0645 334433 for branches

Habitat are still front-runners in the storage stakes. They sell well-made and sturdy boxes in shoe box size and bigger versions with punched studs. The range of colours changes according to what's in fashion. There are always good shelves and great cabinets in stock and smaller items, such as their laundry bins in wicker and canvas, are notably good quality for the price.

The Holding Company
241–245 Kings Rd, London SW3 5EL
tel: 0171 352 1600
and
41 Spring Gardens, Manchester M2 2BG
tel: 0161 834 3400
tel: 0171 610 9160 for mail order nationwide
fax: 0171 610 9166 for mail order nationwide

The Holding Company was the first shop aimed solely at storage to open in the UK. The gap in the market was spotted by retailer Dawna Walter who founded the first London branch in 1995 and has since gone from strength to strength with a mail order business. Their slogan is 'who says storage can't be fun?', and in the shop and catalogue you will find every conceivable storage idea – from the humble sock divider to complete hanging systems. You need never be disorganized again.

Humphrey Newcombe Plastics Co
7c Church St, Dronfield, Sheffield S18 6LZ
tel: 01246 416306 for brochure

Available by mail order only, stackerjacks are tough plastic storage boxes that stack neatly together. Del-ivered to your door in flat packs, they have a wipe clean surface and are extremely tough – even the smallest one can hold up to 100 lb in weight. They would be good for storing toys and books that aren't always needed on a regular basis but that you'd still like to keep.

IKEA
Brent Park, 2 Drury Way, North Circular Rd,
London NW10 0TH
tel: 0181 208 5600 for enquiries and branches

IKEA is great for cheap and cheerful wardrobes and shelving as well as complete storage systems, which can be built on to as your possessions expand. In the 'marketplace' (the area of the shop where smaller bits and pieces are kept) you will find all sorts of good storage ideas. Their simple, cheap, yet stylish files in pale birch and corrugated cardboard have proved highly popular and can't be beaten as well as hat boxes in three sizes that fit neatly inside one another. One of their most successful ideas has been selling different sized plain wooden boxes with drawers which you can decorate yourself in an infinite number of ways. Every home should have one.

Ikino

Brocastle Avenue, Waterton Industrial Estate,
Bridgend, Mid Glamorgan CF31 3YH
tel: 01656 669906 for stockists • fax: 01656 663185

Drawing inspiration from the Japanese approach to living, this company has developed a range of modular storage systems to keep your life pared down. Made of impact-resistant thermoplastic resin (which sounds a mouthful but is tough and flexible) their storage systems can be adapted to suit your needs and come in a range of colours with contrasting handles.

inthebag

3 Lydgate Rd, Shepley, Huddersfield,
W.Yorks HDG 8DZ
tel/fax: 01484 603641 for brochure

If you have to drive to a special occasion with your clothes hanging, rep-style, from the hook by the back seat, inthebag's Walking Wardrobe will allow you to arrive in style instead of crumpled and creased. It also looks so much more stylish hanging on the back of the door at home than the suit carrier you get from the local dry-cleaning shop. The mail order only range was launched in 1994 and the carefully thought out details – such as a ribbon that ties at the neck to prevent the clothes from slipping off the hangers inside, proved such a success that there is now a Wedding Wardrobe – wider than the norm, in gold or cream, that comes with a co-ordinating range of accessories such as padded hangers.

Key Industrial Equipment

Blackmoor Rd, Ebblake Industrial Estate,
Verwood, Dorset BH31 6AT
tel: 01202 825311

This company is really an industrial supplier who manufactures packing crates and shelving. However, they will take orders for the domestic market depending on the size of that order. Good if you've

got a really serious storage problem and you'd quite like that 'I'm just in the middle of moving' look.

Lakeland Ltd

Alexandra Buildings, Windermere,
Cumbria LA23 1BQ
tel: 01539 488100 for branches and mail order
fax: 01539 488300

Lakeland, who are known for their fab range of plastic goods, have a whole mail order catalogue devoted to storage with tons of good ideas. Their plastic stacking boxes and crates are perfect for keeping children's toys tidy and *HomeFront* designer Fiona Samler even transformed one of their boxes into a portable coffee table! There are trolleys on wheels, shoe racks, and instant wardrobe organizers all mostly in plastic but you will find some products in wicker and steel. New products are always being introduced; there are some branches – phone the main number for details.

McCord

London Rd, Preston, Lancs PR11 1RP
tel: 0870 908 7070 • fax: 0870 908 7050

McCord, who do mail order only, is one of the lesser-known mail order catalogues but this shouldn't really be the case as they have some great ideas. Try one of their brilliant PVC portable wardrobes which looks like a mini tent. They are easily assembled and can be dismantled just as quickly. They also do a Rolling Underbed Wheelie Box, which is great for instantly hiding all that clutter. Look out also for their stylish wastepaper bins and boxes. If you like the rattan look, they make virtually anything you could want for your home office from in-trays to letter racks.

Muji

187 Oxford St, London W1R 1AJ
tel: 0171 437 7503 for branches

If you 'yen' for simplicity, this shop sells 'no-brand no-nonsense' goods manufactured in Japan and East Asia. The four London shops are devoid of colour – virtually everything comes in a neutral buff, white polypropylene or steel, but it creates a very tranquil atmosphere and a pleasing uniformity. Particularly good is their range of cardboard storage in lots of different sizes which can either fit neatly under the bed or look equally good on display – perfect for minimalists. There are also perforated steel shelving, plastic trolleys, and acrylic boxes with drawers which you can use for literally anything.

Nomad Box Company
Rockingham Rd Industrial Estate,
Market Harborough, Leics LE16 7QE
tel: 01858 464878

If you've got an awkward-sized space that you want to utilize for storage but can't find anything to fit, this manufacturer will make 'one offs' to size. The storage boxes come in resin fibre board, aluminium or polypropylene and are built to last.

Ocean Home Shopping
Freepost LON811, London SW8 4BR
tel: 0800 132985
tel: 0870 848 4840 for mail order

This mail order company, which boasts next-day delivery, offers a range of modern and stylish designs to clear your clutter including chrome magazine racks, wastepaper bins and CD racks. There are also lots of smaller items which make ideal presents. They will gift wrap for an extra charge no matter how big the item.

Paperchase
213 Tottenham Court Rd, London W1P 9AF
tel: 0171 580 8496 for branches and mail order

Paperchase has loads of fun and ever-changing ideas for storage, although what you will find largely depends on the size of the branch. The biggest London one in Tottenham Court Rd has four floors where you start with pencil cases and stationery on the ground, and work your way up to

bins and plastic and mesh boxes, including some lovely hand-made paper boxes. Depending on what's currently in vogue, you can find anything from polypropylene stationery in acid colours, to files covered in raffia and hessian.

The Pier
200 Tottenham Court Rd, London W1P 0AD
tel: 0171 637 7001 • fax: 0171 637 3332
tel: 0171 814 5004 for stockist and mail order
tel: 0171 814 5020 for branches

The Pier might not be the first place you think of when it comes to storage, but they do have some good, reasonably priced ideas. Their rattan and metal chests in various sizes would look good anywhere from a bedroom to a conservatory.

Slingsby Commercial and Industrial Equipment
Preston St, Bradford, W.Yorks BD7 1JF
tel: 01274 721591 for branches

Slingsby is really an industrial supplier but they do cater for personal customers. They make huge stacking containers, which can come in red resin fibreboard with smart steel rivets, as well as aluminium containers and galvanized stacking baskets. You will need a catalogue first to give you some idea and, once you have chosen, it's best to place your order with the nearest regional office to you (there are eight nationwide) or by post. The head office will be able to tell you which one is most convenient.

salv

Salvage could be called a nineties phenomenon and the interest in making something new out of the old shows no signs of slowing down into the next millennium. More and more people are recognizing that this is a valuable way of recycling and rescuing things, as well as guaranteeing that your neighbours won't have the same as you. In the past fifty years, hundreds and hundreds of period features have been ripped out and it is only the foresight of salvage companies that have prevented examples of some items being lost forever.

Salvage yards are an excellent source of old baths and sanitary ware, fireplaces, period doors, old-style radiators, as well as raw materials such as brick, slate, quarry tiles and reclaimed wood. There is still, however, a certain mystery surrounding them. People are a bit wary of the unknown and it is easy to be unsure about how to put salvage to use in your home, or whether it will be possible for the item to be restored to good enough condition to be used before parting with your cash.

Home Front's salvage expert, Neville Griffiths, definitely has the eye. He has transformed all sorts of unlikely objects into covetable things – making a dirty old boot scraper into a shiny dish for sweets, a rusty hopper (a piece of guttering) into a candleholder, as well as furnishing a hallway entirely from found objects and fitting an entire salvage bathroom. He can pick up things, that most people would discard, and make something out of them. It can all look so easy on television when a quick wander round a yard seems miraculously to uncover something wonderful that just happens to fit. But, rest assured, these things *are* there and are just waiting to be discovered. With some patience and practice, you will learn what to discard and what to snap up.

age

sourcing salvage

If you are a salvage novice, there are a few points it is worth keeping in mind before you go on the hunt. Always phone first to make sure the place is open before making a wasted journey. We have included opening hours specially in this chapter, but it's best to make doubly sure. Salvage yards keep rather odd hours as their staff are often out themselves picking stuff up from all over the country to replenish their stocks. Be prepared to get dirty and preferably wear old clothes. Take a pair of gardening gloves for rummaging around for things that may be hidden under piles of other stuff. If you're looking for something specific like a fireplace or a door, make sure you take accurate measurements with you.

Look at every piece for its hidden potential, but don't get carried away as some things are just past repair. That beautiful thirties radiator you're dying to spray a lovely shade of silver may have hidden cracks. The cost of having that beautiful Edwardian fireplace may be just too prohibitive – and, anyway, make sure it's got all the bits with it. When choosing a bath try to find taps to go with it at the same time, as modern ones are unlikely to fit. If the bath is in a bad condition, it can always be re-enamelled, but decide first if it's worth it. Think also about its compatibility with your modern fixtures and fittings and whether it could run off a modern gas boiler. Finally, if you fall in love with a heavy Victorian cast-iron bath with beautiful claw feet, find out first whether your bathroom floor will be able to take the weight. You don't want to end up on the floor below!

The beauty of salvage is that you don't have to use the object for the means it was originally intended for. An old door mounted on trestle table legs can become a table; a Belfast sink can become a herb garden; and then there are all sorts of decorative objects – glass balls, gutter coverings, wooden printers' trays. In fact, almost anything can be turned into something else or simply displayed as a beautiful object in its own right with a little bit of imagination.

The way salvage yards operate varies wildly. In some, things are helpfully sorted out into categories and fairly clean, whereas in others it's all piled on top of each other. Be prepared to barter – it's the done thing. Knowing that what you are buying is honestly procured and has not been removed from a listed building without permission can be helpful. An organisation called Salvo can provide advice if you are in doubt (see p.274 for further details).

Happy hunting!

south west

Ace Demolition & Salvage

Pineview, Barrack Rd, West Parley, Dorset BH22 8UB
tel: 01202 579222 • fax: 01202 582043

A very tidy yard. You will find a hugely diverse selection of salvage items here including pieces from the heavier side such as timber, bricks, doors and quite unusual windows; and some on the lighter side like tiles, statues, butler's sinks, stoves and fireplaces. Open Mon–Fri, 8.30 a.m.–5 p.m. and Sat, 9 a.m.–4 p.m.

Architectural Heritage

Taddington Manor, nr Cheltenham, Glos GL54 5RY
tel: 01386 584414 • fax: 01386 584236
e-mail: puddy@architectural-heritage.co.uk

Set in the grounds of the Manor, this is at the top end of the salvage market. Expect to find good antique garden statuary, chimney pieces and other stone artefacts. They also have quite a lot of wooden panelling from the seventeenth, eighteenth and nineteenth centuries. Open Mon–Fri, 9.30 a.m.–5.30 p.m. and Sat, 10.30 a.m.–4 p.m.

Au Temps Perdu

5 Stapleton Rd, Easton, Bristol, Avon BS5 0QR
tel: 0117 955 5223

Although this company has some reclaimed building materials, they tend to concentrate on the lighter side of internal fixtures and fittings. They specialize in fireplaces and old sanitary ware in particular. When *Home Front* was following the renovation of a 1930s semi in Bristol belonging to the Perry family, salvage expert Neville Griffiths managed to unearth some period radiators perfect for the style of the house, as well as a fireplace that was brought back to life. It is well set out, neat and tidy, with helpful staff, but if you like to rummage to find your bargains, there is also scope for that. Open Mon–Sat, 10 a.m.–5.30 p.m.

Bridgwater Reclamation

Old Co-op Dairy, Monmouth St, Bridgwater, Somerset TA6 5EJ
tel: 01278 424636 • fax: 01278 453666

A big yard where you are welcome to rummage at your leisure. This company has been established for over fifteen years and specializes in reclaimed building materials such as floorboards, tiles and bricks. They

also offer internal fixture and fittings including fireplaces and some furniture. Open Mon–Fri, 8 a.m.–5 p.m, Sat, 8 a.m.–12 noon and Sun by appointment.

Castle Reclamation

Parrett Works, Martock, Somerset TA12 6AE
tel/fax: 01935 826483

This is a large yard that also has some showrooms attached. They offer all kinds of architectural antiques from bricks and beams, through fireplaces and statuary, down to the smallest items. Stone masons are at work here and they do a lot of stone cutting and carving. Open Mon–Fri, 8.30 a.m.–5 p.m. and Sat, 10 a.m.–1 p.m.

Chauncey's

15–16 Feeder Rd, Bristol, Avon BS2 0SB
tel: 01179 713131 • fax: 01179 712224

This is a specialist centre for timber, some of which has been salvaged, and some of which is new. If you want old timbers, they specialize in old pitch pine and oak. They have wide and narrow floorboards and block flooring in stock. Open Mon–Fri, 8.30 a.m.–5 p.m. and Sat by appointment only.

Colin Baker

Crown Hill, Halberton, Tiverton, Devon EX16 7AY
tel: 01884 820152

This place specializes in old timber whether it be floorboards in oak or pine, reclaimed joinery or old beams and joists. You will also find good wood if you want to make your own furniture, doors and some windows. Open by appointment only, so ring first.

Cox's Architectural Salvage Yard

10 Fosseway Business Park, Moreton-in-Marsh, Glos GL56 9NQ
tel: 01608 652505 • fax: 01608 652881

This salvage yard has a huge selection of pieces, mainly on the lighter side. You will find masses of gates, doors and fireplaces in all materials. More unusually they also have a wide selection of church and pub fittings. On top of this there are floorboards, lights, stained glass and oak and elm beams. Open Mon–Sat, 9 a.m.–6 p.m.

Dorset Reclamation

Cow Drive, Bere Regis, Wareham, Dorset BH20 7JZ
tel: 01929 472200

This is a highly organized salvage yard where you can find real treasures for your house. If you are looking for garden pieces they also have a fair selection of these. They are open five days a week and on Saturday until 4 p.m.

Elmtree Reclamation
Site 45, Victory Rd, West Wiltshire Trading Estate, Westbury, Wilts BA13 4JL
tel: 01373 826486

Some architectural salvage yards feel bric-à-brac is beneath them, but not this one, where you can browse to your heart's content among many of the smaller items of past times. There is also a large selection of larger items to give something for everyone. Elmtree is open five days a week and on Saturdays until 5 p.m.

Farm & Garden Bygones at Padstow Antiques
23 New St, Padstow, Cornwall PL28 8EA
tel: 01841 532914

This retail shop and the surrounding grounds hold a feast of architectural salvage pieces which would look good in your garden. Many of them have an agricultural past, which makes them especially interesting. If you are looking for a particularly large piece, there are local barns and yards full of these. Open from Mon–Sun, 10 a.m.–5 p.m.

Frome Reclamation
Station Approach, Wallbridge, Frome, Somerset BA11 1RE
tel: 01373 463919 • fax: 01373 453122

If you are looking on the heavier side for reclaimed building materials, this place is a good bet. They specialize in roofing materials, old clay tiles, natural slates, flagstones and other types of flooring. They also have some fireplaces, garden pieces and sanitary ware. Open Mon–Fri, 8 a.m.–5.30 p.m. and Sat, 8 a.m.–4.30 p.m.

Grate Expectations
77 Agar Rd, Illogan Highway, Redruth, Cornwall TR15 3EJ
tel: 01209 314234

As you would expect from the name, this is one of the places to come if you are looking for anything to do with fires and fireplaces. They do indeed have a lot of old fireplaces, but also baskets, dogs and other fire-

place paraphernalia. On the more unusual side, you will also see rare Cornish ranges – in fact they are one of the few places to offer these. Open Mon–Sat, 9 a.m.–5 p.m.

Marcus Olliff
26 Redland Court Rd, Redland, Bristol BS6 7EQ
tel: 0117 942 2900 • fax: 0117 944 2400
e-mail: aah69@dial.pipex.com

Marcus Olliff deals in some fascinating pieces of salvage which have been rescued from sites around the country. Things that have passed through his portals include a revolving door from the Jaguar car factory in Birmingham, and a triple-arched limestone loggia, from Bruton Manor in Somerset (priced at over £12 000!). There are some more usual items as well, such as cast iron radiators and fireplaces. The stock is not kept at the above address so please do not turn up to visit – phone for an appointment and for further details.

Northend Reclamation
Northend, Luckington, Chippenham, Wilts SN14 6PN
tel: 01666 841040

This is a compact reclamation yard that mainly concentrates on the heavier side of building reclamation materials. They specialize in bricks, timbers, roofing materials and copings. They do, however, have some bathroom sanitary ware on offer. Open Mon–Fri, 7.30 a.m.–5 p.m.

The Original Reclamation Trading Co
22 Elliott Rd, Love Lane Industrial Estate, Cirencester, Glos GL7 1YS
tel: 01285 653532 • fax: 01285 644383

You will find everything except building and roofing materials in this neatly set out salvage yard. Fireplaces, doors and bathroom sanitary ware with fittings, etc are much in evidence as are some of the more decorative pieces such as stained glass, decorative windows and busts. Open Tues–Fri, 9 a.m.–5p.m., Sat, 9 a.m.–4 p.m.

Reclamation Services
Catbrain Quarry, Painswick Beacon, Painswick, Glos GL6 6SU
tel: 01452 814064 • fax: 01452 813631

Set in a picturesque spot overlooking the Cotswolds, this salvage yard specializes in traditional building materials and garden ornaments. They have a big timber-flooring section, lots of fireplaces and a good bathrooms section. Open Mon–Fri, 8 a.m.–5 p.m., Sat, 9 a.m.–4 p.m.

Robert Mills
Narroways Rd, Eastville, Bristol, Avon BS2 9XB
tel: 0117 955 6542

If you fancy an old Gothic window somewhere in your house, or even as a garden decoration, this is a good place to try as they specialize in Gothic pieces, many of which have been reclaimed from churches. They also have some interesting pub fittings. Open Mon–Fri, 9.30 a.m.–5.30 p.m.

Salisbury Demolition
35 West St, Wilton, Wilts SP2 0DL
tel: 01722 743420 • fax: 01722 744325

A large old pub has been converted to house the showrooms of this architectural salvage centre and there is half an acre of outside storage as well. You can find practically everything you would ever want salvage-wise here from building materials like bricks, slates, tiles and timber to fireplaces, sanitary ware and door furniture. Open Mon–Fri, 7.30 a.m.–4.30 p.m. and Sat, 9 a.m.–3 p.m.

Source
93–95 Walcot St, Bath, Avon BA1 3SD
tel: 01225 469200 • fax: 01225 832800

The owner freely admits this is the 'scruffiest antique shop in Bath', but it is at the more decorative and lighter end of the salvage market. Lighting, panelling and fireplaces are all on offer here as well as more unusual pieces such as bar sittings and fronts and ecclesiastical pieces. Open Tues–Sat, 10 a.m.–5 p.m. and Sun 9 a.m.–5 p.m.

South West Reclamation
Gwilliams Yard, Edington, Bridgwater,
Somerset TA7 9JN
tel: 01278 723173

You will be able to source reclaimed products from the roof down here. They do all sorts of building materials, flooring, windows and doors. They also have a good garden section with local staddle stones, artefacts and old pumps. As an interesting addition to this salvage yard, they have some furniture made from reclaimed wood. Open Mon–Fri, 8.30 a.m.–5 p.m. and Sat, 9 a.m.–1 p.m.

Toby's
Brunel Rd, Newton Abbot, Devon TQ12 4PB
tel: 01626 51767

A real pick-it-over yard where you will come across such gems as old telephone boxes cheek by jowl with the more usual architectural salvage pieces. You will find everything from doors to bathroom fittings and from slates to windows. They can also arrange a pine stripping service for you. Open Mon–Fri, 8.30 a.m.–4.30 p.m. and Sat, 9.30 a.m.–4 p.m.

Wells Reclamation Co
The Old Cider Farm, Coxley, nr Wells,
Somerset BA5 1RQ
tel: 01749 677087 • fax: 01749 671089

Come with your walking boots on as there are nearly four acres of architectural salvage on offer here. Choose from flooring, beams, fireplaces and bricks. They have a good stock of old quarry tiles and flags as well. Open Mon–Fri, 8.30 a.m.–5.30 p.m. and Sat, 9 a.m.–4 p.m.

south east

Alfred G Cawley
Havering Farm, Guildford Rd, Worplesdon,
Surrey GU4 7QA
tel: 01483 232398

On the heavier side of reclamation here, this company does its own demolition jobs and has built up a good stock of floorboards, roof tiles, windows, doors, beams and doors. They also have a selection of bathroom fittings. Open Mon–Fri, 8 a.m.–5 p.m. and Sat, 8 a.m.–1 p.m.

Antique Buildings
Hunters Wood Farm, Dunsfold, Surrey GU8 4NP
tel: 01483 200477

This is one of the few places you can buy off-the-peg buildings! Old timber-framed buildings are dismantled and stored by this company after they have made records of what they looked like. If you don't fancy a whole building you can buy anything in the building materials line right down to half a dozen bricks. Open Mon–Fri, 8.15 a.m.–4.30 p.m.

Architectural Rescue
1–3 Southampton Way, London SE5 7JH
tel: 0171 277 0315 • fax: 0171 277 0315

This company concentrates more on the internal and decorative fittings rather than on building materials. They specialize in fixtures and fittings such as doors, fireplaces, baths, sinks and stained glass. Much of their stock is Victorian. Open Mon–Sat, 10 a.m.–5 p.m.

Architectural Salvage Centre
30–32 Stamford Rd, London N1 4JL
tel: 0171 923 0783

There are all kinds of salvaged period fixtures and fittings here, mostly for interiors. There is a good selection of fireplaces, furniture and door fittings and also some garden pieces including chimney pots and garden benches. Open Mon–Sat, 9 a.m.–6 p.m.

The Architectural Salvage Store
Unit 6, Darvells Works, Common Rd, Chorleywood,
Herts WD3 5LP
tel: 01923 284196

This is more a shop than a yard but it is packed with some real gems including period windows, doors, garden pieces and a whole collection of original door and window furniture which can sometimes be hard to find. Open Tues–Sat, 9.30 a.m.–6 p.m.

Brighton Architectural Salvage
33/34 Gloucester Rd, Brighton, W.Sussex BN1 4AQ
tel: 01273 681656

This is an old coalyard which has itself been rescued and now contains an enormous, highly organized stock of old stained glass, ironmongery, fireplaces and flooring. It is open from Mon–Sat, 10 a.m.–5 p.m.

Brondesbury Architectural Reclamation
The Yard, 136 Willesden Lane, London NW6 7TE
tel: 0171 328 0820

This cavernous old stable block has a well-laid-out stock of old architectural treasures, so if you are the kind who doesn't like to turn over piles of dirty junk in a muddy yard, this could be one of the places for you! There is also a large yard alongside for the more adventurous. Open Mon–Sat, 10 a.m.–6 p.m. and Sun, 10 a.m.–4 p.m.

Churchill's Architectural Salvage
186–188 Old Kent Rd, London SE1 5TY
tel: 0171 708 4308

The speciality here is salvaged cast iron, marble or wood fireplaces. They also have a few reproductions. Another speciality is decorative ironwork such as garden gazebos, balconies and rose arches. They have a good selection of old brass and iron beds and cast-iron radiators. They will undertake restoration work if you need it. Open Mon–Sat, 10.30 a.m.–5.30 p.m. and Sun by appointment.

Dackombe
5 Wulwyn Court, Link Way, Crowthorne, Berks RG45 6ET
tel: 01344 779155

This is a very specialized service, which sources old oak beams, mainly from French barns, to be incorporated into people's houses. There are also old oak railway sleepers that are generally used for landscaping in gardens, often used for dramatic decking or for patios. Open by appointment only so please call before setting out.

Drummonds of Bramley
Horsham Rd, Bramley, Guildford, Surrey GU5 0LA
tel: 01483 898766

A real treasure trove of architectural antiques, Drummonds have a huge selection on offer covering just about everything you would need to rebuild and refurbish a house from the chimneypot to ornaments for the garden. They have a particularly good bathroom section. Open Mon–Sat, 9 a.m.–6 p.m. and Sun, 10 a.m.–4 p.m.

Fens Restoration
46 Lots Rd, London SW10 0QF
tel: 0171 352 9882

If you have something old that is in desperate need of restoration, this is a good place to bring it. They specialize in tasks such as the stripping of furniture, metal and wood that you often don't want to undertake yourself. They also make furniture from reclaimed wood in a traditional style. Open Mon–Fri, 9 a.m.–5 p.m.

The House Hospital
9 Ferrier St, London SW18 1SW
tel: 0181 870 8202

Set in an industrial unit, this salvage yard is a good place to buy anything from reclaimed school cast-iron radiators, to columns and panelled rooms. They also have a good selection of rolltop baths, fireplaces, doors and bathroom sanitary ware. Open Mon–Sat, 10 a.m.–5 p.m.

LassCo
St Michael's Church, Mark St, off Paul St, London EC2A 4ER
tel: 0171 739 0448 • fax: 0171 729 6853
e-mail: lassco@zepnet.co.uk

This is London's largest salvage store and it has a huge range of architectural antiques. Set in an old church it has a fascinating range of salvage and more decorative items. There is also a separate flooring company – phone for details. Open from Mon–Sun, 10 a.m.–5 p.m.

Lazdan
218 Bow Common Lane, London E3 4HH
tel: 0181 981 4632

It's often the small things that are frustratingly difficult to get hold of when you are restoring an old house and this salvage yard has really useful items such as sash weights for old windows. They also have larger items like second-hand bricks, chimney pots and reclaimed slates. Open Mon–Fri, 8 a.m.–5 p.m. and Sat, 8 a.m.–12.30 a.m.

Newbury Salvage
Calvin Rd, Newbury, Berks RG1 4DB
tel: 01635 528120

This is a classic, stock-everything salvage yard with everything from roof tiles right down to floor tiles. They also have fireplaces, chimneys, doors and much more. For the garden they have a small stock of garden ornaments and old stone archways. Open Mon–Fri, 8 a.m.–5 p.m. and Sat, 9 a.m.–1 p.m.

Old Cottage Things
Broxmore Park, Off Bunny Lane, Sherfield English, nr Romsey, Hants SO51 6FU
tel: 01794 884538

If you are looking to replace the doors in your house with something a little older, this is a good place to visit as they offer up to about 1000 pine doors at any one time. If your doors just need a little TLC, they also have a stripping service. In addition, they have a good

stock of other interior architectural salvage materials. Open Mon–Sat, 9 a.m.–5 p.m.

The Old Pine Works
Cross Lane, Hornsey, London N8 7FA
tel: 0181 348 7344

This is the kind of salvage yard where you will find plenty of reclaimed wood including floorboards, old joists and beams. They also have a rich vein of old fireplaces and radiators on offer. Open Mon–Fri, 7.30 a.m.–4.30 p.m. and Sat, 10 a.m.–12 p.m.

Peco
72–76 Station Rd, Hampton, Middx TW12 2BT
tel: 0181 979 8310 • fax: 0181 941 3319

If you are looking for doors or fireplaces you can choose between about 2500 doors and 500–600 fireplaces here in this two-storey warehouse. Most of the doors are original and restored although some of them are reproductions. On the fireplace side, they are all fully restored. They don't offer installation but do offer gas fires and hearths. Open Mon–Sat, 8.15 a.m.– 5.15 p.m.

Pew Corner
Artington Manor Farm, Old Portsmouth Rd, Guildford, Surrey GU3 1LP
tel: 01483 533337

This is a centre for ecclesiastical reclamation which generally means pews, lecterns, pulpits and panelling. They also make bespoke furniture out of reclaimed timber like oak, pitch pine, mahogany and African opepe. Open Mon–Sat, 10 a.m.–5 p.m.

Retrovius
32 York House, Upper Montagu St, London W1H 1FR
tel/fax: 0171 724 3387

Not a salvage yard, as such, but a design duo who use architectural salvage in unusual ways. Adam Hills and Maria Speake run the company and make frequent trips to Scotland to source stuff so they can offer some wonderful pieces for interiors and exteriors. These pieces are really works of art, some of which double up as having a practical use and some are purely decorative. They say they are 'bridging the gap between destruction and construction'. They also undertake specialist dismantling and restoration work. Phone them for an appointment.

Robinson's Reclaim Yard
Colne Way, Watford, Herts WD2 4WZ
tel: 01923 661885

This is one of the places to come for reclaimed wood
such as Victorian flooring in pitch pine, oak and pine,
joists and Victorian doors and window frames. They also
have a large stock of Victorian baths. Open Mon–Fri,
8.30 a.m.–5.30 p.m. and Sat, 8.30 a.m.–2.30 p.m.

Ryde Demolition
17 St John's Hill, Ryde, Isle of Wight PO33 1EU
tel: 01983 564721

This reclamation yard covers the whole lot from large
to small items. They have a fairly large stock of old
timber, bricks, roofing materials and doors on the
heavier side, down through fireplaces and sanitary
ware to smaller items such as window furniture. Open
Mon–Fri, 8 a.m.–5 p.m. and Sat, 8.30 a.m.–1 p.m.

Southern Architectural Salvage
The Pump House, The High St, Lyndhurst,
Hants SO43 7BD
tel: 01703 283300

There is a really good selection of salvage here
although they specialize in fireplaces, rolltop baths
and garden statuary – originals and reproductions.
Other salvage pieces include doors, windows, leaded
lights and taps. Open seven days a week 9 a.m.–5 p.m.

Symonds Salvage
Colts Yard, Pluckley Rd, Bethersden, nr Ashford,
Kent TN26 3DD
tel: 01233 820724 • fax: 01233 850677

You will find the larger items of salvage here such as
bricks, oak beams, slates, tiles, doors and furniture.
The smaller items like door furniture are sold in a
sister shop. It is all set in a huge site of several acres
with lots of buildings. Open Mon–Fri, 8 a.m.–5 p.m.
and Sat, 8.30 a.m.–12.30 a.m.

Totem Interiors
81 Tottenham Lane, Hornsey, London N8 9BE
tel: 01621 784075 (weekdays)
tel: 0181 340 5607 (weekends)

Not really a salvage yard, but a fascinating business
that designs and makes furniture using salvage
materials from the yards. Bring your measurements
and your ideas as you can have quite a bit of input into
the design of your furniture. Open Sat, 11 a.m.–7 p.m.
and Sun, 1 p.m.–6.30 p.m.

Townsends
81 Abbey Rd, London NW8 0AE
tel: 0171 625 6762
and
106 Boundary Rd, London NW8 0RH
tel: 0171 372 4327

Between the two yards you will find a good selection
of reclaimed stained glass windows and antique
fireplaces. They have a survey and fitting service and
can also restore old stained glass if you have some old
gems you want to bring back to prime condition. Both
branches are open Mon–Fri, 10 a.m.–6 p.m. and Sat,
10 a.m.–5.30 p.m.

Victorian Wood Works
International House, London International Freight
Terminal, Emple Mills Lane, London E15 2ES
tel: 0181 534 1000

This is a well-known place to buy reclaimed wood floors
including wood block flooring and parquet. You can
even get such things as inlaid parquetry here. They also
have a selection of old beams in a variety of woods.
Open Mon–Fri, 8 a.m.–5 p.m. and Sat, 8 a.m.–1 p.m.

east

Cobar Services
Stowmarket Rd, Ringshall, Stowmarket,
Suffolk IP14 2JA
tel: 01473 658435

This one is for people doing fairly major jobs as they
specialize on the heavy side. You will find plenty of
bricks, timbers, tiles and slates here as well as
landscaping materials. Wander round the yard and
choose your 'weapons'! Open Mon–Fri, 8 a.m.–5 p.m.

GC Reclamations
Drury Lane, Carbrooke, nr Watton, Norfolk IP25 6SJ
tel: 01362 850411

If you are undertaking some heavy work, this is one of
the places you could look for all the heavier building
fittings you might need. These include oak beams, York
flagstones, old flooring, brick flooring, slates and
doors. By appointment, usually on a Thurs or Sat.

Heritage Reclamation
1a High St, Sproughton, Suffolk IP8 3AF
tel/fax: 01473 748519

This is a huge and fascinating selection of salvage from taps, butlers' sinks and sanitary ware, through fireplaces, floors and wood-burning stoves and old cooking ranges. Their real speciality is ironmongery and they have a simply enormous stock of door knobs and window furniture. If you need advice for your project you will get plenty of that as well. There are also several really useful products such as stripping agents, waxes and special varnishes. Open Mon–Fri, 9 a.m.–5 p.m. and Sat, 9.30 a.m.–5 p.m. and other times by appointment.

Phoenix of Battlesbridge
Heritage Dock, Battlesbridge, Essex SS11 7RE
tel: 01268 768844

This salvage store mainly carries Victorian and Edwardian fireplaces, which they restore. They also have a reasonable selection of Belfast sinks and the occasional rolltop bath. Open seven days a week 10.30 a.m.–5 p.m.

Solopark
Station Rd, nr Pampisford, Cambs CB2 4HB
tel: 01223 834663

One of the largest and best-known salvage yards in Britain. This enormous concern covers six acres and has a giant-sized indoor showroom, so bring your walking shoes. It's all made much easier than it sounds by being meticulously organized into sectors with different kinds of salvage and recycled building materials. Open Mon–Thurs, 8 a.m.–5 p.m., Fri–Sat, 8 a.m.–4 p.m. and Sun, 9 a.m.–1 p.m.

Tony Hodgson & Partners
The Forge, 2 Wesley Rd, Terrington St Clement, nr King's Lynn, Norfolk PE34 4NG
tel: 01553 828637

If you have some ironwork that needs restoring this is the place to come as they offer a full service. They also have an excellent selection of ironwork on offer from quite small pieces up to large gates. Open Mon–Fri, 8 a.m.–5 p.m.and by appointment at the weekends.

Tower Reclamation
Tower Farm, Norwich Rd, nr Mendlesham, Suffolk IP14 5NE
tel: 01449 766095 • fax: 01449 766095

There is everything here at Tower Reclamation, from bricks to beams and chandeliers to garden rollers.

Other items they have include flooring, new terracotta and slate tiles and gazebos. There is an open yard and some outbuildings which contain some of the stock. By appointment or by chance if you are passing.

central

Architectural Heritage of Northants
Heart of the Shires, A5, 2 miles North of Weedon, Northants NN7 4LB
tel: 01327 349249 • fax: 01327 349397

There is a simply amazing range of gems from the past here at Architectural Heritage. Church fittings such as pews, pulpits and Gothic windows rub shoulders with Victorian sanitary ware and fireplaces. There is also stoneware, statues, cast-iron gates, carved work and panelled rooms. The pristine show-room and yard are part of a shopping complex with a tearoom. Open Tues–Sat, 10 a.m.–5 p.m. and Sun, 11 a.m.–5 p.m.

Baileys Architectural Antiques
The Engine Shed, Ashburton Industrial Estate, Ross-on-Wye, Herefordshire HR9 7BW
tel: 01989 563015

Baileys has a wonderful selection of garden antiques and tools, including a massive choice of old watering cans. They also have statuary, stonework, ironwork and garden furniture as well as bathrooms, fireplaces, Belfast sinks and other pieces for interiors. Open Mon–Sat, 9 a.m.–5 p.m.

Britain's Heritage
Shaftesbury Hall, 3 Holy Bones, Leicester, Leics LE1 4LJ
tel: 01162 519592 • fax: 01162 625990

The intriguing address comes from the fact that the nearby church contains (allegedly) the bones of Richard III, which is appropriate as this business concentrates on former glory too. Their main speciality is restoring and selling antique fireplaces, with all the fitting services and accessories. Britain's Heritage have fireplaces from the 1750s through to ones from the 1930s with more than a hundred fireplaces in many different materials. Open Tues–Sat, 10 a.m.–5 p.m. and Sun, 11 a.m.–5 p.m.

Cawarden Brick Co
Cawarden Springs Farm, Blithbury Rd, Rugeley,
Staffs WS15 3HL
tel: 01889 574066 • fax: 01889 575695

There is a huge selection of salvage here so don't run
away with the idea it is just bricks. They do offer
reclaimed bricks, but also a whole host of other things
such as doors, flooring, beams, fireplaces, sinks,
sanitary ware and furniture. The owners describe it as
an organized mess with the largest stock in the
Midlands. Open Mon–Fri, 8 a.m.–5 p.m. and Sat,
8 a.m.–4 p.m.

Conservation Building Products
Forge Lane, Cradley Heath, Warley,
W.Midlands B64 5AL
tel: 01384 564219

It is well worth a journey to this architectural salvage
site to get the pick of garden and building gems. You
will also benefit from sound advice from the staff.
Open Mon–Fri, 8 a.m.–4 p.m. and Sat, 8 a.m.–noon.

Dickinsons Architectural Antiques
140 Corve St, Ludlow, Shropshire SY8 2PG
tel: 01584 876207

If you are a born rummager, you will love this shop
with its scruffy but welcoming atmosphere. It excels
in bathroom fittings, doors, lighting, fireplaces and
internal fittings from all eras. Open Mon–Sat,
9.30 a.m.–5 p.m.

North Shropshire Reclamation &
Antique Salvage
Greystone Barn, Petton, nr Burlton, Shrewsbury,
Shropshire SY4 5TH
tel: 01939 270719 • fax: 01939 270895

Expect a long rummage here as they have a barn, a
yard and various garages full of reclaimed materials.
The stock covers the whole gamut from bricks, beams,
quarry tiles and fireplaces to garden statuary, sanitary
ware, stained glass windows and window furniture.
Open Mon, Thurs, Fri and Sat, 10 a.m.–5 p.m.

Nottingham Architectural Antiques
531 Woodbrough Rd, Nottingham, Notts NG3 5FR
tel: 0115 960 5665

You will not find any of the heavier building materials
here as this shop, with yard attached, specializes in

fireplaces and surrounds. In addition it does have
some old doors and bathroom sanitary ware. Open
Mon, Thurs, Fri and Sat, 10 a.m.–5 p.m.

The Original Choice
1340 Stratford Rd, Hall Green, Birmingham,
W.Midlands B28 9EH
tel: 0121 778 3821

Good old stained glass windows can sometimes be hard
to find, but here you will find that they are specialists
in the subject. Their stock includes windows from the
mid-eighteenth century through to the mid-twentieth
century. They also have old fireplaces. Open Mon–Sat,
10 a.m.–6 p.m. and Sun, 12 noon–4.30 p.m.

Oxford Architectural Antiques
16–18 London St, Faringdon, Oxon SN7 7AA
tel: 01367 242268

Don't be deceived by the antique pine furniture shop
that fronts this establishment, there is a whole
warehouse full of architectural salvage behind. This is
mainly full of fireplaces, lights, baths, stoves and
French and Hungarian wood burners. Open Tues–Sat,
9 a.m.–5 p.m. and Sun, 11 a.m.–3 p.m.

Ransford Bros
Drayton Way, Drayton Fields, Daventry,
Northants NN11 5XW
tel: 01327 705310

If you like your salvage yards well organized, this is
one for you. Ransford Bros has an impressive stock of
bricks, slates, roof tiles, quarry tiles and flooring all of
which is cleaned and palleted ready for use. Open
Mon–Fri, 8.30 a.m.–5 p.m. and Sat, 9 a.m.–noon.

Reclaimed Building Supplies
Lower Farm, Brandon Lane, nr Coventry,
W.Midlands CV3 3GW
tel: 01203 639338

Looking for a reclaimed floor? These people specialize
in both reclaimed and new hardwood floors. You can
choose from a selection including reclaimed Oregon
pine, reclaimed pine, pitch pine, new kiln-dried oak,
Cyprus pine and maple old and new. They also have
doors, fireplaces, railway sleepers and they specialize
in polishing reclaimed oak beams. Open Mon–Fri,
8.30 a.m.–5 p.m., Sat, 9 a.m.–4.30 p.m. and in the
summer, Sun, 11 a.m.–3 p.m.

Rococo Architechtural Goods & Furnishings
5 New St, Lower Weedon Beck,
Northants NN7 4QS
tel/fax: 01327 341288

This is *Home Front*'s salvage expert Neville Griffiths'
own yard. It is a delightful old Georgian house
crammed with restored pieces spilling over into a big
yard to house the less petite pieces. Full of all sorts of
goodies that Neville has brought back from his travels,
it is definitely worth a visit. If Neville himself is there,
he will no doubt dispense some of his invaluable
advice on all things to do with salvage. Open Mon–Fri
by appointment, Sat, 10am–5pm and Sun, 12.30–5pm.

north east

Borders Architectural Salvage
2 South Rd, Wooler, Northumberland NE71 6SN
tel: 01668 282475

This yard specializes in fireplaces, stonework,
bathroom sanitary ware and doors. Open Mon–Fri,
9 a.m.–5 p.m., Sat, 10 a.m.–4 p.m.

Havenplan
The Old Station, Station Rd, Killarmarsh, Sheffield,
S.Yorks S21 1EN
tel: 0114 2489972

Quite a selection for the garden here including stone
troughs, furniture, edging tiles and chimney pots. You
will also find interior flooring, doors, pews, bathroom
fittings and fireplaces. Open Tues–Sat, 10 a.m.–4 p.m.

Kevin Marshall's Antique Warehouse
17–20a Wilton St, off Danson Lane South, Hull,
Humberside HU8 7LG
tel: 01482 326559

Chock-a-block with stock from antique bathrooms to
door furnishings. It is all housed in an enormous
Victorian warehouse and is the kind of place where you
can rummage to your heart's content. Open Mon–Sat,
10 a.m.–5 p.m. and Sun, 10 a.m.–4 p.m.

Shiners
123 Jesmond Rd, Newcastle upon Tyne,
Tyne and Wear NE2 1JY
tel: 0191 281 6474

This is not just a run-of-the-mill salvage yard but
offers several useful services as well. These include a

blacksmith, a French polisher, a picture framer and a
stained glass repair expert. All this is in addition to a
wealth of architectural salvage pieces. Open Mon–Sat,
9 a.m.–5 p.m. and Sun, 10 a.m.–2 p.m.

Woodside Reclamation
Woodside, Scremerston, Berwick-upon-Tweed,
Northumberland TD15 2SY
tel: 01289 302658/01289 331211 • fax: 01289 330274

An old estate yard has been turned into a tidy salvage
yard here, complete with Victorian pit and an old
winding house. The stock varies across most of the
traditional building materials including doors,
bathrooms, timbers, stone lintels, Georgian brick and
door furniture. They also offer a stripping, polishing
and waxing service. Open Mon–Sat, 9 a.m.–5 p.m. and
Sun, 11 a.m.–4 p.m.

York Handmade Brick Co
Forest Lane, Alne, York, N.Yorks YO6 2LU
tel: 01347 838881

If you want to match some old handmade bricks or just
buy a whole new load, this company still makes them
in all kinds of shapes and sizes. They also make pavers
and terracotta floor tiles. Open Mon–Fri, 8.30 a.m.–
4.30 p.m. and Sat, 9 a.m.–12 noon.

north west

Andy Thorton Architechtural Antiques
Victoria Mills, Stainland Rd, Greetland, Halifax,
W.Yorks HX4 8AD
tel: 01422 377314 • fax: 01422 310372

One of the largest and best yards in the country with
literally thousands of doors, windows and fireplaces in
stock at any one time. They are also one of the
founders of the Salvo code. Open Mon–Fri, 9 a.m.–
5.30 p.m., Sat, 9 a.m.–5 p.m. and Sun, 11 a.m.–5 p.m.

Bruce Kilner
Ashton Fields Farm, Windmill Rd, Worsley,
Lancs M28 3RP
tel: 0161 702 8604

If you are looking for the kind of place that will give
you the scope to restore items yourself, this could be
it. The stock is general salvage, including doors,
windows, bricks, beams, baths, sinks and stone flags.
Open seven days a week, but ring before you come.

Cairn Building Products
Carrington Business Park, Carrington,
Manchester M31 4YR
tel: 0161 442 4433 • fax: 0161 776 4540

Specialists in reclaimed paving for inside and out, this
company mainly concentrates on Yorkstone. They have
a CAD (computer aided design) facility to cut them to
exactly the size you want. There are also some
other salvaged building supplies. Open Mon–Fri,
9 a.m.–5 p.m. and Sat, a.m. by appointment.

Cheshire Brick & Slate Co
Brook House Farm, Salters Bridge, Tarvin Sands,
nr Chester, Cheshire CH3 8HL
tel: 01829 740883 • fax: 01829 740481

Quite a large range of architectural salvage on offer
here from brass door handles and hinges to lamp-
posts. In between you will find bricks, tiles, bathroom
fittings, beams and garden ornaments. They also have
some old ranges and fireplaces. Open Mon–Fri,
8 a.m.–5.30 p.m., Sat, 8 a.m.–4.30 p.m. and Sun,
10 a.m.–4 p.m.

Cumbria Architectural Salvage
Birks Hill, Raughton Head, Carlisle, Cumbria CA5 7DH
tel: 01697 476420

This yard specializes in old fireplaces and a small stock
of Victorian kitchen ranges, which are all fully
restored. They also have other salvage items such as
doors, beams, bricks and stone dressings for windows
and doors. Open Mon–Fri, 9 a.m.–5 p.m. and Sat,
9 a.m.–12 noon.

Great Northern Architectural Antiques
New Russia Hall, Chester Rd, Tattenhall,
Cheshire CH3 9AH
tel: 01829 770796 • fax: 01829 770971

Bric-à-brac fans will find plenty to choose from
here, but you can also discover other architectural
antiques right up to complete panelled rooms. Doors,
stained glass, garden furniture and bathroom fittings
are just some of the rest of the selection. Open
Mon–Fri, 9.30 a.m.–4.30 p.m, Sat and Sun,
9.30 a.m.–5 p.m.

Ken Howe Natural Stone Supplies
Mount Spring Works, Burnley Rd East, Waterfoot,
Lancs BB4 9LA
tel: 01706 210605 • fax: 01706 228707

Natural stone is the main item on offer here from
fireplaces through window frames, walling, flooring
and stone flags. The majority of the stock is Yorkstone
but there are other choices including granite and
marble. Open Mon–Fri, 8.30 a.m.–5 p.m. and Sat,
9 a.m.–12 noon.

R&R Renovations & Reclamations
Canalside Yard, Audlem, Cheshire CW3 0DY
tel: 01270 811310

This is the kind of place where you will find everything
from door knobs to Gothic arches amongst the
enormous stock of architectural antiques. The staff
always have time to give you good advice, so you will
pick up some good tips as well as salvage. Open
Mon–Fri, 8 a.m.–5 p.m. and Sat, 10 a.m.–4 p.m.

Reclaimed Materials
Northgate, White Lund Industrial Estate, Morecambe,
Lancs LA3 3AY
tel: 01524 69094

Most of the materials here are on the real building
side, rather than interior decoration. Chief among the
stock are slates, roof tiles and chimney pots, which are
joined by timber, flooring and flagstones. Open
Mon–Fri, 8 a.m.–5 p.m. and Sat, 8 a.m.–1 p.m.

Tricklebank
The Malthouse, off Green Lane, Ormskirk,
Lancs L39 1QR
tel: 01695 570503

This is good-sized working salvage yard with a large
showroom. The stock is impressively well organized
and they specialize in pine floorboards, doors, bricks,
old beams and pews. Open Mon–Fri, 8.30 a.m.–5 p.m.,
Sat, 9.30 a.m.–4.30 p.m. and Sun, noon–3 p.m.

Wilson Reclamation Services
Yew Tree Barn, Low Newton in Cartmel, Grange-over-
Sands, Cumbria LA11 6JP
tel: 01539 531498

This is a deluxe reclamation yard as they also have a
café and other services such as a soft furnishing
department and upholstery service. On the real
salvage side they specialize in beams, bathroom
fittings and fireplaces. Open Mon–Sat, 10 a.m.–5 p.m.
and, in the summer, Sun, 12 noon–6 p.m.

wales

Adferiad Gwent of Monmouthshire
nr Monmouth, Monmouthshire
tel: 01291 690709

You will have to ring for an appointment and directions to visit this yard, but it is well worth the trouble as you will find a huge stock of old timber including floorboards, panelling and beams. There is also a selection of church fittings and, in particular, pews from demolished churches. By appointment only.

Architectural Reclamation
Unit 1, Forest Business Centre, Queensway, Fforestfach, Swansea SA5 4DH
tel: 01792 582222 • fax: 01792 582222

They describe themselves as the builders' merchants among architectural antiques dealers and they do seem to have a bit of everything. Alongside the normal building materials you will find church pews, farmhouse kitchens, tiles and parquet flooring. Open Mon–Fri, 9 a.m.–5 p.m. and Sat, 9 a.m.–1 p.m.

Cardiff Reclamation
Tremorfa Industrial Estate, Rover Way, Cardiff CF2 2FD
tel: 01222 458995

Victorian salvage is a speciality here. There is quite a bit reclaimed from churches, such as pews and windows, and some repro and original garden furniture and ornaments. They have a strong vein of restored cast-iron fireplaces and marble, stone and slate surrounds. Open Mon–Fri, 9 a.m.–5 p.m., Sat, 9 a.m.–1 p.m. and Sun, 10 a.m.–1 p.m.

D&P Theodore Sons & Daughters Building Salvage & Reclamation
North Rd, Bridgend Industrial Estate, Bridgend, Mid-Glamorgan CF36 5NH.
tel: 01656 648936

This must win the prize for the friendliest and most helpful salvage yard in Britain. It is run as a family business and there is a real rummage atmosphere where you can spend as much time as you like picking things over to find what you want. There are several thousand items here ranging from old dressed stone to telegraph poles and many, many more. Open Mon–Fri, 8 a.m.–4.30 p.m. and Sat–Sun 8 a.m.–1 p.m.

Dyfed Antiques & Architectural Salvage
The Wesleyan Chapel, Perrots Rd, Haverfordwest, Pembrokeshire SA61 2JD
tel: 01437 760496 • fax: 01437 760496

This is an old chapel full of all kinds of salvaged household fittings from doors, windows and shutters through wood panelling and old timber, to bricks, slates, slabs and roof tiles. They also use salvaged timber to make traditional-style furniture and have another yard where they have cast-iron items. Open Mon–Fri, 9.30 a.m.–5.30 p.m. and Sat, 10 a.m.–5 p.m.

Heritage Restorations
Llanfair Caereinion, Welshpool, Powys SY21 0HD
tel: 01938 810384 • fax: 01938 810900

Not strictly a salvage yard, this business specializes in good antique pine furniture. Nearly all the pieces are fully restored and there are also some reproduction items, but their real speciality is good, unusual pieces. Open Mon–Sat, 9 a.m.–5 p.m.

Radnedge Architectural Salvage
41 Pemberton Rd, Llanelli, Dyfed SA14 9BG
tel: 01554 755790

You can get some unusual flooring materials here such as Rhodesian teak and Burmese teak, which is all salvaged. They also specialize in cast-iron fireplaces and marble surrounds. There is a little garden furniture and quite a few baths and radiators. Open by appointment only, so please call first to arrange one.

Welsh Salvage
Isca Yard, Milman St, Newport NP9 2JL
tel: 01633 212945 • fax: 01633 213458

These specialists in the restoration of Victorian fireplaces also have a very unusual service to offer. They have on site an interior design studio, complete with a paint effect artist who specializes in faux marbling on slate fireplaces. Alongside all this, they have an acre of reclamation yard where everything is immaculately laid out. Open Mon–Fri, 8.30 a.m.–5 p.m., Sat, 8.30 a.m.–4 p.m. and Sun, 11 a.m.–2 p.m.

scotland

The Angus Architectural Antique Co
Balmain House, Balmain St, Montrose,
Angus DD10 8AZ
tel: 01674 674291

A company that steers clear of the heavy side of
architectural salvage, they are actually specialists in
fireplaces. Alongside these, they also have a lot of old
pine furniture for kitchens and bedrooms, lighting and
bathroom fittings. Open Mon–Sat, 9 a.m.–5 p.m.

Auldearn Architectural Antiques
Lethen Rd, Auldearn, Nairn, Inverness IV12 5HZ
tel: 01667 726673

This is a very large showroom housed in an old
converted church. The stock includes old furniture and
all kinds of other salvage items. There is also a
separate stable complex selling old linen and bric-à-
brac. Open Mon–Sun, 9 a.m.–5.30 p.m.

Burnthills Demolition
Floors St, Johnstone, Renfrewshire PA5 8QS
tel: 01505 329644

This salvage yard specializes in reclaimed timber,
slates and steel. It also carries stone slabs and
occasionally you will find bathroom ware and Belfast
sinks. Smaller items, such as ornaments and brass,
make up the stock. Open Mon–Fri, 8 a.m.–5 p.m.,
Sat, 8 a.m.–12 noon and Sun, 8 a.m.–4 p.m.

Edinburgh & Glasgow Architectural
Salvage Yards
Unit 6, Couper St, Leith, Edinburgh EH6 6HH
tel: 0131 554 7077

This is one of Scotland's biggest and best salvage
yards with a wide range of all the usual kind of salvage
stock but also including a rich vein of church fittings.
Open Mon–Sat, 9 a.m.–5 p.m.

Holyrood Architectural Salvage
Holyrood Business Park, 146 Duddington Rd West,
Edinburgh EH16 4AP
tel: 0131 661 9305

If you are looking for a cast-iron bath, this is one of
the best places in the area to go. Specialists in
Victorian and Edwardian pieces, they can even paint
the exterior in a colour of your choice. They also carry
a huge selection of turn-of-the-century interior
fittings and the occasional Georgian piece. Open
Mon–Sat, 9 a.m.–5 p.m. and Sun, 12 noon–5 p.m.

Taymouth Architectural Antiques
49 Magdalen Yard Rd, Dundee DD1 4NF
tel: 01382 666833 • fax: 01382 666833

Reclaimed fireplaces are the bread and butter of this
company, but they also have a significant stock of
church fittings, kitchen ranges and old doors. They
don't have any of the heavier building materials but
they do have some carved stone pieces. Open
Tues–Sat, 9.30 a.m.–5.30 p.m.

Tradstocks
Duneverig, Thorn Hill, Stirling FK8 3QW
tel: 01786 850400 • fax: 01786 850404

This company's speciality is all kinds of stone, whether
it be local or not. They have large stocks of reclaimed
stone walling, flags, cobbles, setts and coping stones.
Open Mon–Fri, 9 a.m.–5 p.m. and Sun, 9 a.m.–1 p.m.

northern ireland

Alexander the Grate
126–128 Donegal Pass, Belfast BT7 1BZ
tel: 01232 232041

They specialize in old fireplaces here as well as
all kinds of other architectural salvage including
leaded windows and doors. Seasonally they will
offer old garden furniture as well. Open Mon–Sat,
10 a.m.–5 p.m.

Andy Jones Salvage
37 Ballyblack Rd, Newtonards, Co Down BT22 2AS
tel: 01247 822722

You will find everything you need here to completely
rebuild a house or to do a minor makeover. They
specialize in fireplaces, bricks, slates, garden pieces
and old timber. Open Mon–Fri, 9 a.m.–5 p.m. and Sat,
9 a.m.–1 p.m.

Architectural Salvage
4–50 Jenny Mount St, York Rd, Belfast BT15 3HW
tel: 01232 351475

This place is definitely worth a journey if you are looking for the beautiful old Belfast bricks of which they have large stocks. They also offer all kinds of other architectural salvage. Open Mon–Fri, 9.30 a.m.–5 p.m. and Sat, 9.30 a.m.–1 p.m.

Arksal

541 Saintfield Rd, Carryduff, Belfast BT8 8AS
tel: 01232 815191 • fax: 01232 815255

A specialist in reclaimed timber flooring, this salvage yard also offers new wood floors. In addition there is a good selection of other salvage including roofing, sandstone facades, granite kerbs, cobblestones and other architectural pieces. On the lighter side they cover all the usual areas such as bathrooms and kitchen sinks. Open Mon–Fri, 8 a.m.–5 p.m. and Sat, 8 a.m.–12 noon.

Wilson's Conservation Building Products

123a Hillsborough Rd, Dromore, Co Down BT25 1QW
tel: 01846 692304 • fax: 01846 698322

Reclaimed floors are big news here. The materials range from reclaimed pine and maple through to Bangor blue slates. They also have stocks of pub furniture such as bar fronts, and cast-iron radiators and old reclaimed bricks. One of, if not, the biggest salvage yard in Ireland, they have an enormous premises and several showrooms. Open Mon–Fri, 8 a.m.–5 p.m. and Sat, 8 a.m.–12.30 a.m.

heat

Keeping your home cosy in winter and cool in summer is one of those things that most people don't give much thought to. Boilers, whether newly installed or inherited, are only given attention when they go wrong or pack up. The majority of people in the UK have standard panel radiators running along the walls and although you might have a fan in the office, at home most of us simply open a window when things start over-heating. If you do want to think about your heating and cooling systems around the house, in both practical and aesthetic terms, there is plenty of scope.

Going back to basics, nothing beats the endless fascination of a real fire, but it is often something everyone wants but few people can be bothered with. Instead of the hearth being the focal point of the room, the television has usurped it (check whether your furniture is angled towards the black box in the corner!). Emphasis is gradually shifting back towards the fireplace though and, whether it's real or fake, a fire creates a wonderful atmosphere. If you decide you want a real fire, check first with your local authorities about rules (pollution, safety, etc) that may apply to your area. Ensure that your chimney is properly swept and lined by a professional. There are plenty of really life-like imitation fires available that give you the visual pleasure without the mess and hassle. If you want to create or replace an existing fireplace, this chapter can tell you where to start looking, whether your taste is modern or traditional. It is worth looking in the Salvage chapter (see p.190) too.

The choice of radiators now available is huge, with ones shaped, for example, like coils and springs that go up or along the wall. Read through the list to find something you like the sound of – most of them should be available from a local stockist. We have also listed the best selection of fans around today – from desk to ceiling, they come in all shapes and sizes.

me up

and cool me down

key: 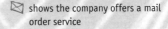 shows the product has appeared on *Home Front*

✉ shows the company offers a mail order service

fireplaces

The Victorians treated their fireplaces not only as an integral part of a room but almost like a piece of furniture. That is why there are so many different examples from this period – they designed them to suit every style whether it was Georgian or Queen Anne. Fireplaces were highly ornate with decorative tiles on the surround and the hearth, probably an overmantel, and accessories in brass. The smaller the room, the less ornate the fireplace, but even the servants would have had some sort of fireplace in their attic rooms.

If you yearn for an original fireplace, there are some points to remember. Firstly, and it may sound obvious, do check that there is not one lurking there already, hidden away, perhaps just the hole or even one with the backplate intact, somewhere behind all the wallpaper or panelling. If you tap on the walls, it should sound a bit hollow. With the invention of central heating, many fireplaces were either regarded as unnecessary or unsightly and were bricked up or ripped out, to be replaced with modern gas fires. It's quite easy to knock a hole through yourself if it's just been panelled over, but get a professional in if you're not sure. You'll also need a chimney sweep to clean the chimney and check the flue first if you're planning on using the fireplace. The inside of your chimney probably needs lining and the flue may have been sealed, which will create billows of nasty smoke back into the room – dangerous as well as dirty.

Measure the chimney breast and the opening before you start looking for an original fireplace. Depending on the period of your house and your own personal taste, decide what style you are going to go for. It's best not to choose one that will dominate the room. When you're hunting round salvage yards for old fireplaces, it's easy to fall in love with one but always check that it's going to fit. The staff are there to help and usually they can give helpful advice, although occasionally they might be more interested in making a sale. Make sure the fireplace has got all its bits with it – if the lugs that will hold the screws to the wall are broken or missing you will have trouble fixing it. If all is intact (i.e. you have the lugs, backplate, gratebars, ash can and mantelpiece) remember that, even if it looks really grotty, it can be restored marvellously with some hard work. Of course, if the tiles are broken or missing, you can replace these quite easily. Alternatively, you could opt for a reproduction fireplace. There are some fantastic ones around with tiles that are excellent versions of the real thing. You will also get a guarantee that the fireplace works.

Finally, what do you do if you don't like the period look but would still like a focal point? There are some groovy alternatives about these days, like steel and glass. We've included these in this fireplaces section, too.

south west

Aarrow Fires Ltd
The Fireworks, North Mills, Bridport, Dorset DT6 3BE
tel: 01308 427234

If you love the smell of woodsmoke but don't want the mess to go with it, Aarrow Fires have developed a range of environmentally friendly woodburners, which sounds like a contradiction in terms. You can look at the fire burning away through the glass-fronted panel. They have also developed an ingenious system whereby the glass door remains clean and doesn't get all blacked up and sooty. There are various models available, some of which are multi-fuel.

Architectural Heritage
Taddington Manor, Taddington, nr Cutsdean,
Cheltenham, Glos GL54 5RY
tel: 01386 584414 • fax: 01386 584236

Top-of-the-range stone fireplaces can be found here from the sixteenth to nineteenth centuries. Helpful staff will be able to give you advice about would suit your home and budget.

Ashburton Marbles
Great Hall, North St, Ashburton, Devon T Q13 7QD
tel/fax: 01364 653189

This massive showroom has a huge range of stock – mostly eighteenth- and nineteenth-century fireplaces. They will also restore your fireplace *in situ*. If you need a coal or gas fire, they can also arrange this.

Au Temps Perdu
5 Stapleton Rd, Bristol, Avon BS5 0OR
tel: 0117 955 5223

They specialize in fireplaces here and provided *Home Front*'s Neville Griffiths with a fireplace when he was renovating a 1930s semi in Bristol. The staff are very helpful but you are also welcome to rummage to find your own bargains.

Clarke's of Buckfastleigh
rear of 32 Fore St, Buckfastleigh,
Devon TQ11 0AA
tel: 01364 643060

Original Victorian and Georgian fireplaces in marble and wood. They also do reproductions that are

simple but authentic. It's best to phone first as they don't have a vast range of stock at any one time. Most of their fireplaces are timber, but they also do cast iron.

Farmington Fireplaces
Farington Stone, Northleach, Cheltenham,
Glos GL54 3NZ
tel: 01451 860280 • fax: 01451 860115

You usually find fireplaces made out of the same stone as the area from which they originate and this Gloucestershire company stocks ones in Bath stone – a wonderful honey colour – and Cotswold stone.

Fine Art Mouldings
Unit 6, Roebuck Rd Trading Estate, 15–17 Roebuck Rd,
Hainault, Ilford, Essex IG6 3TU
tel: 0181 502 7602 • fax: 0181 502 7603

Plaster fire surrounds in a choice of classical styles from a plain Tudor one to a highly ornate Large Louis. Fashioned from a specially hardened plaster reinforced with wood and canvas, the surrounds come in white so that you can paint them any colour of your choice (matt emulsion is recommended). Alternatively, you can opt for one of their specialist finishes such as 'dragging' or a fake but life-like marble effect in a choice of ten colours.

Hayles & Howe
Picton House, 25 Picton St, Bristol, Avon BS6 5PZ
tel: 0117 924 6673

This company specializes in reproduction fireplaces in plaster and you can choose from their stock or have one made to order.

Stovax
Falcon Rd, Sowton Industrial Estate Exeter,
Devon EX2 7LF
tel: 01392 474055 • fax: 01392 474011

Stovax is one of the leading names in the fireplace industry and every one of their stoves is made from cast iron – a material which has been used for this purpose for over 250 years. There are traditional log-burning stoves, which suit older-type homes and will give your room an instant homely feel. They also do a good range of fire accessories such as wrought iron log baskets.

south east

Acquisitions
24–26 Holmes Rd, London NW5 3AB
tel: 0171 482 2949 for stockists • fax: 0171 267 4361

Handmade period fireplaces using traditional methods. They can either be highly decorative or stylishly simple and they use marble, stone, wood or cast iron.

Amazing Grates
61–63 High Rd, London N2 8AB
tel: 0181 883 9590 • fax: 0181 365 2053

A good selection of Georgian, Victorian, Edwardian and Art Deco fireplaces in stock. They also operate a restoration service.

The Antique Fireplace Warehouse
194–202 Battersea Park Rd, London SW11 4ND
tel: 0171 627 1410 • fax: 0171 622 1078

There is a good range of both antique and reproduction fireplaces here – usually over one hundred in stock at any time.

Brighton Architectural Salvage
33–34 Gloucester Rd, Brighton, E.Sussex BN1 4AQ
tel: 01273 681656

If you're a fan of the Art Nouveau or Regency periods, you should be able to pick something up here. They usually have both cast-iron inserts and some marble surrounds, although make sure all the pieces are there.

Capital Fireplaces
The Old Grain Store, Nupend Business Park,
Old Knebworth, Herts SG3 6QJ
tel: 01438 821138 for stockists • fax: 01438 821157

If you are a fan of Art Deco and William Morris, but can't find or afford an original, this manufacturer makes very good reproductions that are sold at outlets around the country. They're normally in keeping with these styles and made from wood or cast iron.

The Chiswick Fireplace Company
68 Southfield Rd, London W4 1BD
tel: 0181 995 4011 • fax: 0181 995 4012

In the showroom you will find some good examples of fireplaces from bygone ages, particularly Victorian and Edwardian. It is always worth asking if they have any more in stock or are likely to be getting others in, if you cannot see what you want on display.

Design Fireplaces
113 Walnut Tree Close, Guildford, Surrey GU1 4UQ
tel: 01483 503333 • fax: 01483 570013

Stone mantlepieces don't always come cheap, especially if the stone they are fashioned from is quarried in France. But for something that will last a lifetime, they can definitely prove a worthwhile buy. As well as these, Design Fireplaces make and sell their own range.

The Edwardian Fireplace Company
1a Stile Hall Parade, London W4 3AG
tel: 0181 995 2554 • fax: 0181 742 8974

Period antique and reproduction Georgian, Victorian and Edwardian fireplaces. They also have branches in Wandsworth and Dulwich, phone the above number for details.

Grate Fires
5 Church Rd, London SW13 9HH
tel: 0171 748 8622

The shop itself is tiny but there are lots more fireplaces – both original and repro – in stock in their showroom. Phone and ask for an appointment to be shown round. There is a good choice of pine fireplace surrounds with roundels and rosettes set into the wood, and fancy grates. There's one that looks like an open chestnut and ornate ones from the Georgian period, as well as plainer ones. They also do outdoor fires, which look like giant insect pods or beehives on stick legs.

House of Steel
400 Caledonian Rd, London N1 1DA
tel: 0171 607 5889

As well as lots of antique fireplaces, you will find a good range of antique coal buckets, toasting forks, coal boxes, and brass chestnut roasters which, when given a polish, will come up gleaming. They are open during Monday to Friday, but on Saturdays by appointment only.

King's Worthy Foundry
London Rd, Winchester, Hants SO23 7QG
tel: 01962 883776

Here you will find fireplace accessories for both solid fuel and log-burning fires. If you're after a fireback or a basket in a traditional design, you will find plenty to choose from.

Marble Hill Fireplaces
70–72 Richmond Rd, Twickenham, Middx TW1 3BE
tel: 0181 892 1488 • fax: 0181 891 6591

On offer here is a good range of both French and English marble surrounds as well as hand-carved wooden mantels.

Modus Design Ltd
16 The Warren, Radlett, Herts WD7 7DX
tel: 01923 210442 • fax: 01923 853486

These are truly amazing fireplaces in glass, stainless steel, or lacquered metal. You can suspend them from the ceiling, have them freestanding or mount them on the wall. They're functional, and guaranteed to be a talking point.

Peco
72 Station Rd, Hampton, Middx TW12 2BT
tel: 0181 979 8310

This two-storey warehouse has a vast selection of doors and fireplaces – you will have a choice of about 500–600 of the latter. All the fireplaces are fully restored and, although they do not offer installation, they do have gas fires and hearths too.

The Platonic Fireplace Company
40 Peterborough Rd, London SW6 3BN
tel/fax: 0171 610 9440

If you want something ultra-modern, this is the place to come. If you don't want to mess around with dirty black coal, this fire comes with ceramic 'fuel' in the geometric shapes. Anne McKevitt used one on the programme to create a really different fireplace that was still the focal point of the room.

Real Flame
80 New King's Rd, London SW6 4LT
tel: 0171 731 5025

This company's sales gimmick is that it has supplied gas log and coal fires to such salubrious addresses as 10 Downing Street and Chequers. If you want to be in good compnay, visit their showroom – they have a big range of fires and accessories.

Townsend's
81 Abbey Rd, London NW8 0AE
tel: 0171 624 4756

Antique fireplaces are to be found here, made of cast iron, wood and marble. There are also reproduction ones, lovingly finished with the appropriate tiles, available.

Valantique
9 Fortis Green, London N2 9JR
tel: 0181 883 7651

All sorts of particularly interesting accessories for the hearth can be found here. Root around for Georgian fire irons, trivets, companion sets, and old scissor tongs. Call before visiting as they are not open on Mondays or early morning.

Winther Browne & Company Ltd
Nobel Rd, Eley Estate, Edmonton, London N18 3DX
tel: 0181 803 3434 for stockists • fax: 0181 807 0544
e-mail: sales@wintherbrowne.co.uk

If you'd like a very simple, unfussy fire surround Winther Browne make plain ones in pine, mahogany and MDF.

east

Anglia Fireplaces & Design Ltd
Anglia House, Kendal Court, Cambridge Rd, Impington CB4 4NU
tel: 01223 234713 • fax: 01223 235116

If you visit the huge showroom, one of the largest (if not the largest) in East Anglia, you will find a large range of off-the-peg fire surrounds in marble, wood and stone. They will also undertake commissions for specific designs if you have something particular in mind and can't find it among their shop stock.

Cervo Masonry
Belvoir Way, Fairfield Estate, Louth, Lincs LN11 0LQ
tel/fax: 01507 602197

This company specializes in the restoration of marble chimneypieces, and can supply marble, slate and stone fireplaces.

central

A Bell & Co Ltd
Kingsthorpe Rd, Northampton, Northants NN2 6LT
tel: 01604 712505 for stockists • fax: 01604 721028

Marble is the main material used for Bell's high-quality fire surrounds, which are polished to a gleaming finish. They also manufacture traditional log baskets and grates for either real fires or coal effect ones.

Clearview Stoves
More Works, Bishops Castle, Shropshire SY9 5HH
tel: 01588 650401 for stockists • fax: 01588 650493
Showroom at Dinham House, Ludlow,
Shropshire SY8 1EH
tel: 01584 878100

Clearview Stoves are designed to be multi-fuel; one model will take logs as big as 18 inches/45 cms, which will keep burning safely all night without you having to put the fire out. Other models take solid fuel. Whichever one you choose – and they come in an array of colours from traditional Black to Welsh Slate Blue – you are sure to be cosy.

Firecraft
1159 Melton Rd, Syston, Leics LE7 2JS
tel: 0116 2697030

If you'd like something really special, Firecraft can hand-build you a new stone fireplace from scratch. However, it is a very skilled job so be prepared for it to be quite costly.

Flavel-Leisure
Clarence St, Royal Leamington Spa, Warks CV31 2AD
tel: 01926 427027 for stockists • fax: 01926 450526
e-mail: flavel-leisure.market@dial.pipex.com

Flame-effect fires can solve the problem of creating that lovely warm glow if you live in a built-up area where real fires aren't allowed by law, or if you can't be bothered to clean the grate every day. Flavel-Leisure make a wide range of models, some in period designs, which will look like the real thing.

Nottingham Architectural Antiques
531 Woodborough Rd, Nottingham, Notts NG3 5FR
tel: 0115 960 5665

If you have a Victorian house and would like a fireplace from the period, this is definitely the place to come. They have a huge selection, but are not open on Wednesdays.

north west

I Bradbury & Son
3 Rouse Mill Lane, Batley, W.Yorks WF17 5QB
tel: 01924 471300

Their showroom has a good selection of reproductions of rather opulent and dignified mantelpieces on display, with names like 'The Mayfair' and 'The Dorchester'. As it says in their brochure, if you want to give your home that 'old baronial look', this is the place to come.

north east

Robert Aagaard
Frogmore House, Stockwell Rd, Knaresborough,
N.Yorks HG5 0JP
tel: 01423 864805 • fax: 01423 869356

If you are looking for a fireplace from the eighteenth or nineteenth centuries, you could start your search here. There are often quite a few originals in stock and they also do reproduction ones, as well as installing them for you too.

Modena
Be-Modern Group, Western Approach, South Shields,
Tyne & Wear, NE33 5QZ
tel: 0191 455 3577 • fax: 0191 456 5556

This group of fireplace manufacturers, which includes Be-Modern, Simcraft and Marcraft as well as Modena, offer modern solutions to heating your home. Whether it's electric fires that simulate real flames or reproduction fireplaces in marble effect, they have a lot to offer.

radiators

Radiators are normally something that you just inherit when you buy a property. Give them a lick of paint and that's it. The only real decision is whether you paint them white or paint them the same colour as the walls – a contentious issue! But occasionally you will need to buy a new radiator. Perhaps you are having your bathroom refitted or an entire new one installed. Warehouse-style lofts call for a radiator that will not be dwarfed by the room's proportions, and standard panel radiators can sometimes jar the eye in a period home.

If you're looking for a new radiator for a bathroom, there are lots of types to choose from depending on your needs. If authenticity is a priority in a period home, column radiators (manufactured in sections so that your exact requirements can be calculated and a radiator made to fit your space) are in keeping with most periods, and many companies now make these new. They also give out more heat than panel radiators. Nothing beats the joy of warm soft towels when you step out of a bath or shower and a combination radiator, which is operated by your central heating, will both heat the room and dry your towels. Ladder towel rails, which go up the walls, are great for saving floor space and now come in a huge range of colours and finishes so you can choose one to fit into your colour scheme. Freestanding ones, several feet high, can even act as a partition between open-plan spaces.

If you really hate the look of panel radiators, or live in a large open-plan space and need something unobtrusive, coil radiators are an option. They're low down on the floor so they're space saving and virtually unnoticeable, and they heat the air as it rises. For industrial-style lofts, you can get ones that look like giant springs. They can be fitted either underneath a window or in a corner where they'll look like a piece of art.

Don't forget that radiators can be covered with radiator covers, which are not dangerous and allow the warmth to circulate as long as they have in-built ventilation or fretwork on the front. A radiator underneath a window will do its job adequately as long as the curtains or blinds do not hang down over it, causing the hot air to become trapped in the fabric. Instead, make sure any window dressings stop short a couple of inches above it. Underfloor heating is another option but as it's quite specialist it's not something we have covered here. You will, however, find all types of radiators in both traditional and modern designs. As most of the companies tend to supply radiators to others, like bathroom outlets, throughout the country we have listed them alphabetically rather than regionally.

Acova Radiators
30 Rowland Way, Hoo Farm Industrial Estate,
Kidderminster, Worcs DY11 7RA
tel: 01562 753001 for stockists • fax: 01562 69413

If you find normal panel radiators unsightly, this
company manufactures both horizontal radiators,
which can be positioned fairly unobtrusively along
walls and under windows, as well as vertical radiators,
which can be transformed into towel-dryers.
Alternatively, if you want to make a feature of a
radiator rather than hide it, there is an ingenious
model called Fassane which has a mirror set into the
middle and looks great in bathrooms. There are also
six traditional towel rails with regal sounding names –
Balmoral, Windsor and Sandringham.

Bisque Radiators Ltd
15 Kingsmead Square, Bath, Avon BA1 2AE
tel: 01225 469244 for stockists • fax: 01255 444708

A range of unusual bow-fronted radiators, with names
like Yucca, which are available in the normal chrome
and white but also in bold primary colours.

Clyde Combustions Ltd
Cox Lane, Chessington, Surrey KT9 1SL
tel: 0181 391 2020 for stockists • fax: 0181 397 4598

There are six different styles of radiator to choose
from, all equally stylish and elegant.

Heating World Group Ltd
Eyre St, Birmingham, W.Midlands B18 7AD
tel: 0121 454 2244 for stockists • fax: 0121 454 4488

A large range of stylish radiators that come in a variety
of finishes including gold, chrome, nickel, and enamel.

Hudevad
Hudevad House, 130–132 Terrace Rd,
Walton-on-Thames, Surrey KT12 2EA
tel/fax: 01932 247835 for stockists

If you have a particularly awkward space, Hudevad can
make radiators to specification to fit round bay windows
or to curve round a wall, or even to stretch up the stairs.

Merriott Sales
Spinning Jenny Way, Leigh, Lancs WN7 4PE
tel: 01942 263466 for stockists • fax: 01942 260684

Choose from lots of primary colours in a variety of
models – either column, horizontal or vertical. This

company prides itself on being able to solve all your
heating design problems.

MHS Radiators
35 Nobel Square, Burnt Mills Industrial Estate,
Basildon, Essex SS13 1LT
tel: 01268 591010 for stockists • fax: 01268 728202

This manufacturer makes a wide range of radiators but
if you live in a period property or listed building, or
simply hate the look of modern radiators, their Liberty
Radiator will be perfect. It looks like an original
Victorian radiator and is floor-mounted to protect
fragile wood panelling.

Myson
Victoria Works, Nelson St, Bolton,
Lancs BL3 2DW
tel: 01204 382017 for stockists • fax: 01204 398920

If you like your towels warm and fluffy, invest in one
of their heated towel rails, which come in 22ct gold. If
that's too glitzy, they also have brass, chrome and a
selection of other colours.

Radiating Style
Unit 15, Derby Rd Industrial Estate, Hounslow,
Middx TW3 3UQ
tel: 0181 577 9111 for stockists • fax: 0181 577 9222

Radiating Style has some really unique and imaginative
radiators which can turn your bathroom into a fun
place to soak in. There's even one that looks like a
silvery eel.

Vogue (UK) Ltd
Units 9 & 10, Strawberry Lane Industrial Estate,
Strawberry Lane, Willenhall, W.Midlands WV13 3RS
tel: 01902 637330 for stockists • fax: 01902 604532

Stocked in the best bathroom shops, Vogue have
established themselves as an unusual supplier with a
good range of contemporary designs for modern
living. Look out for their Art Deco-inspired radiator, as
well as one that looks like a banjo.

Zehnder Ltd
Unit 6, Invincible Rd, Farborough, Hants GU14 7QU
tel: 01252 515151 for stockists • fax: 01252 522528

You're sure to find a radiator that matches your
bathroom's colour scheme as there are over one
hundred colours in Zehnder's range, which is stocked
by many bathroom outlets.

fans

Not essential in the British climate, but fans can be a stylish accessory. They come in all colours and finishes and can be floor or wall-mounted, freestanding, or small enough to fit on a desk.

Aero

96 Westbourne Grove, London W2 5RT
tel: 0171 221 1950 • fax: 0171 221 2555
tel: 0181 981 1066 for mail order

Aero is a good source for those American-style industrial fans that always look so stylish. They have both the floor and wall-mounted versions.

After Noah

121 Upper St, London N1 1QP
tel: 0171 359 4281
and
261 Kings Rd, London SW3 5EL
tel: 0171 351 2610
e-mail: mailorder@afternoah.demon.co.uk

After Noah hunt for original 1930s fans and restore them to full working order. If you'd like something a little different, with no doubt an interesting history attached to it, this is the place to come.

Fantasia

Unit B, The Flyers Way, Westerham, Kent TN16 1DE
tel: 01959 564440 for stockists • fax: 01959 564829

This company has hundreds of fans in traditional designs. There are brass and chrome ones, white ones, ones fashioned from wood and cane. Their chrome ceiling fans, some of which are operated by remote control, will definitely keep you cool when the heat is on.

Freud

198 Shaftesbury Avenue, London WC2H 8JL
tel: 0171 831 1071 • fax: 0171 831 3062

This trendy little shop above a good bar has a small, but good, range of desk fans in 1930s and 1950s styles in black or chrome, and pedestal and ceiling versions

IKEA

Brent Park, 2 Drury Way, North Circular Rd,
London NW10 0TH
tel: 0181 208 5600 for enquiries and branches

Don't forget IKEA if you're after reasonably priced fans. Look out for the Taifun table fan, which has that industrial feel at a fraction of the cost.

Mellerware Sona

Talbot Rd, Mexborough, S.Yorks S64 8AJ
tel: 01709 579044 for stockists • fax: 01709 579028

Mellerware Sona has a large and varied range of fans. Choose from fans with three oscillating speeds and remote control in stylish metallic blue or grey, reproduction 'antique' ones in brass and chrome, or coloured fans in yellow, lime or cornflower blue.

Mr Resistor

82 New Kings Rd, London SW6 4UL
tel: 0171 736 7521

If you like the colonial style, this wholesaler keeps large ceiling fans. They also do ones with a 1950s industrial feel plus more ordinary fans.

Out of Time/Metro Retro

21 Canonbury Lane, London N1 2AS
tel: 0171 354 5755 • fax: 0171 354 5755

This retro shop specializes in reconditioned fans which are imported mostly from America. There are ones from the 1920s right through to the 1950s.

Pifco

Head Office, Wombourne Factory, Balesworth,
Manchester M35 0HS
tel: 0161 681 8321 for stockists

If you like something fun, Pifco are the experts for the Jellybean fan, which comes in lots of colours and sizes from tiny desk versions to floorstanding models.

Themes & Variations

231 Westbourne Grove, London W11 2SE
tel: 0171 727 5531 • fax: 0171 221 6378

Black Bakelite fans still look really classy. Themes has a good stock of reconditioned, mostly 1930s, ones.

14 the global

Over the years *Home Front* has travelled to places as far afield as Mexico, Sweden and India to investigate what makes up that particular country's style. Everyone has a special place in their heart for a particular country no matter which country happens to be in fashion in the style magazines, and *Home Front* has always attempted to show viewers how to re-create the look for themselves in their own homes. It can be as simple as punching sheets of silver tinware and attaching them to cupboard doors to get the feel of Mexican style, or finding reproduction furniture to recreate the Gustavian opulence of a grand Swedish house. You needn't spend a fortune either. If you know where to look you can pick up some real bargains, whether it's a length of sari for an eastern flavour or metres of ticking and checked fabrics to create that Swedish look. Whatever your penchant, the shops listed below will give you a taste of the exotic.

Most of the shops listed in this chapter sell items from many different countries rather than just one exclusively, but they have been listed under the country that dominates.

village

key: 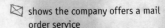 shows the product has appeared on
Home Front

✉ shows the company offers a mail
order service

african style

African style is all about earthy colours – think browns, rusts, oranges and yellows. Prints are bold and highly patterned or stark black and white. Buying authentic ones from African textile warehouses can work out relatively cheaply and you can use them for cushion covers, bedspreads or wall hangings. Look out for hand-carved wooden statues and artefacts like masks and spoons.

The African Craft Centre
38 King St, London WC2 8JT
tel: 0171 240 6098

The window is awash with all sorts of items in this little shop in the heart of London's Covent Garden. There are lots of hand-carved ornaments and masks, textiles and smooth stone statues.

African Escape
1 Westbourne Grove Mews, London W11 2RU
tel/fax: 0171 221 6650

All sorts of interesting artefacts can be found here from exquisitely carved masks and statues, to hand-blocked textiles and prints.

David Champion
199 Westbourne Grove, London W11 2SB
tel: 0171 727 6016 • fax: 0171 792 2097

Here you will find a jumble of things from all over the world but inclined towards Africa. Choose from wooden spoons, North African ammonite fossils, and Indian carvings.

Karavan
167 Lordship Lane, London SE22 3HX
tel: 0181 229 2524 • fax: 0181 229 2524

This shop is crammed with home furnishings largely imported from Morocco and Trinidad, though Iran and Columbia feature here too. There are also some great handcrafted ceramics in bold designs.

indian style

To add a touch of spice to your home in Indian style, look for goods that originate from India itself. (This is not to be confused with English Colonial, which is all cane blinds and overhead fans.) Use woven rugs in natural colours on the floor and even on the walls. If they are true dhurries, they will have been hand-dyed with natural dyes. Don't rule out ones from high-street stores – they often are made in India as well. Find hand-blocked textiles to use for wall hangings and soft furnishings. Seek out simple wooden tables with chunky legs, often jointed with black iron, known as Thakat tables. Look for inexpensive ceramics in blue and white, and lots of brassware – particularly candlesticks. Saris, worn by many Indian people, have been appropriated by interior designers for use in the home and their beautiful colours and patterns can look stunning used in a variety of ways, from canopies to cushions.

Country & Eastern
8 Redwell St, Norwich, Norfolk NR2 4SN
tel: 01603 623107
and
34–36 Bethel St, The Old Skating Rink Gallery,
Norwich, Norfolk NR2 4SN
tel: 01603 758108
and
3 Holland St, Kensington, London W8 4NA
tel: 0171 938 2711

The old skating rink branch in Norwich has five floors bursting with block textiles, hand-woven fabrics, lighting, wood carvings, oriental rugs, crewel fabrics, and jewellery. It was one of the first companies to start importing and it supplies to many other retail outlets. The ceiling is also worth a look as it is one of the most unusual in the country and architects come from far and wide to see it.

Emily Readett-Bailey Ltd
St Lukes Old Rectory, 107 Grange Rd, London SE1 3BW

As well as the Orient, many of the goods are imported from Morocco and Bali. There are lots of Buddhas in jade, marble, wood and iron as well as larger items such as carved tea chests.

India Jane
133 King's Rd, London SW3 4PW
tel: 0171 730 1070
and
140 Sloane St, London SW1 9AY
tel: 0171 351 1060

Very classy top of the range imports with Thakat tables, large ornamental mirrors, lots of porcelain, and ironwork with price labels to match.

The India Shop
5 Hilliers Yard, Marlborough, Wilts SN8 1NB
tel: 01672 515585 • fax: 01380 728118

This company supplies a good range of Indian fabrics and furnishings including lots of hand-woven dhurries, hand-blocked cotton cushion covers, and smaller items of furniture such as Thakat tables.

The Indian Collection
4 Castle St, Wallingford, Oxon OX10 8DL
tel: 01491 833048 for stockists • fax: 01491 839590

A major importer/wholesaler who has been working in conjunction with Indian tradesmen for more than twenty years. The company searches out skilled craftsmen in out of the way places and has a commitment to be ecologically friendly, using traditional production techniques and natural vegetable dyes. They supply numerous outlets nationwide. There are wonderful Kalamkari quilts made from hand-blocked cotton, cushions, bedspreads, throws, dhurries and tablecloths.

The Modern Saree Centre
26–28 Brick Lane, London E1 6RF
tel: 0171 247 4040

Sari fabric can be used in all sorts of spectacular ways within the home. *Home Front* designer Fiona Samler visited this shop and chose lots of beautiful silks to create cushions and bolsters to turn a girlie bedroom into a seductive boudoir. To crown it all she created a sumptuous canopy hanging over the bed made by suspending lengths of sari fabric from doweling rods. It is sold by the sari length which is about five metres and can be remarkably inexpensive, although expect to pay more for ones that have gold thread or are heavily embroidered.

Oliver Bonas
tel: 0171 627 4747 for enquiries and branches
fax: 0171 622 3629

Oliver Bonas have a small but good range of Thakat coffee and dining tables, and stock Indonesian furniture too. There's a very unusual pyramid-shaped chest of drawers, apothecary chests, and drawer chests, all handmade. Available in all branches (see p.117 for shop locations).

Partap Textiles
86 Ilford Lane, Ilford, Essex IG1 2LA
tel: 0181 478 0529

A very good stockist of silk-mix fabrics in jewel-like colours that are reasonably priced.

Pukka Palace
Seifton Depo, Culmington, nr Ludlow,
Shropshire SY8 2DH
tel: 01584 861393 • fax: 01584 861604
tel: 0345 666660 for mail order

Their mail order catalogue, called Pukka Brief, is loosely divided up into rooms. It includes antique and repro colonial style – glass bell jar lamps, and quilts inspired by the dura inlay of the marble in the Taj Mahal. The antique furniture is genuinely the actual pieces which were used by military families in the days of the Raj. If you want to see more phone the Colonial Furniture Warehouse on the number listed above. It is open Mon–Fri by arrangement only.

Rainbow Textiles   **hf**

98 The Broadway, Southall, Middx UB1 1QF
tel: 0181 574 1494

An excellent supplier of sari fabrics, which were a favourite with *Home Front* designer Nishma Chande when she created an Indian-themed bedroom for

Caroline Lewsey at her Norfolk barn. If you live in an area where there is a large Indian/Asian population, there are likely to be some good wholesale sari shops near you.

Warris Vianni

85 Golbourne Rd, London W10 5NL
tel: 0181 964 0069

Rolls and rolls of both Indian and Thai fabrics are kept in stock here and you will be spoilt for choice.

mexican style

The Mexicans have always loved colour and using vivid fuchsia, purple, cobalt blue, bright yellow and turquoise on their walls is nothing new to them. If you have fallen in love with this look, it can easily be imitated with the range of chalky paints available in this country but remember that, in the cold English light, it may not always quite come off. Instead, try painting the walls white with just one wall picked out in a vibrant colour or, if you're more adventurous, try walls of the same colour but in different shades such as orange and red, or even clashing colours. Add details such as enormous cacti in large earthenware urns, woven mesh baskets, ceramics decorated with geometric patterns, punched silver tinware, hand-painted clay ornaments and lots of recycled glassware – the more irregular the better.

Corres Mexican Tiles Ltd

Unit 1A Station Rd, Hampton Wick, Kingston, Surrey KT1 4HG
tel: 0181 943 4142 • fax: 0181 943 4649

For more than 130 years this company has been producing mainly handmade tiles with a Mexican feel. They come in all types of terracotta with painted designs.

Designer's Guild

267–271 & 275–277 Kings Rd, London SW3 5EN
tel: 0171 243 7300 for the store• fax: 0171 243 7710
tel: 0171 351 5775 for general enquiries

Down in the basement, you will find little Mexican candles with paper wrappers. As the candle burns, the wax glows through the paper giving off an an eerie glow.

Elon

66 Fulham Rd, South Kensington, London SW3 6HH
tel: 0171 460 4600 • fax: 0171 460 4601

Elon's unique range of hand-painted tiles have been much imitated but these are the real thing; and no two tiles are identical. Choose from hand-painted Mexican designs. (They also do Provence wall tiles that have exquisitely painted flower designs in soft delicate colours, and floor tiles reminiscent of being in a Tuscan farmhouse.) Mexican-style terracotta and slate floor tiles are also available.

Emma Bernhardt

301 Portobello Rd, London W10 5TE
tel: 0181 960 2929

Lots of little trinkets from Mexico such as mesh bags in acid colours – use them for shopping, for storing vegetables, or for going out. There are also lots of Mexican candles, transparent door knobs with flowers and Madonnas inside, and paper flower garlands. It's a fun, bright place. You'll need your sunglasses.

Fifth Corner
17–18 Parsons St, Banbury, Oxon OX16 8LY
tel: 01295 266531 • fax: 01295 266531

Large and small items of furniture imported from Mexico, plus lots of ceramics, pottery and vases. They also have a great many artefacts from India and Indonesia.

The Lemon Tree
103 King St, Knutsford,
Cheshire WA16 6EQ
tel/fax: 01565 751101

Here you will find pottery from Mexico plus an eclectic range of furniture from Morocco, Thailand, India and

Indonesia. It's all handmade in the country of origin and imported to this country.

Mexique
67 Sheen Lane, London SW14 8AD
tel: 0181 392 2345

This is a tiny shop but it is jam-packed with Mexican items including hand-painted clay, recycled glassware and lots of punched tinware, in colours as well as silver. There are some nice wall decorations such as portal mirrors – tiny three-way mirrors with two doors that open up to reveal the central mirror.

Verandah
15b Blenheim Crescent, London W11 2EE
tel: 0171 792 9289

A little shop off Portobello Rd which is crammed with lovely things like Mexican tinware, glassware, ceramics, terracotta pots. It's not exclusively Mexican but an eclectic mix of bits and bobs culled from all over.

moroccan style

For a flavour of Moroccan style, create a palette of strong earthy colours in reds, browns and yellow ochres combined with flashes of brilliant pinks and oranges. Use it everywhere from walls to fabrics and picked up in small details such as handmade tiles and ceramics. If you can afford it, contrast this with cool stone floors. Lighting is highly ornate with lots of hanging lanterns with detailed filigree work. Heap masses of sensuous cushions on the floor, in velvets, silks, and leather, and cover unsightly areas using screens with highly ornate fretwork. For a truly authentic look you could even have window shutters made to order. Lastly, no Moroccan room would be complete without a set of tea glasses – tiny thimbles with a rim of painted glass in jewel-like colours with delicate flowery patterns. If you don't partake of tea, you can always use them for displaying a single flower.

Color 1 Ceramics
404 Richmond Rd, Twickenham,
Middx TW1 2EB
tel: 0181 891 0691 • fax: 0181 296 0491

If you like the hot spicy colours of Morocco and the Mediterranean, they do a great range of wall tiles

called Maroc Rustic, which has contrasting items called Marakesh and Kasbah.

dar
No 11 The Arches, Miles St, London SW8 1RZ
tel: 0171 720 9678 • fax: 0171 627 5129

This company makes table tops in zellige – the traditional Moroccan art form of using hand-cut pieces of wood-fired ceramic tiles. The table bases are made from forged iron and you can have a console, coffee or occasional table with the zellige top. They can do mail order and they do have a showroom but please ring first. They also do lighting, tiles, and accessories made by Moroccan craftsmen.

Maryse Boxer Chez Joseph
26 Sloane St, London SW1 9NH
tel: 0171 245 9493

A very classy range of those little Moroccan tea glasses which have coloured glass round the rim and patterns etched into the glass.

oriental style

Oriental style always seems to be popular, particularly for interiors, but at the end of the nineties it was absolutely everywhere. It is predicted by the style gurus to last well into the next millennium. If you like this look, use red and black with flourishes of gold, keep all the furniture low, look for paper screens, anything lacquered, and try coir matting on the floor with bamboo accessories. Hang Chinese lanterns in clusters or individually, arrange peacock feathers in simple vases or on the wall, and remember you can pick up all sorts of things in Chinese supermarkets.

The Cross
141 Portland Rd, London W11 4LR
tel: 0171 727 6760 • fax: 0171 727 6745

This trendy little shop is frequented by lots of movie stars shopping for clothes but it also has a small range of Oriental-style accessories including large Chinese lanterns, bags and slippers.

Minh Mang
182 Battersea Park Rd, London SW11 4ND
tel: 0171 498 3233 • fax: 0171 498 3353

Specializing in silks and fabrics from Vietnam and Cambodia which are beautifully embroidered and made into everything from notebook covers to handbags. They also supply to Designer's Guild and The Cross (see above).

Muji
157 Kensington High St, London W8 6SU
tel: 0171 376 2484
tel: 0171 323 2208 for mail order

The products are all manufactured in Japan and East Asia and the company is committed to only using quality raw materials. If you fancy having bath salts and soaps

adorned with Japanese writing there are lots to choose from, as well as rice bowls and shallow finger bowls in delicate porcelains but without any fancy patterns. (See also Furniture p.158, and Storage p.188.)

Neal Street East

5 Neal St, London WC2H 9PU
tel: 0171 240 0135

An Aladdin's cave of treasures containing four floors of inexpensive goods. You will need to rummage around as it's absolutely jam-packed. In the basement, you will find masses of great ideas for presents from paper lanterns, Japanese water flowers and cookery ware, and upstairs you will find everything from authentic Chinese dresses to fabrics and cushion covers.

Sebastiano Barbagallo
15–17 Pembridge Rd, London W11 3HL
tel: 0171 792 3320 • fax: 0171 792 3320

This shop specializes in antiques and handicrafts from India, Tibet, South-east Asia and China. There are hundreds of Buddhas in marble, stone, wood and ceramic, panels of embroidery, and framed pictures. A fascinating place to browse around in.

shaker style

The Shakers were an American religious sect who lived at the beginning of the eighteenth century. The philosophy of the Shaker craftsmen was that the quality of their work was a testament to their lives and that their work was dedicated to God believing that, 'the peculiar grace of a Shaker chair is due to the maker's belief that an angel might come and sit on it'.

Today, original Shaker items fetch massive sums at auction and the look has filtered down to the high street, although the term 'Shaker style' is bandied about to apply to almost anything that looks naïve and primitive with a few patchwork hearts stuck on it. As long as you make the distinction between the high-street look and those companies who make reproduction furniture using traditional skills and craftsmen, you will know what sort of prices to expect.

If you want to achieve the Shaker look stick to a few basic rules. Look for strong and simple shapes in furniture. For the colour scheme, stick to a limited palette of colours – red, light and dark blue, a warm yellow, and a bluish green. Use matt emulsion not sheen and look out for milk or casein paints; some companies import their paint, which is made using traditional methods, from America. The Shaker look is all about clean lines, no clutter and simplicity, and remember you don't have to go the whole hog and stick your chairs on peg rails around the walls.

Appalachia

14a George St, St Albans, Herts AL3 4ER
tel: 01727 836796

American folk art is represented in this small shop. All the goods are made and imported directly from the States and not through a wholesaler. Expect to find small items of furniture – stools, cabinets etc. in eight different stain finishes, copies of samplers, peg boards, bird houses, limited edition prints and dolls, wood carvings, American scented candles, antique hand-made quilts.

Index Catalogue

tel: 0800 401080 for branches and catalogue

This high-street home catalogue offers two Shaker-inspired furniture ranges which are at the lower end of the price bracket. The Mayflower is a chest made from Scandinavian pine which comes in either a lacquered

finish or a blue/green wash. Alternatively, there is the Boston Shaker range which you assemble yourself.

Lakeland Ltd

Alexandra Buildings, Windermere,
Cumbria LA23 1BQ
tel/fax: 01539 488100 for branches and mail order

Amongst all their storage items, Lakeland do a good, reasonably priced range of Shaker peg boxes – oval boxes that stack up in varying sizes.

Lawrence T Bridgeman

1 Church Rd, Roberttown, Liversedge,
W.Yorks WF15 7LS
tel: 01924 413813 for stockists and mail order
fax: 01924 413801

For a traditional Shaker or American Colonial look, this company has a range of Buttermilk, Old Village and Vintage paints, which are based on traditional recipes in use in America since 1816. Imported from America, the Buttermilk paints are the only milk paints authenticated by the Colonial Williamsburg Foundation.

New England Direct
PO Box 5221 Broomsgrove, Worcs B61 0BY
tel: 01527 577111 for mail order • fax: 01527 578070

This mail order only company have a catalogue which is not strictly Shaker, more American Country, but the two styles have quite a lot in common, both adopting that charming 'naive' style. Within its pages, expect to find copies of embroidered samplers, quilt kits in Amish style, homespun quilts and tin candle holders.

Shaker
25 Harcourt St, London W1H 1DT
tel: 0171 724 7672 • fax: 0171 724 6640
and
322 Kings Rd, London SW3 5UH
tel: 0171 352 3918

Shaker furniture such as trestle tables, dressers, and chairs are made using the traditional joinery skills so expect to pay accordingly. The larger items are made to order and can be adapted. There are various mail order catalogues. Smaller items like peg rails, boxes, pictures and Christmas decorations feature in their Home Accessories catalogue. If you fancy having a go, there are Shaker Kits containing all you need to assemble some of the chairs and smaller tables yourself. The woven seat pads are made of tape and there's a choice of twelve colours.

Shaker Village
PO Box 14195, Eltham, London SE9 2ZU
tel: 0181 850 0675

This company makes Shaker-style furniture to commission, as well as Shaker boxes, peg rails and smaller items of Shaker furniture. All the items are handmade and beautifully finished.

swedish style

Swedish style embraces two looks – traditional Scandinavian style, and Gustavian style, which is more opulent and would have been found in grander houses. For both looks, bare, scrubbed, wooden floorboards are essential and the paler the wood the better. Use simple throws and rugs over them for warmth. Stick to white for the walls but use antique white rather than brilliant whites to give a much softer effect.

For a traditional Scandinavian look, paint furniture in greys and soft blues, and for a Gustavian style use the same colours but pick out detail using fine lines of gold or silver leaf. Alternatively, paint furniture in bright primary colours with simple stencils. Curtains should be kept plain and simple, preferably in checks and ginghams or plain colours. Leave the woodwork free of paint or use the same colours as the walls but in a matt finish and add stencils as borders. Place fabric runners across the table, and look out for wall sconces in brass and gold.

The Blue Door
74 Church Rd, London SW13 0DQ
tel: 0181 748 9785 • fax: 0181 563 1043

Housed in a pretty courtyard, this delightful shop is a haven of tranquillity. Having moved from cramped premises, they now have room to display things in all their splendour. There is an elegant table set for dinner, books for sale are ranged in Swedish painted cabinets, piles of antique linens and fabrics lie casually on pine tables. Handmade reproduction furniture in the Gustavian style is available to order, painted using traditional Swedish paints.

Codrington Furniture
Arch 80, Chelsea Bridge Business Centre,
Queenstown Rd, London SW8 4NE
tel: 0171 498 9960 • fax: 0171 498 9961

Furniture designer Sasha Waddell was inspired by Swedish style, particularly Carl Larsson's house at Sundborn, which led her to produce a line of furniture distributed by Codrington. Rather than making faithful copies, Waddell extracts some of the period details, which she then refines to create an original piece. Motifs such as fretwork patterns taken from the house recur in the work. Some designs are held in stock but the majority are commissioned.

The Household Goods Trading Company
135 Turney Rd, London SE21 7JB
tel: 0171 274 3507 • fax: 0171 274 3507

This mail order only company makes Swedish-style reproduction furniture, including a Gustavian-style Stromsholm chair, all hand-crafted by a small but well-established firm of Scandinavian craftsmen. They use traditional skills and materials and make beds, chairs, cabinets, stools and mirrors with a choice of finishes. You can also order the items unpainted (at a lower price than the painted versions).

Ian Mankin
109 Regents Park Rd, London NW1 8UR
tel: 0171 722 0997 • fax: 0171 722 2159
and
271 Wandsworth Bridge Rd, London SW6 2TX
tel: 0171 371 8825

Metres and metres of reasonably priced material in ticking, stripes and gingham, muslin, checks – all essential to achieve the Swedish look.

Nordic Style
109 Lots Rd, London SW10 0RN
tel: 0171 351 1755

This lovely shop stocks Sasha Waddell's Swedish Country Classics range of furniture as well as their own bespoke furniture painted in colours like Baltic Blue, Gustavian Grey and Buttermilk. They also have a good range of accessories such as candle sconces, mirrors and linens.

Paint Magic
48 Golborne Rd, Notting Hill, London W10 5PR
tel: 0181 960 9960 • fax: 0181 960 9655

This is where to come to get all the paints, stencils, and woodwashes you will need to create that particular Scandinavian look. Founder and *Home Front* designer Jocasta Innes is herself an expert in Scandinavian style and her staff are all knowledgeable about what products to use to create a particular effect.

The Swedish Chair
91a Crescent Rd, Caterham, Surrey CR3 6LE
tel: 01883 341756 • fax: 01883 627549

Hand-painted reproductions of both Gustavian-style and country-style furniture. Items can be painted in the colour of your choice in Scandinavian antique style.

Tobias & The Angel
68 White Hart Lane, London SW13 0PZ
tel: 0181 878 8902

This beautifully laid-out shop is good for inspiration alone, selling a mixture of old and new. Here you will discover genuine enamel kitchenware, quilts and cushions made from faded antique patchwork scraps, and silk cords threaded with rare old beads, buttons, shells and nutmegs.

back

Trends come and go but it seems that every few years one particular era is resurrected and is suddenly interpreted everywhere from fashion to film, filtering right down through to interior design. Traders report a sudden upsurge of interest in items from that decade, style magazines are full of new things inspired by it, and auctions at places like Bonham's and Christie's are suddenly very well attended. It is difficult to pin down precisely what triggers these trends but it seems wise never to get rid of anything as, no doubt, it will come round again!

Home Front is not, however, about slavishly recreating the look of a bygone era down to every last period detail, because that would smack of regression. It is rather about mixing the best of design from that period with new contemporary items. In this chapter we have decided to concentrate on post-war design – namely fifties, sixties, and seventies. The shops listed here often sell a mix of items from a range of periods, perhaps specializing in one in particular. It would be too commercially risky for them only to concentrate on one decade, and it is difficult to differentiate exactly between eras as styles tend to merge into one another. So, even if your thing is solely sixties, it's worth checking out as many of these shops as you can because you might just find what you have been looking for.

Half the enjoyment of rooting round these sorts of shops is that you will see all kinds of things you might have had in your house as a child or even in your granny's house – it all comes flooding back. Looking at the prices and knowing that you've got one very similar at home is also great fun. Remember too that jumble and car boot sales, junk and second-hand shops, can also be brilliant hunting grounds for genuine retro bargains. And don't forget the attic!

to the
future

 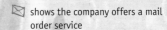

returning decades

Fifties style for interiors was all about optimism. After the austerity of the Second World War people wanted bright colours and there was a temptation to get rid of everything old and start afresh. Although materials were in short supply and still regulated by the Government, it didn't stop many more affluent people from completely re-doing their homes. It was during this time that fireplaces were ripped out and picture and dado rails came down. Even curtain poles were thought to be outmoded and were replaced with new curtain track.

So if you want to inject some fifties style into your home, use lots of bright colours – particularly yellow, red and orange, and also off-set with black. Try keeping three of your walls plain and just paint one in a vivid colour. Look for lots of funky animal prints for cushions, fabrics and throws. America was a huge influence on British design in the 1950s and diner-style furniture, cocktail cabinets, and huge fridges were much in demand. All these things, many of them original, can still be found or you can pick up things that look similar in high-street stores.

The sixties continued with this explosion in colour and massive experimentation. Plastic and PVC abounded and there was some really kitsch stuff around. It is difficult to separate the sixties from the seventies in design terms as many of the influences cross over. In the seventies more and more people were seeing their homes as somewhere to relax in and have parties. To get the right atmosphere, try and keep everything low on the ground. Either invest in low, modular seating, or lounge about on beanbags. There was a huge emphasis on lighting. Arc lights in chrome and steel were like pieces of architecture in their own right and many fine specimens can still be found today. Many of today's lighting designers are mimicking what was around in the seventies because they know that the poise and grace of these lights can't be bettered, so if you can't get hold of an original, you will probably be able to find something appropriate in an upmarket lighting shop (see also modern and groovy lighting section p.113). Furniture was often fashioned from plastic in sculptural shapes and names to look out for include Verner Panton and Charles & Ray Eames.

After Noah
121 Upper St, London N1 1QP
tel: 0171 351 2610
and
261 Kings Rd, London SW3 5EL
tel: 0171 359 4281
e-mail: mailorder@afternoah.demon.co.uk

After Noah has all sorts of original fifties goods including an entire kitchen called English Rose. Supplies of these are sometimes limited but it's worth asking if you want the total retro look. There are normally one or two Coca-Cola fridges on display and they can probably get their hands on more if you ask.

Alfie's Antique Market
13–25 Church St, London NW8 8DT
tel: 0171 723 6066

This is one of London's biggest covered markets. There are lots of individual stalls selling genuine pieces from the fifties, sixties and seventies and you just have to hunt around to compare prices and get the best deals. It's only open on Saturdays and by special appointment during the week. They will consider buying stuff from you if they think it will sell but don't take things in uninvited, especially at weekends, because they're far too busy selling it.

Boom
53 Chalk Farm Rd, Camden, London NW1 8AN
tel: 0171 284 4622

Bursting with colour and fun, the objects, which are all genuine retro pieces and a good mix of fifties, sixties and seventies, are all laid out in room sets. Everything appears to be in mint condition and there are some wonderful arc lamps by famous Italian designers, such as Regianni, which have been imported, rewired and restored to gleaming perfection.

b2
121 Water Street, Castlefield, Manchester M3 4JU
tel: 0161 834 1113 • fax: 0161 834 1119

This company specializes in producing 1950s and 1960s furniture but it is all newly made. They are very good replicas – with American diner chairs and tables, topped with the coloured laminates and pieces made with lots of chrome and features typical of that time. You can choose a table top from their range of colours and a coloured vinyl for the upholstery.

Cath Kidston
8 Clarendon Cross, London W11 4AP
tel: 0171 221 4000 • fax: 0171 229 1992

Apparently, Cath Kidston grew up in the fifties and, once she became a designer, tried all sorts of contemporary styles but eventually went back to what she was familiar with. The shop, therefore, is full of 1950s-style fabrics, fablon and wallpaper. Floral sprigs on striped backgrounds in candy colours are typical but they still manage to look fresh and modern. As well as fabrics there are all sorts of bits and bobs from padded hangers to ironing-board covers.

Century Design
68 Marylebone High St, London W1M 3AQ
tel: 0171 487 5100 • fax: 0171 487 5100

Tucked away in the basement of a hairdresser's on the Marylebone Rd, it's easy to miss. This is top-of-the-range retro furniture. Owner Andrew Weaving goes on regular jaunts to the USA bringing back such marvels as original Charles Eames and Arne Jacobsen furniture. It is all beautifully displayed and, as well as classics, there are some items of contemporary design.

The Classic American Fridge Company
Unit 1, Darvells Yard, Common Rd,
Chorleywood Common, Herts WD3 5LP
tel: 01923 490303 • fax: 01923 480303

Giant American-style fridges have been popular in the high-street stores for a few years now but if you want something really unique, this company actually renovates original ones to their former glory. Makes such as Frigidaire, LEC and Prestcold are rechromed, fitted with new compressors using CFC-free gas, and then sprayed in bold colours. However, all the distinguishing features such as the original lettering are kept intact and each fridge has its own identity tag and certificate of authenticity.

Flying Duck Enterprises
320–322 Creek Rd, London SE10 9SW
tel: 0181 858 1964 • fax: 0181 852 3215

If you're looking for an old fifties fridge, this shop in London's Greenwich district usually has a few in stock. There is a good mix of old and new here with things carefully chosen to fit in with the style, even if they're not genuine. Smaller items can be purchased by mail order – including the eponymous flying ducks.

Focus on the Past
25 Waterloo St, Bristol, Avon BS8 4BT
tel: 0117 973 8080

Lots of sixties- and seventies-style stuff is packed into this shop – some of it genuine and some of it imitation. Popular with Bristol's large student population, it's all a bit haphazardly displayed so be prepared to root around.

The Ginnell Gallery
18–22 Lloyd St, Manchester M2 5WA
tel: 0161 833 9037

This is a huge antiques centre housing all sorts of collectables but with a good representation from the fifties including ceramics, lighting and furniture. They have one of the largest collections of the famous Midwinter pottery in the country.

The Home Service
Unit H34, Camden Stables Market,
London NW1 8AH
tel: 0171 267 0620

A small but beautifully maintained unit within the covered area of Camden Market, which comes alive at weekends. There are examples of fifties, sixties and seventies retro – mostly smaller items such as radios, clocks, pictures, a good selection of lighting, china displayed in fifties dressers, and funny postcards. Open at weekends only.

Igloo
34 Silver Arcade, Silver St,
Leicester, Leics LE1 5FB
tel: 0116 251 4066

This little shop has a very good range of furniture and lighting, which is all original and reflects the more kitsch side of the sixties and seventies with inflatable furniture and day-glo colours. They are closed on Mondays and Sundays.

Jerry's Home Store
163–167 Fulham Rd, London SW3 6SN
and
57 Heath St, London NW3 6UG
tel: 0171 794 8622
tel: 0171 581 0909 for mail order catalogue

This shop, which also has branches in Kingston upon Thames, Surrey and within London's Harvey Nichols store, has lots of new but fifties-influenced stuff. Upstairs you could be in an American deli with gumball machines, cocktail shakers, Coca-Cola paraphernalia, and is a good place to go if you yearn for Oreos and Hershey's chocolate. Downstairs are larger items of furniture including some very stylish steel cabinets which are quite retro. They launched a mail order service in autumn 1998.

Les Couilles Du Chien
65 Golbourne Rd, London W10 5NP
tel: 0181 964 8192

A gem of a shop that it might be easy to dismiss as just another junk shop. On closer inspection, there are all sorts of treasures. Owner Jerome Dodd trawls the country looking for genuine seventies lighting and furniture and there are some fantastic bargains to be had. It's worth asking if he's got anything else stashed away and if you've got your eye on something, it's best to buy it there and then because stock is sold rapidly. As well as seventies items, there is all sorts of other stuff – from stuffed moose heads to cowskins. The shop is not always open on a Monday so it's best to check first.

Luna
23 George St, Nottingham, Notts NG1 3BH
tel: 0115 924 3267 • fax: 0115 924 3267

If you can beat off the rest of Nottingham's design-conscious crowd, you can pick up some great bargains here. Concentrating on fifties, sixties and seventies design, there are all sorts of collectibles that are aimed to be used rather than to be admired in a glass case. It's particularly good for small items that can really make a room – lamps, telephones, ashtrays. There are some larger items of furniture and the occasional complete fifties kitchen. If you see something you want, it's advisable to snap it up as the stock rotates rapidly.

Mathmos
179 Drury Lane, London WC2B 5QF
tel: 0171 404 6605 • fax: 0171 404 6606

No sixties room would be complete without a lava lamp and, although many little gifty shops now sell them, Mathmos was really the frontrunner. It has been making them since 1963 and they come in all different shapes, sizes and colours. They also sell fibre optic lamps – some of which change colour on a four-second cycle.

Out of Time/Metro Retro
21 Canonbury Lane, London N1 2AS
tel: 0171 288 1086 • fax: 0171 288 1086

Two shops operate out of the same premises here and you will find a real treasure trove of stuff from the forties and fifties including wallpaper, lighting, glass, fridges in pastel colours, chrome fans, and telephones.

Planet Bazaar

151 Drummond St, London NW1 2PB
tel/fax: 0171 387 8326

A small but colourful shop selling collector's items
from the kitschy pop end of the sixties and seventies.
The stock changes regularly and owner Maureen
Silverman has built up an impressive collection such as
original lights from Heals' and Habitat, Verner Panton
chairs in sculptural plastic, Whitefriars glass, BIBA
posters – in fact, the more you look, the more you see.
The shop featured on *Home Front* when designer Kevin
Allan made over a room in seventies style. The shop is
open Tues–Sat, 12–8 p.m.

Squawk

51 Topsfield Parade, Tottenham Lane,
London N8 8PT
tel: 0181 245 3147 • fax: 0181 245 3147

This is a colourful shop with a good mix of genuine
retro from the thirties to the seventies nicely blended
in with contemporary items. The owners have
consciously decided to find and sell beautiful pieces of
design from each era but not by the well-known
names, wisely figuring that this market is already
saturated. The result is a fine range of stock,
particularly of original lighting.

Stuff & Co

1 Heathcoat St, Hockley, Nottingham,
Notts NG1 3AF
tel/fax: 0115 988 1780

Rather than concentrating on designer names, this
shop concentrates on everyday products from the
fifties, sixties and seventies (with the sixties
predominating). It's popular with students who want
the look but can't afford prices of the design classics.
It's good for large items such as dining room furniture,
particularly in chrome, as well as telephones and
lighting. A mix of new names work well with the retro
stuff as they've been chosen specifically to fit in –
look out for Alessi, Inflate, Guzzini, and Bliss.

Tab

7 Kings Rd, Brighton, Sussex BN1 1NE
tel: 01273 239687

This is really a shop for retro clothes but there are also
some interior things from the sixties and seventies,
particularly wallpaper, tables, and accessories.

Tom Tom

42 New Compton St, London WC2H 8DA
tel: 0171 240 7909

Although the shop can seem more like a small art
gallery than somewhere to browse and is somewhat
intimidating, if you're after some really classy
seventies classics – with price labels to match – this is
definitely worth a visit. There are some spectacular
examples of Italian arc lights, and downstairs there
are often original Verner Panton chairs.

Twentytwentyone

274 Upper St, London N1 2UA
tel/fax: 0171 288 1996

An almost reverential feel pervades this small shop
which is tastefully furnished with design classics from
such notables as Charles & Ray Eames, Arne Jacobsen,
and Alvar Aalto. The furniture is a mix of originals,
reproductions and licensed reproductions, as well as
new designs from names such as Tom Dixon. Nothing
has a price tag, which can be a bit off-putting and
suggests, if you have to ask, you probably can't afford
it. A good range of books on twentieth-century design
is also for sale.

Visto

41 Pembridge Rd, London W11 3HG
tel: 0171 243 4392

You will find mostly 1950s paraphernalia here with a
good range of clocks and lights. Smaller items, such as
ceramics and genuine fifties fabrics, are displayed
upstairs. Larger pieces of furniture are kept
downstairs. They could all do with a bit of a clean and
brush-up but the prices are reasonable.

kids'

Home Front has shown nurseries for new-born babies, playrooms for toddlers, right through to virtually self-sufficient apartments for teenagers. Decorating children's rooms can be great because you can really let your imagination run wild. The most important consideration is that, whatever their age, you need to create an exciting, stimulating room that will grow with them. You don't necessarily have to spend a lot, but the room should be somewhere they will enjoy spending time to play, work and be with their friends.

Safety in a child's room is of paramount importance although it's mainly down to common sense. There are lots of safety gadgets available and planning a room to avoid potentially lethal hazards can be as simple as keeping furniture well away from windows, to buying covers to obstruct dangerous electrical sockets and fitting proper window locks. When choosing paint, always make sure it is non-toxic – lead paint is now banned from use unless you live in a Grade I or II listed building – and choose a finish such as eggshell that wipes clean easily. Wallpaper can easily be picked off by little fingers!

Be wary of giving in to your child's latest craze – cartoon character or pop group. Matching wallpaper and bed linen is expensive and may soon be tired of! It's tempting to use lots of pastels with matching accessories but if you opt for plain walls in bright colours, you can then have fun with changeable accessories that can be swapped as tastes change. Lilliputian-sized furniture looks cute but it's soon grown out of. As they get older, kids will want more of a say in how their rooms are decorated, and a few well-chosen bits of furniture at the start, that can be revamped over the years, will give you the basis for an ever-adaptable room. Anne McKevitt transformed a cluttered, boring teenager's room into a stunning fifties boudoir by giving cheap junk-shop furniture an overhaul, and covering everything from wardrobes to mirrors with lots of fake fur. This chapter is full of furniture, fabrics, accessories and all manner of stuff designed with kids in mind.

stuff

Alexanders Rocking Horses & Hand Crafted Toys
68 Aylesbury Rd, Bedford, Beds MK41 9RE
tel: 01234 364658 • fax: 01234 364658

If you want to bring a rocking horse into the family, Alexander Adams makes quite a range of traditional wooden horses in oak or walnut. If you already have one in need of repair, he also restores them.

Anna French
343 Kings Rd, London SW3 5ES
tel: 0171 351 1126 for stockists • fax: 0171 351 0421

Anna French has a fairly extensive choice of bright and more muted fabrics to suit the tastes of your child from the nursery through to teenage. Fabrics are complemented by lace, wallpapers and borders to give the full effect.

Bundles Design
21 Victoria St, Liverpool, Merseyside L1 6BD
tel: 0151 236 8727 for stockists
fax: 0151 236 8727

Choose from quite a wide selection of nursery bed linens including a stylized safari theme, owl and the pussycat in *toile de jouy* style (a particular type of nineteenth-century pastoral or country scene with people and animals), ginghams, bunnies and soldiers. They also offer a range of accessories including nappy stackers, changing mats, lamps and covered Moses baskets.

The Children's Cottage Company
The Sanctuary, Shobrooke, Crediton, Devon EX17 1BG
tel: 01363 772061 • fax: 01363 777868

These are garden playhouses for the truly lucky child. They include models that have thatched or tiled roofs and window-boxes and there is even a castle. Made by craftsmen, they are built to live permanently outdoors.

Community Playthings
Darvell, Robertsbridge, E.Sussex TN32 5DR
tel: 0800 387457 • fax: 0800 387531

This religious community makes a huge range of wooden products for children including furniture, toys, nursery gyms for toddlers and storage units. The emphasis is on simplicity and all the products are designed to be functional and suit the way children play.

The Conran Shop
Michelin House, 81 Fulham Rd, London SW3 5EN
tel: 0171 589 7401 for branches
fax: 0171 823 7015

Next time you're in the Conran Shop to pick out something stylish for yourself, check out their small but equally stylish children's section, as there are some charming things for tiddlers here. Look out for a range of scaled-down enamelware, which is perfect for picnics or everyday use, with a cat or penguin motif, and some delightful crafted toys and pint-sized furniture.

Countrywide
Brynteg, Llandovery, Carms SA20 0ET
tel: 01550 720414 • fax: 01550 720525
e-mail: countryww@aol.com
This charitable trust makes children's wooden furniture including painted ottomans, toy boxes, desks, blackboards and rocking horses. They also make a huge range of wooden toys, children's clocks and brightly coloured mobiles.

Crown
Belgrave Mills, Belgrave Rd, Darwen,
Lancs BB3 2RR
tel: 01254 704951 for stockists

Crown offers a range of wallcoverings and curtains in muted colours. Some of them such as Gardening Teddies and Country Companions are clearly destined for the nursery, while others like African Animals, which supports the work of the World Wildlife Fund, will last your child into their teens. Phone for details of your local stockist.

Descamps
197 Sloane St, London SW1 9QX
tel: 0171 235 6957 for stockists
fax: 0171 235 3903

Part of the larger Descamps range of bed linen and accessories, Petit Descamps is a range of adorable cot sets, bed linen and robes that would please even the most style-conscious tiny tots.

Designer's Guild
267–271 & 275–277 Kings Rd, London SW3 5EN
tel: 0171 243 7300 for the store
fax: 0171 243 7710
tel: 0171 351 5775 for general enquiries

Designer's Guild has made a great contribution to children's fabrics and wallpapers with their imaginative, stylized designs, which are never soppy. They use bright and unusual colours, avoiding too many pastels or primaries and have several, very different, collections as well as accessories. These designs will often live on long after the nursery years.

Dico Furniture

Constantine St, Oldham, Lancs OL4 3AD
tel: 0161 665 1445 for stockists
fax: 0161 627 2048

If your child wants a bed that no one else will have, then Dico have two that may fit the bill. Turby the Car Bed is literally a bed on wheels and shaped like a simple car and may make the bedtime blues just a little easier. Puppy is a pine bed of fairly traditional shape, but that has a puppy and a bone painted on to the foot and headboard.

Dragons of Walton St

23 Walton St, London SW3 2HX
tel: 0171 589 3795 • fax: 0171 584 4570

If you want to spoil your child a little how about a piece of hand-painted furniture from this shop? All the furniture comes in pine or white and there is a huge choice of designs that can be painted on this base. Dragon's artists can also copy from toys, photographs of pets or furnishings to give your child a really unique piece. There are also fabrics, wallpapers and borders on offer.

Elephant Industries

Unit 14, Lansdowne Workshops, London SE7 8AZ
tel: 0181 850 6875 • fax: 0181 850 6875

If you have a child who is mad on animals they will really appreciate some of this wooden furniture which is made in the shape of different animals. All the pieces are handmade and painted to order.

Emma Jefferson

16 Cross Bank, Great Easton, Market Harborough, Leics LE16 8SR
tel: 01536 772074 • fax: 01536 772074

These wonderful wooden height charts and lamps are bound to become favourites in the nursery and may

even turn into heirlooms. The height charts include animals, teddies, dinosaurs and soldiers, while you can choose between ballerinas, cowboys, knights, clowns and many other wooden figures for the lamps. Phone for mail order details.

Farmer Foster

Tuff-Link House, Green Rd, Colne, Lancs BB8 8EL
tel: 01282 873100 for stockists • fax: 01282 873101

Choose from the Children's Patio Range that includes a pint-size picnic table, a wooden sandpit and a rustic bench available in Forest Green or natural timber. The sandpit can be used as a raised children's garden as they grow up.

Gautier

Globe House, Lower Rd, Chorleywood, Herts WD3 5LQ
tel: 01923 285606 for stockists • fax: 01923 285607

France's largest manufacturer of teenage and children's bedroom furniture offers a huge range of different styles which are mostly modern, in wood finishes and bright colours. The furniture ranges from cots to quite grown-up looking designs, so children of all ages can be suited. Phone for details of your nearest stockist.

Geoff Bates

First Floor, Unit 1, Highfield Industrial Estate, Camelford, Cornwall PL32 9RA
tel: 01840 212141

Geoff Bates specializes in designing and making imaginative children's beds, which he describes as the kind of thing you might see in a fairy tale book. He makes sure they are not ridiculously expensive but they are intended to become the family heirlooms of the future. He can make them in MDF or solid timber depending on your budget. He also makes Tall Ships playframes.

Glover & Smith Ltd

Maker's Cottage, 14 London Rd, Overton,
nr Basingstoke, Hants RG25 3NP
tel/fax: 01256 773012 for stockists

An unusual range of door handles your child will love. You could also hang their dressing-gown from a hook in the shape of a rabbit's head, or put knobs in the shape of teddy bears on their furniture.

The Great Little Trading Co
134 Lots Rd, London SW10 0RJ
tel: 0171 376 3337

Mail-order paradise for parents as this company offers a wide-ranging collection of storage items, play furniture and gadgets that will make your life easier from the moment your little bundle arrives home from the hospital! Call for mail order details.

Habitat
196 Tottenham Court Rd, London W1P 9LD
tel: 0171 255 2545
tel: 0645 334433 for branches

Habitat have some seriously trendy and very appealing children's goodies ranging from beds and bedroom furniture to smaller items like toys. Christmas time is a real treat as they ship in masses of extra stocking fillers, many of which are simply irresistible.

The Hambledon Gallery
42 Salisbury St, Blandford, Dorset DT11 7PR
tel: 01258 454884 • fax: 01258 454225

The House, their mail order catalogue, has a small but interesting selection of children's toys and clothes which range from the nursery upwards. Wooden trains rub elbows with glockenspiels and boules sets, with something to suit everyone. Phone for a mail order catalogue.

Hamilton McBride
Shorten Brook Drive, Altham Business Pk, Accrington, Lancs BB5 5YP
tel: 01282 777000 • fax: 01282 858205

The Soft Wear Collection is a whole range of bright and breezy childrens bed linen and matching curtains, featuring Snatch the Dog, Paper Bears, jungle scenes and Budgie the Helicopter.

IKEA
Brent Park, 2 Drury Way, North Circular Rd, London NW10 0TH
tel: 0181 208 5600 for enquiries and branches

IKEA has a wonderful selection of children's furniture, toys and safety items so it's perfect for your children's needs and for presents. Everything is practical, well made and cheap and they have a large section for babies as well. Some of the furniture changes as your child does, for instance a baby changing chest of drawers becomes a bureau with shelves.

Iron Design Company
Summer Carr Farm, Thornton Le Moor, Northallerton, N.Yorks DL6 3SG
tel: 01609 778143

Although they only make one item of children's furniture, it is such a special item that it is well worth taking a look at it before you decorate your child's room. It is the Jester Bed, which has a simple but wacky design, shaped a bit like a jester's hat, that will definitely attract children. The iron bed is available in thirty-four different paint finishes. Call and ask to be sent some details.

Joshua Jones
Whitemill Barn, Sturminster Marshall, Wimborne, Dorset BH21 4BX
tel/fax: 01258 858470

If you want well-made but imaginative bedroom furniture for your children's rooms, the artists and traditional furniture makers work together here to produce just that. There is a wide range of painted designs on offer, or your own ideas can be used.

Kidsville
Chanon House, Waddensbrook Lane, Wednesfields, W.Midlands WV11 3SF
tel/fax: 01902 733000

Teletubbies, Winnie the Pooh and the Looney Tunes characters are just some of the children's favourites which appear on this furniture. Interchangeable doors means that a new bedroom theme can happen practically overnight and there are co-ordinating soft furnishings.

Laura Ashley

PO Box 19, Newtown, Powys SY16 1DZ
tel: 0990 622116 for mail order and branches
tel: 0800 868100 for their Home Furnishing Catalogue

If you are looking for some unusual and not too twee things for your children's rooms, Laura Ashley has some crackers. In a range of lighting, bed linen, wallpaper and curtain fabrics there are stylized teddies, boats, cool mice on the beach and background ginghams and checks. Lots of stuff to please the little ones.

Lion, Witch & Lampshade
89 Ebury St, London SW1W 9QU
tel: 0171 730 1774

This imaginatively named shop specializes in antique rocking horses. If you – or perhaps your parents – had one yourself as a child, or you have an idea of the one you want, they will try and track down a similar one for you. They will also put the 'rock' back in your existing rocking horse if it's in need of some love and care.

Little Bridge
56 Battersea Bridge Rd, London SW11 3AG
tel: 0171 978 5522 • fax: 0171 978 5533

Whether you're looking for a hand-painted stool, a blanket box or a larger piece, Little Bridge offers a wide range of children's furniture in over 1000 colours. There is a choice of painted designs including teddies, racing cars, dalmatians and Noah's ark. Items of furniture can also be commissioned and painted designs adapted from fabric.

Mark Wilkinson Furniture
Overton House, High St, Bromham, nr Chippenham,
Wilts SN15 2HA
tel: 01380 850004 for branches • fax: 01380 850184

This is children's furniture to die for. There are two ranges called Goldilocks and Tom Thumb and they have been designed very much from a child's perspective, but are still beautifully made in first-class materials, mainly wood. The Goldilocks range has an enormous range of pieces from a crib to a four poster, while the Tom Thumb range, which is slightly more masculine, ranges from a child's bed to a computer desk.

Melin Tregwynt
Tregwynt Mill, Castle Morris, Haverfordwest,
Pembrokeshire SA62 5UX
tel: 01348 891225 for stockists • fax: 013485 891694

A family-owned textile mill, which has been in production since the eighteenth century, this is the source of many beautiful blankets including pram and cot blankets. Continental-sized blankets are also available in baby- and child-size and in irresistible colours and designs.

Monogrammed Linen Shop
168/170 Walton St, London SW3 2JL
tel: 0171 589 4033

Spoil your or someone else's children with some of the very upmarket children's clothes and bed linen from this shop. They can all be monogrammed to order and there is a whole host of other nursery accessories.

Nursery Window
83 Walton St, London SW3 2HP
tel: 0171 581 3358 • fax: 0171 823 8839

Fabrics, bed linen, curtains, bathrobes and accessories that are all designed to be good enough quality still to look new by the time they reach the third baby! They offer quite a range of different designs, some of which are more suitable for older children or even adults.

Osborne & Little
304 Kings Rd, London SW3 5UH
tel: 0171 352 1456 for stockists
fax: 0171 351 7813

Famous design company Osborne & Little specializes in what they call adult children's collections. They mean you will find no flopsy bunnies here! The designs are aimed at being suitable for the nursery but stylized and stylish enough to suit the children as they grow. The Charades collection includes topiary trees and celestial themes, while the Scrapbook collection has strong Shaker influences.

Purves & Purves
80–81 & 83 Tottenham Court Rd,
London W1 9HD
tel: 0171 580 8223 • fax: 0171 580 8244

You will find a mixture of children's furniture here and wooden educational toys. The furniture is Danish bedroom furniture and is designed to 'grow' with the child. They also have wonderful trikes and stocking fillers. Phone for the mail order catalogue.

Shelfstore
Frognal Parade, 158 Finchley Rd,
London NW3 5HH
tel: 0171 794 0313 • fax: 0171 435 3927

It's very difficult to get children's furniture just right, especially as their needs change as they grow. This is where the system range of solid pine furniture which this shop offers comes in. It has a great emphasis on practicality and storage and, like a giant Lego set, will adapt to your child's needs as they grow.

Simon Horn

117–121 Wandsworth Bridge Rd, London SW6 2TP
tel: 0171 736 1754 for stockists
fax: 0171 736 3522

An object of serious desire for many parents, the Simon Horn Cot will change to suit the child's needs, first metamorphosizing into a child's bed and then into a sofa. The cot is made in the classical Louis Philippe style and is designed to become a family heirloom. There is a whole range of metamorphic furniture to complement it including a wardrobe that becomes a TV/video cabinet and a toy box that becomes a filing cabinet.

SKK

34 Lexington St, London W1R 3HR
tel: 0171 434 4095

If your child has trouble getting to sleep at night, why not let them count sheep with one of SKK's revolving lights? They're based on a simple zoetrope model featuring sheep, or half a dozen other designs, which can be left safely on as a nightlight. These lights are now seen in most of the bigger department stores, but SKK still have the best range.

Stockwell Carpets

24 Harcourt St, London W1H 1TT
tel: 0171 224 8380 for stockists • fax: 0171 224 8381

This company makes one-off carpets for adults but they also do some more fun ones for children. They can adapt your child's favourite design or their own painting into a rug, which is handmade in 100 per cent wool. There is no limit on size.

Stompa Furniture

The Old Mill House, Dockfield Rd, Shipley,
W.Yorks BD17 7AE
tel: 01274 596885 for stockists • fax: 01274 588741

This company offers all kinds of pine bunk beds, cabin beds and children's furniture to suit the needs of your brood as they grow up. Produced in Norway with wood from managed forests, there has been a lot of thought put into the storage options in these bed systems, which include wardrobes, desks and play areas.

Tidmarsh & Sons

32 Hyde Way, Welwyn Garden City, Herts AL7 3AW
tel: 01707 886226 • fax: 01707 886227
e-mail: blinds@tidmarsh.co.uk

This company can hand-paint children's designs such as rainbows on to wooden venetian blinds. They can also laminate pictures and letters on to roller blinds and, if your child is a bad sleeper, they offer black out blinds in all shapes and sizes. They do mail order too!

Touch Design

51 High St, Sixpenny Handley, Salisbury,
Wilts SP5 5HD
tel: 01725 552888

Introduce your tots to the joys of DIY early by buying them a blank Plywood house that they can then paint themselves. It's a basic model but you can buy extras for it, such as shutters and window boxes. A novel idea that will give them hours of fun.

Toy Planet

The Basement, 45 Tollington Park, London N4 3QP
tel/fax: 0171 281 2763 for stockists

Which child could resist a tiger desk, a zebra chair or a duck rocker? These bright, appealing pieces of furniture are just part of a range which also includes wooden toys. All are made in the UK from recycled woods, decorated with non-toxic colours.

TP Activity Toys

Severn Rd, Stourport-on-Severn, Worcs DY13 9EX
tel: 01299 827728 for stockists • fax: 01299 827163

This is an exciting range of activity toys for children. They are sturdy as they are made from wood or galvanized steel. They have the added advantage of being able to add to them, so you can build up a whole playground, as and when you can afford it.

The Wadham Trading Co

Wadham, Southrop, nr Lechlade, Glos GL7 3PB
tel/fax: 01367 850499

You can buy distinctive iron garden furniture and accessories from this company, as well as some well-designed conservatory furniture. In addition, they also make some child-sized metal benches, chairs and tables and some wonderful wire topiary animals which are bound to appeal.

The White Company

Unit 19c, The Coda Centre, 189 Munster Rd,
London SW6 6AW
tel: 0171 385 7988 • fax: 0171 385 2685

For the thoroughly pampered baby there are tiny luxury towelling robes, hooded towels, bath towels with elephant and hippo motifs and delicate cot sets. You can also choose from soft-coloured, checked blankets and gingham-trimmed bed linen.

Wilson & Garden

17–21 Newtown St, Kilsyth, Glasgow G65 0JX
tel: 01236 823291 for stockists • fax: 01236 825683

Although this company generally supplies grown-up companies, they have a small selection of smart blackboards including the Abacus Board which has reversible black and white boards and two abacus frames, and the Nursery Chalkboard which will accept magnetic symbols.

Zoffany

Unit G12, Chelsea Harbour Design Centre, Chelsea Harbour, London SW10 0XE
tel: 0171 349 0043 for stockists • fax: 0171 351 9677

Zoffany offer some unusual and innovative designs for children's wallpapers, borders and fabrics including alphabets, soldiers, ships and butterflies.

17

in the

Home Front in the Garden, an offshoot of Home Front, was launched in June 1998 but is not a programme about gardening. Instead it took the seed of the idea of Home Front and replanted it outdoors – namely treating the garden like a room and giving it defined areas as a natural extension to your house. Even the familiar faces of the designers from Home Front were brought in to see if they could apply the same principles to the outside, with the addition of plant expert and top garden designer Diarmuid Gavin to be the green-fingered one amongst the crew.

With the flourishing crop of garden programmes aimed at true gardeners, Home Front in the Garden soon found its niche for those people who want a low-maintenance, almost instant, garden. The series has proved that you can have a stylish and well-designed garden without spending all your time in a garden centre. It is not denying the importance of plants, but rather treating them as the icing on the cake.

In this chapter, therefore, you won't find lists of garden centres but you will find all sorts of oddities and useful things that have been used on the programme – a water fountain, unusual containers and planters, even alfresco dining furniture. Many are products that are used elsewhere in the house, such as spray paints, glass blocks and mosaic. Also included in this chapter is where to go to find different types of garden furniture, where to get good outdoor lighting, and salvage companies specializing in things like brick or quarry edging tiles or timber suitable for the garden.

garden

key: **hf** shows the product has appeared on
Home Front

hfg shows the product has appeared on
Home Front in the Garden

✉ shows the company offers a mail
order service

garden furniture

There is nothing quite so pleasant as dining outside: the food really does seem to taste better. And sitting under the shade of a tree, admiring your handiwork in the garden is also a joy. But whether you have a tiny patio or several acres, what should you look for in a piece of garden furniture? Something that will withstand all the elements, especially rain in the British climate, is imperative if you want to be able to leave it outside and not have to keep carting it indoors every time dark clouds gather. Teak and oak are the best woods to look for and they can look even better as they age and weather. If you want your furniture to stand the test of time, look for sturdy, well-made shapes with proper joints rather than ones merely glued together. Classic shapes will not go out of fashion and will suit any garden. There are also lots of great wrought-iron designs around which shouldn't rust if you leave them outside and, if they do, sometimes the 'distressed' look can add to the charm of a piece. Many French, café-type chairs and tables can look just as good outdoors as in, although you may need a cushion or two for added comfort! This section tells you where to look for the best garden furniture around at all price levels.

Anthony de Grey Trellises

Broadhinton Yard, 77a North St, London SW4 0DQ
tel: 0171 738 8866 for examples of previous work
fax: 0171 498 9075

If you've always wanted something really special for your garden, such as a pavilion, pergola or arbour, this company will make up a unique design for you. They don't have a catalogue as such as each design is custom made but will happily show you work they have carried out for other clients and discuss your require-ments with you. If you live within the catchment area of the M25, they'll also come and put it up for you.

Ascott Designs

Units 4–6, Marley Way, Banbury, Oxon OX16 7RL
tel: 01295 270848 for stockists • fax: 01295 270965

This company manufactures Italian-style wrought iron furniture, which would look stunning on a patio or terrace. The designs are quite ornate with scrolls and curves and, as well as tables and chairs, there are rose arches, Victorian gazebos, and a beautiful arch – complete with two facing seats – for the garden.

Ashton Products

Satco House, Claylands Rd, Bishop's Waltham, Hants SO32 1BH
tel: 01489 894666 for stockists • fax: 01489 896289
e-mail: satco@satco.telme.com

If you're looking for classic garden furniture in teak and aluminium, there are many ranges to choose from here, including a good line of extendable tables and collapsible chairs for dining outside. They are the sole agents for the Spanish company Kettal who do stylish sun loungers and loom furniture. They have a showroom in Winchester, too, so ring for details.

Barlow Tyrie

Springwood Industrial Estate, Braintree, Essex CM7 2RN
tel: 01376 320051 for catalogue and stockists
fax: 01376 347052

This family business, which has been in operation for over eighty years, concentrates on the design and manufacture of outdoor furniture in teak. Traditional styles are built by a team of skilled craftsmen and each piece looks like it will stand the test of time in all weather conditions. Their products are stocked in the larger branches of John Lewis and although they don't do mail order, they do a catalogue to view their range.

Barnsley House GDF

Barnsley House, nr Cirencester, Glos GL7 5EE
tel: 01285 740561 for stockists • fax: 01285 740628

If you like the traditional look with no frills or flounces, this manufacturing company makes solid, yet elegant, teak furniture. Relax on one of their classy steamer deckchairs or sit in the shade on one of their wooden benches.

Bisca Design

Shaw Moor Farm, Harome, York, N.Yorks YO6 5HZ
tel: 01439 771 702 for catalogue • fax: 01439 771002
e-mail: bisca@easynet.co.uk

A very stylish range made of wrought iron, bordering on the hi-tech, which comes in either a zinc or a cornflower blue finish. By mail order only, there are round tables with a toughened glass or mesh top and co-ordinating, oval-backed chairs. Expect to pay more than the norm as these products are hand-forged and are quite unusual.

Chatsworth Carpenters

Edensor, Bakewell, Derbys DE45 1PJ
tel: 01246 582394 • fax: 01246 583464

If you want something handmade and crafted, then this team of experienced carpenters should be able to oblige. The designs are traditional and should last a lifetime. A garden bench, particularly if you have a plaque attached, can make a wonderful present.

The English Garden Collection

Cowley Bridge Rd, Exeter EX4 5HQ
tel: 0870 606 0304 for mail order • fax: 01392 431025

Available by mail order only, rattan chairs and tables, teak benches and French café-style folding chairs are the staples of this mail order service. There is a whole host of other treats for green fingers everywhere – from birdfeeders and wooden hanging lanterns to galvanized buckets.

English Hurdle

Curload, Stoke St Gregory, Taunton,
Somerset TA3 6JD
tel: 01823 698418 • fax: 01823 698859
e-mail: hurdle@enterprise.net

English Hurdle are the largest and, indeed, one of the only surviving growers of Somerset willow, which makes an ideal natural fencing material. Hurdles are made by weaving pliable and strong withies (strips of willow) into panels and their colours change subtly according to the weather. They act as a perfect screen for plants as well as looking charming. The owner and his son are the fourth generation of the same family to carry on this traditional skill and their work was featured on *Home Front*.

Frolics of Winchester

82 Canon St, Winchester, Hants SO23 9JQ
tel: 01962 856384 • fax: 01962 844896

If you want a garden seat with something a little different from wooden slats, this company makes seats with ornate backs cut out in a variety of designs. If you're an animal lover, choose from carved horses, trout, cockerels, and cats amongst others. There are also pineapples, vine leaves and olive branches. If you're looking for a large circular seat to fit round the trunk of your tree, this is where to come.

Gaze Burville Ltd

Plain Farm Old Dairy, East Tisted, Hants GU34 3RT
tel: 01420 587467 for stockists or direct order
fax: 01420 587354

Gaze Burville uses the sturdy oak to make their classic garden furniture. Choose from benches and tables, both large and small, and a wide variety of seats.

George Carter

Silverstone Farm, North Elham, Norfolk NR20 5EX
tel: 01362 668130 • fax: 01362 668130

If you'd like something really special commissioned for your garden, George Carter could be your man. A talented garden carpenter who can make to order quality and unusual furniture and fixtures, in the past he has made seats with a Baroque feel, obelisks based on seventeenth-century Dutch prototypes, and even a Gothic Chinese Aviary. Phone first for details.

Habitat

196 Tottenham Court Rd, London W1P 9LD
tel: 0171 255 2545 for the store
tel: 0645 334433 for branches

Don't forget Habitat when it comes to reasonably priced garden furniture. There are deckchairs with coloured slings, wooden steamer chairs, plus smaller items such as parasols, garden flares, glazed pots, stone planters, and lots of other bits and bobs.

Holloways

Lower Court, Suckley, Worcs WR6 5DE
tel: 01886 884665 for catalogue • fax: 01886 884796

This company are specialists in conservatory furniture and have a massive showroom, set in two floors of what used to be hop kilns, to prove it. They use only the top-quality rattan, often from the Far East, so you can be confident it won't easily break and unravel like some cheaper makes do. If you'd like cushion pads or seating made, you can choose from more than 2000 fabrics from many of the top names – traditional prints from Sanderson and Malabar to more contemporary styles from Designer's Guild.

Indian Ocean Trading Company

155–163 Balham Hill, London SW12 9DJ
tel: 0181 675 4808 for catalogue and showrooms
fax: 0181 675 4652

All the benches and chairs made by this company are crafted using traditional methods and have mortice and tenon joints rather than glue, and are fine sanded for a smooth finish. Expect to find slatted sun loungers and steamer chairs as well as a good range of outdoor lighting. They deliver nationwide.

Lloyd Loom of Spalding

Wardentree Lane, Pinchbeck, Spalding, Lincs PE11 3SY
tel: 01775 712111 for stockists • fax: 01775 761255

The only European company still producing the British classic Lloyd Loom furniture in-house. Invented in 1917, the popularity of this woven furniture still endures, probably because it looks good in any setting. Chairs, beds, tables and laundry baskets come in a variety of twenty shades – from white and fawns to shocking pinks and icy blues. It's ideal for the conservatory, but should not be left outside.

Marston & Langinger

192 Ebury St, London SW1W 8UP
tel: 0171 824 8818 • fax: 0171 824 8757

A classic colonial-style wicker sofa always looks good in a conservatory and this outlet has a top-quality range. There are wirework chairs, ones made from English willow, which has been bleached or painted for a country look, and an assortment of garden paraphernalia.

McCord

London Rd, Preston, Lancs PR11 1RP
tel: 0870 908 7020 • fax: 0870 908 7050

McCord's do mail order only, but their catalogue is full of useful things. Their garden furniture is no exception and they have items like a reasonably priced range of granite-black chairs with a matching table, which needn't be confined to the garden.

Neptune Classics

Industry Park, Cricketts Lane, Chippenham, Wilts SN15 3EQ
tel: 01249 657100 • fax: 01249 657200

These are timeless classics for the garden. The wooden furniture comes in simple but well-crafted designs – from a small bistro table to an enormous one with extension leaves that can comfortably sit twelve people for dining alfresco. For a bit of added comfort, there is the option of cushions in green or cream. There are also parasols and hammocks.

Prestige Garden Furniture

Unit 67, Halliwell Mill, Bertha St, Bolton, Lancs BL1 8AH
tel: 01204 363563 for stockists • fax: 01204 363563

Prestige use an African hardwood called iroko to make all their garden furniture, which comes in more than 200 designs. It is one of the largest ranges of garden furniture available in this country today.

Rusco

Little Faringdon Mill, Lechdale, Glos GL7 3QQ
tel: 01367 252754 for stockists • fax: 01367 253406

A wide range of teak furniture, plus elegant French café-style wrought iron chairs and tables can be found here. Their umbrellas and parasols are top quality and are made from canvas with wooden spokes. They also have hammocks, outdoor heaters, sundials, birdbaths and urns.

Stuart Garden Architecture

Burrow Hill Farm, Wiveliscombe, Somerset TA4 2RN
tel: 01984 667458 for brochure • fax: 01984 667455

Exporting throughout the world, this company is one of Europe's leading manufacturers of hardwood landscape structures. If you dream of something really special and have the budget for it, they will construct a beautiful pagoda, gazebo, or even a picturesque ornamental bridge. There is also a range of planters, garden furniture and trellis work for the upmarket garden. You can visit their site and see the products for yourself.

Summit Furniture
198 Ebury St, London SW1 8UN
tel: 0171 259 9244 for stockists • fax: 0171 259 9246

This manufacturer specializes in teak garden furniture made from Tectona Grandis – a premier teak that can be used indoors as well as out. The wood is cut under strict regulations and for each tree cut, three new saplings are planted. There are some beautifully designed dining armchairs, which look sturdy but sleek.

outdoor lighting

Outdoor lighting is primarily about safety and security. It is a sad indictment of our society that more and more people seem to be installing lights that come on automatically as soon as so much as a cat approaches the driveway. However, you can also use lighting for outside areas in more pleasurable ways: you can light a pathway; a particular plant or tree lit from beneath can look stunning; and you can create a truly spectacular water feature with the clever use of underwater lights. However, make sure you always choose fittings that are suitable for use outside and that they are installed by a qualified electrician with proper circuit breakers – particularly if they are going anywhere near water.

Don't forget that the humble garden flare, which is now available in an array of gorgeous colours, can also make a garden look truly magical at night. On *Home Front in the Garden*, designer Anne McKevitt made some cheap and cheerful outdoor lights by getting empty and washed-out tin cans – catering-sized ones are best so ask your local restaurant or café if they'll save some for you – and punching holes all round, either at intervals or in patterns. You can either paint them, or leave them as they are and place a nightlight inside. As long as you don't leave them unattended with children around, they are a brilliant way of creating lovely flickering light outside.

Chelsom
Heritage House, Clifton Rd, Blackpool, Lancs FY4 4QA
tel: 01253 791344 for stockists • fax: 01253 791341

Chelsom supply hundreds of different styles of light to retail outlets all over the country, including a good range of lights suitable for outdoor use.

Deltalight (UK)
Unit 7, Kings Rd Industrial Estate, Haslemere, Surrey GU27 2QH
tel: 01429 651919 for stockists

Deltalight have a good range of uplighters that are small enough to be hidden at ground level, as well as wall-mounted lights to highlight paths or doors.

Garden & Security Lighting
39 Reigate Rd, Hookwood, Horley, Surrey RH6 0H9
tel: 01293 820821

The name of the company tells you exactly what it does but it needn't be just about practicality and security. If you have a particular architectural feature you would like to light up, or perhaps a tree or two, then here are lights big and powerful enough to perform the task.

John Cullen Lighting
585 Kings Rd, London SW6 2EH
tel: 0171 371 5400 • fax: 0171 371 7799

As well as interior lights, John Cullen has a good range of low-voltage lights which can be placed unobtrusively in the garden. The demonstration studio within the shop is useful for seeing just what sort of effect they will provide.

Louis Poulson
c/o Outdoor Lighting, 6 Kingston Business Centre, Fullers Way South, Chessington, Surrey KT9 1DQ
tel: 0181 974 2211 for stockists • fax: 0181 974 2333

This company specializes in underwater lighting for pools and ponds, and has some swish flood and spot lights, including some designed by Arne Jacobsen.

Noral
c/o Elstead Lighting Ltd, Mill Lane, Alton, Hants GU34 2QG
tel: 01420 82377 for stockists
fax: 01420 89261

This Norwegian company has developed a range of outdoor lighting that has a twenty-year anti-corrosion guarantee as they are confident the lights will be able to withstand all weathers from rain and snow to sun and even salt-spray from the sea. There are lamp-posts, pedestal lanterns in traditional shapes, and clean, crisp white fittings for wall-mounted lights, which not only look stylish but will keep snoopers away.

garden salvage

The companies listed below specialize mainly in antique garden statuary and wrought ironwork but remember that salvage can be anything and needn't just be restricted to the obvious. Old chimney pots, old quarry tiles and bits of railway edging can all be utilized for planters or lawn edgings. Use these addresses in conjunction with the main chapter on Salvage (see p.190) where opening hours for many of the companies listed here are also given. Salvage yards often keep odd hours so always call first to check they are open.

south west

Architectural Heritage
Taddington Manor, Taddington, nr Cutsdean, Cheltenham, Glos GL54 5RY
tel: 01386 584414 • fax: 01386 584236
e-mail: puddy@architectural-heritage.co.uk

A fascinating place to browse round even if you're not really looking for anything in particular. The statues are some really fine examples of stonemasonry from bygone centuries including such things as a pair of Flemish stone lions, an eagle from the eighteenth century, and a statue of Mercury dating from the nineteenth. Set in the beautiful Cotswolds, there's lots to see and there's even a nearby landing pad if you've come in a helicopter!

Castle Reclamation
Parrett Works, Martock, Somerset TA12 6AE
tel/fax: 01935 826483

This is a large yard which also has some showrooms attached. They offer all kinds of architectural antiques from bricks and beams, through fireplaces and statuary, down to the smallest items. Stone-masons are at work here and they do a lot of stone cutting and carving.

Dorset Reclamation
Cow Drive, Bere Regis, Wareham, Dorset BH20 7JZ
tel: 01929 472200

If you're looking for old statues or garden ornaments, Dorset Reclamation has a good selection.

Farm & Garden Bygones at Padstow Antiques
21–23 New St, Padstow, Cornwall PL28 8EA
tel: 01841 532914

This is a huge site for rummaging around looking for salvage that could be used in your garden. Many of the pieces have an agricultural past, such as corn grinders and hayracks. As well as barns and yards holding larger pieces, there is a shop.

Reclamation Services
Catbrain Quarry, Painswick Beacon, Painswick,
Glos GL6 6SU
tel: 01452 814064 • fax: 01452 813631

Set in a picturesque spot overlooking the Cotswolds, this salvage yard specializes in traditional building materials and garden ornaments, both large and small.

South West Reclamation
Gwilliams Yard, Edington, Bridgwater,
Somerset TA7 9JN
tel: 01278 723173

This large salvage yard has a good garden section where you will find local staddle stones, garden artefacts and old pumps. There is also some furniture made from reclaimed wood which you could use outdoors.

Wells Reclamation Co
The Old Cider Farm, Coxley, nr Wells,
Somerset BA5 1RQ
tel: 01749 677087 • fax: 01749 671089

This is a good place to come if you're after old quarry tiles or flagstones to make a patio or to edge your garden. They also have lots of old bricks and beams you could put to good use outside with a bit of imagination. The site covers four acres so be prepared for a walk.

south east

Architectural Salvage Centre
30–32 Stamford Rd, London N1 4JL
tel: 0171 923 0783

Old garden benches, chimney pots and the odd garden ornament are all featured here, although they do tend to concentrate more on salvage for interiors. It's still worth a visit, though, as you never know what you might find.

Churchill's Architectural Salvage
186–188 Old Kent Rd, London SE1 5TY
tel: 0171 708 4308

Lots of decorative ironwork for outdoors can be found here from gazebos to rose arches. They will undertake restoration work if you need it, but most pieces look charming in their original state.

Crowther of Syon Lodge
Syon Lodge, Busch Corner, London Rd, Isleworth,
Middx TW7 5BH
tel: 0181 560 7978

They claim to be the oldest specialists in architectural antiques in the country and have a vast range of garden statuary and ornaments. This is where you'll find something really unusual like a summer house in Gothic style or an armillary sphere.

Dackombe
5 Wulwyn Court, Link Way, Crowthorne, Berks RG45 6ET
tel: 01344 779155

Dackombe has a good supply of old railway sleepers made from oak, which are much in demand these days for use outdoors as decking. They also have old beams and planks. Open by appointment only.

Drummonds of Bramley
Horsham Rd, Bramley, Guildford, Surrey GU5 0LA
tel: 01483 898766

Old chimney pots, which would make great planters, plus more usual ornaments for the garden can be found in this huge yard.

Fens Restoration & Sales
46 Lots Rd, London SW10 0QF
tel: 0171 352 9883

Amongst the old doors and furniture waiting to be restored, you will find a selection of antique garden implements, terracotta pots, and bits of furniture made from old wood.

Newbury Salvage
Calvin Rd, Newbury, Berks RG1 4DB
tel: 01635 528120

For the garden, Newbury Salvage has a small stock of garden ornaments and old stone archways, but you will also find building materials, such as bricks, that you could use for patios and edgings.

Romsey Reclamation

Station Approach, Romsey Railway Station,
Romsey, Hants SO51 8DU
tel: 01794 524174 • fax: 01794 514344

Decking in gardens is very 'in' and this reclamation company specializes in railway sleepers, which make brilliant outdoor decking. You have to order a minimum of ten for home delivery. (*Home Front in the Garden* designer Diarmuid Gavin used them to create a fabulous extension of the living room for a family garden.) You can also find other useful bits and pieces here, such as telegraph poles, bricks, roof tiles and Yorkshire flagstones.

Southern Architectural Salvage

The Pump House, The High St, Lyndhurst,
Hants SO43 7BD
tel: 01703 283300

Original and reproduction garden statuary is one of the specialities at this charming site. You can also pick up small *objets d'art* and bric-a-brac, so it's worth having a good look around.

central

Baileys Architectural Antiques

The Engine Shed, Ashburton Industrial Estate,
Ross-on-Wye, Herefordshire HR9 7BW
tel: 01989 563015

Baileys has a wonderful selection of garden antiques and tools, including a massive choice of old watering cans. They also have statuary, stonework, ironwork and garden furniture and Belfast sinks which make great outdoor herb containers.

Ransford Bros

Drayton Way, Drayton Fields, Daventry,
Northants NN11 5XW
tel: 01327 705310

A good place to come for bricks, slates, roof and quarry tiles – all of which can be used to great effect in the garden for everything from rockeries to patios. It's all very well organized, too, which is a real bonus.

north east

Havenplan

The Old Station, Station Rd, Killarmarsh, Sheffield,
S.Yorks S21 1EN
tel: 0114 2489972

There is quite a selection for the garden here at Havenplan including furniture, stone troughs, edging tiles and chimney pots.

north west

Cheshire Brick & Slate Co

Brook House Farm, Salters Bridge, Tarvin Sands,
nr Chester, Cheshire CH3 8HL
tel: 01829 740883 • fax: 01829 740481

As their name suggests, this company has a good range of old bricks and slates that could be used just as well outdoors as in. They also have a selection of garden ornaments, and old lamp-posts, which could become a talking point in any garden.

R&R Renovations & Reclamations

Canalside Yard, Audlem, Cheshire CW3 0DY
tel: 01270 811310

There is a vast selection of architectural antiques on offer here and you're bound to pick up something you could use in an unusual way for the garden, whether it's purely decorative or functional.

Reclaimed Materials

Northgate, White Lund Industrial Estate, Morecambe,
Lancs LA3 3AY
tel: 01524 69094

Chief among the stock are slates, roof tiles and chimney pots, which are joined by timber, flooring and flagstones. Great for creative gardeners.

wales

Cardiff Reclamation

Tremorfa Industrial Estate, Rover Way, Cardiff CF2 2FD
tel: 01222 458995

Reproduction and original garden furniture and ornaments can be found here and, if you can make use of an old church pew somehow, there is often quite a bit picked up from churches – all above board, of course.

D&P Theodore Sons & Daughters Building Salvage & Reclamation
North Rd, Bridgend Industrial Estate, Bridgend, Mid-Glamorgan CF36 5NH.
tel: 01656 648936

There are several thousand items here ranging from old dressed stone to telegraph poles. Be prepared to rummage around for treasures.

scotland

Tradstocks
Duneverig, Thorn Hill, Stirling FK8 3QW
tel: 01786 850400 • fax: 01786 850404

This company's speciality is all kinds of stone, whether it be local or not. They have large stocks of reclaimed stone walling, flags, cobbles, setts and coping stones.

northern ireland

Andy Jones Salvage
37 Ballyblack Rd, Newtonards, Co Down BT22 2AS
tel: 01247 822722

Bricks, slates, garden pieces and old timber are the chief mainstays of this salvage yard.

miscellaneous

Here you will find all the more unusual products that have been used on *Home Front in the Garden* – and more – from underwater pumps that help create stunning water features, to spray paint and wacky ideas for planters.

Adam Booth
4 Victoria St, Kirkpatrick Durham,
Castle Douglas, DG7 3HQ
tel: 01556 650513

Adam Booth makes some wonderful one-offs such as weather vanes and sundials, which are really special and make ideal presents for that individual touch. Have something appropriate fashioned for the top of your weather vane and people will not only be able to see it for miles, they'll be talking about it too!

After Noah
121 Upper St, London N1 1QP
tel: 0171 359 4281
and
261 Kings Rd, London SW3 5EL
tel: 0171 351 2610
e-mail: mailorder@afternoah.demon.co.uk

The two London shops don't sell a very big range of garden stuff but, if you hunt around, you might find an old-fashioned stripy canvas deckchair, or a galvanized tin cabinet with a chicken wire mesh front that could be ideal for storing packets of seeds. Some of the products are also available by mail order.

Arrowtip Expanded Polystyrene Ltd
30–37 Stannery St, London SE11 4AA
tel: 0171 582 2718

You might wonder what you can do with a bagful of polystyrene chips in the garden but *Home Front in the Garden* expert Diarmuid Gavin used them to go in the bottom of metal planters on a roof terrace. Because everything on a roof has to be light as possible, they did the trick.

Avant Garden
77 Ledbury Rd, London W11 2AG
tel: 0171 229 4408 • fax: 0171 229 4410

This shop offers a huge range of terracotta and lead planters, and classical wrought iron furniture which would look great in both classic and contemporary settings. Its speciality is wirework, which is fashioned into everything from wall sconces, baskets, candle sticks and chandeliers. They also sell topiary frames in the guise of cockerels, swans and geese, as well as more traditional topiary shapes.

British Play Sand Company
Longfield, Dunstew, Oxon OX6 4JR
tel: 01869 340224 for suppliers • fax: 01869 347474

Brilliant for creating a safe, clean sandpit for the garden, you can order bags of sand in any amount you like although it usually comes in quantities of half a ton to a ton. Order direct from the company or go direct to Argos, branches of Children's World and selected toy shops.

Browns Living
26 South Molton St, London W1Y 1DA
tel: 0171 491 7833

Browns Living sells lots of stylish garden paraphernalia including things that you might not even know you needed. What about a barbecue that folds up into a suitcase?

The Conran Shop
Michelin House, 81 Fulham Rd, London SW3 6RD
tel: 0171 589 7401 for branches • fax: 0171 823 7015

As you walk into the store from the Flower Van entrance, you come straight into the garden department. Everything is laid out well and you will find lots of smallish, stylish items made from galvanized steel, hanging lanterns, garden flares, bird houses, and bags of pebbles.

Cuprinol Ltd
Adderwell, Frome, Somerset BA11 1NL
tel: 01373 465151 for stockists • fax: 01373 474124

Available from most large DIY outlets, Cuprinol's name has become synonymous with paint for use outdoors. If you fancy giving your garden shed, trellis work, or outdoor woodwork a makeover, they have some great colours from hyacinth blues to mossy greens, without

being too gaudy. Cleverly used, and once they have weathered a bit, they can really add character to your garden, giving it a Mediterranean feel or being reminiscent of Monet's Giverny.

General Trading Co
144 Sloane St, London SW1X 9BL
tel: 0171 730 0411 • fax: 0171 823 4624

For the upmarket gardener, check out their range of garden ornaments and accessories, including a nice line in bamboo furniture.

Homebase
Head Office, Beddington House, Wallington, Surrey SM6 0HB
tel: 0645 801800 for enquiries and branches

Homebase is obviously a haven for everything for the garden but there are some products that are a real mainstay of *Home Front in the Garden*. If you want to take inspiration from Anne McKevitt, try using their terracotta pots as a starting point. To jazz them up a bit, she sprayed them with paint, and stuck glass pebbles and mirror tiles on them. Also look out for their bags of Cornish cobbles for creating water features, good barbecue sets and tools, and cheap ceramic tiles if you want to smash them up to create your own mosaic barbecue.

LBS Horticulture Ltd
Standroyd Mill, nr Colne, Lancs BB8 7BW
tel: 01282 873311 • fax: 01282 869850

All sorts of useful things for the garden from wheelbarrows to bubble film for insulating the greenhouse. They are a good supplier of underwater pumps for ponds and fountains plus plastic bowls in varying sizes for creating your own pond.

Neal Street East
5–7 Neal St, London WC2H 9PU
tel: 0171 240 0135

You will have to hunt around amongst everything else, but if you do you'll find lots of exciting and reasonably priced things for the garden such hurricane lamps, bamboo accessories and multi-coloured hammocks in different sizes – perfect for lazing around in.

Ocean Trading Company
155–163 Balham Hill, London SW12 9BJ
tel: 0181 675 4808

Outdoor decking made from kiln-dried plantation-grown teak will give an outdoor area a classy feel. It's easy to lay as long as the surface is hard and level, and comes in boxes of eight squares, each square measuring 20 x 20 inches/50 x 50cm. You could also lay it indoors. Products available by mail order only.

RK Alliston [hf]
183 New Kings Rd, London SW6 4SW
tel: 0171 731 8100

RK Alliston is a small florist and garden design shop, but they also have all sorts of items, such as topiary balls, which you can use for decoration inside and out.

Ronseal [hfg] [hf]
Ronseal Technical Services, Thorncliffe Park, Chapeltown, Sheffield, S.Yorks S35 2YP
tel: 0114 246 7171 for stockists

Ronseal do a good range of woodwashes specifically developed for wood so why not give your garden shed or your trellis a makeover? There is a choice of eight colours, from Ocean Blue to Lavender, but they still allow the grain to show through no matter how many coats you put on.

Sadolin
Akzo Nobel Woodcare, Meadow Lane, St Ives, Cambs PE17 4UY
tel: 01480 496868 for stockists

Exterior woodwork often gets forgotten about but just as much attention should be given to the outside as in. Treat your garden like a room in its own right and, instead of paint, try woodstains in unusual colours such as Faded Denim and Celery Leaf, which are perfect for joinery or cladding. The Sadolin Scenic and Sadolin Classic are ideal for fences, trellis, sheds and garden furniture and come in more natural shades.

Tropical Surrounds
4 Middle Conholt, Conholt Park, Andover, Hants SP11 9HA
tel: 01264 730408 • fax: 01264 730483
e-mail: tropicalsurrounds@msn.com

To give your garden, or indeed your house, an Oriental feel bamboo screens are perfect. They come in rolls of 1m, 1.5m and 2m lengths and in heights of 3 or 5m. You can either have them free-standing or use them to cover ugly fencing. There are other unusual materials – willow, heather, split cane and peeled reed. Available by mail order only, they deliver within the UK mainland for a charge.

Vallti Specialist Coatings
Unit B3, South Gyle Crescent Lane, Edinburgh EH12 9EG
tel: 0131 334 4999 for stockists • fax: 0131 334 3987

Exterior wood and trellis work can be given an unusual finish with Vallti's range of wood finishes in Scandinavian-inspired colours. Imported from Finland, the paint allows the grain of the wood to show through.

bits

The finishing touches for a room are vital and choosing them can often be the most fun part of redecorating. It's the attention to detail that can really bring everything together and *Home Front* uses many products to dress the rooms and give them that high degree of style and finish. As we compiled this book, it became obvious that there were lots of companies who deserved a mention, such as those who provide nearly all of the accessories we use to dress the rooms but who rarely get a specific mention on the programme.

It became obvious, too, that some of the most popular features on *Home Front* (and which trigger lots of enquiries) are those where the designers use a very ordinary material in an extraordinary way, or those where they use something that is designed for one purpose but used in another unusual and unlikely way – like coloured Perspex used for a bathroom cabinet. We needed to list the places where you can get materials like shrink-to-fit mirror, Fablon or frosted film, so this Bits 'n' Bobs chapter was expanded to include them, too.

Lastly, we have also included in this chapter companies that defy any of the obvious chapter categories but that are nevertheless a vital part of *Home Front* – companies that make products like waxes, oils and stains for use on wood, or who will make you a reproduction key for your period property. Because of the bitty nature of this chapter, you will see we have opted to list the entries alphabetically – you never know, as you scan through, you might find something you didn't even know you needed!

'n' bobs

key: **hf** shows the product has appeared on
Home Front

hfg shows the product has appeared on
Home Front in the Garden

✉ shows the company offers a mail
order service

Acca Kappa
tel: 0171 372 4101 for stockists

Acca Kappa make lovely bathroom products in beautiful packaging, such as frosted glass bottles, and soaps in muted colours. These are often seen in the background of *Home Front* bathroom features and help to give a revamped bathroom that glamorous feel.

AeroMail
46 Weir Rd, Wimbledon, London SW19 8UG
tel: 0181 971 0066 for mail order • fax: 0181 971 0033

For those of us who can't get to Aero's two branches in London, you can now order the goods by post (although the stores still have more besides). Helpfully divided into sections of the house (Aero Kitchen, Aero Office, etc) the catalogue shows the products off to their full advantage and you can order something as large as a shelving system or something as small as a corkscrew.

All About Art
31 Sheen Rd, Richmond Surrey TW9 1AD
tel: 0181 948 1277

A good place to go for lots of craft materials including handmade paper, gilding materials, real gold leaf and books of gold leaf transfer, materials for decoupage, varnish, stencils, spray paints, glass paints and a good selection of craft books.

Amari Plastics
2 Cumberland Avenue, London NW10 7RL
tel: 0181 961 1961

Sheets of coloured plastic are Amari Plastics' speciality and you can use them for whatever takes your fancy. Anne McKevitt used them on a roof terrace to create screens, which then had lights embedded into them to give an unusual effect.

Andrew Martin
PO Box 99, Sudbury, Suffolk CO10 6SN
tel: 0800 328 1346

For top quality bed linen and soft furnishings, Andrew Martin have a good mail order only range, with linen and cotton in subtle colours and patterns. It mostly comes in corrugated cardboard packaging, which doesn't sound glamorous but is actually very stylish.

Argos
tel: 0870 600 3030 for catalogue and stores

Don't forget Argos – it's still great for bargains and they have some natty ideas. They sell everything from phones to barbecues and groovy kitchen scales. You can pick the items up in the Argos stores or order them through the post.

The Bead Shop
21a Tower St, Covent Garden, London WC2H 9NS
tel: 0171 240 0931

The place to go for beads of every size, shape and colour. *Home Front* designer Fiona Samler used them to create hanging threads to decorate a canopy draped over a bed.

Bliss (Flights of Fancy Ltd)
Paradise Works, Arden Forest Estate, Alcester, Warks B49 6EH
tel: 01789 400077 for stockists

Bliss is great for little quirky accessories such as mirrors and clocks, but all with an unusual twist in shape and style. They also make some traditional items that you thought had disappeared such as a galvanized basket you leave on your doorstep for the milkman. Mail order only from this address or call for details of stockists.

Brodie & Middleton
68 Drury Lane, London WC2B 5SP
tel: 0171 836 3289

A great little shop crammed with all sorts of goodies. Right in the heart of London's theatreland, so it's useful for the theatrical set designers who go there frequently to stock up on pigments suitable for mixing up your own paint (which the public can buy mail order) and chemicals to fireproof backcloths, etc.

Cologne & Cotton
791 Fulham Rd, London SW6 5HD
tel: 01926 332573 for branches

If you like sleeping in crisp cotton sheets, Cologne and Cotton sell piles of linen, all beautifully folded, which will make you wish your life was just as ordered. There are also pretty eiderdown covers, bedding, tablecloths and napkins.

Colour Blue
Beckhaven House, 9 Gilbert Rd, London SE11 4NL
tel: 0181 942 2525 for catalogue
tel: 0171 820 7700 to place an order
fax: 0171 793 0537 to fax an order

Inspired by the Mediterranean lifestyle, Colour Blue sell by mail order only but their catalogue is brimming with lovely things. There are small and large items – from galvanized jugs and milk pitchers, to dining tables big enough to seat twelve comfortably.

Conran Collection
12 Conduit St, London W1R 9TG
tel: 0171 399 0710 • fax: 0171 399 0711

The Conran Empire is still going strong and this range was launched in 1998 to give us a chance to order the goods by post. Some of the items are exclusive to mail order only and some available in the stores. You can visit the store at Conduit Street.

Corkery Mackay
5 Pembroke Buildings, Cumberland Park, Scrubs Lane, London NW10 6RE
tel: 0181 960 5612 for stockists • fax: 0181 964 2614

Bursting with fun and imaginative ideas, this company made the headlines in the style magazines. Singling out two of their many products is difficult but their 'plug icons' – stickers with pictures of toasters and radios and kettles – ensure you need never pull out the wrong plug again. They also do ingenious rubber placemats, with a inner circles that pop out to use as coasters.

Craft Depot
Somerton Business Park, Somerton,
Somerset TA11 6SB
tel: 01458 274727 • fax: 01458 272932
e-mail: craftdepot@aol.com

Available by mail order only, there are more than 8000 different items on offer here that have been imported from the States. If you fancy trying glass painting either on windows to create fake stained glass or on drinking glasses, they sell the type of paints you need.

Dylon
Dylon International Ltd, Worseley Bridge Rd,
London SE26 5HD
tel: 0181 663 4296 for stockists

If you're bored with your loose covers on your sofa, why not give them a new lease of life and change the colour by dying them? Dylon make various dyes, which can go in the machine or in a hand wash, in an array of colours. They also do fabric paints – use them on canvas to create original designs for blinds, curtains and cushions.

Egg
36 Kinnerton St, London SW1X 8TS
tel: 0171 235 9315

The setting for this shop is a converted dairy and the items the sell blend in beautifully with its simple, rustic feel. They have a range of goods from wooden bowls and ceramics to shawls. Some of the items are available by mail order to existing customers but they don't do a catalogue as such.

Elephant
230 Tottenham Court Rd, London W1P 9AE
tel: 0171 637 7930 for branches

Elephant sells an eclectic mix of items leaning towards the ethnic, culled from all over the world. Here you will find anything from lava stone balls to galvanized bins covered in Chinese newspaper.

Fablon
Forbo-CP Ltd, Station Rd, Cramlington,
Northumberland NE23 8AQ
tel: 01670 718300 for stockists • fax: 01670 590096

Fablon need no longer just be used for covering exercise books at school as it now comes in all sorts of different patterns and borders and can be used in lots of different ways. The borders are quite fancy and on various themes – everything from Autumn Fruits to Travelling Teddies.

Fiddes Durable Wood Finishes
Florence Works, Brindley Rd, Cardiff CF1 7TX
tel: 01222 340323 for stockists • fax: 01222 343235
e-mail: finishes@fiddes.co.uk

One of the few suppliers in Wales to manufacture durable wood finishes, including a wax polish in six shades, liming paste that simulates the look of an old-fashioned decorative limed finish for oak, and a comprehensive range of shellac sealers and polishes.

Formica Ltd
Coast Rd, North Shields, Tyne & Wear NE29 8RE
tel: 0191 259 3000

Say the name Formica and most people think of work surfaces from the seventies, but it can be groovy. Don't limit it to worksurfaces either – their product Surell, which is made from polymer resin, comes in sheets with either a plain or granite effect, and can be used for shower surrounds.

Get Stuffed

105 Essex Rd, London N1 2SL
tel: 0171 226 1364

This shop is probably terribly un-PC to mention as its full of nothing but stuffed animals. They have pieces like a huge grizzly bear and domestic cats and dogs curled up in favourite poses. Not everyone's taste in ornamentation but definitely the place to look if you are interested.

Glasszone

37 West St, Brighton, E.Sussex BN1 2RE
tel: 0171 351 0060

This company treats glass in a highly unusual way, creating a heavily textured finish with a rippled effect. It is then toughened; you can use it for the smallest splashback or a whole conservatory roof, in place of the more usual plastic corrugated sheeting.

Global Mobility

Camerons Court, Fort William,
Inverness-shire PH33 6RY
tel: 0500 824827 for stockists

This company started out making camping gear but was taken up by the fashion crowd. Now their stuff appears in all the style magazines. Camp out with their Bushtec candle lamps or check out their cushions in suede, leather and sheepskin – not cheap but very luxurious.

House & The Hambledon Gallery

40–44 Salisbury St, Blandford, Dorset DT11 7PR
tel: 01258 454884 (mail order)
tel: 01258 452880 • fax: 01258 454225

House is the name of the mail order catalogue or you can buy the goods in person if you visit the Gallery. There are lots of simple, unfussy but classic, things such as wicker baskets, chicken-wire-fronted cabinets, enamel pitchers, glass tank vases and plain white china.

ICI Acrylics

PO Box 34, Orchard Mill, Darwen, Lancs BB3 1QB
tel: 01254 874444 for stockists

Plastic can be used throughout the house in innumerable ways so let your imagination run riot. ICI manufactures plastic in a whole spectrum of colours – Anne McKevitt used a piece of blue to create the front panel of a bathroom cabinet which, when fitted with a hidden fluorescent tube, gave off a neon-lighting effect for a fraction of the price.

Inventory

26–40 Kensington High St, London W8 4PF
tel: 0171 937 2626 • fax: 0171 938 4079
and
10 Harbour Parade, West Quay, Southampton SO15 1BS
tel: 01703 336141 • fax: 01703 336198
and
Unit 9, Haymarket Towers, Humberstone Gate,
Leicester LE1 1WF
tel: 0116 252 2556 • fax: 0116 253 2557

Inventory, which started life as The Source but changed its name, is a great one-stop shop for your home. Prices, on average, are somewhere above IKEA but below Habitat, and it's particularly good for cheap china and glassware. It has some lovely bedding and cushions in great colours, and it's good for accessories in general (they don't go in for large items of furniture). More stores are gradually opening nationwide.

John Lewis

Cavendish Square, Oxford St, London W1M 9HJ
tel: 0171 629 7711 for branches

You can't beat John Lewis for a one-stop shop and of course there are branches outside London, too, so ring to find out your nearest. *Home Front* has found them an invaluable source of things from eyelet punches to deckchair canvas.

The Keyhole

Pilgrims' Progress, Far Back Lane, Farnsfield,
nr Newark, Notts NG22 8JX
tel: 01623 882590

If you've lost the key to your antique treasure chest or it never had one, this company can come to the rescue. They have hundreds of period keys and their aim is to provide these or a reproduction one in keeping with the style. They will do repair and restoration work on existing keys, they buy and sell period keys, and they will find keys for anything from a tiny jewel box to a huge church door. They do a lot of work for organizations like the National Trust, etc. They specialize in anything pre-1940, and aren't really your general locksmith.

Kiosk

Studio 72, The Big Peg, 120 Vyse St,
Birmingham B18 6NF
tel: 0121 604 3200 • fax: 0121 604 3311
e-mail: bydesignkiosk@btconnect.com

Order stylish accessories for your home by mail order only, over the phone, and then simply wait for them to arrive – there are lots of smaller items from test tube vases to silk scatter cushions and chopping boards.

La Maison Scotts
Corinium Centre, Love Lane, Cirencester, Glos GL7 1FD
tel: 0870 600 4444 • fax: 0990 449800
e-mail: scottsofstow.demon.co.uk

A good collection of furniture and decorative objects for every room in the house. With the emphasis on the traditional, you can order everything from a chenille rug to a mosaic mirror.

Liberon
Mountfield Industrial Estate, Learoyd Rd,
New Romney, Kent TN28 8XU
tel: 01797 367555 for stockists • fax: 01797 367575

A good and varied range of products for use primarily on wood, such as polishes, waxes, and French polish. If you want the look of limewashed floors, they do a great liming wax, which you apply, paint over with a white dye and then take off the excess with steel wool. A good technical leaflet is available. They also do useful pens for touching up scratches. Call for more details.

Lionheart Terracotta Products
Tone Industrial Estate, Milverton Rd, Wellington,
Somerset TA21 0AZ
tel: 01823 666213 for stockists and technical support
fax: 01823 665685

If you're confused as to what cleaning product you should you use on what sort of floor, Lionheart Terracotta have developed a whole range with handy leaflets and good back-up advice. There are cleaners, sealants and polishes for every eventuality and suitable for use on surfaces like marble and quarry tiles.

Mico Printing Supplies Ltd
98 Englefield Rd, London N1 3LG
tel/fax: 0171 354 1431

This company manufactures two products called Glass Mat Cream and Glass Mat Fluid, both of which can be used to give a frosted effect. *Home Front* designer Fiona Samler masked off a design on some glass shelves in a bathroom and used the cream to create a really novel look to them. The fluid is more suitable for smaller items such as vases and ashtrays. Both come in tubs of varying sizes.

Next Homes
PO Box 4000, Leeds LS2 8RZ
tel: 0345 100 500

The high street store known for clothes comes into its own with mail order products such as mohair cushions, chenille throws, and old-fashioned chrome clocks for the home. Call for a catalogue.

Obsessions
151 Cheapside, London EC2V 6ET
tel: 0171 600 7410 for branches

Great for one-off, odd and kitsch things such as heart-shaped hot water bottles and fake fur cushions.

Oliver Bonas
tel: 0171 627 4747 for enquiries and branches
fax: 0171 622 3629

As well as their lighting, Oliver Bonas sell all sorts of accessories for the home from silver magnetic pinboards to chrome bins and ceramics. Available in all branches (see p.117 for shop locations).

Pentagon Auto-Tint
Unit 31, Acton Park Industrial Estate, The Vale,
London W3 7QE
tel: 0181 749 9749

If you'd like some privacy or simply hate net curtains, try using frosted window film, which simply adheres to the window. A great solution for nosy neighbours.

The Period House Group
3 Fold Court, Buttercombe, York YO41 1AU
tel: 01759 373481

If you'd like to revitalize your period furniture, this company have a range of oils and waxes specifically formulated for this purpose. They also do period door latches and nails for period properties.

Philip & Tacey Ltd
North Way, Andover, Hampshire SP10 5BA
tel: 01264 332171 for stockists • fax: 01264 332226

If you fancy having a go at painting your own china, which you then bake in the oven, try Pebeo Porcelaine 150 paints. In loads of colours, they are water-based and therefore non-toxic, and are dishwasher proof. Philip & Tacey distribute Vitrail paints, for use on glass, and they supply a range of kits for doing your own projects like stained glass (with lead foil) and marbling.

Philip Bradbury Glass
83 Blackstock Rd, London N4 2JW
tel: 0171 226 2919

If you'd like a design of your own transferred onto glass, this company can do it for you. They can either use the sandblasting technique or etch it on with acid. The glass has many uses from tabletops to decorative panels.

Planet Organic
42 Westbourne Grove, London W2 5SH
tel: 0171 221 7171

This is actually an organic and natural food supermarket and you may be wondering what it offers for interiors. They do some great things like seed grass which looks great as a houseplant but which you can also eat. Open Mondays to Saturdays until 8 p.m. and Sundays 11 a.m.–5 p.m.

Plascon International
24–30 Canute Rd, Southampton SO14 3PB
tel: 01703 226733 for stockists

If your kitchen cupboards are melamine and need a face lift, this company manufactures a useful primer as well as compatible paint. They also do products suitable for use on wood such as preservative basecoats.

Plasterworks
38 Cross St, London N1 2BG
tel: 0171 226 5355

If you fancy a statue of Aphrodite or Caesar in your room, this company have plaster busts in all shapes and sizes. Some are recognisable figures and some anonymous, but they mostly follow a Greco-Roman theme. Plasterworks also do little roundels which *Home Front* designer Lloyd Farmar painted gold and used in the medieval hall of the Lewsey's barn conversion. They also sell ceiling roses, plaques and Deco pieces.

Plasti-Kote
London Rd Industrial Estate, Sawston, Cambridge, Cambs CB2 4TP
tel: 01223 836400 for stockists

Found in most large DIY outlets, this company specializes in spray paints. Use their red oxide metal primer on metal first before giving it a new lease of life with a car spray paint in a metallic or vivid colour. It has been used on *Home Front* on everything from a tired old filing cabinet to terracotta pots. Plasti-Kote also make stencil paints which dry rapidly.

Preedy Glass
Lamb Works, North Rd, London N7 3QN
tel: 0171 700 0377

This company specialises in all sorts of glass from coloured mirrors to tinted glass. They undertake sandblasting and can make structural items out of glass. They built an incredible all-glass shower surround in a huge curve for Anne McKevitt's hi-tech wet room.

Prices' Candles
Head Office, 110 York Rd, Battersea, London SW11 3RU
tel: 0171 228 3345 for stockists and factory outlets

Seen in the background of lots of *Home Front* programmes, these candles can't be beaten for value and longevity. The classic church candles are the creamy-white ones in tall cylindrical shapes, but they also come in myriad other colours and fragrances. The candles are not only available in lots of shops, but also at factory outlets where they will be at least 30% less than the recommended retail price. Outlets are at Bicester, Bridgend, Cheshire Oaks, Doncaster, Kendall, London, Mansfield, Street and Swindon.

Ray Munn Ltd
861 Fulham Rd, London SW6 5HP
tel: 0171 736 9876 • fax: 0171 384 3723
e-mail: dominick@raymunn.freeserve.co.uk

Ray Munn do a whole range of great products which are available by mail order as well as in person through this London shop (open Mon–Sat, 8 a.m.–5.30 p.m.). If your fridge or cooker needs a new lease of life, try their Varmespray kitchen appliance paint – for fridges it comes in black, white and silver and there is also a paint suitable for cookers which is heat resistant. This is the only place you will find paint by the Swedish company, Beckers, and Ray Munn also stocks Venetian Stucco – Italian-based plaster finishes – and enamel paints for baths that can be tinted to match your suite.

Roscolab Ltd
Blanchard Works, Langley Bridge Rd, Sydenham, Kent SE26 5AQ
tel: 0181 659 2300

If your want to make your room look bigger, try covering the walls with sheets of mirror. Rosco make an ingenious mirror which shrinks when you apply heat to it – you use a hairdryer to shrink it to fit. The effect is not quite as clear as a real mirror and it goes rather cloudy so you can't use it to see your reflection, but it's still very effective and fun.

Russell & Chapple
23 Monmouth St, London WC2E 9DE
tel: 0171 497 0544

Russell & Chapple sells all sorts of useful stuff from canvas to stretcher frames. *Home Front*'s Kevin Allan used these frames to stretch fabric to create pictures.

The Slipcover and Furnishings House
PO Box 1206, Ilford, Essex IG1 4EH
tel: 0870 603 0220 • fax: 0181 518 5170

If your sofa is looking a bit tatty but you can't really afford to shell out for custom-made covers, this company sell loose covers in standard sizes that fit nearly all sofas. They also make macassars (those boxy covers that come right down to the floor) for dining chairs, but they don't fit chairs with arms, winged chairs or recliners. Those aside though, they'll fit virtually anything. The company sells direct to the public rather than through stockists and you can choose from a range of fabrics.

Snappy Snaps
115 Glenthorne Rd, London W6 0LJ
tel: 0181 741 7474 for branches

Next time you go in to pick up your photos, check out the other things this company does that you can put to good use in your house. Have your favourite photos made into placemats or coasters.

Stanford's Map & Travel Bookshop
12–14 Long Acre, Covent Garden,
London WC2E 9LH
tel: 0171 836 1321 for branches

Maps of the world on the wall can look more interesting than a poster (and make you appear well-travelled if you're trying to impress!). Stanford's sells all kinds of maps – world maps, the Americas, etc – which you can get from their shop or by mail order. On *Home Front*, designer Fiona Samler made a feature of a map by sticking it to the wall with wallpaper paste and then giving it an aged look by coating it with a weak solution of tea.

Stuart R Stevenson
68 Clerkenwell Rd, London EC1M 5QA
tel: 0171 253 1693 • fax: 0171 490 0451

A delightful shop with helpful staff where you can buy books of aluminium, gold and silver leaf for gilding as well as artists' acrylics and other craft supplies.

Toast
Llanfynydd, Carmarthenshire SA32 7TT
tel: 01558 668800

This mail order only catalogue sells mostly clothes, but what they do offer for interiors is lovely. Items include poufs in chocolate and blonde suede, suede cushions, pure Irish linen sheets and bedding, and cosy fleece blankets. Everything is gorgeous and highly covetable.

Urban Outfitters
36–38 Kensington High St, London W8 4PF
tel: 0171 761 1001

Urban Outfitters has loads of branches in America and Canada but so far only one in this country. It is seriously trendy with everything from clothes to jewellery. For the home, expect to find bits and bobs depending on what's 'in' – one month it will be giant three-wick candles and sheepskin rugs, the next it will be bamboo accessories. The emphasis is on the throwaway kitsch.

The White Company
Freepost Lon10556, London SW6 6BH
tel: 0171 385 7988

As the name indicates, this company sells things in different shades of white. Choose from pillowcases and sheets to throws and duvet covers – all made from top quality fabrics such as linen and 100% cotton.

Wireworks
Head Office: 131a Broadley St, London NW8 8BA
tel: 0171 724 8856 for stockists

If you've seen unusual fly swats that look like targets, or little silver pegs on stands that double as placecard holders, then they're probably made by this company. Goods are sold through major stores such as John Lewis, The Conran Shop, Heals', etc as well as smaller outlets.

X-film UK
PO Box 37, Unit 3, Dalroad Enterprise Estate,
Luton, Beds LU1 1YW
tel: 01582 453308 • fax: 01582 417528
tel: 0800 7316134 for stockists and sales information

If you have an ugly window or one that is overlooked, and you want to create a stained glass effect, use one of X-film's rolls of self adhesive coloured vinyl. They have all sorts of coloured vinyls and frosted films, matt and opaque, with a matt metallic one amongst others. It provides instant colour from a roll. These are available by mail order only or from other stockists.

cour

Home Front is all about inspiring you to have a go yourself and we do hope that people will try things at home that they have seen on the programme – from weekend projects like making a simple mosaic table top to learning how to colourwash. Hopefully we can also whet your appetite for wanting to know more.

There is nothing quite as satisfying as learning a new skill and being able to bring something home with you that you have made. Reports of people being so inspired that they throw up their jobs and decide to retrain, setting up a small business in their chosen craft, are not unheard of! There are so many excellent courses on offer, covering everything from decoupage to trompe-l'œil, that it can be difficult to choose between them. But, time and money permitting, there is nothing to stop you from going on as many as interest you.

Besides getting expert tuition, often in small enough groups to have individual attention, there is the pleasure of meeting new people from all walks of life who have been brought together by the common denominator of wanting to learn a new craft. Most local education authority or further education colleges now run many of their own courses and they are worth checking out. There would have been far too many to list them all here. Instead, we have picked some of the best courses from all over the country that we know about and, although they haven't all been tried and tested by *Home Front*, they are all run by professional people and have been recommended by word of mouth. Have fun!

ses

south west

Bishop's Tower Specialist Paint Courses

Bishop's Tower, Tower Cross, Honiton,
Devon EX14 8TN
tel: 01404 45699

The days will fly by on these intensive two-day courses, which run through the gamut of paint effects from ageing to rag rolling. They particularly concentrate on effects for furniture and walls. Lunch is included and a list of B&Bs in Exeter is available on request.

Cynthia Greenslade

The Granary, Treviskey, Portloe, Truro,
Cornwall TR2 5PN
tel: 01872 501553

Informal courses in the quiet Cornwall location which was the setting for the television series *The Camomile Lawn*. No previous experience is needed for these courses which include stencilling, paint effects, decoupage and gilding. Day courses and weekend courses are both on offer and the classes are small and friendly. Lunch is provided.

The Eye of the Sun

Beeston Farm, Marhamchurch, Bude,
Cornwall EX23 0ET
tel: 01288 381638 • fax: 01288 381530
e-mail: rbe42@dial.pipex.com

Intensive, small group workshops led by a quilting and patchwork expert. The courses focus on such subjects as the use of fabrics and colouring fabrics, and cover pieces from large wallhangings to small images. The basics are not taught, so you have to be able to sew before you attend. Courses take place all the year round either at weekends or during the week. Accommodation is available at Beeston Farm or in the village.

Janet Shearer

Higher Grogley Farm, Withiel, nr Bodmin,
Cornwall PL30 5NP
tel/fax: 01208 831926

These Introduction to trompe-l'œil courses run for either five or ten days, from spring through to October. The price includes morning coffee, lunch and afternoon tea and accommodation is in local B&Bs. The ten-day course includes at least one visit to a local 'arty' place and possibly two. There is also a separate course on perspective.

The School of Painted Furniture & Creative Arts

The Creamery, The Old Dairy, Pinkney Park,
Malmesbury, Wilts SN16 0NX
tel/fax: 01666 841144

Belinda Ballantine is an artist with a great interest in painted finishes and it is this expertise that she passes on in her decorative finishes classes. The classes mainly concentrate on decoupage and consist of small groups of 6–8 people. They last from 1–5 days and courses run throughout the year. The school is non-residential but a list of B&Bs is available on request.

Stanton Soft Furnishings

12 Lambridge, Bath, Avon BA1 6BJ
tel: 01225 336698 • fax: 01225 318330

Learn the skills and workshop secrets of creating your own soft furnishings on a range of courses including making curtains, blinds, headboards, cushions, stools and loose covers. These one- and two-day courses include coffee and lunch, but overnight accommodation is not provided. You are welcome to stay and finish your work if you run beyond the hours.

south east

Burlow Decorative Arts

Burlow Farm, Milton St, Alfriston, E. Sussex BN26 5RL
tel: 01323 870318

If fooling your friends with a painted Greek folly in your bathroom is your desire, then come along and learn the techniques of trompe l'œil. It helps if you already have an eye for painting and perspective but it certainly isn't a prerequisite, and there are other courses in decorative paint techniques, too. The courses mostly last three days and lunch is included. Accommodation can be recommended on request.

Dee's School of Folk & Decorative Art

The Studio, Glenville Rd, Kingston-upon-Thames,
Surrey KT2 6DD
tel: 0181 549 6827 • fax: 0181 395 3682

Traditional folk art is still popular because of its naive simplicity. These courses will teach you both the history and techniques. Introduce yourself to this fascinating subject with a one- or three-day course. Once you've got the bug you may want to enrol on one of the part-timer courses, specifically on folk art, that last eight whole weeks. You don't need any specific painting skills at all. If you send ten second class stamps to Dee's School address, a mail order catalogue will be despatched. Alternatively, you can phone for a list of classes or even make a personal appointment to view previous students' work. Lunch is provided on weekend courses and a B&B list is available.

Grand Illusions
2–4 Crown Rd, St Margarets, Twickenham, Middx TW1 3EE
tel: 0181 607 9446

There are three courses on offer, namely painting furniture, painting walls and floors, and fabric painting. Each offers a comprehensive and practical guide to the different aspects. For example, the one on furniture demonstrates how to distress and 'age' furniture either in one colour or two, as well as burnishing, waxing and liming and uncovering many other fascinating secrets behind the professionals' techniques. The courses run throughout the year and normally take place on a Saturday but phone for details.

Half A Sixpence
The Art, Craft and Home Interiors Gallery, Evegate Craft Centre, Station Rd, Smeeth, Nr Ashford, Kent TN25 6SX
tel: 01303 814221

Amidst the unusual setting of a converted granary, enrolees can learn how to verdigris (create that coppery greeny look for ageing everything from lampbases to candlesticks). In addition, gilding, mosaic, decoupage, and looking at different ways to paint furniture are some of the other courses on offer. Lunch and materials are included in the cost and, no matter what course you choose, the tutors aim to enable you to take a finished piece of work home.

The Handweavers Studio
29 Haroldstone Rd, London E17 7AN
tel: 0181 521 2281

Enjoy a weekend spinning or weaving course at The Handweavers Studio, which has become recognized as a mecca for devotees of this skill from around the world. Courses include tassel-making, embroidery, tapestry and dyeing as well as spinning and weaving. Group numbers are usually limited to seven and accommodation is not available.

Helen Barnes
3 The Crescent, Pendleton Rd, Redhill, Surrey RH1 6LD
tel: 01737 241549 • fax: 01737 248817
e-mail: harvi@compuserv.com

Helen Barnes is a muralist and specialist paint effects expert and she teaches courses for novices in paint techniques such as basic broken colour work and other effects. The courses last a day and there are no more than ten people to a tutor.

Honey's Green
The Old Farmhouse, Honey's Green, Framfield, E.Sussex TN22 5RE
tel/fax: 01825 841054
e-mail: brenda.parke.@dial.pipex.com

Courses covering the skills of soft furnishings, decorative paint techniques, painted furniture and watercolour painting set in a sixteenth-century farmhouse overlooking two-acre grounds. In addition to the scheduled courses there are chances to indulge in courses tailormade to individual requirements. Courses usually last one or two days. Accommodation is available either at the farmhouse or locally.

Jamie Jeffrys Mosaics
33 Castlemaine, Culvert Rd, London SW11 5BG
tel: 0171 223 5764

Whether you're an absolute beginner or someone with some mosaic know-how, these courses are sure to have something to offer on this ancient art. Using all sorts of different materials from Byzantine smalti to pebbles and vitreous glass, they will hopefully help you to create something wonderful. Call to find out course duration and prices. Lunch isn't included but Jamie can recommend accommodation if you need it.

KLC School of Interior Design
KLC House, Springvale Terrace, London W14 0AE
tel: 0171 602 8592/3

This famous school specializes in Easter and summer schools for specialist paint effects, including ragging, bagging, faux finishes, sponging, stippling and many, many more. You can choose from different length courses for quite reasonable prices and the school can provide a list of local B&Bs.

Lead & Light
35a Hartland Rd, London NW1 8DB
tel: 0171 485 0997 • fax: 0171 284 2660

If you fancy having a go at the wonderful art of stained glass, Lead & Light offer places for beginners as well as those with some previous knowledge. Learn how to cut glass accurately, how to solder and lead a panel, or how to master the copper foil method. By the end of the two-day course you should have something to take away with you. All the tutors are experts and the atmosphere is fun and friendly. They can provide you with a list of local B&Bs on request.

The Lime Centre

Long Barn, Morestead, Winchester,
Hampshire SO21 1LZ
tel: 01962 713636 • fax: 01962 715350

If you live in an old building (built before approximately 1820), the chances are lime has been used in its construction. You may need to know how to look after and maintain it, and the Lime Centre is just the place to contact. Housed in a group of renovated farm buildings, the centre was set up ten years ago when it became apparent that more and more people – not just experts – were interested in how to deal with lime in their homes. A one-day course will give you the general low-down and the emphasis is on getting stuck in – literally – so be prepared for some hands-on work! Classes are small (not more than ten) and there is the occasional, more advanced, course available if you want to go into the subject in greater detail. A two-course lunch with wine is included and a B&B list is available on request. You can also get the lime putty, mortars and limewashes coloured to your liking here – either by doing it yourself or by mail order.

Lizzi Porter

43 Roundwood Rd, London NW10 9TP
tel: 0181 451 1976

Lizzi Porter doesn't run organized courses as such but she is happy to teach by arrangement on a one-to-one basis. Her speciality is painted finishes such as marbling, tortoiseshelling and dragging as well as other skills such as gilding and restoring lacquers.

London Mosaic Weekend

tel: 0181 481 4563

These day workshops are held on the second weekend of every month in London's Wapping. The course begins with a lecture and is more art than product based. It is run by experts and enthusiasts Norma Vondee and Liz De'Ath and suitable for everyone no matter what your level. All materials are included.

Martin Cheek Mosaic & Ceramic Courses

Flint House, 21 Harbour St, Broadstairs, Kent CT10 1ET
tel: 01843 861958

Mosaics expert Martin Cheek teaches direct and indirect mosaic methods using a whole variety of materials including glass and ceramic tesserae. (Indirect mosaiking gives a smoother, less bumpy finish.) Course numbers are strictly monitored so you get individual attention. Courses usually cover a long weekend and an accommodation list of B&Bs or Youth Hostels is available.

Missenden Abbey

Great Missenden, Bucks HP16 0BD
tel: 01494 890294 • fax: 01494 863697

Offers week-long summer school courses or weekends during the rest of the year. The subjects you can study include quilt-making, mosaics, stained glass, picture-framing and the fascinating microwave dyeing course. The Abbey has seminar and lecture rooms as well as plenty of accommodation. Week-long courses run from Sunday afternoon to Saturday morning and evenings offer the opportunity to play sport, make friends in the bar or take part in specialist lectures, music or discussions. Half-day courses are also available.

Mosaic Studio

Unit 4, 159 Southsea Avenue, Leigh-on-Sea,
Essex SS9 2BH
tel/fax: 01702 712111

These two-day courses begin with an informative talk on the practical uses of mosaic, and then proceed to demonstrate cutting techniques on all the different media – ceramic, glass and marble. Participants are asked to bring a suitable object for mosaiking. Think small to begin with (a mirror frame or vase) if you want to have something finished to take home with you. Places are extremely limited, so be prepared to pay a small deposit in advance to secure your place. They are happy to recommend local hotels for overnight courses.

Mosaic Workshop

tel: 0171 263 2997 for London courses
Missenden Abbey (Chilterns Consortium), The
Misbourne Centre, Great Missenden, Bucks HP16 0BN
tel: 01494 862904
West Dean College, West Dean, Chichester,
W.Sussex PO18 0QZ
tel: 01243 811301

Mosaic Workshop runs a range of courses for all levels of expertise. The aim is for you to complete a piece to take home with you. There is a specific course on mosaic for the garden and for outdoor use. There is also one on further techniques in mosaic. Most of them run over a weekend. Phone the place nearest to you for more details on dates. Places are always sought after, so it's vital to book early if you don't want to be disappointed. There is no overnight accommodation on offer at the London venue but the Missenden Abbey and West Dean courses are residential.

Paint Creative
17 Holywell Hill, St Albans, Herts AL1 1EZ
tel: 01727 859898 • fax: 01727 875872

A comprehensive range of courses are on offer here including decoupage, craquelure, scumble-glazing, marbling and painting MDF 'blanks' – such as trugs, umbrella stands and, the company's speciality, cachepots. Classes are always popular so it's best to book well in advance. Please call for details of venues and dates. Lunch is provided.

Paint Magic
48 Golborne Rd, Notting Hill, London W10 5PR
tel: 0181 960 9960 • fax: 0181 960 9655

Regular *Home Front* designer Jocasta Innes published her famous *Paint Magic* book some fifteen years ago and now has fifteen shops throughout the UK and Northern Ireland and two overseas. All of them run workshops in decorative paint effects for both the beginner and the professional with subjects ranging from basic paint effects to trompe-l'œil. One- and two-day courses are available and more Stage 2 courses are being introduced for those who have done the beginner's ones and wish to progress further. Regular tutors include Lloyd Farmar and Aaron Barker. The All About Mosaic course is a one-day workshop that will give you a basic grounding in the principles and techniques of this ancient craft. The course covers both 'in situ' mosaic (which you do on the spot e.g. on a bathroom wall) and offsite mosaic techniques (e.g. panels or tiles done elsewhere and then taken to the site), how to plan and execute mosaic designs and how to grout and clean your piece. You will need to organize your own overnight accommodation if necessary.

The Regent Academy of Fine Arts
153–155 Regent St, London W1R 8PX
tel: 0171 287 8707 • fax: 0171 287 3348

Choose between home study or attendance courses and one-day workshops or week-long courses. New on the agenda is a Successful Interior Design evening course. Other courses include soft furnishings, decorative paint effects and floral design. Most of the courses lead to the Regent Academy Diploma and City & Guilds certificate. On the home study courses you go at your own pace and there is no pressure to have course material completed by a certain date – and no exams either! You can ask for a course refund at any time within the first three months if you change your mind.

Ribbons & Bows
Low Heath Cottage, Low Heath, Petworth, W.Sussex GU28 0GH
tel/fax: 01798 344088

Decoupage, crackle-glazing and tassel-making courses for the initiated – not for beginners! These day courses explore the more complicated side of these arts in classes of no more than four. The classes are available throughout the year and the day includes a lunch cooked in the house.

Stencil Store Workshops
tel: 01923 285577 for local details

These are an offshoot of the highly successful Stencil Store which has over fifty outlets nationwide. Not all the stores do workshops so do check with your nearest branch first. They offer full-day courses in marbling and paint effects and a half-day course on stencilling.

Three 8 Four
66 Eden Park Avenue, Beckenham, Kent BR3 3HW
tel: 0181 650 7730

If you'd like to tackle a new skill, these jam-packed, one-day courses could whet your appetite. Courses on offer include stencilling, crackle paint, decoupage, wax finishes and six different paint effects. The cost is quite reasonable and includes lunch as well as materials. Some of the courses take place at the weekend and some during the week, so phone for details.

West Dean College
West Dean, Chichester, W.Sussex PO18 0QZ
tel: 01243 811301 • fax: 01243 811343
e-mail: westdean@pavilion.co.uk

An enormous range of courses from calligraphy to glass engraving, and from silk painting and batik to woodcarving. The courses cover all ranges of expertise and generally last from two to seven days. Accommodation is available in the nineteenth-century mansion, the old vicarage, the stable block or the dower house.

east

The Activity Superstore Ltd
PO Box 123, Saffron Walden, Essex CB10 1XX
tel: 01799 526526 • fax: 01799 526528

Alongside ballooning and tank driving, this centre offers decorative painting courses including the techniques of distressing, dragging and flogging. The one-day courses look at how to achieve these effects easily and at minimal cost. Courses are generally mid-week and lunch is provided.

Belstead House Education & Conference Centre
Sprites Lane, Belstead, Ipswich, Suffolk IP8 3NA
tel: 01473 686321 • fax: 01473 686664

A whole range of interesting courses is on offer at this beautiful old house set in six acres of mature grounds. Weekend courses include patchwork, silk painting, marbling and rag rug-making. All the courses are run by experts and may be non-residential or residential.

Cambridge Fine Furnishings
Pelham House, 36 Grantchester Rd, Cambridge, Cambs CB3 9ED
tel: 01223 357456 • fax: 01223 355437

These courses offer the use of a real, professional workroom environment for all aspects of learning the secrets of soft furnishings. Students come from all over the world to learn how to master upholstery, lampshade-making, tassel- and cushion-making. Learn for fun or as the basis of a professional career. Two-, three- or four-day courses are on offer and local accommodation can be arranged. There is also an annual lunch with a guest speaker for former students. Courses run through the school year.

Creations
21 Mildenhall Rd, Bury St Edmunds, Suffolk IP32 6EH
tel: 01284 766706

If you are an amateur or a professional wanting to learn some more tricks of the trade, there is a course for you here. These day courses cover various paint effects from rag rolling to gilding. You can also learn the different techniques of making a stencil. The courses are usually on a Saturday and are in groups of six to twelve people.

Feather in Your Cap
Old Bourchiers Hall, New Rd, Aldham, Colchester CO6 3QU
tel: 01206 210724 • fax: 01206 212105

One-day courses which aim to move on from the more traditional styles of decorative finishes to a new interpretation. Subjects include furniture painting, wood washing, liming, ageing and crackle glazing. There are also courses covering wall finishes such as Tuscan-style plaster and stone block effects. Glazing techniques are also on offer. Classes include a maximum of ten people and all you need to bring is enthusiasm! The day courses include lunch.

Friend or Faux
28 Earlsham St, Bungay, Suffolk NR35 1AQ
tel: 01968 896170 • fax: 01502 714246

Learn the basics of decorative paint effects from a paint finishes expert and muralist. The courses start with the basics including the preparation stage or, if you fancy something more advanced, they range up to marbling and wood-graining. Useful short-cut courses such as 'cheater's gilding' are also available. The courses all last a day with lunch thrown in and classes are limited to six people.

Helaine Clare
Prospect Farmhouse, The Heywood, Diss, Norfolk IP22 3TA
tel: 01379 644005

Possibly a unique course focusing on DIY Home Maintenance for women. Helaine learned her skills the hard way restoring a derelict farmhouse and is keen to pass on her knowledge on such subjects as basic plumbing, basic electrics, tiling, grouting, wallpapering, painting and some decorative effects. So if you've ever stood around holding the hammer, now is the time to turn the tables! Choose between ten-week-long courses, day workshops or summer schools. Classes contain up to fifteen people and accommodation can be arranged.

Penny Dog Paints
1589 London Rd, Leigh-on-Sea, Essex SS9 2SG
tel/fax: 01702 474361

A lifetime of hands-on experience make Josh Martin's classes in colourwashing, sponging, stippling, and grain effects very practical. You will also get the chance to buy all the materials you would ever need. Classes are usually in groups of about twelve people and run every other Sunday and every Thursday.

central

Acorn Activities
PO Box 120, Hereford, Herefordshire HR4 8YB
tel: 01432 830083 • fax: 01432 830110

This organization offers a whole range of courses at various locations in central England and Wales. Just a few of those on offer in this region cover calligraphy, papier mâché, glass-making and blowing, interior design, stained glass, furniture restoration and beadwork. Courses generally run over a weekend and sometimes stretch to an extra day. Accommodation can be provided in anything from prestigious hotels to camp sites.

Annie Sloan School of Decoration
Landscape Rd, Weston-on-the-Green, Oxon OX6 8TN
tel: 0870 601 0082 • fax: 01993 813710

Fine artist turned decorative painter Annie Sloan hands on some of her secrets on her courses at her newly opened school. Courses include gilding, faux bois, glazing, stamping, trompe-l'œil and fresco techniques. The courses vary from one day to a week and you will benefit from the teaching of famous experts. The emphasis is definitely on practical application so come with your sleeves rolled up. The courses are not residential but they can offer suggestions for places to stay.

The Gateway Education & Arts Centre
Chester St, Shrewsbury SY1 1NB
tel: 01743 355159 • fax: 01743 358951

Day courses are run throughout the year in the arts of spinning, dyeing, silk painting and embroidery.

Machine embroidery tuition is also on offer. Classes include up to sixteen people.

Paint Inspirations
The Old Baker's Cottage, Duffield Lane, Newborough, Burton-on-Trent, Staffs DE13 8SH
tel: 01283 575303 • fax: 01283 575003

Choose from one- or two-day courses, both aimed at amateurs. On the one-day course you will get inspiration and advice on crackle glazing, verdigris, rag rolling and cutting stencils and will decorate your own pot or picture frame. The two-day course goes into more detail and explores other effects. Groups usually include about six people and there is B&B and a three-course lunch available at a local inn.

north west

Burton Manor College
Burton, South Wirral, Cheshire L64 5SJ
tel: 0151 336 5172 • fax: 0151 336 6586

Courses throughout the year include a wide range of subjects such as patchwork, papier mâché, batik and tie dye, hand-painted furniture, stained glass and paint effects. Curtain- and cushion-making, and salt-dough making are also on offer. Courses run from one day to weekends and there is a nursery for children set in the grounds of the college. Courses can be tailormade for groups or organizations, and accommodation is available.

north east

Angela Beaumont
5 The Stables, Weeton Lane, Harewood, Leeds, W.Yorks LS17 9LT
tel: 01132 886882

From the basic to the professional, these very friendly and fun classes will teach you all you need to know about the latest paint finishes. The classes are often as small as two to three people and can be tailored to the individual's needs. All the latest paint techniques are taught including stone-blocking, marbling and wood-graining.

Chapel House Upholstery

The Chapel House, Great Fryupdale, Lealholm, Whitby,
N.Yorks YO21 2AS
tel: 01947 897601

Beginners and improvers upholstery courses are held
on a long weekend basis and from both you take home
an upholstered piece of furniture. Improvers will
obviously need some upholstery experience. The
courses are run throughout the year with no more than
five in a group. Accommodation is available in the
local pub or in B&Bs.

The Rag & Roll Company

Home Farm, Swinton Grange, Malton, N.Yorks YO17 0QT
tel: 01653 690672 • fax: 01653 698711
e-mail: RagnRoll@AOL.com

The emphasis is on acquiring the desired skills, eating
nice food and having fun on these decorative paint
one-day workshops. The courses cover the basics of rag
rolling, sponging, colourwashing and stencilling or the
more advanced skills of verdigris, vinegar graining and
antiquing. Helen Lucy aims to de-mystify the whole
subject and show how the finishes can be achieved
simply and cheaply. The workshops are run at the
weekends and are kept to five or six people who get a
good lunch and bottle of wine.

Wellfield

Claxton, York, N.Yorks YO60 7SD
tel: 01904 468470

Choose between a beginner's guide to colour and
simple paint effects for walls and furniture and a more
advanced course covering faux finishes and antique
effects. Gilding and stencilling courses are also on
offer, as is a weekend course covering painting on
furniture. Classes are usually in groups of three to four
people and the maximum is six. One- and two-day
courses run from March to November, and they can
supply a list of local B&Bs for overnighters.

West Yorkshire School for Woodcrafters

The Cottage, Gomersal House, Lower Lane, Great
Blackheaton, W.Yorks BD19 4HY
tel/fax: 01274 877498

Weekend or week-long courses cover the skills of wood
turning, making dollshouses, carving and routering
(cutting decorative grooves in wooden doors, etc).
Ideal for amateurs – in fact you are preferred that way!
Courses can be tailored to your individual needs for

skills like picture framing, for example. Groups are
usually as small as three or four people. Ask for
suggestions for local B&Bs to stay in.

wales

The Art House

Pen-y-parc, Llangibby, nr Usk,
Monmouthshire NP5 1NY.
tel: 01633 450320 • fax: 01633 450552

If you want to learn the basic technical skills of
canvas work tapestry, you can learn them here. The
courses also focus on developing people's colour
senses and helping them to create both traditional
and contemporary design. Choose between eight-
week courses (evenings or afternoons) or day
courses. Mixed ability and experience classes have
a maximum of ten to twelve people with two to
three tutors.

Rhallt Restoration

The Rhallt, Castle Caereinion, Welshpool,
Powys SY21 9AT
tel/fax: 01938 850086

Five-day courses, run throughout the year, teach the
skills of furniture making and antique restoration.
The classes are small, just two people, who can be
either slightly experienced or total novices. Any kind
or piece of furniture can be attempted. A local B&B
is available.

Studio Fronceri

Rhydlewis, Llandysul, Wales SA44 5SX
tel/fax: 01239 858945

Qualified design teachers Bill Hughes and Lindsay
Gilbert run a variety of arts and crafts courses for
both beginners and the more experienced. A
flexible timetable means there are no dates written
in tablets of stone, but people are fitted in at their
own convenience. A traditional farmhouse includes
accommodation, a studio and a workshop and the
courses cover silk painting, furniture restoration,
fabric printing and dyeing, and woodworking.

The Upholstery Workshop

Teify View, Llandyfriog, Newcastle Emlyn,
Ceredigion SA38 9HB
tel/fax: 01239 711265

Learn upholstery skills on either a week-long course or a six-week course that can be spread over a year. You will be encouraged to bring a piece of furniture to work on in classes that only take five people at a time. With two tutors you receive good, individual tuition. It doesn't matter whether you are a beginner wanting a new hobby or intending to start a business, everybody is welcome. Accommodation and food are provided apart from the evening meal.

scotland

The Byre
Loch Doon, Dalmellington, Ayrshire KA6 7QE
tel/fax: 01292 551025

Spinning and weaving experts Janet and Lee Reouf-Miller run one- and two-day courses with no more than five in a group. There are courses covering handspinning for beginners, spinning exotic fibres, spinning flax and various types of weaving. Lunch is included and local B&B is available on request. Camping and caravanning space is also available in a scenic area which also offers walks, fishing and a forest.

Decorum
335 Sauchiehall St, Glasgow G2 3HR
tel: 01413 328800 • fax: 01413 327277

A group of interior designers with strong market knowledge run an Introduction to Successful Interior Design course in the surroundings of a furniture, fabrics, gifts and accessories store. The course includes colour theory, accessorizing and planning. The courses comprise two-hour sessions over a four-week period and classes are usually in groups of up to about twelve people. There are

often guest speakers from different companies sharing their expertise.

Renaissance
8 Mansfield Place, Edinburgh EH3 6NB
tel: 0131 557 2762 • fax: 0131 556 8159

You can learn a whole host of skills on these courses including casting in plaster, gilding, gilding on glass, specialist paint effects and decoupage. The courses are run in London, Wiltshire and Edinburgh and are for complete beginners. They last one or two days and you will find yourself in a group of no more than ten people. No overnight accommodation available, but ask for recommendations.

The Wolf's Hearth
Torneveen, by Lumphanan, Aberdeenshire AB31 4PL
tel: 013998 810680

You can be a loner or one of the pack here and learn the skills of textile design, interior decor, stencilling and doing up junk furniture. Day courses are run throughout the year to suit an individual or group and class sizes are from two to four.

northern ireland

Ulster Folk & Transport Museum
Cultra, Holywood, Co Down BT18 0EU
tel: 01232 428428

A wide range of classes are held in Cultra Manor, the museum's education centre. Subjects range from Christmas patchwork to Quaker samplers and from stained glass window and applique to knitting. Choose between evening courses that run once a week for up to five weeks, or day workshops. Accommodation can be obtained through the NI Tourist Board (01232 246609) or Coast of Down (012437 270069).

useful

When you're looking for a good plumber, electrician or decorator, the best way to find one is undeniably recommendation by word of mouth. Knowing that someone you know has been pleased with the standard of work carried out is a great comfort. But failing that, where on earth do you begin to look? How many of us have had to resort to frantically leafing through the *Yellow Pages* in an emergency?

Sometimes knowing where to look is half the battle. There are organizations out there that have been set up to help. With a bit of forward planning, you can rest assured that you can obtain a list of people working in your area who are qualified, 'approved' and have met certain criteria. Of course they can't guarantee that the person will be available, but it's a good start!

Perhaps you live in a period home and have become interested in its history? There are now several societies of experts and enthusiasts who you may want to join. Perhaps salvage is your bag and you want to extend your hunting to countries abroad? There is a wealth of information out there.

This chapter is necessarily a bit of a ragbag collection of addresses, but all are really useful. We've listed them, where possible, under the various themes used for the chapters in this book. We are sure that you will find something of use, whether it's leaflets or advice. Please make sure you know whether the information is free or not, and always include the appropriate payment. Many of these organizations are charitable so help them to help you.

organizations

bathrooms

The Bathroom Showroom Association

Federation House, Station Rd, Stoke-on-Trent,
Staffs ST4 2SA
tel: 01782 844006 • fax: 01782 747161
e-mail: info@bathroom-showrooms.org.uk

Members of this organization are bathroom showrooms
and they have to attain certain standards, so if you
need a recommendation for someone to do your
bathroom, this is a good starting point. They also have
a series of free pamphlets on subjects such as The
Essential Bathroom Guide, The Essential Showroom
Guide and The Essential Manufacturers Guide.

ceramics

The British Ceramic Tile Council

Station Rd, Stoke-on-Trent, Staffs ST4 2RT
tel: 01782 747147 • fax: 01782 747161
e-mail: tiles@netcentral.co.uk

Representing British manufacturers of ceramic tiles,
this organization can give you information about
where to source certain products including more
unusual ones such as architectural tiles, used in
commercial building projects. They also have some free
leaflets about ceramic tiles.

Tile Promotion Board

Forum Court, 83 Copers Cope Rd, Beckenham,
Kent BR3 1NR
tel: 0181 663 1569 • fax: 0181 663 9949
e-mail: tiles@dial.pipex.com

If you're looking for a tiler, the Tile Promotion Board
can send you a list of members of the National Master
Tile Fixers Association. Most companies cover a large
area, so don't worry if the addresses don't seem
terribly local. They also publish a free leaflet called
Living with Ceramic Tiles, which has some handy hints
on how to choose tiles and how to care for them.

first impressions

British Blind & Shutter Association

42 Heath St, Tamworth, Staffs B79 7JH
tel: 01827 52337 • fax: 01827 310827
e-mail: www.bbsa.uk.com

If you are looking for blinds or shutters these people
can give you a list of local members free of charge.
They also have a range of free leaflets that outline
useful subjects such as measuring up and fitting, and
leaflets offering guidance about what's currently
available on the market. They can provide a
publication called The Official Guide to Blinds and
Shutters, which outlines the types of blinds available
and where you'd use them.

flooring

The British Carpet Manufacturers' Association

PO Box 1155, Kidderminster, Worcs DY11 6WP
tel: 01562 747351 • fax: 01562 747359
e-mail: bcma@clara.net

If you have enquiries about carpets, this is one of
the main places to get them answered. As the name
suggests, the organization represents carpet
manufacturers, but also publishes booklets on subjects
such as how to choose a carpet and how to care for it.
The booklets are free and you can also bring other
enquiries here.

National Institute of Carpet and Floor Layers

4d St Mary's Place, The Lace Market, Nottingham,
Notts NG1 1PH
tel: 0115 958 3077 • fax: 0115 941 2238

If you have chosen the type of flooring you want but
are nervous about getting the right person to fit it,
this organization can give you some good, free advice.
They will also respond to more general enquiries about
flooring and supply you with a list of Institute
members in your area.

furniture

British Antique Furniture Restorers' Association
The Old Rectory, Warmwell, Dorchester,
Dorset DT2 8HQ
tel: 01305 854822 • fax: 01305 852104
e-mail: www.bafra.uk.org

If you're wanting to restore a much-cherished piece of furniture, you don't want to make a mistake about who you get to do the job, so it's worth contacting these people to get some recommendations. They publish a guide outlining members and their particular expertise which is £6.25 (at the time of going to print), and they also give free advice over the phone.

The Conservation Unit
The Museums & Galleries Commission,
16 Queen Anne's Gate, London SW1H 9AA
tel: 0171 233 4200 • fax: 0171 233 3686
e-mail: n.poole@mgcuk.co.uk

This Government-funded organization holds the Conservation Register, which is a list of antique furniture restorers and conservators. They can supply names, addresses and details of people offering a restoration or conservation service in your local area.

heating

Council for Registered Gas Installers
1 Elmwood, Chineham Business Park, Crockford Lane,
Basingstoke, Hants RG24 8WG
tel: 01256 372200 • fax: 01256 372310

This is the watchdog society for gas installers and if you are having work done, make sure your installer is CORGI registered. If you ring them, they can recommend a registered member in your area.

National Association of Plumbing, Heating and Mechanical Services Contractors
14 Ensign House, Ensign Business Centre,
Westwood Way, Coventry CV4 8JA
tel: 01203 470626 • fax: 01203 470942
e-mail: aphcuk@aol.com

If you have general plumbing or heating queries, this useful body can give advice over the phone. They will be able to provide you with general technical and sourcing advice and a list of members in your area who could carry out the work.

National Fireplace Association
6th Floor, The McLaren Building, 35 Dale End,
Birmingham B4 7LN
tel: 0800 521611 • fax: 0121 2001306
e-mail: dbrotherton@metcom.org.uk

You can get general information on anything to do with fireplaces and the different kinds of fuels used in fires from here. They also publish technical leaflets that cost £2.50 each and a Yearbook with information about member companies for £3.

kitchens

The Kitchen Specialists' Association
PO Box 311, Worcs WR1 1DR
tel: 01905 726066 • fax: 01905 726469

Choosing a kitchen specialist can be as confusing as choosing the type of kitchen you want, but The Kitchen Specialists' Association have lists of reputable members who all have to live up to certain criteria. They also have a warranty system that ensures that if the specialist goes out of business in the middle of installing your kitchen, they will arrange for another specialist to finish it. Ring or write for free leaflets on the do's and don'ts of buying a kitchen and what to look out for.

lighting

The Lighting Association
Stafford Park 7, Telford, Shropshire TF3 3BQ
tel: 01952 290905 • fax: 01952 290906
e-mail: tla@vital.co.uk

If you have queries about any kind of lighting, this association will point you in the right direction. Its members are manufacturers and suppliers, but they can supply consumers with a free buyers guide or a list of members.

period homes

English Heritage

23 Savile Row, London W1X 1AB
tel: 0171 973 3000 and 0171 973 3434
fax: 0171 973 3001

This is a Government funded organization that deals with various historic properties. They can advise owners of listed properties and scheduled ancient monuments (such things as Roman remains or stone circles, which are protected by law) on various topics including where to get grants for financial help in restoring or maintaining these properties.

Georgian Group

6 Fitzroy Square, London W1P 6DX
tel: 0171 387 1720 • fax: 0171 387 1721

Although this is an organization generally campaigning against the neglect of Georgian architecture, parks and gardens, they can advise members of the public on general topics. They have leaflets on how to source anything from windows to curtain rails for Georgian properties. These currently cost £2.75 for each leaflet, excluding postage, but call to find out more. There is a discount for members.

The Society for the Protection of Ancient Buildings

37 Spital Square, London E1 6DY
tel: 0171 377 1644 • fax: 0171 247 5296

This famous organization offers a free telephone advice-line service, available in the mornings only. They also publish leaflets on how to repair old buildings currently priced from £2 each. There are other information sheets on a range of subjects such as authentic building and decorative materials, how to use them and how to deal with problems such as damp, and these are £1 each. Call to see which will be most helpful for you.

The Twentieth Century Society

77 Cowcross St, London EC1M 6EJ
tel: 0171 250 3857 • fax: 0171 251 8985
e-mail: jill@c20society.demon.co.uk

This is a charitable organization that also receives some Government funding. Although they are mainly a pressure group, they can also offer advice on anything to do with twentieth century buildings such as protecting and preserving them, and have information leaflets that start from £3.50. They also publish a journal every year.

Victorian Society

1 Priory Gardens, Bedford Park, London W4 1TT
tel: 0181 994 1019 • fax: 0181 995 4895

Fundamentally, this is an architectural pressure group, which can't give advice on how to do up your Victorian house, but does offer a series of booklets that cover how to care for houses from this period. The booklets are currently £3 each and cover such subjects like fireplaces, paintwork and doors.

salvage

SALVO

18 Ford Village, Berwick-upon-Tweed, Northumberland TD15 2QG
tel: 01890 820333 • fax: 01890 820499
e-mail: salvo@scotborders.co.uk

This is an organization that is dedicated to salvage in every sense. Salvo is an independent body set up in 1990 by a handful of salvage-yard owners, to help promote good practice. Those that subscribe to the 'Salvo code' promise not to deal in stolen goods or remove items from a listed buildings without permission. (This is not to say that those who *aren't* registered do!) Certificates of Salvo-registered companies are re-issued annually so that standards are maintained, and Salvo-approved yards carry a sign with a crane (the bird variety). Salvo has a very useful website at http:\www.salvo.co.uk, which has individual web pages for particular dealers, lists of stolen items, and much more. They also publish packs both for this country and abroad containing, amongst other things, lists of known dealers. The Salvo Pack, currently priced at £5.75 (including postage and packing), includes two issues of a magazine and detailed information about salvage companies in your area. Alternatively, you can subscribe to a fortnightly newsletter, which costs £50 for 25 issues.

sofas and beds

Association of Master Upholsterers & Soft Furnishers

Frances Vaughan House, 102 Commercial St, Newport, Gwent NP9 1LU
tel: 01633 215454 • fax: 01633 244488
e-mail: amu@easynet.co.uk

This organization is currently having a big focus on consumers and have published a range of free fact sheets that give you loads of information, including the questions you should be asking if you want work of this kind done.

The Sleep Council

High Corn Mill, Chapel Hill, Skipton, N.Yorks BD23 1NL
tel: 01756 792327 • fax: 01756 798789
e-mail: sleepco@daelnet.co.uk

Sponsored by the bed industry, these people have a wealth of useful information for that all important choice of which bed to have. They have leaflets outlining how to buy a bed and how to choose beds for children.

walls

The British Decorators Association

32 Coton Rd, Nuneaton, Warks CV11 5TW
tel: 01203 353776 • fax: 01203 354513
e-mail: bda@primex.co.uk

This association can send out a list of local decorators among their membership. They can also supply, free of charge, a leaflet on how to choose a decorator and the questions to ask before you start!

National Federation of Plastering Contractors

56–64 Leonard St, London EC2A 4JX
tel: 0171 608 5090 • fax: 0171 608 5081
e-mail: michelekavanagh@nfcc.demon.co.uk

If you are at a loss to find a good plasterer, decorator or need someone to do some work on the stonework of your house, this organization can send you a list of approved members who work in these areas. The information is free if you call the number given above.

The Wallfashion Bureau

High Corn Mill, Chapel Hill, Skipton, N.Yorks BD23 1NL
tel: 01756 790730 • fax: 01756 798789
e-mail: wfb@daelnet.co.uk

Dedicated to promoting the charms of wallpaper, The Wallfashion Bureau can give you all kinds of help on the subject including a very useful range of leaflets on how to hang wallpaper, why you should use wallpaper rather than paint or another finish, where to put which kind and how to cope with difficult situations. Send a first class SAE for the leaflets.

The Wallpaper History Society

c/o Gill Saunders, Department of Prints, Drawings and Paintings, Victoria & Albert Museum, South Kensington, London SW7 2RL
tel: 0171 938 8500 • fax: 0171 938 8615

Run by a small group of people who are professionally involved with wallpaper, this society aims to promote the study and conservation of wallpaper. They occasionally publish reviews, organize lectures and visits. In addition they will carry out identification and dating of old wallpapers if you send a sample or photograph, and they can point you in the right direction for people who can help you conserve old papers. The service is free, but if you send in photos or samples and want them returned, enclose the return postage cost.

miscellaneous

British Wood Preserving and Damp-Proofing Association

Building 6, The Office Village, 4 Romford Rd, Stratford, London E15 4EA
tel: 0181 519 2588 • fax: 0181 519 3444
e-mail: bwpda.co.uk

It may not be the sexiest of subjects, but it's vital to any homeowner and this organization can either recommend local companies to carry out work or give you technical advice over the phone. They will also send you a free list of publications on the subject.

The Building Centre
26 Store St, London WC1E 7BT
tel: 171 637 1022 • fax: 0171 631 0329
e-mail: manu@buildngcentre.co.uk

This impressive organization has a telephone facility called Guideline Service, which offers building information for consumers. They avoid giving technical advice as such, but can supply you with product information, product literature and other information including details about self-build. The service is free, but be warned, this is a premium-rate phone line.

Federation of Master Builders
14 Great James St, London WC1N 3DP
tel: 0171 242 7583 • fax: 0171 404 0296

An independent trade association for medium-size building companies, this organization will not be able to give you technical advice, but can send a list of members on a regional basis. They also have a complaints procedure if you use one of their members, and a warranty scheme with a five-year guarantee.

Interior Decorators & Designers Association
1–4 Chelsea Harbour Design Centre, Lots Rd, London SW10 0XE
tel: 0171 349 0800 • fax: 0171 349 0500
e-mail: enquiries@www.idda.co.uk

If you are confused about how on earth to choose an interior designer from the hosts available, this organization can send you a list of your local members. They also publish a directory of their 300-strong membership that currently costs £75.

National Approval Council for Security Systems
Queensgate House, 14 Cookham Rd, Maidenhead, Berks SL6 8AJ
tel: 01628 627512 • fax: 01628 773367
e-mail: nacos@nacos.org

As well as monitoring security companies, this body can give you all kinds of security information, inspect your system and give you a free leaflet explaining their working practice.

National Federation of Roofing Contractors
24 Weymouth St, London W1N 4LX
tel: 0171 436 0387 • fax: 0171 637 5215
e-mail: ww.nfrc.co.uk

If you want a new roof or are having trouble with an existing one, it's worth checking out this organization first. They can send you a free leaflet explaining why you should choose one of their members and also give you a list of those members.

The Royal Insitute of British Architects
66 Portland Place, London W1N 4AD
tel: 0171 580 5533 • fax: 0171 436 9112
e-mail: www.ribafind.org

As the name suggests, the membership of this society consists of architects, but they do offer a limited service to the public that mainly consists of sending out short lists of member architects who are suitable for your specific needs. This is a free service.

The Royal Institution of Chartered Surveyors
12 Great George St, Parliament Sq, London SW1P 3AD
tel: 0171 222 7000 • fax: 0171 222 9430
e-mail: www.rics.org.uk

If you are in a process of buying a new home, this is an excellent source of information because they have a comprehensive range of free leaflets on buying and selling your home, different types of survey and how to look after your home. There is also a bookshop and they can send you a list of members in your local area.

Society of Garden Designers
14–15 Belgrave Square, London SW1X 8PS
tel: 0171 838 9311 • fax: 0171 838 9322

This society can provide a free list of designers, who work to high professional standards, and recommend courses on garden design. Even if you are not a designer you can become a corresponding member (£47 per annum) and receive a regular journal and access to workshops and seminars.

index of suppliers

index